Introduction to Western Concert Music

ARMAND AMBROSINI

MICHAEL LEE

University of Oklahoma

 KENDALL/HUNT PUBLISHING COMPANY
4050 Westmark Drive   Dubuque, Iowa 52002

Dedicated to our brothers and sisters:
Al, Ann, Elaine, and Erica
Cathy, Jodi, Barb, Chris, Patty, and Karen

Contents

CHAPTER 1

Introduction to Western Concert Music and Society

STUDYING MUSIC

The study of music is very old in the West. In the past, studying music enjoyed a most privileged status. Today, the study of music struggles to remain in the curriculum of public schools due to budget cuts and shifting priorities leading society toward a more vocational approach to education. Often music educators find themselves justifying their presence within a modern education. In light of what appears a crisis for music in education, this book will begin by doing what textbooks in the sciences, social sciences, humanities, and most of the fine arts rarely need to do: it will try to justify itself.

Insofar as most readers of this book are enrolled in an introductory college course by the time they are reading this introduction, such a justification may be totally unnecessary. This course clearly fit your schedule, addressed some curiosity, or fulfilled some needed requirement as part of an assigned curriculum. Chances are that the class that prompted the purchase of this book was an elective, or a course chosen from a menu of general education options in the field of Western Civilization. The fact that you're reading this book right now may make any justification of music education seem defensive, but the authors feel it's worthwhile to present music's fine credentials within the traditions of education in the West, even if the audience for this presentation is in some sense already hostage.

Musical Study in Ancient and Medieval Times

Plato, one of the West's most persuasive thinkers, argued that music should form fully one half of a man's education. The other half, he argued, should be gymnastics. Music perfected the mind, so his argument ran, while gymnastics perfected the body. Why would Plato, a man associated with the field of philosophy rather than music, advocate such centrality for music in an education? He felt that music was at once a pleasure (thus it could keep the attention of the student), while at the same time music was a useful illustration of mathematical ratios and formulas in motion. Music's power to illustrate physical properties and potentials would, he hoped, reveal to the student the pleasing order and logic of the natural world. Plato's vision for music education was twofold. On the one hand he advocated learning to play an instrument or sing (although he felt that no man should make this his profession), while on the other he advocated intellectual engagement with music.

During the Middle Ages, Plato's two-part curriculum of music and gymnastics gave way to the study of the trivium (three essential subjects concerning logic and language) and the quadrivium. Music formed part of the quadrivium, along with arithmetic, geometry, and astronomy. These disciplines—closely related in the Western imagination—shaped our understanding of the central proportional movements and relationships of our physical world.

While these two brief illustrations of music's centrality within an education are well and good, this line of justification might seem too antique for practical use. After all, Plato is long gone and the university has long ago abandoned the trivium and quadrivium as the foundation for the curriculum. What this survey of music's past centrality teaches us is simply that music has long been an essential and basic mental discipline in the West. This central role for music points to centuries and centuries of serious human engagement with this art. Music has been important to all civilizations around the world throughout their respective histories. Coming to some understanding of this enormous legacy of human achievement, thought, and discipline can only be achieved through the study of music itself. As a field concerned with the motion of air perceived as sound and understood as music, a means of abstract communication as old as our species, nothing can stand in its place. The only way to study this vastly ancient and impressively living field of human endeavor is through the field itself. Humans are musical and have always been musical. Should we cut ourselves off from the musical in mankind, we would cut ourselves off from part of who we are as a species. Humanity's striving to understand ourselves separates us from the rest of the animals on the planet. Such striving, in short, is the substance of an education.

Formal and Informal Musical Knowledge

Everyone who has never studied music formally still has a relationship with it. An education should lend nuance and insight to those relationships, but it needn't overturn them. Perhaps by looking at another kind of educational relationship, this point might become clearer.

Perhaps by examining the author's informal knowledge of zoology, we might arrive at a contrast of informal and formal study of a thing, as this book presumes to offer a formal study of a thing many people already know a good deal about. I know what a lemur is. Lemurs, arboreal primates with large eyes and long tails, live on the island of Madagascar. In writing this statement, I've now nearly exhausted what I know about lemurs. The study of zoology, biology, and primatology would surely lend nuance and insight into my relationship with lemurs. I can even take this idea a step further and claim that I really like lemurs, even based on the small amount I know about them. They're interesting to look at, and the few I've seen in zoos were behaving in a lively way that pleased me. I'm basically happy with my relationship with lemurs. This informal liking isn't necessary, but it may be the spark that gets me to study them more deeply. In short, the casual relationships we establish with things are good and helpful. That said, I'm still confident that, should I ever study lemurs formally with someone who has developed some real expertise in their behavior, physical morphology, habitat, and so forth, my relationship would deepen and my curiosity would begin to open new avenues for further deepening.

Most people know a good deal more about the music they like best than I know about lemurs. These relationships built on liking and using certain music in one's daily life are both wonderful and healthy. But everything can stand some intensification and widening through education. This book likely won't address very many readers' favorite music, nor should it. Readers don't need an introduction to the things they already know and like, but it should have some *widening* effect on experiences with music as a general field of study. By studying how other people come to like and use music in their daily lives, we may even develop a tool to understand ourselves better. The authors neither want to overturn the readers' already good relationship with music nor to despise that relationship. On the contrary, we'd like to celebrate it. This book provides an added perspective, and certainly not the only perspective of worth. Claims of offering a morally or ethically superior approach could not be further from our intentions.

Studying Music Making and Studying to Make Music

Introductions to the study of music can take many forms. For some, learning to sing or play a musical instrument provides the ideal way to gain an introduction to music. To be sure, much insight can be gained from the practice of one's object of study. In public primary and secondary schools, making music is often the only way to study music. This singular focus on performance is useful, if what you want to gain from your study of music is to sing or play an instrument. The downside is that the student gains only a limited, albeit valuable, perspective. Music is both a performing art and an integral part of the humanities. So, just as English Departments teach both creative writing and the study of literature, Music Departments teach both musicmaking and the study of music. Just as Plato advocated both, the authors present only one approach but advocate both as well. The approach presented in this book resembles what we do in a literature class, where we read, analyze, and debate the meaning of written work. The rough equivalent of the creative writing class, the practical making of music is the province of other classes and different authors.

One crucial difference exists between studying literature and music: literature uses words and is conducive to being written and talked about. By contrast, music is often conceived as an arrangement of abstract sounds toward some human purpose. The abstraction of musical sound separates it from language and forces us to talk about music either through metaphors or through technical language (itself usually metaphoric in nature). If discussing music were a mere matter of measuring the sounds through oscilloscopes, reporting the frequencies of the sounds, and describing their relative placement in time, our job would be comparatively easy. Unfortunately, such precision of description doesn't say anything about what the sounds and their configuration might mean to someone. Instead, we must look not only to the music itself, but to the individuals and the society that gave it life.

Studying Meaning in Music

The search for the meaning or meanings of a piece of music is complicated in the extreme. Not only do we need a technical vocabulary and an understanding of metaphoric ways of talking about music, but we also need to develop a healthy respect for the diversity of meanings that audience members might develop for themselves. Music is a social phenomenon that reveals its identity through encounters. These encounters can take a nearly infinite variety of forms, thus the complexity of searching for meaning. Complexity in educational endeavors is not grounds for giving up. Complexity suggests that we proceed, as we're likely on the path to something useful.

The Birth of Music Appreciation Classes

To help in the arduous path of gaining an introduction to a kind of music, we need to establish the sorts of questions that are important to us. Traditionally, music departments offered a music appreciation class. The first such classes were taught in Vienna in the late 1800s by a man named Eduard Hanslick. He looked at the city where he lived and found the audiences for music insufficiently informed to love the music he loved best: abstract instrumental music. His classes were designed to correct this imperfection in the audience, and to encourage them to value what he valued. He had noble reasons, but his project essentially boils down to correcting the audience so that it might share his values.

Classes configured on the assumption that the students need to be taught how more perfectly to value a body of music deemed valuable by the instructor or the institution sometimes are called "music appreciation classes," in recognition of Hanslick's educational innovation. Obviously a name may not tell everything about a course. You may be reading this book because you are enrolled in a class called "music appreciation," but in using this book, the instructor likely doesn't share Hanslick's goals.

The word "appreciation" serves many fields of study and flows from a connoisseur's sensibility. The connoisseur studies something in order to understand how to value the examples of the thing. Developing connoisseurship is not the goal of this book. This kind of engagement suffers from a central fault line in its assumption. The student is taught to value, on the false assumption that musical practices have absolute values. Unlike the fields of wine-tasting or art-collecting, where there is a free market that the consumer must engage in order to participate in the field, music does not reside within a directly comparable market situation. If you want a certain kind of wine, having developed an appreciation for it through study with a wine expert, you're going to have to compete with a thirsty market of fellow consumers trying to get bottles of the same wine. The wine itself is finite in quantity, so the price reflects how it is valued. The wine in question surely isn't worth the asking price to everyone, but if the seller can command the price from enough consumers to sell his or her stock, then its absolute value in monetary terms has been set by the market.

The wine market is very different from music, where there are only a very small number of instances when scarcity affects pricing. Most music enthusiasts can obtain relatively cheaply recordings and even live experiences of the music that interests them. A particular sold-out performance of an opera may leave you on the outside wishing you could get in, but these situations are quite rare. Recordings don't lend the same pleasure as live concerts, but a facsimile of even the most rare and (by market standards) precious performance can usually be purchased on CD. Music does exist in an economy, but the relative plenitude, and the artificiality of rare moments of scarcity, force us to look upon it rather differently. Unlike a painting, where there's only one original, musical works are reproduced constantly through performance. A single work could, therefore, exist a nearly infinite number of times.

Appreciation in the end has too much to do with the economy of buying and selling scarce objects. One might find a dictionary entry for "appreciation," defining it with words comparable to these: "The act of estimating the qualities of persons or things." This might lead us to look up "estimate" where we might find something comparable to this definition: "To make a judgment as to the approximate cost, quantity, or extent." Clearly this vocabulary comes from the world of buying and selling. That world may have correspondences to the world of understanding, but too often the study of the arts resembles the replication of sanctioned patterns of consumption. The authors of this text aren't much interested in influencing student consumption, although some broadening along those lines might be a happy coincidence of using this book.

Moving Beyond Appreciation

Instead of asking questions of connoisseurship (how valuable is this piece of music), the book takes the study of music as a search for some meaning in the musical practices of the West, just as literature students try to excavate a novel's meaning that lies just beneath the surface story. To accomplish this task in music, we look to the societies that gave rise to the music, to the music itself, and to the world of ideas swirling around the music. The authors, in the end, don't need the student to value in the way we value. The authors want to model a strategy for engaging music as a social practice toward fostering better understanding. Obviously we think the music we have written about in this book is worthy of the readers' attention or we wouldn't have chosen it, but whether the reader appreciates and values it remains largely irrelevant, provided some understanding exists.

Musical meaning resides in relationships between the listener and the creator of the music. Such relationships depend enormously on what the listener has as a frame of reference. That frame of reference may embrace other music that the listener knows and can use for comparison. It may include ideas and beliefs important to the listener. This book will try very hard to connect the music of a particular time and place within the scope of what we call "the West" with the ideas and beliefs circulating in that time and place. By illustrating such connections, our hope is that readers will come to an understanding of music as a social as well as sonic experience. This is by no means the only way to study music. The authors feel it is a way to help readers seeking a more sophisticated way of engaging music to get a start that won't be overburdened with technical language, which often stands between interested students and this vital field of human endeavor.

THE FORMAT OF THE BOOK AND ITS USE

Armed with some sense of the book's basic goal and justification, we can now look at its presentation. Following this introduction, chapters Two through Five of the book deal respectively with the fundamental technical elements of music. The last and largest section of the book (chapters Six through Fifteen) provides a historical overview of music and society.

The fundamentals section provides needed vocabulary and concepts that musicians use in their discussion of music. These chapters could be consulted on an as-needed basis to answer questions and flesh out technical understanding. It could be read from beginning to end as a gateway to a more precise technical knowledge of Western music's internal functioning. It could be selectively referenced when unfamiliar technical vocabulary enters into the historical survey section. The abstract nature of music can be daunting for students seeking an introduction. These chapters are designed to explain as efficiently as possible some of those abstractions central to music's nature.

The historical survey does not by any means provide a comprehensive discussion of musical issues in each of the stylistic periods covered over the course of music's long history in the West. Instead, it was written in a conversational manner as a continuous narrative. Most details, and indeed entire subjects, have been omitted to foster more of a storytelling approach. Each section might be seen as a tip of an iceberg.

In addition to being more like storytelling than a traditional historical chronicle, this survey is designed to initiate a discussion. Instructors using the book and students taking courses for which it is required should feel free to use the historical survey as a point of departure, the beginning of a discussion, sometimes even the path to an argument. It was not written as a last word or the end of curiosity and debate, but as a beginning.

Provocation of debate and discussion was not the only motivation in the organization of the historical survey. The general approach guiding the selection of contents for the historical survey was an illustration of how ideas and structures central to each century informed the making of music in that century. Certainly the lives and choices of individual musicians play a role in that story. Music and musicians do not merely respond to history; on some occasions they seek to shape it, even anticipating important developments.

The historical survey emphasizes the previous century more than any other. The authors feel they have fairly represented Western concert music from antiquity to the present, but feel that the diversity of action during the previous century warrants its emphasis. Far more than half of the human beings who have ever lived on this planet were alive during some part of the twentieth century. From this fact of human population growth we might conclude that more than half of all the musical activity accomplished by the human race took place during the previous century. In light of this situation, some might argue that the coverage of the last century is too skimpy. Whatever the case, four chapters deal with the music of the last century.

MUSIC AND SOCIETY

To facilitate introducing the general approach of the book, we might create a loose formula of questions we might want to ask ourselves about the musical works discussed in this book. These questions certainly informed the writing of this book, although in order to preserve a conversational tone these questions are not always in the foreground nor are all of them addressed with each piece. The questions that inform this book's approach include:

1. Who was the intended audience for this piece?
2. What were the circumstances that led this composer to create a piece for this audience?
3. In what context was this piece performed, and did the context shape the piece in any way?
4. How was the piece received in its day?
5. What disagreements emerged as a result of the piece and what values were at stake in any disagreements?

These questions can help us understand part of the story. But there are related questions that further our cause, such as a network of questions about the larger society in which the interactions questioned above took place. Some of these might include:

1. What ideas were in circulation that might have informed the writing and reception of this piece?
2. What historical circumstances, such as economic arrangements, hostilities and warfare, or the distribution of power, might have impacted the writing and reception of this piece?
3. What was happening in the other arts, such as poetry or painting, that might reveal parallel social stresses placed upon this piece?

In addition to these social questions, we might link the social with the technical. For example:

1. How might the structure of this piece be linked to the world of ideas?
2. What ideas did musicians draw upon to justify their actions?

We might also investigate how pieces were used after the time of their initial creation. Music often outlives its creator, and as a musical work passes into an unknowable future, the work's meaning might shift, along with the ideas and issues of the new audience. What was boldly innovative to one generation can become old-fashioned to the next. These shifts in taste and attitude can tell students of music much about the ways humans engage music and use it to shape their understandings.

We can see this shift in meaning affecting the entire field of Western concert music, often called "classical music." Classical music has come to be linked with prestige, the upper classes, and intellectuals. The particular ambitions of the day when it was first heard have lapsed into a generalized meaning that it never had before recent times. We can see this shift illustrated in how music gets used today. For example, eighteenth-century classical music is far more apt to appear in the soundtrack for a television commercial selling $45,000 sport sedans than $3 cheeseburgers. The music communicates prestige, and advertisers know that. Among the many things this book will need to chronicle, this shift of meaning ranks high, for this shift in meaning has had a negative impact on music itself. If classical music communicates little more than prestige and privilege for many people today, no wonder music educators are having so much difficulty justifying our presence within the curriculum. We've seen this vigorous art slip from one half of the curriculum, to an essential part of the quadrivium, to an elective, to a discipline ripe for cutting when budgets shrink. The book's goal of introducing students to music in a fashion more useful than replicating patterns of connoisseurship serves a twofold purpose: it aids the student in understanding more broadly and meaningfully; and by shedding light on the many things classical music can mean beyond privilege and prestige, it seeks to reverse the damage done to music within the realm of education. Music is much too interesting, and communicates too many diverse ideas, moods, and worthy abstractions, to fall out of the educated person's field of interests and curiosities.

CHAPTER 2

The Elements of Music

SOUND, SILENCE, AND MUSIC

We are exposed to an immense array of sounds each day. Particular sounds may impress us as difficult to ignore; other sounds are so subtle or distant that they go unnoticed. While there are many people who devote a great deal of attention to subtle aural nuances, most go through life ignoring what they hear and asking themselves no more complex questions than "Do I or don't I like the sound?" Quite a few people appear habitually capable of tuning out several sounds, including those extremely loud, irritating assortments such as car alarms or jackhammers. Others are lured in by marketing strategies encouraging the purchase of "white-noise" devices to block out superfluous reverberations.

Regardless of the variety, or the extent to which we notice, sound is produced by a disturbance that causes a sound-producing object to vibrate. A simple knock at the door initiates a pulsating reaction that generates sound. These small but very rapid vibrations are relayed through a medium, which is usually air, and transmitted to our ears. When our eardrums, which are capable of detecting an extensive range of these pulsations, begin vibrating as well, a signal is sent to the brain. This organ then selects, organizes, and interprets those sounds. Particular varieties may stimulate a learned response, such as answering the door when a knock has been heard, or evacuating a building when a fire alarm has been set off. Other sounds are structured linguistically for communication, a means toward getting to know what someone is thinking and feeling. As information is gathered, the brain perceives silence—the absence of sound—as well. For example, a tacit response to a question may lead to assumptions, or outright conclusions. A pregnant pause often heightens expectations in storytelling, or when it takes place just before the punch line of a joke. In any case, our brain begins cataloging sounds and silence from infancy.

Among the rich diversity of aural perceptions experienced daily, music appears an intrinsic part of all human experience. Many expectant parents, keenly aware of hearing as the first of the five senses developed in the womb, begin speaking and singing to their baby before birth. Perhaps lullabies, as well as other types of children's songs, were sung soon after. Most children, to varying degrees, quickly become active participants at home, at the playground, or in school music programs. Whereupon one continues to pursue music as an active performer or observer, it is easily encountered most everywhere we go. Take a moment to consider the ways we encounter it daily, and then imagine what life would be without it.

One goal of studying music is the acquisition of a more precise means of describing musical experiences. Most verbal descriptions of music rarely rise above this level of precision: "It has a nice melody" or " It has a good beat." There's no harm in such generalities, but the goal of college-level study must be more ambitious. This section will provide you with a more precise technical vocabulary and more sophisticated issues to enrich listening. The end of Chapter Five provides a glossary of terms to aid in the acquisition of useful and precise terminology. Just as college-level students of meteorology would never be satisfied to generalize about how certain weather conditions make them feel, students of zoology would never content themselves to call every primate from a lemur to a gorilla "monkeys," students of music need to aspire to greater precision. Precise description of music isn't an empty intellectual game. Making sense of how music is put together affords an entree into discussions of music with musicians. It may even sharpen the way you listen, lending the entire experience of music more pleasure, or at the very least more precision.

Though many noise-like sounds, such as handclapping, foot stomping, bells, and whistles, are often incorporated into music-making, we will begin by observing the difference between noise and musical tone. *Noise* is any sound producing a series of irregular, unpredictable pulsations in the air, causing diffusion in aural clarity. *Musical tone* produces a series of regular, predictable pulsations that possess more definitive characteristics.

Every musical tone consists of four basic properties: *frequency*, *volume*, *timbre* or *tone color*, and *duration*. We will look at each, and observe their various musical applications. Again, music certainly can and does include noise; however, the distinction between a musical tone and noise begins the process toward a more precise vocabulary.

Frequency (Pitch)

The highness or lowness of different sounds may profoundly effect how we interpret them. For example, higher sounds are intentionally used in mechanical devices such as alarm clocks, smoke alarms, or whistles, to grab our attention quickly and to provoke an immediate response. The sound rising from a whistling teakettle lets us know when the water within has reached a full boil. Low rumbling sounds may inform us that a train is approaching, or more dramatically, may warn us to take cover from a frightening stampede of animals or a nearby tornado.

Frequency refers to the rate or speed of vibrations occurring in an object set in motion. Narrow, shorter vibrating bodies generate higher frequencies, which produce higher sounds. The converse is also true. Wider, longer sound-producing bodies produce lower frequencies, resulting in lower sounds. This is why smaller musical instruments sound overall higher than the larger variety. The musical term used in referring to the relative highness or lowness of sound is *pitch*.

Though much larger, instrumental pitch ranges are directly related to vocal pitch registers, and are often used interchangeably. From high to low respectively, we label them *soprano*, *alto*, *tenor*, and *bass*. The soprano and alto registers usually employ both upper and lower female voices in large vocal ensembles, such as a choir. The tenor and bass pitches are sung by the upper and lower male voices. Instrument makers must initially consider the nature of an instrument's sound-producing mechanism and its intended pitch range. Let us contemplate an assortment of instruments traditionally used in a symphony orchestra, though they represent but a few instrumental varieties.

Orchestral String Instruments

String instruments have their sound produced by taut strings, placed over a hollow wooden body that allows the air within to resonate. The strings on their instruments are set into motion by plucking, strumming, or bowing them, usually near the bridge (a device used to lift the strings up from the main body of the instrument) with the right hand. Performers obtain different pitches on each string by shifting and depressing their left-hand fingers on the upper-portioned lengths. Stopping them in various places allows the performer to shorten and lengthen each string to the desired vibrating distance, and corresponding pitch. Furthermore, the violin (fig. 2.1) is specifically constructed with a smaller resonating body, and shorter and thinner strings (under greater tension) than the viola (fig. 2.2). Although the bottom notes of the violin overlap with many notes on the viola, the violin's overall pitch register is higher. Likewise, the cello (fig. 2.3) shares its upper pitch range with the viola's bottom notes, and its lowest pitches with the upper tones on the bass (fig. 2.4).

The violin has a large pitch range that covers soprano and alto registers. As a result, string repertoire often requires two violinists—a first and a second—to play the soprano and alto parts respectively. In such cases, the viola, a member of the violin family, serves as the tenor instrument, though its wide pitch range allows it to be used as an alto voice when only one violin is employed; it is drawn on in a variety of other musical settings. The bass instrument of the violin family is the cello. However, its extensive pitch range covers the bass and tenor registers, and many higher notes as well. Like the violin, it is a favorite solo instrument, as well as an integral member of the orchestra and many other ensembles.

FIGURE 2.1 Violin   **FIGURE 2.2** Viola (@ Arte & Immagini SH/CORBIS)   **FIGURE 2.3** Cello   **FIGURE 2.4** Bass

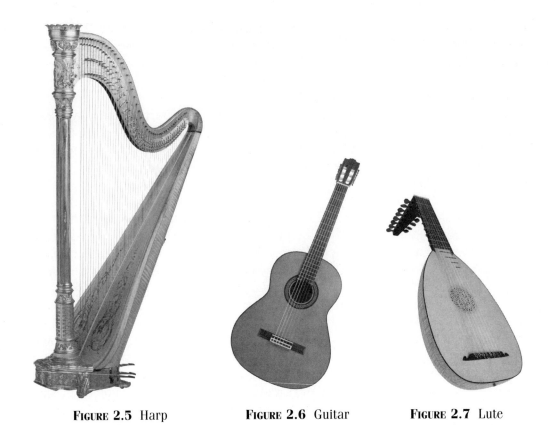

FIGURE 2.5 Harp   **FIGURE 2.6** Guitar   **FIGURE 2.7** Lute

The bass viol, also referred to as the string bass, double bass, or bass, is not a member of the violin family, because of various details of construction. Instead, it belongs to an older instrumental family of strings popular in the sixteenth and seventeenth centuries, the viols. The string bass usually provides deep, rich-sounding support for the upper orchestral strings, as it doubles the cello part in its lower register. Like each of the upper members however, it may also be utilized in an assortment of musical settings, and as soloist. Basses are used in a great diversity of ensembles, from bluegrass to jazz.

The harp (fig. 2.5) requires the performer to pluck or strum its strings, one for each pitch. This instrument can produce several notes at a time, or simply move note to note melodically. They are among the oldest instruments, dating as far back as 3000 B.C., and a great variety of forms have existed throughout history. The orchestral harp is a modern instrument with forty-seven strings, encompassing an enormous pitch range. It is widely used in both solo and ensemble performance.

The guitar (fig. 2.6) and the lute (fig. 2.7) were both used in orchestral ensembles during the Baroque era. In later periods, their use in the orchestra fell out of favor, although there are examples of later works that make use of one or both of them. The guitar has six strings, plucked with the fingertips or with a small pick made of bone, wood, or mother of pearl. Modern picks are often made of plastic. The instrument possesses a wide range, can play both melodies and accompaniments, and is ideally suited to both ensemble and solo performance. In modern jazz ensembles, the guitar has reappeared as a regular part of an ensemble. In order to compete with the louder instruments with which the jazz guitar shares the stage, players now amplify the guitar in many settings. The lute, like the guitar, is plucked with the fingertips. This instrument usually has twelve strings tuned to six different pitches. That is, the instrument is said to be "double strung," since two strings are each tuned to the same pitch. The lute was used in the orchestra during the 1600s and early 1700s. Now it is used only to perform this older repertoire. It is ideally suited for solo performance, for the accompaniment of singers, and in early orchestral music.

Orchestral Woodwind Instruments

The descriptive name "woodwind" indicates that these instruments were previously made of wood, and some still are. Performers of these instruments generate sound by causing the column of air inside their tubular instruments to vibrate. The pitch range of wind instruments is governed by the length and width of its pipe. The longer and wider the tube, the longer the vibrating column of air within, and the lower the pitch. Likewise, the shorter and narrower the tube employed, the higher the pitch. In the woodwind family, there are different vibrating mechanisms to consider.

Flutes are among the most ancient and widespread of all instruments. Older varieties were made of animal bone, clay, and wood. Though some of these materials are still used in various parts of the world, the modern Western European flute is now made of metal. This instrument (fig. 2.8) relies on the performer's ability to direct air in and across an open tone-hole at one end of its long, narrow, cylindrical tube. The sound is produced much in the same way as blowing in and over the top of a pop bottle. The air column is split, causing disturbances or vibrations in the air contained within the instrument. As in all the woodwinds, opening and closing tone-holes achieve a shortening and lengthening of its tube, thus manipulating the air stream inside the instrument. Generally, when fingers are added, the tube is, in-effect, made longer and the resulting sound is lower. Lifting fingers shortens the tube, allowing the air moving inside the instrument to escape through open tone-holes, causing the pitch to be higher. The flute lies comfortably in the soprano pitch range.

The oboe (fig. 2.9) shares much of the flute's pitch range, but because of a wider, longer cone-shaped body, it possesses a powerful low-pitch register and is thereby heard as an alto instrument at various times. Its sound-generating mechanism is a double reed, made from a plant, which is a member of the grass family know as *arundo donax*. The principle used is similar to one many may have experienced after placing two blades of grass together and blowing through them, causing them to vibrate against one another.

FIGURE 2.8 Flute

FIGURE 2.9 Oboe

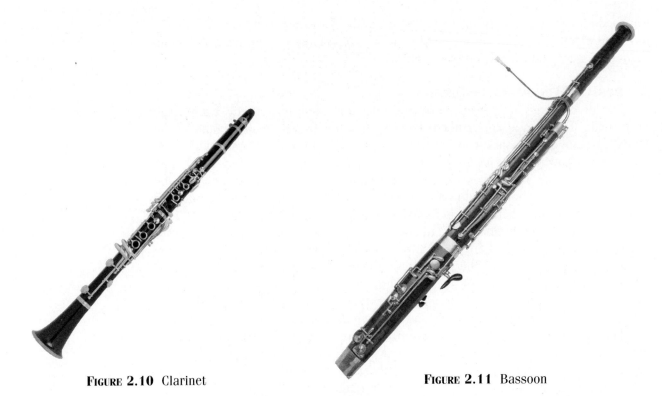

FIGURE 2.10 Clarinet

FIGURE 2.11 Bassoon

With slightly larger dimensions and a conical body, the clarinet (fig. 2.10) boasts a wide pitch range. It shares much of the flute's pitch range and extends several notes below those on the oboe. When performing with its woodwind relatives, it frequently takes the role of tenor. It has one fixed blade, the mouthpiece, on which a single vibrating reed is held by means of a string, metal, or plastic ligature.

Finally, the bassoon (fig. 2.11), like the oboe, is a double-reed instrument. However, its reed is bigger than the oboe's, and its body is much larger than the other woodwinds, easily making it the bass instrument of the woodwind section. In addition to serving as a bass voice, it is equally valued as a solo instrument.

Orchestral Brass Instruments

Modern brass instruments are made of brass or other types of metal, as distinguished from those made of wood. These instruments require the player's lips to serve as a double reed. Air is forced through stretched lips, causing them to buzz or vibrate. Varying lip tension contributes to regulating pitch, and manipulating valves and slides instead of tone-holes accomplish the shortening and lengthening of tubing. When considering the extent of pipe managed on each instrument, we must take into account different wraparound designs, which convenience playing.

The trumpet (fig. 2.12) has the shortest and most narrow tubing in this family, and is the soprano member. Its tube is cylindrical for about three-fourths of its length and then widens out into a moderate-sized bell. In addition to its orchestral role, it is a popular solo instrument in a variety of musical ensembles.

Though the French horn (fig. 2.13) has the largest pitch range of all the brass instruments, it is generally heard in the alto pitch register. The design of its body, commencing with relatively narrow conical tubing which gradually flares to a very wide bell, offers a visual clue to its range. Both trumpets and French horns were used in many ancient cultures. Many early examples were made from animal horns, seashells,

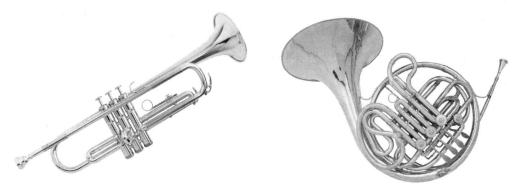

FIGURE 2.12 Trumpet   **FIGURE 2.13** French horn

snail shells, bark, and silver, for the primary purpose of signaling, either in hunting, ceremonial functions, or military duty.

The tenor trombone (fig. 2.14) may provide for the most obvious performance display of tube manipulation. When the slide is extended outward, available pitches are lower; bringing it inward shortens the tube length, and brings into play higher pitches. As its name clearly indicates, its pitches are centered within the tenor range. Instruments fitting more or less the description of the trombone are described in the Bible, making this one of the oldest basic designs for a brass instrument.

Utilizing the widest and longest conical tubing, with a bell pointing upward, the modern orchestral tuba (fig. 2.15) is the bass instrument of the brass family. However, it belongs to a group of instruments that are comprised of many sizes and shapes. The contemporary use of its generic name loosely refers to any bass-pitched brass instruments other than the larger, lower members of the trombone family.

FIGURE 2.14 Tenor trombone   **FIGURE 2.15** Tuba

FIGURE 2.16 Timpani

Orchestral Percussion Instruments

The amount and variety of instruments included in this section of the orchestra have changed dramatically through its history. In Mozart's day, for example, the percussion section only involved one performer, who played two timpani (fig. 2.16) or kettledrums, each consisting of a large copper drum and parchment skin. Presently, orchestral percussionists (usually four, though more may be required for a particular piece) are required to perform on several different instruments, often moving from one to another quickly. Their standard equipment includes a full range of drums, keyboard instruments, bells, and cymbals, as well as gadgets, utensils, appliances, and various implements selected for their unique timbres. This may include incorporating automobile brake drums, whistles, typewriters, radios, washboards, and so on. What categorizes this rich assortment of instruments is the way their sound is produced. Striking a vibrating body produces each sound, though there are few contemporary exceptions made when utilizing such devices as the radio or various whistles. Particular percussion instruments, such as cymbals, tenor (fig. 2.17) and bass drums, have no definite pitch, but a rather conspicuous tone color. Other percussion instruments, such as the marimba (fig. 2.18), xylophone (fig. 2.19), and glockenspiel (fig. 2.20), have a complete series of wooden or metal bars tuned by length and width, to play pitches employed by the other orchestral instrumental families.

FIGURE 2.17 Tenor drum

FIGURE 2.18 Marimba

FIGURE 2.19 Xylophone

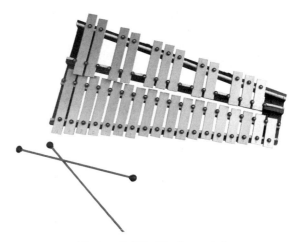

FIGURE 2.20 Glockenspiel

Orchestral Keyboard Instruments

The piano (fig. 2.21) is a relatively new instrument to the symphony orchestra. In earlier times, the orchestral keyboard instruments relied on were the harpsichord (fig. 2.22) and pipe organ. Each keyboard instrument offers the advantage of playing several notes simultaneously, as well as melodies. These instruments do not require other instruments for performance. In fact, they often accompany other single-line or melodic instruments for richer sounding performances. Consequently, a great deal of solo and ensemble music has been written for them. Their distinguishing timbres rest on differences in their sound mechanisms.

Both the piano and harpsichord utilize a full range of strings stretched on a metal frame. The difference in their overall sound is mainly due to the way their strings are forced to vibrate. Depressing keys on a piano's keyboard sets into motion felt hammers that reach up to strike tuned strings. The keys on a harpsichord bring into play little quills that rise to pluck tuned strings.

The pipe organ (fig. 2.23) is the oldest known keyboard instrument, dating back two thousand years. Its sound principles are closely related to the winds, though the instrument remains separate in classification. They have many sets of pipes controlled from several keyboards or manuals, including a pedal keyboard played by the organist's feet. The keys control valves from which air is blown across or through openings in the pipes. The longer and wider pipes produce the lowest pitches, the shorter, narrower pipes the highest. Various sets of pipes are brought into play by pushing and pulling knobs called stops. Each set of pipes possesses a particular tone color. The organist uses each set alone or with others. Pipe organs also come in a large variety of sizes. Some of the earliest designs and sizes allowed the performer to hold them, and were referred to as portative. In particular, the seventeenth century saw the construction of organs, which occupied several stories and rooms within cathedrals. The large pipe organs have a greater range of pitch, volume, and tone color than any other instrument.

What instruments you hear will influence the meaning of what you hear. A pipe organ conveys its tradition in the church. Play the same music on a trumpet and the effect will change entirely. Composers not only choose the instruments they write for, but they can make any combinations they wish.

FIGURE 2.21 Piano   **FIGURE 2.22** Harpsichord   **FIGURE 2.23** Pipe Organ
(University of Oklahoma)

Amplitude (Dynamics)

Dynamics are the second descriptive property of any sound, and refer to its relative loudness or softness. Sometimes the dynamic shifts are sudden and extreme, perhaps moving from loud to very soft, while others may incorporate subtle gradations. Certain instruments, such as the trumpet, are naturally louder than others, and are often reserved for bolder orchestral statements. Nonetheless, all adept performers are considerably capable of varying, and required to vary their dynamics to a large extent. The volume of sound depends on the *amplitude* of its vibrations—how hard the string or air column vibrates. Performers are sometimes encouraged to use their own artistic judgments. More often, composers specify the type and amount of loudness by traditionally using Italian words and abbreviations in the music. Common directives are:

Term	Abbreviation	Meaning
pianissimo	**pp**	very soft
piano	**p**	soft
mezzo piano	**mp**	moderately soft
mezzo forte	**mf**	moderately loud
forte	**f**	loud
fortissimo	**ff**	very loud

Symbols commonly referred to as hairpins, usually indicate more gradual changes in dynamics.

Symbol	Term	Meaning
>	*decrescendo* or *diminuendo*	gradually get softer
<	*crescendo*	gradually get louder

When precise starting and arrival points are desired, the hairpins appear with abbreviated dynamic indications on each end.

The Italian designations for dynamics must all be considered relative to the potentials of each instrument. Singers and string players can make sounds inaudible to anyone standing or sitting even a tiny distance away. By contrast the oboe cannot drop below a certain volume or else the double reed will freeze up and stop vibrating. Oboe players cannot play below a volume sufficient to keep their reeds in motion. A harpsichord or harp or guitar—instruments with plucked strings—are by their nature much quieter than the brass family. A composer can tell a harp to play fortissimo, but the volume produced will be less than a trumpet player told to play mezzo piano. Dynamics are relative to the acoustic potentials of the instruments.

Timbre or Tone Color

Timbre or *tone color* is the third basic property of sound. For many, the concept of color value applies solely to visual realms, though without special training we can appreciate timbre in daily aural perceptions. For instance, the way we distinguish the difference between the sound of a flute and a violin playing the same pitches on a sound recording is by their unique sonorous quality, or tone color. This quality of sound or color depends on the amount and proportion of several simple tones that form and shape the composite tone heard on each. For example, a vibrating string does not only vibrate along its overall designated pitch length, but begins to vibrate in smaller lengths as well. The violin's tone is composed of several softer tones produced by additional vibrating string lengths uniquely related to the instrument. When strings and other sound-producing bodies tend to vibrate simultaneously in halves, quarters, eighths, and smaller fractions, in addition to their full length, softer tones are created and heard as part of the main note. These sounds, called overtones, are very soft on a particular string being plucked or bowed, but when other strings on the instrument begin vibrating sympathetically, the overtones of the first string are reinforced. Overtones are heard as a type of duplication that directly relates to an instrument's tonal character. For example, in a flute, the overtones are much fewer than those of strings. Here, the air column vibrates sturdily along its total length and not very much in halves or quarters. As a result, the flute possesses a whiter tone color than the warm, rich timbre of the violin. Other instrumental timbres are sometimes referred to as bright, dark, mellow, hollow, brassy, and so on.

The unique and arguably the most beautiful and most widely used tone colors belong to the human voice. Consequently, singers' voice types, in addition to pitch range, are often further classified with regard to character and timbre. Some examples are: *dramatic soprano* (a powerful voice with a marked declamatory and emotional ability), *lyric soprano* (possessing a lighter, lyric quality), *coloratura soprano* (possessing great agility and a high pitch range), *dramatic contralto* (producing a powerful sound capable of great dramatic expression), *tenore robusto* (with full voice and vigor), *lyric tenor* (with a lighter, lyric quality), *basso profondo* (low powerful voice and solemn character), *basso cantante* (lighter and more lyric bass), and *basso buffo* (comical, agile bass). In general, Western singers favor an open-throaty timbre. Other cultures favor a more nasal timbre, while still others, such as China, favor a tight throat when singing.

Changes in tone color are sometimes created for variety and contrast. A returning melody can sound expressively different when played by one instrument and then another. Presenting them with a fresh, perhaps bolder, color may highlight new aspects of the melody. Then again, a recurring melody may be appreciated as possessing its own sound signature when kept on the same instrument. There are seemingly infinite possibilities for musical color, especially when we additionally take into account its wider application of bringing together various combinations of instruments and voices. Much like a painter mixing different colors of paint on a palate to arrive at a specific color value, great composers achieve desired tonal colors, in part by varying instrumental and vocal groupings.

Duration

How long a note lasts, its *duration*, is the fourth basic property of musical tone to consider. In musical presentations, tones are perceived within various timeframes. Some may be very short, other quite long. Rapidly performed notes require shorter durations. Longer notes often help to extend slow, beautiful melodies and sustain tonal fields. Hearing low pitches with short durations, interspersed with poignant silences that progress slowly, can sound rather macabre. Strategically used, duration accentuates particular notes as well. For example, a high pitch becomes ever more pronounced as it is sustained. A single pitch may appear to go on into infinity when steadily decreasing its volume to silence over a prolonged period of time. The possibilities seem only limited by imagination, as duration directly affects all aspects of perception.

In a more general sense, timing is the primary concern in all performance arenas. Artistic endeavors such as storytelling, ballet, theater, opera, and so forth, reveal themselves by steps and degrees. In fact, one of the highest artistic requirements in these performance disciplines involves the ability to shape sound and silence through time and space. In music, the organization of sounds and silences through time is called *rhythm*. This organization will be explained in more detail in Chapter Four.

Let's review briefly what we've covered in this chapter, and what it means for serious listeners. Every sound you hear has a *frequency (pitch)*, unless it is a diffused noise. Pitches are discussed as being on a continuum from high to low. In music, the highest pitches are attributed to the soprano range, the lowest to the bass range, with alto and tenor in between. Every pitch has a *timbre* unique to each voice type and instrument. Playing the same pitch on an oboe, a guitar, and a xylophone will result in an important change of timbre. The pitches might be the same, but the way they are heard and interpreted will not be. Every sound has an *amplitude*. Available amplitudes range from deafeningly loud to nearly inaudible. Music stays mostly in the middle of these two extremes. On a guitar, softly plucking a pitch will have an entirely different effect from an amplified guitar plucking the same pitch at extremely high volume. Finally, every sound has a *duration* ranging from so short as to be nearly imperceptible, to so long as to seem infinite. Most music emphasizes note durations ranging from a fraction of a second to several seconds. The important thing to note here is that every musical tone exemplifies all four of these basic properties: *frequency, timbre, amplitude,* and *duration*.

3

Pitch Designations and Relationships in Music

VARIOUS WESTERN EUROPEAN METHODS

Our ears are capable of detecting, within a wide range of perceptible sounds, the slightest incremental differences of pitch. Various types of sirens, slowly sliding pitches up and down, may all too often remind us of this capability. In music, the entire audible pitch range is almost never utilized. Rather, a restricted number of fixed pitches are chosen from this sound continuum.

The Twelve Chromatic Tones

There are many tuning systems to designate pitch preferences used in various parts of the globe, and many methods for arranging them. In the contemporary Western European system, there are twelve basic pitches spaced an equal distance, or *interval*, apart when presented in their respective ascending or descending order. These pitches are given the letter names, A, B, C, D, E, F, G, represented by the white keys on the piano, and A# or B♭, C# or D♭, D# or E♭, F# or G♭, G# or A♭, the black keys (fig. 3.1). The smallest interval in this tuning system is the half step (there are no other keys between the white and black keys). Since a half step is the interval between the closest adjacent notes, the distance from E to F is a half step, just as the distance from F to F sharp (F#), G to A flat (A♭), and so on. Neither a flat (♭) or sharp (#) sign will change the letter name of a note. However, a flat is designated when a pitch is to be altered by *lowering* it a half step (played on the next piano key down), the sharp sign (#) when a pitch is to be *raised* half a step (to the key just above). Clearly, two different labels may be placed on the same black key used to designate the same pitch (for example, A# is the same key used for B♭). Though these notes are spelled differently, we observe that the pitches for each are the same, or that they are *enharmonic*. When the twelve basic pitches, or a portion of them, are heard ascending or descending in order, we say they are moving *chromatically*, meaning "by half steps," up or down.

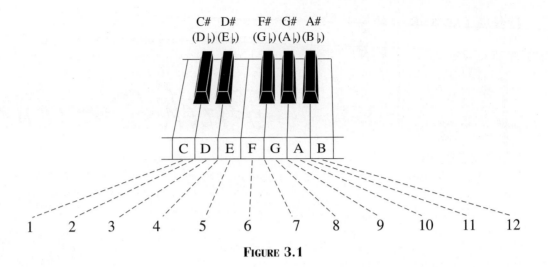

FIGURE 3.1

The Octave

At either end of the twelve basic pitches, a significant sound phenomenon takes place. These arrival points represent intervals in music called the *octave*. The octave refers to the interval span of eight steps, represented by the piano's white keys, and is the place where a pitch is perceived as being "duplicated." For example, each consecutively higher C on the piano strikes a string half as long as the C string immediately lower, causing the upper string to vibrate twice as fast. This mathematical ratio of 2:1 results in pitches sounding so similar that both appear to melt into each other. Its timbre, as well the reinforcement of this duplication, is caused when other strings additionally begin to vibrate in partial lengths, that is, not only along their full length but also in halves and other fractions. The lower octaves produce many more overtones than the upper ones, as there are more strings above them vibrating sympathetically. Eight of the eighty-eight keys on the modern piano keyboard are the pitch C. Likewise, each of the twelve basic pitches on the piano has several octave duplications.

In speaking or singing, it is understood that men's voices will usually be one or two octaves lower than women's voices. When given the same vocal line, they will duplicate each other's singing an octave or two apart. Humans are able to perceive approximately ten octave segments. Most instruments perform within various pitch ranges of two and a half to three and a half octaves. The harp has a pitch range that spans six and a half octaves. Both the pipe organ and piano cover about ten octaves (fig. 3.2).

Various Scales

A *scale* refers to the selected ordering of pitches used for making music, and is in effect a pool of pitches made available. The chromatic scale, consisting exclusively of

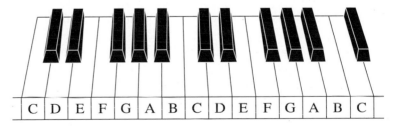

FIGURE 3.2

half steps, gives the sense of wandering, as no one note stands out as more important than any of its half-step neighbors. A performer may start on any of its pitches and move up or down with the same result. Though chromaticism is often incorporated in larger compositions, a good deal of music uses less than the twelve basic pitches and their octave duplications. Instead, a composer often selectively assembles desired pitches from these twelve, into other types of scales that are meant to generate, to various degrees, *pitch hierarchies*.

Diatonic Scales

Among the most widely used are the *diatonic scales*. These scales consist of five whole steps (each whole step equals two half steps) and two half steps, as they are produced on the white keys of the piano—there are no black keys between B and C and between E and F, because they are already half steps. The white keys C to C represent one of the most familiar diatonic arrangements. This particular scale of two whole steps, one half step, three whole steps, and one half step respectively, presents the note C as a central tone. All six other pitches relate and revolve around C, eventually striving to return and to rest on it.

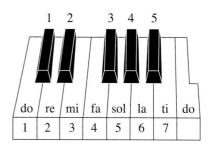

FIGURE 3.3

MAJOR SCALES

C, in this case, is the central note or *tonic* commonly referred to as "do," under a system called "solfege." Singing from low to high using such syllables, they are:

                                                Do

                                      Ti

                                La

                            Sol

                      Fa

                  Mi

            Re

      Do

After singing these syllables up and down, try stopping on a pitch other than "do." You will notice that every other pitch seems to leave matters unresolved. In addition, each pitch appears to take on a specific function as a result of its position in this scale. For example, you may notice the pitch "Re" strongly wants to resolve downward to "Do." "Mi" is in harmonious agreement to "Do," but leaves one hanging if used to conclude. "Fa" usually falls to "Mi." "Sol" strongly wants to jump up to the higher octave "Do," or down to the lower "Do," as either one appears to suffice. "La" is also a good, stable, harmonious pitch, but usually leads to "Ti," which strongly leads upwards to "Do." As the words to the song "Do, a Deer," from the Broadway musical ***The Sound of Music,*** profess:

> **Do**, a deer, a female deer
> **Re**, a drop of golden sun
> **Mi**, the name I call myself
> **Fa**, a long, long way to run
> **Sol**, a needle pulling thread
> **La**, a note to follow sol
> **Ti**, a drink with jam and bread, that will lead us back to **Do**!

This scale, like all scales, can start on any key. By using flats and sharps to adjust pitches so as to maintain the intervallic relationships that make a particular scale unique, represented in this case by the white keys C-C (two whole steps, one half step, three whole steps, and one half step), "Do" may be shifted to any of the other eleven basic pitches, producing the same effect.

MINOR SCALES

Different diatonic varieties, represented solely by the white keys, are achieved by shifting the tonic to any of the other white keys. Starting on various white keys changes the organizational relationships of whole and half steps, which determine its gravitational center. As a result, each diatonic arrangement has been given its own name. For example, much diatonic music presently is also constructed around "La" as the tonic (represented by the white keys A to A), instead of "Do" (the white keys C to C). When the tonic pitch in a diatonic scale is C, it is said to be a *major scale*. With A as its tonic, it is referred to as a *minor scale*. Again, what distinguishes the *major tonality* from the *minor tonality* is their unique intervallic pitch relationships. Both strongly enforce a sense of centrality around their tonic note.

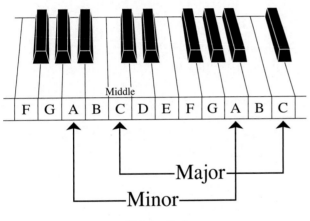

FIGURE 3.4

Unlike the major, the minor consists of one whole step, one half step, two whole steps, one half step, and two whole steps. Though both scales may be experienced with some chromatic alterations, the main difference is in their third and sixth notes. The major scale has its third and sixth notes a half step higher than the minor—thus their respective names; major (larger) and minor (smaller). Consequently, their quality, timbre, and mood differ dramatically. The minor tonality is sometimes referred to as dark, cloudy, or sad, while the major appears more open, cheerful, and happy. Singing some familiar tunes in each tonality may bring to light similar observations. Selections in the major tonality include: "Row, Row, Row Your Boat, "Frere Jacques," "Mary Had a Little Lamb," and "America." Some in the minor tonality are: "Summertime," "God Rest Ye Merry Gentlemen," and "When Johnny Comes Marching Home."

CHURCH MODES

What the major and minor scales share in common is a strong sense of tonality. Other diatonic pitch orderings that can be traced back to the music of ancient Greece orderings which were later used in early Christian church and secular music (often referred to as *church modes*) and are still utilized in a good deal of contemporary music possess to varying degrees a weaker gravitational pull to any one note. These church modes do not sound quite like the major and minor scales more commonly used today. However, we can easily appreciate them for their unique sound qualities and fluid, rich and subtle pitch relationships. Like all scales, each church mode may be referenced by name (fig. 3.5). They are: *Dorian* (represented by the white keys from D to D on the piano), *Phrygian* (E to E), *Lydian* (F to F), *Mixolydian* (G to G), and *Locrian* (B to B).

You may listen to several works utilizing the church modes on [CD 1, numbers 1 through 10].

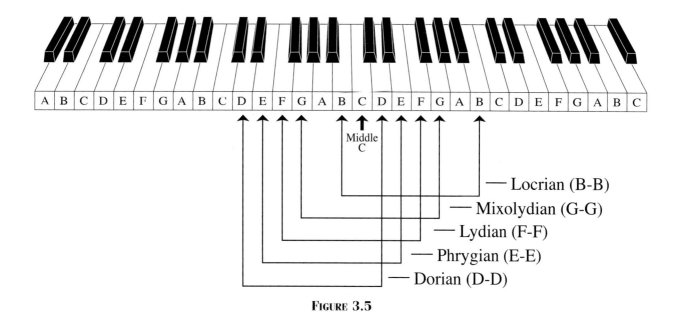

— Locrian (B-B)

— Mixolydian (G-G)

— Lydian (F-F)

— Phrygian (E-E)

— Dorian (D-D)

FIGURE 3.5

Other Scale Patterns

Scale resources considered thus far have mainly focused on those consisting of seven notes, comprising five whole steps and two half steps (the diatonic scales). These scale patterns have dominated Western European music for several centuries, though there is no sound justification for limiting musical resources to them exclusively. Other scale patterns, long favored by non-Western European cultures, have received new attention by Western composers over the past century. One of the most ancient scales is the five-tone *pentatonic scale*, represented in the relation of the black keys of the piano (it is easily reproduced by staying exclusively on the piano's black keys). This scale departs from the diatonic scheme, in that each note may serve as a tonic, and any note that is stressed or on which a musical passage comes to rest will tend to assert itself as such. Its unique timbre is frequently heard in the music of many cultures including China, Indonesia, Polynesia, and much of Africa, as well as that of the Native Americans, Celts, and Scots. In addition, the pentatonic scale frequently occurs in modern Japanese music, and in the music of Impressionist composers such as Claude Debussy (*La Mer, Dialogue of Wind and Waves*) [CD 3, #8] and Maurice Ravel (*String Quartet in F major*).

Another alternative, a six-tone scale often associated with Claude Debussy (he exploited its musical possibilities extensively) is the *whole-tone scale*. As its name indicates, the relationship of the six tones within an octave consists exclusively of whole steps. Like the chromatic scale (all half steps), it immediately creates an impression of wandering, as all of its pitches are uniformly positioned, though it possesses a unique sonorous quality.

The *octatonic scale* is an eight-tone scale alternating between whole and half steps when positioned in ascending or descending pitch order. Like the whole-tone and chromatic scales, its organizational consistency generates a liquid motion, and offers an alternative timbre. This scale figures into the music of Russian composers, especially with Mikhail Glinka, the first to exploit its possibilities.

Alternative Pitch Arrangements

Even though the term *scale* comes from the Latin for "ladder," and people frequently play (or scale) them in their ascending or descending pitch sequence up or down as if they were unadorned melodies, the term does not really imply any particular order of the notes that comprise them. The intervallic pitch relationships of a scale contribute to its character and varying degrees of pitch hierarchy, but once again, the term applies to a collection of pitches chosen for a particular piece, not their ordering. Many twentieth-century composers have realized the value of this concept, and sought to invent new scales for expression that are not necessarily organized by a progression of ascending or descending pitches in the octave. Instead, selected pitches often jump up and down when presented in successive order, and avoid any series of tones, which outline traditional tonal relationships. The primary intent is to deny the importance of tonality, and to renounce it as a desirable quality. Consequently, works utilizing such pitch relationships are referred to as *atonal*, having no tonal center. Nonetheless, since pitch relationships comprising a selected pool of available tones make up its character and timbre, an atonal ordering allows each piece to have a system of pitch relationships that are unique, with each composition possessing its own sound signature. As with all scales, its sound signature serves as a unifying element. There are 479,001,600 possible arrangements of the twelve tones.

Some Alternative Tuning Systems

In addition to alternate possibilities of arranging of the twelve tones, some Western composers make use of the fact that humans can hear an infinite number of pitches within the range of an octave. Designated pitch preferences used by non-Western European cultures offer a hint to the some of the possibilities. For example, in the music of Central Java, the tones of the *pelog* and *slendro* systems (two scales used extensively in Javanese classical music) cannot be replicated on the Western piano. Pitches in these scale systems are much closer together than the half steps used in Western tuning. Instrument makers in Ghana and Uganda do not tune any two flute sets (even two sets owned by the same musicians) alike, so the same tune played on different sets may sound very different, even like a different melody. Here, and in many other countries, it is believed that each instrument possesses a unique spirit, as do human beings. It reveals an approach that is free of a standardized-pitch, tempered-scale tuning system. Music using more than twelve pitches to an octave is called "microtonal."

Though many Western European instruments, like the piano and pipe organ, are designed to produce the twelve particular pitches and their octave duplications exactly, other instruments, such as the human voice, string instruments and the slide-trombone, are easily capable of producing a multitude of microtonal alternatives (as do slide whistles and sirens). A quartertone scale, for example, would include pitches between the half-step keys on the piano, but may be performed by singing them or playing them on an instrument such as the violin, as the performers hand position may easily be shifted up or down to the desired pitch. After all, string players often include expressive slides to some pitches when performing traditional repertoire. A jazz singer occasionally adds a "blue" note, an altered pitch usually slightly beneath the one expected.

Computer-generated sound has already become a viable alternative for producing wide varieties of pitches, dynamics, colors, and durations. Already, we experience synthesized sounds incorporated into the soundtracks of many films, pop songs, and the like. The possibilities seem only limited by the human imagination. These, as well as other post-tonal alternatives, will be explored in more detail in later chapters of this book.

4

Musical Notation

A BRIEF HISTORY

The ability to notate music constitutes an ability to freeze sound in space. This amazing concept has provided the opportunity for someone to open up a musical manuscript and sing or play at sight a piece of music never seen before, just as a literate person might discover and bring to life a new story by reading a book. Whereupon the printed word paved the way for lengthy, intricate novels, plays, and other assorted literature, the practice of Western European musical notation led to the development of extremely complex musical compositions for large ensembles, such as the symphony orchestra and chorus.

Human inscriptions of every kind have a long, extensive history, continuously and dramatically changing in method, style, and meaning. In music, for example, ancient Greek music was notated by two systems utilizing letters, an older one used mainly for instrumental music and a more recent one intended chiefly for vocal music. Archaeological excavations have discovered both systems appearing on papyrus manuscripts, though some were carved into stone. In the Christian era, ensuing developments that led to the modern Western European system of notation are rooted in the much vaguer symbols of Greek and Oriental (Jewish) speech recitation, the grammatical accents of the second century B.C., and similar signs. These symbols evolved into a more elaborate system of stenographic symbols that vaguely signified the outlines of melodic motion. Modifications that took place in the eleventh century led to note shapes that related more accurately to the rise and fall of the melody. The use of the staff—first two lines, then three, and finally four—also stabilized points in melodic contours. In the early twelfth century, the representational appearance of notes acquired square shapes, used to signify more accurately the relative durations of inscribed pitches. Extremely rapid developments followed during the thirteenth and fourteenth centuries, involving frequent changes and innovations that introduced different note values and meter. Remaining almost virtually unchanged, those principles held up until the end of the sixteenth century. The only modification made was the change, around 1450, from black notes (black measured notation) to white notes (white measured notation).

Notation systems most commonly recognized today date from the early seventeenth century. These systems are designed with a five-line staff and solid black or hollow-centered, oval shaped note heads and stems, so as to indicate at the very least (though they often indicate much more) two main properties of musical sounds: pitches and their durations. We will look at some basic techniques encountered in this system of notating sound in time, as well as a few contemporary additions. As in every evolutionary phase of notational practice, however, other types of graphical and even literary methods for notating music coexist.

PITCH NOTATION

A *staff* consists of five lines, and the resulting four spaces, and is used to graphically indicate the relative highness or lowness of pitch. The higher a note is indicated on a line or space, the higher the pitch. Short extra lines added above or below the staff can be used to expand the staff and accommodate a few higher and lower pitches, respectively. These lines are called *ledger lines*.

FIGURE 4.1

In and of itself, a staff only represents the relative relationships between pitches. For example, the beginning note in figure 4.1 is much lower in pitch than the last, although neighboring notes are close. To indicate precise pitches, symbols called *clefs* are positioned at the beginning of each staff to designate a point of reference. Once one pitch is fixed, all other pitches are specifically recognized by name. Multiple clefs may be used, known as the *movable C clefs*, to shift the reference point to every line and space on the staff. We will focus on each of the two most common ones.

The **treble clef** or **G clef** (𝄞), by design, circles around the second line from the bottom of the staff and ends on it. The G clef shows the reader that the note G, just above middle C found in the center of the piano keyboard, is on the second line. This clef is only used to indicate the higher pitch frequencies or treble notes. A pianist's right hand is primarily used for the higher pitch frequencies, all the notes above middle C.

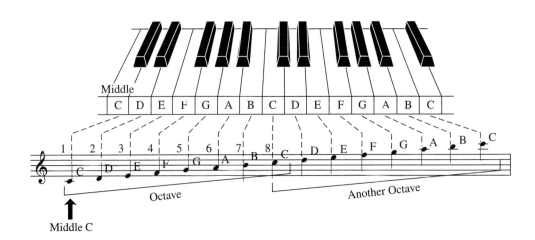

A pianists' left hand mainly takes care of the lower pitch registers on the instrument, from middle C down. To avoid excessive use of ledger lines, it becomes advantageous to shift reference points, or clefs. The **bass clef** or **F clef** (𝄢) has its bulb-shaped portion resting on the fourth line up on the staff. The following two dots accentuate this line by straddling it as well. This line is used to indicate the pitch F, just below middle C. All other bass notes on the staff will be named in relation to this fixed point.

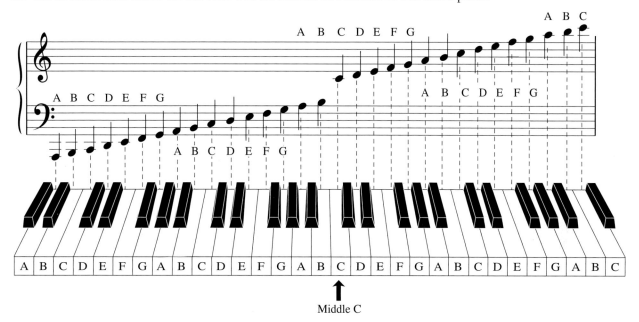

Middle C

As notes with flat or sharp signs added to them do not change their letter names (for example A# or B♭), they do not receive their own line or space on the staff. For example, an ascending chromatic scale is often notated with sharp signs placed on alternating notes with the letter names of their proceeding pitches, which share the same line or space on the staff; flat signs are used in the same way when the scale is descending. Remember, the interval between E-F, and B-C, is already a half step, therefore no sharp or flat sign is required when notating them within an ascending, or descending, chromatic passage.

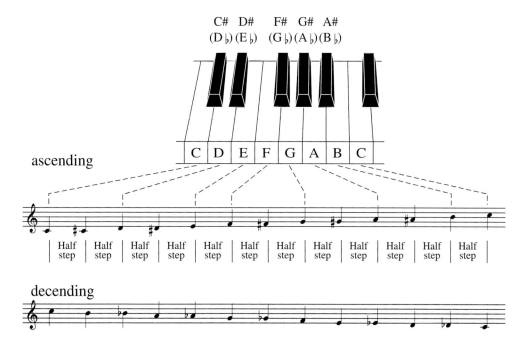

When flats or sharps are used to shift the tonic or "Do" of a diatonic work from its natural white keys, the alterations to the respective note(s) being adjusted are often collectively indicated next to the clef sign. The flats or sharps placed at the beginning of the staff, to indicate the tonality or key applied throughout every measure and in every octave of an entire section or piece of music, are called the *key signature*. A few examples are shown to the left.

RHYTHMIC NOTATION

In musical notation it is also necessary to indicate the relative time placement and duration for every designated pitch. The visual aspects of a note accomplish much of this goal. Various notes have hollow centers; some are all black; particular notes have stems, with or without flags, or beams.

The longest note commonly used in modern music is the whole note. A half note is half the length of the whole, moving at twice the speed. The quarter note divides the half note by two, and so forth. The chart below reflects various relative-durational relationships.

1 Whole Note

2 Half Notes

4 Quarter Notes

8 Eighth Notes

16 Sixteenth Notes

One characteristic feature of the whole note is that it does not have a stem. An eighth note is distinguished from the quarter note by the flag placed at the end of its stem, when it is grouped with other eighths, a beam usually appears. Moving at twice the speed of the eighth notes, the sixteenth note bears two flags or beams. The thirty-second note has three, and so forth.

Since rhythm applies to both sound and silence through time, similar notational values apply to short silences, called *rests* in music. The chart below shows the equivalent relative-durational relationships of rests.

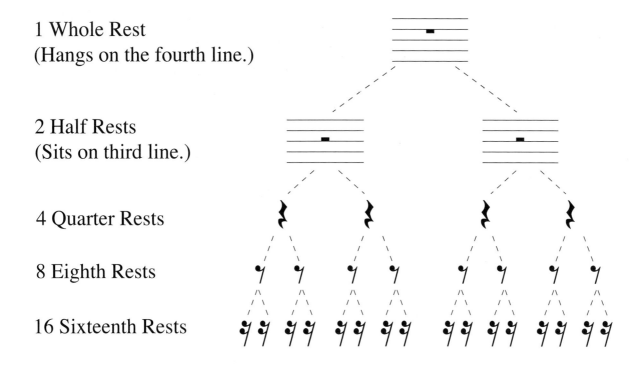

1 Whole Rest
(Hangs on the fourth line.)

2 Half Rests
(Sits on third line.)

4 Quarter Rests

8 Eighth Rests

16 Sixteenth Rests

Durational values of notes and rests are lengthened by 50 percent when a dot is placed after them. For example, a dot on a whole note adds a half note value to it. The dot appearing after a half note extends its length a quarter note, and so on. Some examples of dotted notes and rests are:

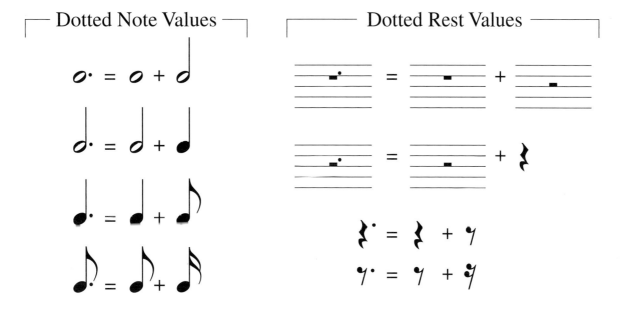

When a note is extended by a dot, a note of shorter value often follows it, though this rhythmic combination is sometimes reversed, putting the shorter note ahead of the dotted note. These amalgamated rhythms are called *dotted rhythms*. We hear and sing them frequently. For example, the "Star Spangled Banner," "America," and "Happy Birthday," makes use of this convention from the very beginning.

Durational pitch extensions may also be achieved by another means. Two notes of the same pitch may be tied together by use of a *tie* (♩‿♩ = ♩) between them. Repeated ties may be used between several consecutive notes of the same pitch to bring about a very lengthy duration. The first note is lengthened by whatever the durational value is of the second, and so on (i.e. ♩‿♩‿♩ = ○).

Rhythmic notation often includes note values that are not multiples of two. Any number of notes may be bracketed together within a specified timeframe. For example, the groupings of three quarter notes, marked with a 3 (♩♩♩ or ♩♩♩ or ♩♩♩) are called a *triplet*. This indication calls for these notes to be performed in the space of two ordinary quarter notes, or 3 in the time of 2. An eighth-note triplet (♫) equals two ordinary eighth notes, or three notes performed in the time of two ordinary eighth notes. This principle is also used for the grouping of five notes, six notes, seven notes, and so forth.

Time Signatures and Measures

As previously stated, the visual aspects of notes can only represent relative time relationships. Just as a fixed point of reference was needed to identify specific pitches on a staff (the clef), a fixed time indication is necessitated. The specific durational unit of measure from which all other rhythmic values will specifically relate, is indicated by the bottom digit of a *time signature* situated to the right of the clef sign. If a 2 appears on the bottom, the unit of measure establishing the pulse will be the half note; a 4 indicates the quarter note as the basic unit of beat; an 8 refers to the eighth note as measurement; and so on. This basic beat will then be grouped into recurring patterns or time units, separated by *bar lines*, relating respective *measures* (or bars) of time. The upper digit of the time signature indicates the length of recurring patterns. If there are two beats to the measure, the upper digit will be 2; when three beats are desired, a 3 will appear; and so forth.

Simple Meter

Depending on whether there are two, three, or four units to the measure, one refers to them as: *duple meter* (2/2, 2/4, 2/8), *triple meter* (3/2, 3/4, 3/8), and *quadruple meter* (4/2, 4/4, 4/8). Collectively, these meters are labeled *simple meters*. As reflected in previous diagrams, some notes of a tune may move faster than the designated beat, some slower. The performer, nonetheless, must feel the steady, continuous pulsation of beats and their groupings.

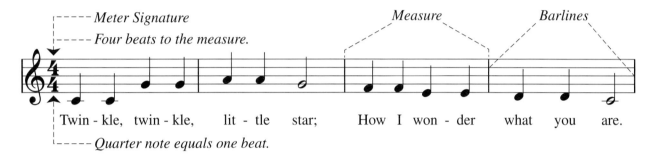

Musical beats are different from mechanized pulses, such as those produced by a clock, metronome, or pendulum. In music, some beats are stronger than other weaker ones. A composer takes this difference into account when determining the length of recurring patterns that will be required in a particular work. The first beat in any metric unit will always be the strongest, and as a result, becomes the determining factor in the length of recurring patterns. For example, listen to where the strongest beat emphasis takes place when singing "Twinkle, Twinkle, Little Star." When singing in a metric pattern of four, you will notice that beat three is also emphasized, but not as strongly as the first beat. Beats two and four are weak. The time signature of $\frac{4}{4}$ is used for this song; a simple meter often referred to as *common time*.

Metric stresses will change within different meters. For example, when writing such works as a waltz or minuet, a metric pattern of three is required, having two weaker pulses following the strong first beat of each measure (a continuous rhythmic pattern that has sometimes been described with nonsense syllables, having an underlining emphasis placed on the first beat, is: <u>um</u> pa pa). Consider this metric pattern in the following familiar melody, "America."

Compound Meter

Exhilarating metric combinations take place in *compound meters*. Compound meters are simple meters, multiplied by three: *compound duple meter* (6/2, 6/4, 6/8), com-

pound triple meter (9/4, 9/8), and *compound quadruple meter* (12/4, 12/8, 12/16). For example, if the time signature is $\frac{6}{8}$, the basic eighth note pulse (indicated by the bottom digit) in recurring groupings of six (designated by the upper number) will often be felt in subdivided patterns of two by means of metric stress, rather than six quick-stressed beats to the measure, or two main beats subdivided into a total of six. (Underlining the two main beats, it is: <u>one</u>-two-three <u>four</u>-five-six). The song "Row, Row, Row Your Boat" clearly reveals the rolling rhythmic nature of this compound duple meter.

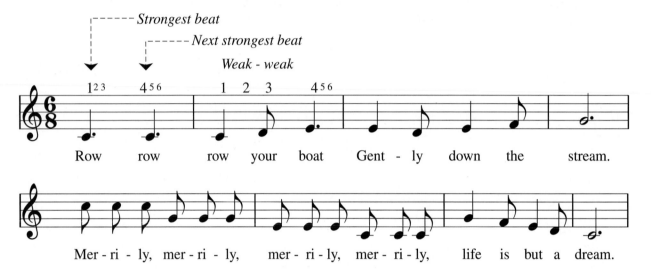

Other Meters

In *quintuple meter* (5/4), the recurring groupings of five are often felt in subdivided patterns of two plus three, or three plus two, depending on where the secondary accent is placed; subdivided patterns for *septuple meter* (7/4), are three plus four, or four plus three. Whatever the case, the basic principles for understanding metric pulse in the examples explored hold true for what appear to be infinite possibilities for metric arrangement.

Tempo

Some works proceed faster than others. *Tempo* is the musical term for the pace at which the rhythmical units progress. When exact time is desired, composers give a numerical metronome indication. For example, the composer might specify above the top-left hand corner of the staff: "quarter note equals mm. 60." This means that the quarter note is the unit of measure, and its pulse will move at the rate of one per second. When more general interpretation is allowed, the tempo indication is traditionally given in Italian. Below are some of the more common terms and meanings.

Term	Meaning
Largo	very slow, broad
Lento	slow
Adagio	slow, leisurely
Andante	slow to moderate walking pace
Andantino	little faster than *andante*
Moderato	moderate
Allegretto	less lively than *allegro*, moderately fast
Allegro	fast (literally means lively)

Vivace   very fast (literally means very vivacious)
Prestissim   very quick

Additional Notations

Like all notational systems, this one remains in constant flux. Various contemporary additions to this notational system are necessitated by the desire to incorporate additional pitches, rhythms, colors, and techniques. Though they are not yet standardized, some notational examples for additional pitches used are:

Perform pitch a quartertone higher when symbol appears in front of note:

$$(\sharp) \text{ or } (\flat)$$

Perform pitch a quartertone lower when symbol appears in front of note:

$$(\sharp) \text{ or } (\flat)$$

The pitch is to be raised any amount less than a half step:

The pitch is to be lowered any amount less than a half step:

A few notational examples involving rhythms are:

Pitches to be performed in any order

Each note becoming faster (accelerating) within the timeframe of a half note:

Each note becoming slower (retarding) within the timeframe of a half note:

Pauses indicated in relative order of short to long:

6" (specific time)

There are many notational directives reserved for specific instruments, as many extended techniques directly relate to only one instrument, or sometimes a family of instruments. A few added performance directions involving non-traditional performance techniques, now commonly used for woodwind instruments, are:

Key-slaps un-pitched (without producing sound by putting any air through the instrument, the player produces percussive timbres on the instrument by slapping on its keys):

Normal notes with key-slaps (sticking the keys hard to create added percussive colors to the pitches being played):

As artists search for new tools to express themselves, notational symbols to represent them will almost surely be added to the extensive vocabulary of signs already utilized. Clearly, not all aspects of music can be notated, nor, perhaps, should they. The most obvious trait is perhaps musical expression. The printed page can only serve as a roadmap to personal interpretation and expression. This aspect becomes very apparent when listeners demonstrate a preference for one performance over another, on any given work. It simply isn't enough to execute the right note at the right time. Anyone can sing the notes of "Hound Dog," but it was Elvis who made music out of it!

CHAPTER 5

The Structures of Music

SIMPLE AND COMPLEX MUSICAL RELATIONSHIPS

Basic musical properties such as pitch, dynamic, timbre, and duration do not exist in the abstract. Consequently, music is made up of both simple and complex structures that utilize various combinations of these fundamental elements. This chapter explores a wide-range of possibilities for expressing diverse musical relationships.

Melody

When the term "melody" is used, it appears most everyone understands its meaning in relation to music. Yet this term can be rather difficult to put into words. Even so, a *melody* is often recognized as a succession of single pitches going somewhere with an appeal to the senses, heard as a recognizable whole. No matter the style, voice type, instrument, or pitch register used, it is usually the most pronounced linear aspect of music—that "tune" one goes home singing.

The melodic line may be confined to a relatively narrow pitch range. At the same time, there are many times when its curve may include several large leaps, in addition to several occasions when it progresses by small intervals, covering a rather wide pitch range. Some melodies contain notes that have relatively long durations, while others are characterized by notes that are quite short. Various melodies may move forward using a rhythmic pattern that is repeated, while others will change dramatically. Melodies are sometimes sung or played very softly, other times loudly. Of course, subtle and bold dynamic gradations may exist as well. When a composer takes into account the selection of pitches, or the scale, that will comprise a melody, it is in addition a contemplation that will profoundly contribute to its quality and timbre.

Indeed, there are numerous considerations involved in creating a unique melodic character, as melodies are often used to express an infinite variety of moods, colors, and images. For example, some melodies may convey the blues, while others communicate joyfulness, playfulness, love, horror, fright, action, celestial contemplation, meditative states, and so forth. Nevertheless, what most melodies appear to hold in common is their potential to encourage the listener's interest in where the succession of notes leads that comprise them, and what moods they relate.

A melody, like any good story, is communicated by a progressive series of thoughts, feelings, or ideas. In literature, for example, words are chosen and organized for a particular purpose. Grammatical structures such as sentences are often based on a linear sequence of words that make up structural units, called phrases, with each one leading logically to the next. Likewise, melodies often consist of smaller parts called *phrases*. A phrase is a sequence of notes grouped together to form a unit in music, each leading sensibly to the next. When text is used in music, the string of words that grammatically form a unit often dictates the musical phrase length and place of pause. For example, when lyrics end with a rhyming word and punctuation mark, the musical phrase will often coincide with, and emphasize, those features. A few examples of two rhyming lines, also marking two symmetrical musical phrases, are:

Twinkle, twinkle, little <u>star</u> [comma]
How I wonder what you <u>are</u> [comma]

OR

Ring around the <u>rosy</u> [comma]
Pocket full of <u>posy</u> [comma]

Frequently, all phrase lengths in a particular piece are two, four, eight, and sixteen measures (or bars). The blues, for example, are fundamentally made up of three, four-bar phrases; commonly referred to as "twelve-bar blues." A familiar folk tune, "By the

FIGURE 5.1 | *Au Clair De la Lune*

Moon's Faint Light" ("Au Clair De la Lune") continuously repeats the rhythmic patterns of the first four bars, which are made up of two smaller units of two symmetrical bars. All of its phrases add up to sixteen measures or bars. You may notice (fig 5.1) that lines one, two, and four, are also comprised of identical pitches, though the text changes. This kind of musical repetition may be indicated by means of lower-case letters, signifying the internal relationships of phrase lengths, as opposed to capital letters often used to refer to larger organizational relationships. Hence, the structure of this melody is **a a b a**, its **b** material providing the only contrasting phrase.

In much music, as in much speech, phrase lengths are not always equivalent. The melody "America" has phrases that are not of equal length. Its first phrase is six measures long, consisting of three, two bar units; bars three and four repeat the rhythms of the first two. The second phrase begins by repeating the rhythms of the first four measures of the melody, but suddenly introduces different rhythms that cause this phrase to be extended to eight full bars. The melody is fourteen bars long, made up of a six-bar phrase and an eight-bar phrase, with their respective subdivision of units. The melodic form is **a b**.

"America"

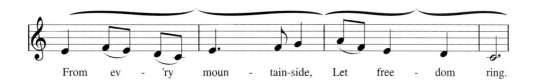

When following a melody's linear contour and mood, we often notice that it builds to a high point, or climax, arriving approximately three-quarters of the way into a song, resolving its tension near the end. Sometimes its climax is the result of a steady melodic progression to a high note. Other times, it may be expressed by one large leap upwards. A whole passage may otherwise be used to build to, and sustain climactic action. The *climax* is the most exciting or important moment, or the point toward which a melody strove. In "The Star Spangled Banner," the climax is boldly professed with the phrase, "and the land of the free." So important is the word "free" that it is assigned the highest note of the song, and the singer or instrumentalist is afforded the liberty to hold it for a very long time, to extend (a musical metaphor) and thus heighten the climax even more. The tension wanes immediately after, with the phrase, " and the home of the brave." Here, the music also leads to a sense of conclusion. Such stopping places in music are called *cadences*. Of course, as in grammatical punctuation, musical stopping or pausing points may reflect many different degrees of finality. Consequently, musical punctuations are found at the end of phrases, melodies, entire sections of larger works, and at their finish.

A melody is often used as a central feature in large, complex structures, generally written for ensembles such as the string quartet, symphony orchestra, or choir. When this happens, the melody is referred to as a *theme*, which means "subject" or "topic." As a theme, it usually gets manipulated in various ways. It may have its rhythms exaggerated in length (*augmentation*), or shortened (*diminution*). It may have its overall phrase length shortened repeatedly, reducing it to just a few basic notes (*fragmentation*). It may be presented in different tonalities, or played by different instruments to achieve different colors. In addition, such genres generally include more than one theme, presented as an emotional, tonal, and color contrast. All the same, each principal or basic melodic subject is considered a theme, and is open to thematic exploration.

Motives

Though the term "theme" may apply to a full-blown melody, as "topic," it may also serve to reference a short musical idea. This thematic material, consisting of at least two notes forming the basis for development in a piece of music, is also more specifically labeled a *motive*, or *motif*. One way to appreciate the power a musical motive may possess is to initially compare the entire concept to the business world's use of a logo. The most basic of symbols (such as an upward-curved line) can potentially conjure up a company's entire line of products, the places they are sold, their production, and their marketing strategies, as well as any other preexisting knowledge about it. In music, once a motive is introduced, all musical material contributing to its initial mood, character, and capacity is automatically associated with it, even when the briefest and most basic glimpse of its return takes place. The introduction of a motive may also serve as the seed or germ from which an entire piece unfolds. Arguably; the most famous musical motive in classical music repertoire comes from the opening of Ludwig van Beethoven's *Fifth Symphony*. In this case, the rhythmic motive

(Rhythm: short - short - short   —   long)

represents in Beethoven's words, "fate knocking at the door," and provides the basis for his entire symphony. For those readers who are not familiar with this symphony, and who can find the courage to reflect on, or to view, or review, the movie *JAWS*, you will quickly appreciate the power that can be generated by a half-step motive presented in a low pitch register. This motive is introduced and developed at the beginning of the film and utilized throughout, to represent a gigantic shark's imminent appearance and savagery, or at various times to simply, but dramatically, lead the viewer to "only" imagine it. If there are any doubts that remain about the enormous power this particular motive holds after viewing this movie, try rewinding your video machine to a place where you know the shark is about to appear, and watch that segment again without audio. Need more evidence? Another, and perhaps more terrifying, example still may be the motive associated with Alfred Hitchcock's famous "shower scene," in his movie *Psycho*. The musical motive here, which simply constitutes repeating a succinct high note, is so poignant that it is sometimes borrowed out of context, by someone often singing it with gestures mimicking a stabbing, to make a very stark point.

Though the examples used in this section may all appear rather bleak, they were selected to demonstrate to the reader that the musical brevity of a motive should in no way suggest its potential, for motives could carry with them a rather serious emotional and psychological wallop. The reader should also realize that motives in music are used to represent any number of things, some involving non-extra-musical associations (instrumental music that is self-contained, showing no reference to outside sources), but with no less poignancy. Then again, following recurring motives and their transformations may simply help guide the listener through musical journeys that are otherwise vague or ambiguous, but endlessly suggestive.

Texture

The term "texture" comes from the word "textile," where it refers to the weave of assorted threads in a piece of cloth. In music, *texture* is a term used to describe the various sounds and melodic lines taking place concurrently. The musical term is often used in the same way one generally describes clothing. The texture of music may be described as thick, when several voices, instruments, or their combination are simultaneously active; a thinly textured work is the opposite. If a piece appears dominated by brass instruments, one might say the work's texture is "brassy"; the texture of another work might simply be described as smooth," or "rough," and so on. Another sense of texture refers to a specific interactive approach utilized.

Monophony

When there is only one unaccompanied melodic line, its texture (or weave) is *monophony*. "Mono" means "one" channel carrying "sound," ("phony"). One may experience this texture quite often, especially if one is prone to sing alone, perhaps while driving a car or taking a shower. In musical repertoire there exist many wonderful melodies that have been intentionally written for unaccompanied voice or instrument. For an example, please listen to "Alleluia," from the "Mass for Christmas Day," [CD 1, #2].

Polyphony

Polyphony is a texture that describes two or more melodies being sung or played simultaneously. "Poly" means "two or more" channels conveying "sound." The interest here is how each independent melodic line weaves in and out of the other. Many may have experienced using this texture while singing children's songs. A few examples include: "Row, Row, Row Your Boat" and "Frere Jacque." Both songs are intentionally written so that they may be sung with staggered vocal entrances. For example, in "Row, Row, Row Your Boat," after the first person or group begins, the second joins in from the beginning of the melody after the first person or group has completed singing the first two measures. A third person or group may begin after the second group has finished singing the first two measures. Each person or group, once arriving at the end, may repeat the entire song as many times as desired. The example on the next page illustrates how this works. The bracketed staffs show the individual parts, occurring simultaneously.

Clearly, after singing the same melody, one person or group cannot justifiably claim that the melody they sang was any more important than another. Instead, the overall result from singing this polyphony hopefully produced a richer sonority and greater attention to how the individual parts functioned together, compared to singing

this melody monophonically. Because all voice parts sang the same melody, one person or group imitated each of the others. *Imitative polyphony* takes place when two or more simultaneous melodic lines use the same or quite similar melodies, but with staggered entrances. Often, composers or performers will use imitation for short musical ideas. Sometimes they do not use the same or similar melodies when incorporating polyphony. Instead, they may use very different melodies. This texture is called *nonimitative polyphony*. A familiar nonimitative performance practice occurs in jazz, when each instrumentalist begins improvising (making up music on the spur of the moment) at the same time as another. An example of nonimitative polyphony in jazz may be heard in Louis Armstrong's, "Hotter Than That," [CD 4, #13]. An early notated use of this technique may be heard in Guillaume Dufay's, "Nuper Rosarem Flores," [CD 1, #7].

Homophony

Another kind of texture takes place when only one melody of real interest is presented with other sounds that do not really stand up on their own, but are used in such a way as to be harmoniously supportive of the melody. This texture is called *homophony*, and is perhaps the most commonly used today. Most pop songs, folk songs, blues songs, as well as textural sections within larger works such as a symphony, utilize it.

The subordinate sounds of the "accompaniment" often consist of chords. A *chord* is comprised of three or more notes played or sung simultaneously to harmonize and embellish a melody. When presented in their respective pitch order, each tone is usually the interval of a third apart. Sometimes the harmonic style outlines each chord by playing the notes one at a time. Sometimes the harmony will only consist of an interval (two pitches), suggesting an entire chord. Nonetheless, when we begin to focus our attention on the harmonic progression of chords, we will notice that some chords appear to demand resolution to another chord that seems at rest. Such examples are perhaps most obvious at the very end of a piece, as the listener is often led to a sense of final conclusiveness. The term *dissonance* or *discord* is used in such cases to describe intervals or chords, or any other musical sounds, that sound relatively unstable and needing resolution. *Consonance* refers to intervals or chords, or any other musical sound combinations, that sound free of tension or discord.

Even so, we will come to understand in the historical chapters of this book how the meanings of the terms "consonance" and "dissonance" have changed profoundly through time. To serve as an example, a general survey would look something like this:

In ancient Greek culture, the numerical system of musical sounds and rhythms epitomized the harmony of the cosmos and thus corresponded to it. Any pitch that was not in agreement with the natural order of the universe was viewed as discordant, or a disturbance within it, and was therefore perceived as something producing chaos. In early medieval times, the concept of consonance and dissonance was appreciated by the relationship of any two successive notes in a melodic line. They even held superstitious notions about certain intervals. For example, the "augmented fourth" or "diminished fifth" (an interval constituting seven half-steps; for example the notes "C" to "F sharp") was seen as the "devil's interval," and most certainly avoided.

Renaissance composers were certainly concerned about the pitches that make up a melody, but focused as well on maintaining consonant pitch relationships between two or more melodic lines occurring at the same time. Later, Baroque musicians looked to the relationship existing between the pitches occurring in a melody, as well as all others, to those in the bass. It was Classical period composers who really shed attention on particular chord qualities and their progressions, as discussed above. Toward the end of the Romantic period, chord progressions had begun serving as a vehicle for extended harmonic journeys (achieved by suspending their succession in various ways, so as to avoid resolutions, and returns back "home" to the tonic). As most are aware, by the early twentieth century, all traditional distinctions representing dissonance as something so unstable that it needed to be both anticipated and resolved relatively quickly to a consonance has been completely abandoned. In addition, generalized labels assigned to consonance and dissonance, such as "pretty" and "harsh," become inappropriate. For example, the medievalists' interval "which belonged to the devil," is now used to begin Leonard Bernstein's very famous and "beautiful" song, "Maria," from *West Side Story.* Also, the half-step motive utilized in the movie *Jaws*, already explained in some detail, would never be described by anyone as "beautiful," "peaceful," or musically stable. As the twentieth-century composer Igor Stravinsky so eloquently stated:

> *Dissonance is no longer tied down to its former function. Having become an entity in itself, it frequently happens that dissonance neither prepares nor anticipates anything. Dissonance is thus no more an agent of disorder than consonance is a guarantee of security.*

This said, an appreciation of consonance and dissonance in musical repertory is now largely dependent on the listener's ability to decipher the composer's intent, or to experience a specific work with some preexisting knowledge about the composer's style.

Finally, the listener should be aware that the texture of any given work might, and often does, change. This is especially true of lengthier compositions, for changes of texture sustain interest as they create variety and contrast.

Musical Style and Form

To varying degrees, all human expression takes place within the cerebral, spiritual, emotional, and visceral realms. Utterances of any kind can be expressed freely, subtly, or boldly, and without any pre-thought or consideration. Yes, a simple "grunt" can be a means of meaningful communication! Even the boldest outcries could often be impulsively expressed by making use of recognized structural patterns. For example, when someone spontaneously yells out "I hate this!", we may still observe the declaration as an outburst; because the person professing it utilized known linguistic speech patterns, we are more aware of its specific emotional meaning, as the statement also intimates that the particular person or group to whom it is generally directed understands what "this" is referring to. Recognized units of expression often serve as a more direct or specific means of communicating human ideas and feelings.

Human expression through music may be understood and appreciated by means of a performer freely articulating sounds used solely for their unique quality and purpose. Musical compositions are often assembled into specific structural patterns, easily recognized as a learned means of communication. Sometimes a composer will alternate the methods and of course, both manners may successfully coexist. A few concurrent examples are when a musical manuscript directs a performer to execute a foot-stamp within an otherwise traditional sounding instrumental piece, or, when we hear the great soul-singer, James Brown, freely sing, "OW! I feel good," at the beginning of his tune. The initial vocalization by James Brown in the last example could have easily been interpreted in a variety of ways. It was only after he vocally professed, "I feel good," that the intent was somewhat qualified. Clearly, the initial outcry not only captures the listener's attention from the beginning, but also proves to be an integral, meaningful, and exuberant addition to what might have otherwise appeared as a mundane musical phrase in the hands of another singer. In the first example, we observe that an instrumental piece (a musical work without text lines sung or spoken) cannot in and of itself be as specific as a work utilizing text. Instrumental sounds may nevertheless be appreciated as free from the strict definitions of words and syntax of sentence (much like a good deal of poetry and visual art), and may therefore become infinitely suggestive. Essentially, then, in the instrumental example specified, interjecting a foot-stamp within a more traditional, learned means of interaction could effectively accent, color, and dramatize other musical material associated with it.

Interactions of every kind mostly rely on generating recognizable shapes for expression, appearing in infinite variety and size. We have already explored how the basic elements of music may be used to construct larger shapes such as a phrase, melody, or texture. These musical constructions frequently become the building blocks for still larger contemplations, incorporated into the overall shape or planned design of a large musical composition. The ways in which the various musical sections are deployed in linear time dictate the composition's form.

Form in music is often associated with any musical interactions that produce a sense of overall shape and structure. This effect may be achieved by any of the methods described above. Sometimes music is spontaneous; other times it may be predetermined, while still other means reflect combinations.

Because such considerations deal with large, integrated structural forms, calling to mind various structural differences in housing construction might make a helpful comparison. Upon completion, we readily recognize the overall shape or form of the composition as a house. We also understand that houses appear in an assortment of shapes and sizes, and that each is made up of several smaller parts, which may be appreciated separately. For example, the type of wood and the nails that hold it together are a few of its fundamental elements. Larger units—the windows, the roof, entranceways, and so forth—all maintain unique shapes as well. Essentially, the overall form (the house) is recognized as a complex structure that represents a synthesis of several smaller shapes. *Style* is the recognized way in which the formal elements (the form) of a composition have been handled so as to provide the whole with expressive effect.

When the concept of form is applied to music, it could represent the overall shape of a relatively short work such a folk song or pop tune. Form can also apply to the organization of a large, self-contained unit within a sizable work such as a symphony. In such cases, the term *movement* is used in referring to one of these sections. The meaning and purpose of a movement's relationship to a larger work might be thought of in much the same way we appreciate the connection that a "chapter" has to a novel (as opposed to a short story, which may perhaps equate to the pop tune). If the reader prefers to return to the initial analogy, a movement may be compared to a self-contained housing unit within a larger composition such as a duplex or triplex.

In any case, the overall plan or method of organization relies on our memory to recognize various parts of music and how they relate to each other when they return. They generally return by exact repetition, altered recurrences, or within contrasts taking place among other material. The pleasure the listener receives by recognizing the return of a musical pattern, such as an entire melody, becomes a useful tool for organizing entire sections of a particular work. The time it takes for a passage to return influences the listener's reaction to it. For example, when a melody that is introduced at the beginning of a lengthy work does not return in its entirety until the end, the melody is not strictly appreciated as repetition, but more importantly with an added sense of balance, symmetry, and, in some cases, resolution.

The word "return" most obviously suggests some kind of departure. This may simply be reflected by a shift of mood in the music, often achieved by a change of tempo, dynamics, color, mood, a new melody, and so on. Sometimes the idea is demonstrated by outright musical conflict. Simply, the music must create noticeable *contrast,* for the listener to perceive a sense of departure from earlier material, and to then appreciate when that musical material returns.

Let's consider a few well established, pre-determined methods for structuring musical forms. For purposes of introduction, the forms are explored as basic outlines. Hopefully, the reader has already begun to appreciate that musical interactions of every kind are subject to artistic license and integrity. In addition, significant modifications to each have resulted from prevailing historical preferences. A medieval house has a roof, walls, windows, doors, and so on, but it appears much different stylistically from more modern versions.

Various Types of Musical Structure

Theme and Variations Form

As the structural name clearly indicates, a melody will be introduced at the beginning of a composition, or movement within a larger piece, to serve as theme. This opening material will then be followed by multiple sets of variations on it. The intent is also to allow the listener to recognize the theme presented over and over again, although various decorative notes are often added to it as the variations proceed. In addition, interest is sometimes sustained in variations by contrasting the texture, timbre, tempo, and so on. Sometimes the particular ordering of variations will lead progressively to variations that are more and more animated, creating a sense of climax. Regardless, the number of variations differs from work to work, since they may continue until the composer feels he or she has fully explored all of the musical possibilities a particular theme may hold, or when the numbers of variations following a theme are composed in proportion to the length of other movements.

Like all forms, small musical sections may be tagged on to the beginning, as well as the end. A section added to the beginning is called an *introduction*. The section placed at the end is called a *coda*, Italian for "tail." Both introduction and coda do not represent part of the described form, but serve as additions to it. In theme and variations form for example, an introduction would not be used to introduce the theme, nor would a coda placed at the end be used to represent another variation. This musical concept may be appreciated by using our earlier analogy, for it is very much like the optional front and back porch an architect may choose to add to the overall structure of a house.

The third movement of Wolfgang Amadeus Mozart's **Piano Concerto Number 17,** is in theme and variation form, and can be found on [CD 2, #7]. Mozart adds a coda section to conclude this movement. (The term "concerto" is explained under ritornello form. Also, all musical examples used in this chapter with CD references will be explored in more detail in corresponding historical chapters.)

Ritornello Form

Typically, the *ritornello form* is applied to the first and last movements of a baroque style concerto. The term *ritornello* has a double meaning. It refers to the orchestral material introducing the ritornello theme in homophonic texture at the beginning of the movement. Also, because its name means "little return," the opening material will come back throughout the movement, but in fragments ("little"), and in different keys until the end, when it is usually presented again in its entirety, and in the original key.

The word *concerto* means, "to contend." When utilizing a small group of soloists in a baroque style *concerto grosso* ("group"), additional contrast, or contention, is provided between the varied orchestral returns of the ritornello. Though the soloists often utilize ritornello material as well, they toss various ideas and embellished treatments of it back and forth between themselves in imitation, as opposed to the homophonic orchestral returns. Contrast between the orchestra and group of soloists is also achieved by dynamic variance, since the small group of soloists will naturally sound softer than the orchestral *tutti*, meaning that everyone plays. As wind instruments were not a standard part of the baroque string orchestra, they offered further contrast in timbre when employed as soloist.

Essentially, this form encourages the listener to anticipate the orchestral returns of the ritornello, though altered in treatment, as recognized phrases between contrasting material provided by the group of soloists. As this form is frequently applied to the first and last movements of a baroque concerto, the composer often has the orchestral ritornello build to an emotional climax three-quarters through the movement, where one soloist is traditionally featured. Here, the soloist is asked to play an improvised passage, unaccompanied, that is usually based on previous material. An improvised solo within a larger work such as a concerto is called a *cadenza*.

The outline below reflects the general scheme of this form, and may be a helpful listening tool. For a musical example, please listen to the first movement of **Brandenburg Concerto Number 2,** by Johann Sebastian Bach, on [CD 2, #1].

Ritornello Form:

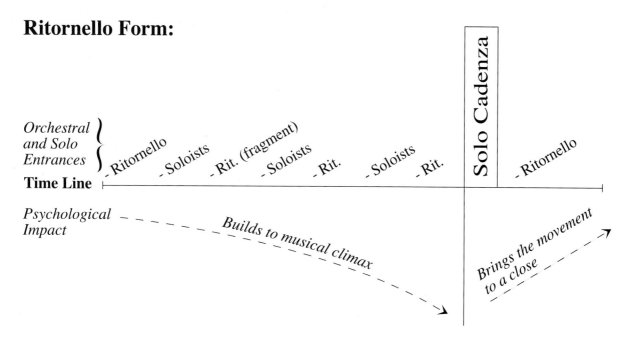

The Fugue

The fugue is more of a style, or technique, or way of writing, than a specific form. As a result, it is extremely flexible and varied. A fugue could represent a single work, a movement within a larger composition, or a section within any movement. It could be written for various voices or instruments, or for a solo keyboard instrument, utilized to execute multiple melodic lines. In any case, each linear line in a fugue is referred to as a *voice*.

The *fugue* is a polyphonic composition for an established number of voices, built on a single principal theme called the *subject,* as all parts will be based on the same linear material. The fugue subject is relatively brief, but distinctively bold, usually consisting of relatively few pitches and clear rhythms, for easy recognition. In addition, the subject is almost always noticeably presented in one voice at a time at the beginning, with each entrance staggered. The opening section of the fugue, in which all the voices introduce the subject in an orderly manner, is called the *exposition.* If a particular fugue is comprised of two parts, each voice will commence with the subject in turn. If it is a three-part fugue, or four-part fugue, and so on, the exposition will systematically continue until all voices have entered with the subject.

Each voice utilizes a different pitch register, the highest being the soprano and the lowest the bass. The introductory orderings of the subject will not necessarily be from the bottom voice part up, or top voice down. Instead, it may originate in any voice. For example, in a four-part fugue, the first entrance may very well commence in the alto voice, the second in the bass, and the third in soprano, followed by the tenor. Irrespective of their arrangement, the first voice entrance is always in the tonic or home key, while the second voice, often called the *answer,* enters in a second key as contrast. When a fugue incorporates multiple voice parts, the following entrances will usually continue to alternate between the tonic and second key, which is frequently the dominant, located five scale steps higher in the chosen key.

After the subject in the exposition is stated, the melodic line usually moves to a *countersubject*, making room for another subject entrance to be heard. The countersubject is a distinctive polyphonic line that recurrently accompanies the subject in another voice. It almost always proceeds with quicker notes, and with rhythms that are not as poignantly defined as the subject. Though the countersubject is distinctive, its function is descriptively captured by its lesser role of accompanying, or countering, the subject in another voice. Once again, the intent is for the subject to be heard as it is passed from one voice to another. After all the voices of a fugue have entered in turn with the subject, the first section, the exposition, of the fugue is concluded

Diversionary music called an *episode* follows. Here, the fugue often appears to wander, since all the melodic lines start to move freely, and the tonality constantly modulates. Fugal features may include holding a single note in the bass while other voices progress with a succession of changing harmonies against it. This technique is called *pedal point*, as it most often pertains to an organist's foot ("pedal"), which manipulates a pedal keyboard, used for bass notes on an organ. At times, harmonic resolutions are prolonged by repeatedly holding over one or more pitches from a preceding chord into the next, which would have otherwise resolved the prior harmonic tension. This is called a *chain suspension*.

Though diversionary material is sometimes derived from the subject or countersubject, an episode's particular quality brings contrast to later subject entries. This section of other material seems less solid than the subject entries, as it freely explores harmonic textures and colors. The freedom generated may even cause the listeners to lose the ground beneath them, because there is nothing solid to hold onto. Various returns of the subject are anticipated.

The fugue falls into an alternating pattern of new subject entries and episodes. There is no strict rule as to how the subject returns. Unlike the exposition, it does not return in all voices, nor does it usually return in its entirety. Instead, it appears in fragments, and in different keys. Sometimes one voice will overlap with another, as a second voice may enter before another has finished, a feature called *stretto*. The rhythms of the subject may be lengthened (augmentation) or shortened (diminution). There are times the subject is played note for note in reverse order, or in *retrograde*. Subjects may undergo a process known as *inversion*. Here, if the subject originally moved up a whole step from the first note, the inversion will move down the same interval. This technique continues, with each interval comprising the subject, as all will be reversed in direction, turning or inverting the subject upside-down. No matter the treatment, later subject entrances serve as structural stepping-stones, in an otherwise free-flowing fugal texture. Alternations between subject entrances and episodes continue until the composer, or performer (if the fugue is being improvised), has explored the subject material fully.

Johann Sebastian Bach's "Contrapunctus III, from **Art of the Fugue**, may be found as an example on [CD2, #3].

Sonata Form

Sonata form has so frequently been used for the first movements of sonatas, symphonies, string quartets, overtures, and so on, that it is sometimes referred to as "first-movement form," or "sonata-allegro form." Nonetheless, these labels may be misleading, since this form is often used for other movements in many works as well.

A movement structured in *sonata form* consists of three traditionally indicated sections: exposition, development, and recapitulation. These labels are a little misleading as well, since the exposition, which introduces all of the musical ideas before they are developed and afterwards recapitulated, consists of two groups, and is repeated in almost all early applications, causing it to be experienced as a four-part structure. In such cases, the sectional scheme may be indicated as: **A A B A**, with each **A** section being made up of two parts.

The exposition introduces two main themes (though sometimes more), which usually contrast each other in mood and key. The *first theme* is always presented in the tonic key, and is often dramatic or agitated in quality. The *second theme*, usually lyrical, in a second key from the first, commences the second part or *group*. These themes and tonalities are connected by a *bridge*, which is a modulating passage that moves from the tonic key to the second key, normally the key of the dominant if the tonic is major, or the relative key if the tonic is minor. The exposition is closed with a *cadence theme*, or "closing material" that is usually less distinct, sometimes consisting of only descending scales or chords.

The psychological impact is one that moves the listener from a sense of stability (even though the first theme may be agitated) to an awareness of conflict, as the melodic lines, moods, and keys are sharply contrasted. Repeating the exposition is aesthetically important, because it helps the listener to remember the themes that serve as bases for the entire movement; the repeat also accents the conflict by literally reiterating its existence. In essence, the listener is led into heightened developmental tension with familiar thematic material. The development section, now positioned as the third of four sections, will be experienced as the climax, taking place three-quarters of the way into the movement.

The emotional impact of the development section is achieved by musically developing any or all thematic material introduced in the exposition. As discussed earlier in this chapter, various themes may be juxtaposed, augmented, and fragmented, while harmonies rapidly modulate. Various themes, or the motives that comprise them, will often be in inversion, retrograde, and so on. There are no set rules for how a composer will develop thematic material, as artistic freedom, ingenuity, and imagination are employed. Once again, this unknown developmental journey of possibility may give the listener pleasure in following thematic manipulation, while psychologically generating a need, thus anticipation, for resolution. At the end of this section, a modulating passage of *re-transition* leads to the recapitulation.

As the name indicates, recapitulation restates the main points of something, and in this case, all the thematic material of the exposition returns in its original order. However, all of the themes now appear in the tonic, as opposed to moving to the second key utilized in the exposition. Though the first theme remains more dramatic than the lyrical second theme, their harmonic qualities have come together in the home key of the tonic. The listener not only appreciates the return of the exposition's thematic material as a welcomed and conclusive arrival, generating stability, but the tonic commonality of the themes provide for them a similar character, which gives the listener an added sense of resolving all of the confliction that had taken place between them.

A coda is usually added to this form as an additional closing statement, though in the hands of composers such as Beethoven (for example, the first movement of his **Eroica**) it is utilized as another development section, saving any feeling of conclusiveness and resolution for the last movement.

The schematic roadmap of this form shown on the following page may be a helpful listening tool. **Symphony #56** by Joseph Haydn may serve as an example from the recorded anthology, [CD 2, #6].

Sonata Form:

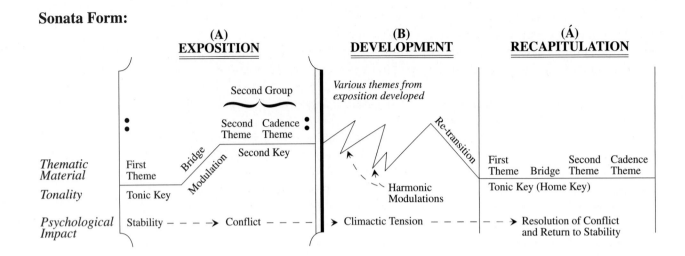

Rondo Form

The *rondo* is a relatively joyful, simple form that was frequently used (along with theme and variations form) for the last movements of multi-movement classical period works such as sonatas, symphonies, and concertos. Its often lighthearted playfulness provided a desired contrast to the dramatic sonata scheme of the first movement, the slow, lyric quality of the second movement, and the third movement's minuet. The psychological and emotional effect of the concluding rondo would send their aristocratic audiences away with a smile. Of course, composers would sometimes require more intense and gripping finishes, and choose other structures, such as sonata form to conclude; the overall scheme of a movement, with its relationship to other movements, has always remained a primary consideration for artistic expression.

In rondo form, the fundamental principle is the unvaried repetition of a main theme, commonly called the *tune*, because of its typical playful character. The tune is almost always presented in homophonic texture. The recurrent tuneful section is frequently called *rondo*. Intermediate sections are labeled *episodes*, or *diversions*. When the internal phrases of the tune fall into a typical ⁝ a ⁝ ⁝ b́ ⁝ pattern (the middle phrase indicated as **b** reflects new material, while the last phrase **a'** shows a return of the first phrase, slightly altered), subsequent returns may only come back with a portion of it. For example, it may return simply as: **a b a'** (no repeats), or **a b**, or **b a'**. Whatever the case, the tune's distinctive nature will always be easy to recognize.

Common patterns for rondo form are **A B A C A** and **A B A C A B' A**. The latter ordering is really an extension of sonata form, inasmuch as the middle section **C** is used as development, with the first and last groupings, respectively **A B A** and **A B' A** corresponding to the exposition and recapitulation. When used for such purposes, it is more appropriately called, sonata-rondo form. Composer Robert Schumann uses sonata-rondo form for his "Aufschwung" from ***Fantasiestucke***, found on [CD 2, #12].

Chapters 2–5 Vocabulary

Alto: the lowest female vocal range, also called contralto; an instrument that performs in a range similar to an alto voice

Amplitude: the furthest distance a vibrating object travels; the displacement of an object

Atonal: having no tonal center; avoiding any sense of tonality

Augmentation: the repetition of a theme, using notes that are lengthened in value, thus slowing it down

Bar lines: vertical lines through the staff, used to show measures

Bass: the lowest male voice register; an instrument that performs in a range similar to a bass voice

Bass clef or F clef: a clef indicating that a note on the fourth line of the staff represents the F, an interval of a fifth, below middle C

Bridge: a modulating passage moving from the tonic key to a second key, connecting to main themes

Cadence: notes that give pause or end, to a passage, or work, with some degree of conclusiveness

Cadence theme: closing material that is usually less distinct than other themes in a piece; sometimes consisting of only descending scales or chords.

Cadenza: an improvised solo within a larger work such as a concerto

Chain suspension: when harmonic resolutions are prolonged by repeatedly holding over one or more pitches from a preceding chord into the next, which would have otherwise resolved the prior harmonic tension

Chord: three or more notes played or sung simultaneously to harmonize and embellish a melody

Chromatic: pitches moving by half steps

Church modes: pitch orderings that date back to ancient Greece, represented by several pitch orientations of the diatonic scales with D, E, F, G, and B, as tonics; instead of the tonal scales represented by C and A

Climax: the most exciting or important moment, or point toward which a melody or entire piece strove

Clef: symbol used to designate pitch

Coda: "tail"; it is a musical section placed at the end of a piece or movement that does not represent part of a described form such as Theme and Variations form

Common time: commonly used meter; four beats to the measure; quarter note equals the beat

Compound meter: simple meters, multiplied by three: *compound duple meter* (6/2, 6/4, 6/8), *compound triple meter* (9/4, 9/8), and *compound quadruple meter* (12/4, 12/8, 12/16)

Concerto: "to contend," it is an instrumental work for soloist or group of soloists and orchestra

Concerto grosso: "large concerto"; it is an instrumental work that requires a group of solo instrumentalists rather than just one, and orchestra

Consonance: intervals or chords, or any other musical sound combinations, that sound free of tension or discord

Countersubject: a distinctive polyphonic line that recurrently accompanies the subject of a fugue in another voice

Crescendo: to gradually get louder

Decrescendo or diminuendo: to gradually get softer

Development: the practice of manipulating themes and motives in various ways; it also refers to the section of Sonata form in which themes from the exposition undergo this process

Diatonic: the natural scales consisting of five whole steps and two half steps, produced by the white keys on the piano

Diminution: the repetition of a theme, using notes that are shortened in value, thus speeding it up

Dissonance, discord: intervals or chords, or any other musical sounds, that sound relatively tense, harsh, biting, or unstable.

Dominant: the note, or a triad built on the fifth degree of a diatonic scale

Dotted rhythms: an amalgamated rhythm produced when a dotted note is followed by a shorter note, or vice versa

Duration: the length of time a particular sound or silence lasts

Dynamics: the loudness or softness of sound, or volume of a musical passage

Enharmonic: used to describe notes spelled differently, but having the same pitch

Episode: diversionary music in a fugue that often appears to wander, since all the melodic lines start to move freely and the tonality constantly modulates

Exposition: the first section of a fugue or a Sonata-form movement

Form: associated with musical interactions that produce a sense of shape and structure

Fragmentation: the process of reducing a theme to fragments

Frequency: the speed of vibrations occurring in a sound-producing body

Fugue: a polyphonic composition for an established number of voices, built on a single principal theme called the subject, since all parts are based on the same material

Harmony: a combination of musical notes that usually form chords; the vertical aspect of music

Homophony: a musical texture that describes only one melody of real interest presented with other sounds used to harmoniously support it

Imitative polyphony: a musical texture describing two or more simultaneous melodic lines using the same or quite similar melodies, but with staggered entrances

Interval: the distance between two pitches

Introduction: a musical section added to the beginning of a piece or movement that does not represent part of the described form such as Theme and Variations form

Inversion: reading or playing a musical line or series upside-down; reversing all its upward intervals downward and vice versa

Key signature: a group of flats or sharps printed on the staff at the beginning of a piece to show the key in which it is to be played

Ledger lines: short extra lines added above and below the staff used to accommodate a few higher or lower pitches

Major scale: a diatonic scale represented by the white keys on the piano keyboard, oriented around C as the tonic; characterized by half step intervals between the third and fourth tones and seventh and eighth tones, with whole tones between all other consecutive steps

Measure: a unit of meter, consisting of a principal strong beat and one or more weaker ones

Melody: a succession of single pitches going somewhere with an appeal to the senses, heard as a recognizable whole.

Minor scale: a diatonic scale represented by the white keys on the piano keyboard, oriented around A as the tonic; the third and usually sixth and seventh notes are lower by a half step from those in the major scale, giving it a less bright quality

Monophony: a texture describing one unaccompanied melody

Motive, motif: a short musical idea consisting of at least two notes, forming the basis for development in a piece of music

Movement: term used for a large, self-contained section within a larger work, such as a symphony

Musical tone: sound producing a series of regular, predictable pulsations, which possess four basic definitive characteristics; frequency, volume, timbre, and duration

Noise: any sound producing a series of irregular, unpredictable pulsations, causing diffusion in aural clarity

Nonimitative polyphony: a musical texture that describes two or more simultaneous melodic lines that are quite different

Octatonic scale: an eight-tone scale alternating between whole and half steps

Octave: an interval of eight notes, represented by the white keys on the piano, where a pitch is perceived as being duplicated

Pedal point: as a term that most often pertains to an organist's foot ("pedal"), which manipulates a pedal keyboard, it is used for holding a single bass note while other voices progress with a succession of changing harmonies against it

Pentatonic scale: an ancient five-tone scale, represented in the relation of the black keys of the piano

Phrase: a sequence of notes that form a unit in music, each leading sensibly to the next

Pitch: the highness or lowness of musical sound

Pizzicato: using fingers to pluck the strings of an instrument that is usually bowed, such as a violin

Polyphony: a texture describing two or more melodies played or sung simultaneously

Rests: short silences in music

Re-transition: a modulating passage that leads to the recapitulation in Sonata form

Retrograde: reading or playing a musical line or series backwards

Rhythm: in general terms, the organization of sound and silence through time

Ritornello: orchestral material that is introduced at the beginning of a movement of a work such as a concerto, which always returns, usually in fragments and in different keys throughout

Ritornello form: a Baroque form that utilizes the recurrences of a ritornello theme

Rondo: a relatively joyful, simple form; the fundamental principle is the unvaried repetition of a main theme, commonly called a "tune," spaced by diversionary material called episodes.

Scale: a collection of pitches chosen for a particular piece

Simple meters: metric groupings in *duple* (2/2, 2/4, 2/8), *triple* (3/2, 3/4, 3/8), and *quadruple* (4/2, 4/4, 4/8), time

Sonata form: sometimes referred to as "first-movement form" or "sonata-allegro form," this structure incorporates an exposition, development, and recapitulation

Soprano: the highest female voice register; an instrument that performs in a range similar to a soprano voice

Staff: the five lines and four spaces used to indicate graphically the relative highness or lowness of pitch

Stretto: when one voice in a fugue overlaps with another; entering before another has finished

Style: the recognized way in which the formal elements (the form) of a composition have been handled so as to provide the whole with expressive effect

Subject: the single principal theme of a fugue, as all parts will be based on the same linear material

Tempo: the pace at which rhythmical units progress

Tenor: the highest natural adult male singing voice; an instrument that performs in a range similar to a tenor voice

Texture: a term used to describe the various sounds and melodic lines taking place concurrently in a piece of music

Theme: "topic," a principal or basic subject of a piece of music

Theme and variations form: a form that consists of a theme followed by a series of variations on it

Tie: a symbol connecting two notes of the same pitch, used to extend the durational value of the first note by the durational value of the second

Timbre or tone color: the sonorous quality of tone of a particular voice or instrument, or group of voices or instruments, dependent on the amount and proportion of overtones present

Time signature: a sign used to indicate meter, represented by a fraction in which the upper figure shows beats per measure and the lower figure shows the time value of each beat

Tonality: the feeling of centrality of one note to a passage of music

Tonic: the central note commonly referred to as "do," in a diatonic scale

Treble clef or G clef: a clef that puts G above middle C on the second line of the staff, used for the higher pitch frequencies

Triplet: a group of three notes played in the time usually taken by two notes of the same value

Whole-tone scale: a six-tone scale consisting exclusively of whole steps

CHAPTER **6**

Ancient Greece

STUDYING MUSIC FROM ANCIENT TIMES

This book is designed as an introduction to Western concert music, yet we begin our historical survey in ancient times, with music that is almost never performed in concerts today, and some that is simply impossible to perform. Why should we study music that is almost never performed today? Partly because the ideas about music held during the origins of Western civilization shaped the ideas of musicians from subsequent periods. These ideas include notions about the function of music in society. As an abstract means of communication, musical activity reveals much about how people of a particular time and place conceive of themselves in relation to ideal and physical experience, and tells us much about what they valued. From ancient times to the present, we can observe common concerns and common ways that music is used.

The impact on the present of ancient musical practices described in this chapter may at first glance appear abstract, but these abstract connections are important. Much of modern practice is based on certain formulas and ideas first conceived in remote times. The debates of today, such as music's appeal to the intellect or the emotions, were well practiced in the homes and academies of long-ago Greece.

THE EARLIEST EVIDENCE OF MUSIC IN THE WEST

When one thinks of archaeologists, one seldom imagines that their work contributes to what we know about music. Yet the study of music in the ancient world has largely been left up to archaeologists rather than musicians. Archaeologists are specialists in locating, and developing theories about, the physical evidence of past times. Their excavations have uncovered considerable evidence of musicmaking associated with virtually every ancient civilization. In some cases they have found musical instruments or the remains of broken instruments. Instruments made from the bones of megafauna (giant mammals such as the woolly mammoth now extinct) and dating to approximately 20,000 B.C. were discovered among the artifacts associated with humans living during the

Ice Age, in what is now known as the Ukraine. Sadly, the humans of the Ice Age left no instructions on how or what they performed on their bony instruments, but these discoveries demonstrate that humans have been musical for many thousands of years.

Some archaeological discoveries of more recent societies include small examples of musical notation. These musical notes are usually carved in stone, and virtually all the examples from ancient societies are indecipherable today. Perhaps the oldest written music from the West dates from roughly 2300 B.C. and the ancient civilization of Ugarit, located in what is now the nation of Syria. All we can know is that this music was certainly important to the people who took the time to carve notes into raw stone. What we would learn if we could hear it today remains a mystery. Indeed, the study of ancient music primarily attracts people who don't mind adding a little bit of knowledge toward solving problems that will likely remain unsolved for many lifetimes. Musical archaeology requires patience.

Other evidence of music and its making emerges through literary references. Clay tablets found in Mesopotamia contain mention of garments specially made for professional singers. This tiny fragment of information provides one more small clue into the values and concerns of ancient Mesopotamians and another shred of evidence to add to the case that music has mattered to people for a very long time.

MUSIC IN ANCIENT GREECE

The most complete musical record from the ancient West comes from the Greek city states that rose around 800 B.C. By 64 B.C., all Greek-speaking lands had been conquered by Rome, and the most influential flourishing of Greek civilization was over. What we know today about ancient Greek music is far from complete, but there is a large amount of evidence we can consult to inform our understanding. Moreover, many ideas and practices associated with ancient Greek music were influential on modern musical practice in the West.

At the time of this writing, there are only fifteen examples of ancient Greek written music. To supplement this limited repertory of musical pieces, we have a wealth of pictures of music being made. We call these pictures *iconographic evidence*. Perhaps most valuable of all, we have a tremendous amount of literary evidence, ranging from stories and plays mentioning musicmaking, to philosophical tracts outlining the importance of music for ancient Greeks. Perhaps most useful for musicians who wish to recreate the music of ancient Greece, we have detailed theoretical writings on the modes or scales used by ancient Greek musicians. This theoretical writing provides clues into how music was used during these remote times. Among the many intriguing possibilities stemming from the literary and theoretical evidence is that certain modes may have been used to heal the sick.

The sources of musical notation mostly appear in papyrus manuscripts and date after the Greek city states were in decline. Among the oldest examples are two Delphic hymns to Apollo that date from approximately 130 B.C. These two hymns are both incomplete. They were carved in stone and have been so damaged over the centuries that much of the notation has decayed into dust. To further complicate our understanding, each of the hymns was written using a different notational system. So while we have fifteen pieces of music available for study, all of them bring their own complications and limitations to the table.

Older still than the two Delphic Hymns is a fragment written around 200 B.C., containing a few lines of a chorus written for the play *Orestes* by the brilliant Greek dramatist Euripides. This piece of music may have been written by Euripides himself, to accompany a performance of his play. We now know from literary evidence that the great achievements of Greek drama were mostly sung when performed in ancient times. In later chapters, we will see how certain musicians working during the Italian Renaissance in the city of Florence used this knowledge to inspire their invention of the opera. Like the tragedies of ancient Greece, modern operas are sung from beginning to end.

THE EPITAPH AT SEIKILOS

Comparable in age to these early examples of Greek music is a song that was carved into the tombstone of a Greek who once lived on what is now the coast of Turkey. The occupant of the tomb must have been an interesting person, as the song carved on his tombstone is an example of a Skolion, a kind of Greek drinking song. This tombstone features both the text and musical notes carved into it, providing historians of this period an excellent example of Greek music. What further elevates this example in importance are the rhythmic values of the notes, which are also inscribed into the stone.

For all the precision in the notation of this example, performing this music is no easy accomplishment. The notes themselves are not difficult to sing, however, there is much about music that notation cannot express. This notation, known as Greek "vocal" notation, tells us nothing about what a Greek singer should sound like. Among other things, we don't know if ancient Greeks sang with a nasal or open-throated timbre. We can guess based on how modern Greeks sing, but we cannot rule out the possibility of changes in taste during the last 2100 years. Having notation and knowing how to read it does not mean that we automatically understand how to perform the music. Even the most intricate notation systems leave much to the performer to decide. But just as archaeologists sometimes form reasonable opinions based on the limited data they possess, musicians also form reasonable opinions based on incomplete records.

In the recorded anthology accompanying this text, there is a reasonable guess as to how this drinking song sounded more than 2000 years ago [CD 1, Track 1]. In the recording, not only do we hear a singer who sings the words and notes found on the tombstone, but we also hear two instrumentalists. The musical notation found on the tombstone makes no mention of instrumentalists, yet ancient Greek pictures of singers often show them accompanied by instruments. In this case, we hear a plucked string instrument called a lyre. The inclusion of the small metallic instruments is a matter of pure speculation on the part of the modern performers. Archaeologists have found such instruments. Using them in this context may or may not reflect how they were used during ancient times.

FIGURE 6.1 | *Man Playing Kithara and Singing. Fifth Century B.C. Greek Vase.* The Kithara was one of the most popular instruments of ancient Greece. It consisted of a square, wooden sound box and two curved arms connected by a crossbar. Five to eleven strings were stretched between the sound box and crossbar, and were plucked with a plectrum (a small, thin piece of bone, metal, or wood). Its primary use was to accompany the voice. The musicians on the accompanying CD 1, track 1 justify their use of such an instrument through iconographic evidence such as that found on this vase. (The Metropolitan Museum of Art, Fletcher Fund, 1956. All rights reserved, The Metropolitan Museum of Art.)

Like all the existing examples of Greek musical notation, this piece is monophonic, being comprised only of a melody. In actual practice, ancient Greek musicians may have improvised accompaniments for their melodies. Indeed, the existence of so many pictures of singers joined by instrumentalists makes this a highly probable conjecture. Literary evidence suggests that the instrumentalists played the melody along with the singer. In this recording, the lyre is used to complement the singer by presenting a drone. Drones are commonly used to accompany singers in many societies, so this surmise also seems reasonable on the part of the modern performers.

In addition to the words of the drinking song on the tombstone, we also learn from it that the text of the song is by Seikilos. Thus the song has come to be known as *The Epitaph of Seikilos*. Seikilos wrote this short poem for his wife in an apparent attempt to cheer her up.

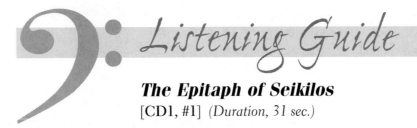

Listening Guide

The Epitaph of Seikilos
[CD1, #1] *(Duration, 31 sec.)*

0.00 Throughout your life, be lighthearted.
0.09 Let nothing trouble you.
0.16 Life is too brief,
0.23 And time takes its toll.

Throughout this historical survey, each piece found in your recorded anthology will be discussed. Each example will be presented with a Listening Guide. These guides are designed to help readers follow what is happening in the music. Vocal works will be presented with translations of their texts into English. Instrumental works will feature descriptive guides to the structure of the piece. The timings listed in Listening Guides refer to the timings of the tracks of the compact discs that accompany this book.

GREEK MUSICAL THEORY AND PHILOSOPHY

While the *Epitaph at Seikilos* and the small number of other surviving Greek songs serve the study of ancient Greek music extremely well, we must be cautious about pretending to know more than we do. Drawing generalizations based upon such a small sample, spread over such a vast period of time, can lead students of music to draw false conclusions. With that in mind, musicologists interested in ancient Greek music have concentrated much of their efforts on studying the writing about music and its meaning. On that topic, the existing record is large, indeed too large to summarize in an introductory book. The following discussion of ancient Greek musical theory and philosophy is general, and emphasizes issues that will be taken up during the discussion of later periods.

One of the most influential ideas of the ancient Greeks on later Western music was the concept that among the nearly infinite possible tones the human ear can perceive, some were more useful to musicians than others. To organize and access the useful tones, Greek thinkers turned to mathematics, astronomy, and physics for guidance.

Pythagoras and Greek Musical Theory

The Greek mathematician Pythagoras (d. 497 B.C.), famous in the study of geometry for the Pythagorean theorem, was keenly interested in the study of music. He heard in music the logical unfolding of mathematical truths in a pleasing form. Typical of his times, Pythagoras believed that certain pitches, or musical notes, when sounded together formed a pleasing combination called a "consonance." The antithesis of consonance is dissonance, or two pitches that sound harsh when sounded together.

Legend has it that while passing a blacksmith's shop, Pythagoras heard pitches that sounded pleasing when the smiths struck the anvil simultaneously with different-sized hammers. He investigated this phenomenon and learned that hammers of differing weights produced different pitches. More importantly, hammers having simple ratios of weight, one to the other, formed consonances. For example, when two hammers, one half the weight of the other, sounded together, they form the consonance of an octave. In Western music, two notes an octave apart are considered so similar that we give them the same name. The modern piano, for example, has 88 keys, but eight of them sound the note "C." Each successively higher "C" strikes a string half as long as the "C" string immediately lower. The length of the strings, like the weights of the hammers, indicates that the ratio of 2:1, the simplest ratio, creates the most basic consonance, the octave.

The ancient mathematician's observations in musical consonance went further. He discovered that two hammers sounding a perfect fourth apart

FIGURE 6.2 | *Pythagoras, Inventor of Music. Thirteenth century. From manuscript containing the treatise* De musica *by John of Cotton.* This illustration from the Middle Ages depicts the legend of Pythagoras observing the pitch relationships of hammers while passing a blacksmith shop. It also expresses his willingness to contemplate any and all sound, as discoveries are often made in the most unlikely ways. (Bayerische Staatsbibliothek München)

(for a detailed discussion of pitch in Western music see Chapter Two of this book) had the weight ratio of 4:3 with one another. The consonant interval of the fifth results from the ratio of 3:2. For many ancient Greeks, Pythagoras included, numbers were crucial to understanding all things material and spiritual. That musical consonances resulted from a sequence of simple arithmetic ratios demonstrated the purity and logic of music, and stimulated far-flung inquiry into music's nature and power. Furthermore, Pythagoras' discovery and subsequent rationale for emphasizing pitch relationships based on simple arithmetic ratios helped determine how Western musicians for centuries to come create hierarchies of pitches. Despite important changes in recent centuries that have strayed from the precise tuning of consonances associated with Pythagoras, the importance of certain consonant intervals in Western music has rarely been challenged. Other cultures have developed sophisticated and persuasive concepts of pitch wholly different from the concepts of Pythagoras. These alternate developments help explain the tremendous diversity of music on our planet.

Ptolemy and the Music of the Spheres

The Greek astronomer Claudius Ptolemy expanded on Pythagoras' ideas. Ptolemy noted that the proportional relationships between certain musical pitches, as discovered by Pythagoras, corresponded to the ratios found in the movement of heavenly bodies, most notably the planets. He argued that music of a certain character and emphasizing certain pitches could channel the powers associated with the planets and result in music specially suited to sway the audience in predictable and valuable ways. Ptolemy, like most Greek thinkers on the topic of music, believed that music had a moral power that could affect the character and actions of the listener. In later centuries, the philosopher Plato gave the poetic name *Music of the Spheres* to Ptolemy's ideas concerning music emulating the movements of the cosmos. Musicians would return to this

FIGURE 6.3 | *The Parthenon. 447–438 B.C.* Greek certainties about the importance of mathematical symmetries and simple ratios can be seen in their architectural ideals as well. The Parthenon's symmetric plan and simplicity of line represent the perfect balance of physical forms. Consonant, internal harmony is expressed in the likeness of each of column, spaced equidistantly from its neighbor, with slight adjustments to accommodate the corners. The structure's emphasis on form, idealization and simplicity appeal to the intellect more directly than to the emotions.
(© Bettmann/Corbis)

idea periodically throughout subsequent centuries. You may have come in contact with contemporary arguments that certain music promotes corruption of the moral fiber of the nation. Such arguments are most often started by the parents of teenage children. Ptolemy and the Greeks had much more complex ideas concerning the impact of music on the moods and actions of listeners.

Greek Modal Theory

Over time, Greek musicians developed a complex system for regulating what pitches sound pleasing together and work well in forming melodies. There was diversity of opinion among them, but some general points were held in common. The central concerns in this system were the modes, or scales. Greek modes differ from the modern major and minor scales, but like them are comprised of seven different pitches and end on the note an octave above the first note of the mode. Here are a few examples for comparison:

Greek Modes

Mixolydian: E F G A B-flat C D E

Dorian: E F G A B C D E

Hypophrygian: E F# G# A B C# D E

Modern Scales

Major: E F# G# A B C# D# E

Minor: E F# G A B C D E

Each of these different modes or scales exhibits a distinct musical flavor. These distinctions were decisive in the thinking of ancient Greek musicians, and prompted much writing about the effect each had on the moods, character, and behavior of listeners.

Plato, Aristotle, and Philosophical Approaches to Modes

The philosophers Plato and Aristotle wrote about the power of music and its role in ordering a just and moderate society. Here is a tiny sample of Aristotle's ideas concerning the three Greek modes presented as examples above.

The musical modes differ essentially from one another, and those who hear them are differently affected by each. Some of them make men sad and grave, like the so-called Mixolydian; others enfeeble the mind, like the relaxed modes; another, again, produces a moderate and settled temper, which appears to be the peculiar effect of the Dorian; Phrygian inspires enthusiasm.[1]

---

[1]Aristotle, *The Politics*. Translation from Donald J. Grout and Claude Palisca, *A History of Western Music*, 5th ed. (New York: W. W. Norton, 1996), 13.

Figure 6.4 | *Banqueting Scene, Center medallion of a red-figured cup. 460-450 B.C.* In this banqueting scene, the reclining figure holds a drinking cup similar to the one this image decorates as he listens to a youthful musician perform. While some Greeks such as Plato saw music as solely connected to the contemplation of truth and beauty, others favored music as entertainment. So is the figure in this picture locked in deep contemplation, or indulging in the sort of professional entertainment Plato despised? (Rèunion des Musèes Nationaux/Art Resource, NY)

Such writing fueled the passions of music theorists and composers during the Italian Renaissance as they tried to recreate these effects. Readers who play an instrument or sing may want to improvise melodies using the modes mentioned in this excerpt, and see if Dorian prompts a moderate and settled temper, as Aristotle claimed. Modern musicians largely ignore the modal theories of ancient Greece, but as medical science begins its exploration of the healing potential of music, the writings of Aristotle and others have served as an entrée into this important line of inquiry. Literary evidence from ancient Greece mentions numerous instances of musical modes serving doctors in the cure of illnesses. Rather than assuming that these scientists of long ago were deluded, a few modern scientists now look to them for the occasional clue. Perhaps some readers can point to times when they have used modern music to elevate their mood, or to inspire them to action. These activities are the modern residue of ideas formulated about music thousands of years ago in Greece. Modern athletes often use music to prepare them emotionally for competition, or to help them endure tedious and difficult training. The modes used in the music they choose probably aren't the element that inspired the choice, but the idea is very similar to ideas circulating before the first Olympic games held in Athens thousands of years ago.

Plato on Music and Society

The writings of Plato (c. 380 B.C.) tell us much about music in ancient Greek society. Plato was an idealist who praised music's power to sober and quiet the mind, even going so far as to outline an ideal educational system in which music occupied half of a man's time. Plato felt that music was perfectly suited to discipline the minds of the young. Being pleasurable, it would serve as an excellent object of study, and would not become too tiresome for his young students. The rest of his educational system was occupied with gymnastics, to discipline the body. Plato's idealism made him a fierce critic of musical practices of which he disapproved. Plato's writings often turn to his contempt for professional entertainers. Here is an example from the dialogue *Protagoras*:

Second-rate and commonplace people, being too uneducated to entertain themselves as they drink by using their own voices and conversational resources, put up the price of female musicians, paying well for the hire of an extraneous voice — that of the pipe — and find their entertainment in its warblings. But where the drinkers are men of worth and culture, you will find no girls piping or dancing or harping. They are quite capable of enjoying their own company without such frivolous nonsense, using their own voices in sober discussion and each taking his turn to speak or listen — even if the drinking is really heavy.[2]

In addition to his contempt for hiring professional singers, Plato feared all musical innovation. His idealism, like so much idealism, turned to nostalgia for an order he hoped would never change, but that inevitably did. He was especially wary of changes in the system of modes. In his *Republic*, Plato wrote, "A change to a new type of music is something to beware of as a hazard to all our fortunes. For the modes of music are never disturbed without unsettling the most fundamental political and social foundations."[3] Plato saw any disruption to musical purity as the path to social chaos.

Plato's criticisms point to the fact that not all Greek musicians seem to have taken to heart the theories and practices associated with the highest ideals of the time in their daily practice. After all, why would Plato need to criticize activities that weren't happening? The practices having little to do with the ambitions of Pythagoras, Ptolemy, or Plato include drumming, music without singers, and professional virtuosos who played for hire. Throughout history there have been interesting disputes

FIGURE 6.5 | *Bust of Plato.* (Scala/Art Resource, NY)

between the guardians of a system that has traditionally served society well and those people who would introduce innovations to the system. In Plato's time, the stakes of this conflict were nothing short of the survival of Greek society as he knew it. Unfortunately for Plato, music did change, and the Greek city states he sought to preserve passed into history. Who can say if there was any correlation?

Some Questions for Discussion

1 Today most people don't make their own music as Plato argued they should. What are the dangers of depending exclusively on professionals for musicmaking? What does our modern dependence on professionals tell us has changed since ancient times? Has this change been for the better?

2 The *Epitaph of Seikilos* is in the Phrygian mode, which Aristotle describes as inspiring enthusiasm. Why might an enthusiastic mode be appropriate to the text of the song? What effect does listening to the song have on your conduct or character? Given that this song is extremely remote from our lives, what current music affects your

---

[2]Protagoras 347 c-d translation from Piero Weiss and Richard Taruskin, *Music in the Western World: A History in Documents* (New York: Schirmer, 1984), 6.

[3]Republic 424 b-c translation from Piero Weiss and Richard Taruskin, *Music in the Western World: A History in Documents* (New York: Schirmer, 1984) 8.

FIGURE 6.6 | *Depiction of Apollo playing a lyre and Artemis holding an aulos. C. 490 B.C. Attrributed to Eucharides and found at Amphora.* Though they are not mutually exclusive, the struggle between intellect and emotion is one of the most significant, ongoing struggles in the history of Western arts. For the Greeks, the battlefield of this struggle was often musical. The depiction illustrates the story of Artemis challenging Apollo to a musical contest. Artemis found an aulos (a double-reed instrument remotely like the modern oboe and associated with emotion and pleasure in the Greek imagination) discarded by the goddess Athena, who disdained the instrument because it distorted her beautiful face when she played it. Armed with a divine instrument and confident that emotions should rule the intellect, Artemis challenges the god Apollo, patron of the rational arts. For his instrument, Apollo chooses the lyre (a string instrument vaguely akin to the modern harp and associated with reason and moderation in the Greek imagination). According to the legend, Apollo defeated Artemis and demonstrated to all the dominance of intellect over the passions. For the ancient Greeks and the many Western artists who would seek to revive Greek ideals in the arts, intellectual appeal serves as the cornerstone of classical arts. (The Metropolitan Museum of Art, Rogers Fund, 1907. All rights reserved, The Metropolitan Museum of Art.)

conduct or character and how is this effect achieved? Is it the mode, or something else about modern music, that moves your character or behavior?

3 If your bedroom turned out to be the only thing that survived the ravages of time, what musical materials would be available to future students of music 2000 years from now. Would they find a musical instrument? Would it be obvious how to play it? Would the recordings they found be representative of all the music available during the early 21st century? What would the literary and iconographic evidence you left behind teach them about music and its importance to our times? Would future students conclude that you favored appeals to the intellect or emotions in your choices of music?

7

The Middle Ages (c. 476–1452)

THE MIDDLE AGES

The period addressed in this chapter goes by many names: the Medieval Period, the Middle Ages, the Dark Ages. All of these names were applied during the late 1400s by people who looked back on their recent past with disdain. They saw nothing of lasting value stemming from the period of history immediately preceding their own time. These critics viewed their own times as capable of splendid accomplishment, and revered the distant accomplishments of ancient Greece and Rome. The term "Middle Ages" stems from their sense that the intervening centuries were the middle between two highs. In their eyes, the Middle Ages were a time to regret as barbarous and unworthy. The term "Dark Ages" captures this sentiment of contempt for the roughly 1000 years from 476 A.D., when the last Roman Emperor was overthrown, to 1452, when Constantinople, the capital of the eastern half of the Roman Empire, fell to the Turks. This sense of regret echoes even today. In modern slang, saying that you will "get medieval" on someone is a way of announcing your intention to act cruelly or viciously toward him or her.

The truth about this period is that, while there were certainly deprivations both material and ideational, it by no means held a monopoly on famine, war, ignorance, or disease. The history of humanity finds such evils flourishing in every age, including our own. The Middle Ages saw tremendous cultural achievements, ranging from the construction of architectural monuments such as the gothic cathedrals at Chartres and Notre Dame in Paris, to literary works of immeasurable importance in every language spoken in Western Europe. In short, this period can boast achievements comparable in scope and ambition to any other period. The accomplishments of medieval civilization need no condescension, and are not valuable solely for pointing the way to greater achievements in the future. In other words, the people of the Middle Ages were not striving to become us but simply lacked the intelligence, ingenuity, and virtue to do so. Their age is an expression of their concerns and desires, which differed from ours in fundamental ways. Consequently, students of history must at least temporarily set aside assumptions about the Middle Ages while examining how the music of that period reflects the distinct understandings and ideals of the time. A brief comparison between medieval methods of understanding the world and those prevalent today can serve as an entry to our discussion of music.

THE MEDIEVAL MIND

The medieval imagination was far more able to embrace and celebrate mystery and uncertainty than most moderns can. During the 1000-year span of the Middle Ages, comparatively little energy was spent in challenging received wisdom. Much more was taken on faith, compared to today. To be sure there were moments of opposition to dominant ideas, but for the most part these were swiftly ended by the dominant political and religious institutions. Rather than instantly concluding that this condition was a fault, we might consider the unexpected virtues of stability and order that stem from the medieval premium on faith. For 1000 years the essential hierarchies of the church and state endured largely untested. At least revolution and partisan intrigue could not be counted among the upheavals common within the Middle Ages. Today we like to test ideas and systems through logical debate. The Middle Ages weren't wholly immune to such concerns, but they represent the methods of the tiniest of minorities. A logical criticism of this mentality is the stultifying effect it might have on the sciences, or on social reform needed to ease the suffering of the weakest people in society. Yet the Middle Ages was not without its scientific advances or its charitable programs. Later critics of this time have managed to replace much of the record of human achievements during the Middle Ages with their generalizations about its filth and ignorance.

FIGURE 7.1 | *Roman de Fauvel*, depicting Fauvel's wedding night with Vaine Gloire. The medieval imagination was little impressed with what we today pass off as logic. This page from a medieval manuscript for the famous ***Roman de Fauvel*** might appear chaotic to modern viewers. No attempt has been made to depict the human figures with any degree of realism nor with any care for proportion. We would be foolish to conclude that the artist responsible was trying to render his subject realistically. He was instead concerned with depicting the story, in this case the noisy wedding night celebration for poor Vaine Gloire, the young woman in the bed. She has foolishly wished to marry someone wealthy. To her surprise, her wish is granted. However, the wealthy someone turns out to be the magic donkey Fauvel. Notice how the figures fill the floors of the tiny house. Meanwhile, the people occupying the towers are impossibly small compared to the other figures. With no door depicted, we can only guess how the guests enter and exit. Such petty concerns of realism never bothered medieval artists. (Bibliothèque nationale de France)

The Medieval Mind and Politics

Politically, the medieval mind favored stability and rigid hierarchy. Western Europe was organized using the feudal system. Under this system, the vast majority of people were serfs. They owned no land, but worked the lands of their feudal lord and gave a generous amount of the fruits of their labor to him. The relationship was not wholly one-sided. The feudal lord in turn provided, to the extent he could, protection against invaders and the stability of an unquestioned central authority. This relationship was certainly more advantageous for the lord. Above the feudal lords, who had titles of nobility such as "baron" or "count," was an aristocracy of increasing power. Each feudal lord was in turn sworn to share his profits and powers with a noble higher in rank than himself. This process continued until the ultimate regional authority was reached, usually a king, but in some places where several kingdoms shared an imperial affiliation, an emperor. Mobility between ranks, such as a serf working hard and rising to the level of feudal lord, was unheard of during this time.

Most of the art that survives from the Middle Ages was created for the edification of the highest ranks of this system. Feudal lords, especially in poorer regions, sometimes lived rather austere lives. The most revered artistic achievements were created even higher within the hierarchy, for the duke or king.

We would be mistaken to assume that the lives of the serfs were pure torment. While they certainly suffered severe deprivations in times of famine or plague, they enjoyed leisure time greater than that available for the modern middle class with its ethos of consumption. Rebellions started by the serfs were not unheard of, but for the most part stability reigned within the system. Even the most drastic rebellions sought redress of immediate grievances rather than sweeping changes to the system. Perhaps the serfs

FIGURE 7.2 | *St. Mark, depiction on the Gospel Book of St. Medard of Soissons, France,* early ninth century. By the end of the third century, Christians were numerous enough to count as a political force within the Roman Empire. With converts from the ruling and upper classes, its survival seemed secured. Every major city within the Mediterranean region had a substantial Christian community, presided over by a bishop assisted by priests and deacons. The Church's system of vassalage served as a model for the feudal system and is depicted in this artistic account. St. Mark is shown as a vassal of Pope Leo III, depicted above as a lion, supposedly responsible to, or vassal of, the Christ figure in the upper-right corner. There is an angel in the upper-left corner acting as Christ's messenger. (Bibliothèque nationale de France)

were conditioned to accept their very bad lot, or accepted it purely through fear of retribution. It seems doubtful that a system could survive 1000 years based on fear alone. Whatever the case, the serfs certainly were not lying about dreaming of democratic revolutions during their modest leisure time. They had other ways to occupy their minds and different priorities from Europeans of later centuries.

The Role of Faith for the Medieval Mind

The impact of faith and acceptance without questions was considerable on medieval scholarship in fields as far flung as chemistry and music. Past accomplishments were held in reverence and seldom challenged. Treatises on every subject depended enormously on copying passages from past treatises on the same subject. Today scholars are prized in all fields for their originality. In the Middle Ages scholars were prized for their sagacious consultation of previous scholars.

For the medieval mind, faith in the Christian God provided a central organizing principle around which most ideas flowed. The Christian Church grew gradually from its embattled beginnings. When the last Roman emperor fell in 476, Christianity had been the majority religion within the Empire for less than 100 years. It was known mainly in the more heavily populated parts of the Empire along the Mediterranean Sea, and in the larger communities of what are now France, Germany, and England. The first 500 years of the period under study saw Christianity supplant various pagan religions, until all of Western Europe and the Italian and Balkan Peninsulas were almost exclusively Christian. Only Judaism maintained an important presence in Europe among the religions that predate Christianity, although Jews often endured terrible persecution for their beliefs. The next 300 years (900–1200) saw Christianity embraced throughout Scandanavia, Northeastern Europe, and Russia.

FIGURE 7.3 | Scene of Medieval Peasant Life. Peasant life in the Middle Ages certainly witnessed its share of severe deprivations, yet ironically, the medieval peasant likely enjoyed more unstructured leisure time than the modern middle class. Little evidence remains concerning the particulars of music made by medieval peasants, yet evidence that they made music abounds in both written accounts and pictures from the period. (© Bettmann/Corbis)

Medieval Christianity

Medieval Christianity emphasized mystery and faith over the more rationalized approaches to Christianity advanced after the advent of the Protestant Reformation during the early 1500s. Among the differences between some modern Christians and medieval Christianity is the belief that each celebration of the Mass witnesses not a symbolic, but a miraculously literal, reoccurrence of the transformation of bread and wine into the body and blood of Christ. This belief, still very much alive within Roman Catholicism, tested the credulity of some later Christians, such as the reformer Martin Luther. Yet this tenet of medieval Christianity was reinforced by the more general belief that the entire calendar of church activities was comprised of similar miraculous reoccurrences. This difference may seem unimportant to some, but it illustrates a key difference between the medieval mind and the tendency to rationalize (rightly or wrongly) by the modern mind. For medieval Christians, rationalizing their faith was irrelevant. The mysteries of faith were sufficient.

Another interesting glimpse into the medieval mind can be seen through the considerable stock they placed in the power of holy relics, such as the bones of especially holy personages, or slivers of wood from the cross on which Christ died. Possession of these relics within the local church was a matter of considerable pride, and many miracles were attributed to them. Pilgrimages taking believers vast distances to behold holy relics were a common event during medieval times. Among the many important destinations was Santiago de Compostela in Northern Spain, where the bones of St. James are believed to reside. Pilgrimages of this sort were most important during times of famine, plague, and war, when believers sought to change the fortunes of their community through pilgrimages, heroic acts of self-sacrifice, and religious devotion. Many modern Christians, especially in Roman Catholic communities, continue to make pilgrimages to holy sites and venerate the artifacts of Christianity's leaders and heroes.

The Medieval Mind and the Arts

The profound faith of many people living during the Middle Ages led to a general sense of the ephemeral nature of existence. These early Christians took comfort in the promise and anticipation of rewards in the life to come. One implication of this belief within the field of the arts was a much greater appearance of anonymous works during the Middle Ages compared to modern times. For example, the architects responsible for the great cathedrals of Europe constructed before 1500 are mostly unknown. Many of these architects knew that they were embarking on a construction project they would never live to see completed. The great cathedral at Chartres, for example, took nearly 200 years to construct. The men and women responsible for the early stages of construction knew that they would never live to see their devotion rewarded with a finished structure. Such selfless anonymity in the arts is totally unknown today, and reflects the medieval sense that this temporary realm of existence was relatively unimportant.

As with architecture, much of the music of the early Middle Ages was composed by men and women who made no attempt to sign their work and enjoy the admiration of future generations. They neither sought nor could even conceive of earning royalties or enjoying fame beyond their most immediate community. Instead, monks and nuns worked in service to God, even as they engaged in creative activity such as com-

FIGURE 7.4 | The ***cathedral in Chartres,*** France, reflects the change from the bulky and fortress-like architecture of the Romanesque period to the more ornate style of the Gothic period. The men and women who began work on the cathedral knew they would not live to see it completed. The majority of artistic and architectural accomplishments of the Middle Ages were anonymously made. (© Ruggero Vanni/Corbis)

posing music. Pride, one of the Seven Deadly Sins articulated during the Middle Ages, was a deterrent for these devout believers.

Hierarchy and the Medieval Church

The importance placed on religion within the medieval mind established the general tendency to accept absolute authority. Just as Christianity admits the absolute authority of God, the medieval church was organized around a rigidly held hierarchy of authority. This system, like that of the feudal system, is one of vassalage. As the head of the Catholic Church, the Pope was (and still is for Catholic communities) seen as an intermediary between God and man. Receiving divine revelation and guidance from the Holy Spirit (part of the Christian Trinity), the Pope holds the power to speak infallibly on matters of belief, and to insist on adherence to his determinations. The Bishops are responsible to, or vassals of, the Pope. Priests are next, serving the common people much like the vassal lord who provided protection for the serfs and to whom they paid direct tribute at times of harvest. During the Middle Ages, no mass communication existed, so regional practices and beliefs often arose that could not be checked by any central authority. Although the Pope's power appeared absolute, in actual practice it could not have been. We must not be fooled by the rhetoric of absolute power.

FIGURE 7.5 | *Pope Gregory the Great* directed a codification of music and texts deemed suitable for worship services. He is commonly depicted writing down the music that would come to be known as Gregorian Chant with a dove on his shoulder directing his activities. The dove represents the Holy Spirit. (Bibliothèque nationale de France)

The Pope often found himself enmeshed in intrigues with wayward congregations who chose to ignore his power. Similarly, the seemingly absolute power of the political elite was sometimes questioned through peasant revolts and, more often, in palace intrigues. Perfectly rigid hierarchy may have inspired the medieval mind, but every age enjoys its contradictions.

GREGORIAN CHANT

For the purpose of musical study, Pope Gregory the Great (540–604) was perhaps the most influential person to hold the office of Pope. During his reign, he sought to codify Christian practices so that Christians throughout Europe would worship in the same manner. To achieve these ends, he depended mightily on the vast networks of monasteries and convents where much of the literate population dwelled. He hoped that through the literacy of monks and nuns, the practices of Christianity could be brought into universal conformity. His project certainly did not reach fruition during his lifetime. Regional celebrations and practices flourished throughout the Middle Ages. Generations later, Pope Gregory's project had a great ally in the Frankish king Charlemagne (742–814), who worked to codify Christian practice within his vast realm. Charlemagne ruled much of what are now France, Germany, and Italy.

Among the facets of Christian worship that Pope Gregory and subsequent reformers who shared his ideals sought to enforce was a uniform repertory of religious chant. Christian services in the Middle Ages were almost entirely sung. In monasteries and convents throughout Western Europe, chanting began in the hours before dawn, and would not be finished for the day until late in the evening. In between the singing of these chants, the monks or nuns would go about their duties of maintaining and sustaining the monastery. The most learned and literate at the monastery devoted themselves to adding to their collection of written texts, and educating themselves and one another.

The Medieval Liturgy

The Christian services of the Middle Ages, or *liturgy*, took many shapes and served many functions. Within the walls of the monasteries, the more minor services were celebrated with minimal fanfare. The most important of these lesser services, or canonical hours, were Matins (celebrated just prior to sunrise) and Vespers (celebrated at sunset). The most important service by far was the Mass. Each Mass was made up not of one continuous chant, but of many chants, each fulfilling a separate function. The texts that were sung fall into two types. The *Mass proper* were those texts that changed from day to day, dictated by a church calendar that was built around three annual cycles. The remainder of the chants form the *Mass ordinary*. These texts are present in every celebration of the Mass. Here is the order of chants used in a typical medieval celebration of the Mass.

The Mass	
Proper	*Ordinary*
Introit	
	Kyrie
	Gloria
Collects	
Epistle	
Gradual	
Alleluia	
Sequence	
Gospel	
Sermon [not sung]	
	Credo
Offertory	
Preface	
	Sanctus
	Agnus Dei
Communion	
	Ite, missa est

Each of these sections of the Mass serves a distinct function. For example, the Credo is a recitation of the beliefs central to the teachings of the Church. It is followed by the

Offertory, which is sung while the bread and wine are prepared for the miraculous transformation into the body and blood of Christ. The Preface is comprised of a very few words designed to lead into the Sanctus, a brief evocation of the mysteries of faith.

A Particular Gregorian Chant

Taken together, Christian chant from the Middle Ages has come to be known as *Gregorian Chant* taking its name from Pope Gregory the Great. Actually, almost none of the chant that has survived to the present day was composed during Gregory's time. Literally hundreds of hours of original music comprise the Gregorian repertory, yet almost all of it remains of anonymous authorship. The Gregorian Chant in your recording anthology is one of the oldest existing chants. It is the Alleluia from the Mass for Christmas Day (CD 1, #2). Like all Gregorian Chant, the text is in Latin, the official language of the medieval church and also the official language of the sciences, law, scholarship, and much literature of the Middle Ages. The value of Latin was twofold for people of the Middle Ages. It aided in communication across national boundaries and provided a link back to the Roman Empire.

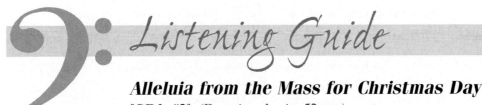

Alleluia from the Mass for Christmas Day
[CD1, #2] *(Duration, 1 min. 52 sec.)*

0.00	Alleluia. Alleluia	Alleluia. Alleluia.
0.17	Dies sanctificatus illuxit nobis: venite	A sanctified day hath shone upon us: come
0.49	gentes, et adorate Dominum: quia	ye Gentiles, and adore the Lord; for this
1.00	hodie descendit lux magna super terram.	day a great light hath descended upon the earth.
1.32	Alleluia	Alleluia.[1]

The word "Alleluia," found in the Old Testament, means "to adore God." The significance of this text for Christians is considerable, as it marks the appearance of Christ on earth.

The music for this example might be among the oldest composed during the Middle Ages. This chant was probably written during the ninth century. Its extreme antiquity stems from its importance within the Christian faith. No later composer of new chants wished to replace such an important melody associated with such an important text as the Alleluia for Christmas Day.

The mode of this example is rooted in the modes of ancient Greece. Medieval scholars of music took great care in studying the musical ideas of ancient Greece. The most famous of these musicians was Anicus Manlius Severinus Boethius (c. 480–524). Known today only as Boethius, his treatise *De institutione musica* served as the model for the vast majority of medieval musical theory. In this treatise, Boethius outlines eight

[1]Translation by Claude Palisca in *The Norton Anthology of Western Music, Volume 1.* (New York, W.W. Norton, 1996), 14.

modes, all of them based on modes used in ancient Greece. When used in Gregorian Chants, they came to be known as the "Church Modes," and are found in all medieval music, both sacred and secular. The mode of this particular chant is Dorian, it uses the following pitches:

D E F G A B C D

Its status as Dorian is solidified by the fact that almost every melodic phrase ends on the pitch D, thus lending that pitch the highest status in the hierarchy of pitches. A mode is, after all, an expression of a hierarchy among pitches, ranging from the complete absence of some and the nearly constant return to another, with all statuses available in between.

In addition to using a mode commonly found in ancient Greece, there is a surprising similarity between this chant and the Skolion examined in the previous chapter in terms of rhythm. Rhythmic notation in both the early Middle Ages and ancient Greek vocal notation was not much more precise than indicating the difference between a long note and a short note. Nonetheless, this flexible rhythmic system suited the church's beliefs and practices perfectly. Any music that led to the sensual encouragement of foot-tapping would have been viewed as blasphemous, were it used in the church. In addition, making contact with the earth would have also been in direct opposition to the purpose of worship. The idea here was to give full attention to the spiritual world, not the physical. This rhythmic quality appears to make the chants sound as if they float in the air. Even so, over the course of this chapter, we will observe Europeans developing notational systems allowing for more complex rhythmic relationships, by generating note shapes that indicate how many beats or partial beats are allocated to a particular note. Through this innovation, every possible relationship of duration is available to composers.

When the Alleluia for Christmas Day was performed, it was only presented on Christmas Day, and only during the appropriate moment within the Mass. Gregorian Chants were never intended as concert pieces and were not performed outside their intended context. They functioned solely as part of the religious life of believers. Aesthetic judgment of this piece seems almost totally irrelevant, if the standards of modern concert life are applied. The idea of the modern concert, a time set aside exclusively for music to be performed in an environment specifically designed for listening to music, won't dawn until the 1800s. The particular social function of music was therefore tremendously important during the Middle Ages and should shape our understanding of that music's meaning.

FIGURE 7.6 | *Saints, jamb-statues, The West Portal of the Cathedral at Chartres, c.1145–70.* With heads and eyes serene, bodies distorted through an exaggerated lengthening that lends them an emaciated look, and feet that dangle, these saints appear to emerge from some mystical vision. Gregorian Chant, likewise, seems otherworldly. This otherworldly effect stems from their flexible rhythms, which discourage foot-tapping, their modes which avoid a strong sense of resolution, and their monophonic texture. This repertory makes no clear attempt to appeal to the emotions or the crude senses, instead creating an ambiance for worship. The music serves the all-important text, just as these saints inspire reverence rather than draw attention to the craft that made them. (© Craig Aurness/Corbis)

Musical Performance and Illiteracy

One of the most interesting mysteries surrounding Gregorian Chant performance centers upon the issue of transmission. How did medieval monks, most of whom were illiterate, know what notes and words to sing? After all, no one at the monastery had performed the Alleluia for Christmas Day since the previous Christmas. Moreover, how did the remote parts of Christendom know to sing the same chant? The second question is easier to answer. Monks traveled from monastery to monastery. They carried with them manuscripts. Slowly, perhaps over the course of centuries, the approved chants were disseminated throughout Western Europe. Local customs, imprecise copies of manuscripts, and likely a measure of plain stubbornness lent medieval Christian practice a pleasing variety from place to place, despite these efforts toward uniformity. Given the lack of any means of mass communication, the marvelous accomplishment is that there was as much uniformity as there was.

The first and more difficult question, how mostly illiterate monks knew what to sing, has puzzled scholars. Among the interesting theories advanced in recent decades is the idea that there are mnemonic devices imbedded within chants. That is, composers drew upon certain recurrent patterns found in many chants in order to stimulate the memories of singers. There certainly are recurrent formulas that help to explain how singers knew what to sing. These mnemonic devices are usually specific to a particular mode and to a particular part of the Mass. Many cultures outside Europe boast elaborate music that is passed from generation to generation by purely oral means. These repertories often feature recurrent patterns that allow performers to rely on certain memorized formulas. We can also surmise that the literate monks at the monastery served a leadership role for the others. Iconographic evidence supports this idea. You can sing along with a song you don't know if you're clever and listen to the person next to you who might have a better recollection or an ability to read the notes. Following along and singing not too loudly can help anyone join in chanting. During the 1960s, the Roman Catholic Church largely abandoned the use of Gregorian Chant. In some modern Catholic monasteries that have special permission to continue using medieval chant, monks who do not read music find that the repertory is still possible to sing, thanks to the more skilled brothers sitting next to them.

THE RISE OF POLYPHONY

One of the remarkable features of Western music is the presence of polyphony. Polyphony occurs when two or more musical lines of more or less equal importance unfold simultaneously. The two examples of music we have heard so far are not polyphonic. The Ancient Greek Skolion features only a melody and a drone, while the Gregorian Chant example features only a melody.

Embellishing Gregorian Chant

The earliest polyphonic music resulted from the desire of medieval musicians to augment the music of their services. The first manifestations of this desire did not result in polyphony. Instead, medieval composers initially added new chant melodies to existing chant melodies, setting religious poetry in order to augment the services associated with days of particular importance to the region. This sort of practice resulted in additions, but not of the sort that results in polyphony. To achieve polyphony, the composer must layer new material upon other material intending for them to be performed simultaneously rather than consecutively. A typical example of additional material being added to the chant repertory requiring consecutive performance can be seen in the addition of chants venerating a saint of special regional or local importance. In Paris, for example, St. Denis is a specially revered personage. He was the Bishop of Paris, martyred for his beliefs. It is said that after being decapitated for his faith, he collected his severed head and walked up a hill on the northern edge of Paris. There he died. Medieval Christians living in Paris celebrated his Feast Day. In order to make his Feast Day more special, an anonymous musician composed a lengthy chant celebrating this saint, which leaders of the church adopted into the service. Such additions came to be known as *sequences* and *tropes*. Sequences (sequential passages) and tropes (musical and textual additions to the established repertory of the Mass) were the most common form of non-polyphonic additions to the chant repertory.

Sequences and tropes became fertile ground for further augmentation, insofar as they were already additions rather than the sacred chants codified by Gregory the Great and his followers. Augmentation of someone else's pre-existent augmentation was a hugely popular form of creativity during the Middle Ages. Today, adding to someone else's work is seen as less original or possibly even illegal, but that was definitely not the attitude of the medieval mind. While the earliest augmentations entailed adding on new material after the original, eventually the idea became a common practice of adding layers of new material to be presented simultaneously.

FIGURE 7.7 | St. Denis, patron saint of the city of Paris. Patron saints exist for most major cities, for virtually all nations, for most professions, and for the cure of most illnesses and afflictions. Local customs celebrate these revered personages to this day in most every city with a significant population of Roman Catholics. St. Patrick's Day, for example, reflects the continuation of this practice into the 21st century. St. Patrick is revered by Irish Catholics as the patron saint of Ireland. Many non-Catholics join in the fun each March 17th when St. Patrick's Feast Day comes around. (© Bettmann/Corbis)

The Notre Dame Composers

Constructed between 1163 and 1235, the cathedral of Notre Dame in Paris housed a large number of scholars who had taken holy orders and become monks or priests or even higher-ranking church officials even before the cathedral itself was completed. This center of learning in medieval Europe was the home to the most robust activity in terms of additive composition, that is, the layering of new material onto old.

Among the outstanding composers from the Middle Ages who worked at Notre Dame were Leonin (c. 1135–1201) and Pérotin (c. 1180–1238). Leonin embarked during his life on the creation of the *Magnus Liber Organum* (*The Great Book of Polyphonic Music*). He intended to compose, along with his students, polyphonic additions for a whole host of pre-existent chants. Fragments of this book can be found copied down in manuscripts scattered throughout Western Europe. Unfortunately, a complete copy of the original no longer exists, and may never have existed at all. It's quite possible that Leonin's project resulted only in fragments of his grand design. Leonin's student, Pérotin, continued and expanded on his teacher's methods. In our recorded anthology is a short example of Pérotin's polyphonic music, "Ysaias cecinit" (CD 1 #3). Unlike the work of Leonin, this composition is not so much an addition of new material on old, but a newly composed piece for three voices. Such compositions were frequently used at Notre Dame to accompany religious processions, and came to be known as *conductus*, in English we still use the word "conduct" to indicate moving from place to place.

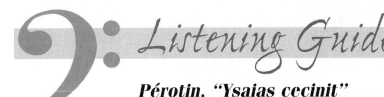

Pérotin, "Ysaias cecinit"

[CD1, #3] *(Duration, 1 min. 39 sec.)*

0.00	Ysaias cecinit;	Isaiah sang,
0.03	synagoga meminit	the synagogue remembers,
0.07	Jesse radix exeret	that the root of Jesse would emerge,
0.11	virgam virga proferet,	that the root would sprout a root,
0.14	florem flos amigdala,	that the almond tree would blossom,
0.18	synagoga scandala.	the synagogue aghast.
0.22	Aridula virguncula	The withered little root
0.26	vivicet, florificat, fructificat.	revives, flourishes, bears fruit.
0.33	Ecce ministerium,	Behold the ministry:
0.37	virgo verbo peperit	the virgin gave birth to the word,
0.41	verum Dei filium	the true son of God.
0.47	Hec est illa virgula	This is that wand,
0.51	Moysi miracula,	the miracle of Moses,
0.55	colubros percutiens,	striking the serpents,
0.58	sibi se reficiens.	remaking itself.
1.02	Hec divisit maria	This divided the waters,
1.06	nova ministeria,	new ministries,
1.10	cum lavimur,	when we are washed,
1.12	renascimur, colligimur.	we are reborn, we are gathered.
1.16	In vipera mens extera	The alien mind [is read] in the viper,
1.22	et in forma baciuli veri	and in the form of the true staff
1.26	vera legitur figura signaculi.[2]	is read the true symbol of the seal.[2]

[2]Translation by Laura Gibbs, University of Oklahoma.

FIGURE **7.8** | Even before its completion in 1235, the ***Cathedral of Notre Dame in Paris*** served as a center of learning in the Middle Ages. Unbelievably, the city fathers of Paris planned to destroy the edifice during the 1800s, so the novelist Victor Hugo wrote his book *The Hunchback of Notre Dame* in an attempt to draw needed sympathy for the building. His efforts succeeded and the building was spared demolition for being a literary rather than architectural landmark. (© Christie's Images/ Corbis)

Among the remarkable features of this piece is the pleasing way that the three voices join together to form a series of shifting, consonant sonorities. Early polyphonic composers felt that they should not simply superimpose pitches indiscriminately upon one another. They looked to the models of the past, especially thinkers from ancient Greece, and used the consonant intervals that had been advocated since the time of Pythagoras and recounted by Boethius and his many imitators. Through a mixture of *parallel* (voices moving in the same direction) and *contrary* (voices moving in opposite directions) motion, Pérotin configures the consonances of the fourth, fifth, and octave in ever-changing combinations.

Contemporaries of Pérotin very much admired Pérotin's ability to create pleasing polyphonic pieces. They admired the sophistication of his innovations and found his works sumptuous compared to earlier polyphonic experiments. One admiring contemporary wrote of Pérotin "this master introduced an abundance of refinements to the art of music and was in every way superior to Leonin." This admiring student's notes contain the only surviving reference by name to Pérotin. Apparently medieval enthusiasts of the arts in Paris were not solely devoted to the ideals of continuity and stability. Like the anonymous student quoted above, they held that innovation and seeming improvement upon the past were also useful. Strangely, we know so little about Pérotin as a person that we cannot say with certainty that this piece was even written by him. It may well be the product of one of his students.

Notation at Notre Dame

In addition to creating works with multiple voices, Pérotin's generation perfected a system of notation that allowed for interesting rhythmic variety. They called their system "the rhythmic modes." In this piece, we hear a steady flow of long notes alternating with short notes followed by a brief pause. The resulting pattern of long-short-long-short-long-short-long-pause was a favored rhythmic mode at Notre Dame during the thirteenth century. Normally musicians reserve the word "mode" to refer to scales of pitches. In this case, it refers to rhythmic patterns. In time, other innovations in musical notation would eliminate the need for rhythmic modes and end this confusing use of the word "mode" to mean both a collection of pitches and a rhythmic pattern.

Each subsequent generation of composers in Paris added new layers of potential complexity. Their innovations included dreaming up new methods of organizing rhythm so that different patterns of accented and unaccented beats, or meters, could be used. They also perfected a method of notation allowing for the subdivision of any beat into as many sub-beats as the composer desired. These innovations are still in use today. By the end of the Middle Ages, composers were creating works of such intense rhythmic complexity that they would have no equals until the 1900s.

SECULAR MUSIC

So far we have only examined music in the church. Certainly the churches and monasteries of the Middle Ages were sites of considerable creative activity, but the noble courts also witnessed the blossoming of music.

Secular song, that is, song not meant for the church, flourished during ancient times, as we heard in our example from ancient Greece. The Middle Ages witnessed a tremendous outpouring of secular song. The nobility took the lead in creating the secular songs that are still known today.

The Troubadours

Some of the most important repertories of secular song belong to the *troubadours*, poet-composers who flourished primarily in southern France during the twelfth and early thirteenth centuries. Troubadours should not be confused with the lower-class *jongleurs*, who were itinerate entertainers. Troubadours entertained the upper classes, and often found kings and queens among their ranks. Their primary poetical concern was the articulation and celebration of the idea of courtly love. Courtly love idealizes the relations between men and women, and imparts a nobility and beauty to interactions between the sexes. Men are celebrated under the codes of courtly love for being steadfast, courageous, and devoted, while women were lauded for being chaste, reverent, distant, and willing to submit to the adulation of the courtly man.

Figure 7.9 | *Richard coeur de lion,* or lion hearted, was a direct descendant of William the Conqueror. He inherited the English throne in 1189 and soon thereafter embarked on the ill-fated Third Crusade. He typified the troubadours in that he was educated in southwestern France, wrote poetry and music, patronized other poets and musicians, and championed the cause of chivalry and courtly love. (© Bettmann/Corbis)

An example of troubadour song is included in our recorded anthology (CD 1, #4). The song was composed by Bernart de Ventadorn (c. 1150–1180), a troubadour of aristocratic background. Composed near the height of the troubadours' influence, this piece is among the most frequently discussed and recorded examples of twelfth-century song. The language of the troubadours was Occitan, a close relative of French, still spoken with pride in its modern form within some remote districts of southern France. The text itself, also composed by Ventadorn, speaks of the age-old problem of unrequited love.

Listening Guide

Bernart de Ventadorn, "Can vei la lauzeta mover"
[CD1, #4] *(Duration, 1 min. 38 sec.)*

0.00	Can vei la lauzeta mover	When I see the lark beating
0.06	de joi sas alsas contral rai,	its wings joyfully against the sun's rays,
0.12	que s'oblid' e's laissa chazer	which then swoons and swoops down
0.18	per la dousser c'al cor li vai,	because of the joy in its heart,
0.24	ai! tan grans enveya m'en ve	oh! I feel such jealousy
0.30	de cui qu'eu veya jauizon,	for all those who have the joy of love,
0.36	meravilhas ai, car desse	that I am astonished
0.40	lo cor de dezirer no' m fon.	that my heart does not immediately melt with desire.
0.50	Ai, las! tan cuidava saber	Alas! I thought I knew so much
0.56	d'amor, e tan petit en sai,	of love, and I know so little,
1.02	car eu d'amar no' m posc tener	for I cannot help loving a lady
1.08	celeis don ja pro non aurai.	from whom I shall never obtain any favor.
1.13	Tout m'a mo cor, e tout m'a me,	She has taken away my heart and myself,
1.18	e se mezeis e tot lo mon;	and herself and the whole world;
1.23	e can se'm tolc, no'm laisset re	and when she left me, I had nothing left
1.28	mas dezirer e cor volon.	but desire and a yearning heart.[3]

The music of this piece reflects in part the Church's influence on secular music. It is vaguely similar to Gregorian Chant, in that it is monophonic and uses a Church Mode. This song happens to be in the same Dorian mode as the Alleluia for Christmas Day. The form of the piece is strophic, in that the same melody is sung with each new verse of poetry. More important than these purely technical characteristics is the piece's delicious sensuality as it fits the curve of the poetry and allows the singer's ardent passions to pour forth.

Secular Polyphony

Just as with sacred music, medieval composers eventually introduced polyphony to secular music. The earliest instances of secular polyphony were created by composers associated with the Church. The invention of additive processes led eventually to adding secular material on top of pre-existing sacred material. These musical compositions were called *motets*. The motet enjoys a long history, thriving in the last centuries

[3]Translation from Hendrik van der Werf, *The Chansons of the Troubadours and Trouvères.* (Utrecht, 1972), 91–93.

of the Middle Ages and still occasionally attracting new composers today. Strictly speaking, motets are polyphonic, secular compositions with at least one Latin text.

Philippe de Vitry (1291–1361) was typical of composers of his age. He was a composer, a poet, and the Bishop of Meaux. He wrote mainly secular music, but maintained close ties to the Church through his important role within the Church's hierarchy. His secular creations include important contributions to one of the most celebrated books of the Middle Ages, the *Roman de Fauvel*. This large poem satirizes the foibles of the day. Fauvel is a donkey with magical powers to grant wishes when anyone combs or curries his coat. The modern English phrase "to curry favor," which means to seek some advantage from someone by fawning upon them or complimenting them, is a bastardization of the phrase "to curry Fauvel," which means to comb Fauvel's coat. In each section of the poem, a person from a different segment of medieval society encounters Fauvel, combs his coat, and makes a wish that immediately comes true. Unfortunately for them, their wishes reveal their sinful impulses, and invariably backfire. This poem was printed in a magnificent illuminated manuscript and peppered with musical compositions. De Vitry was a leading contributor of pieces for the collection. The listening example "Garrit Gallus/In nova fert/Neuma" (CD 1 #5) was written by De Vitry for the *Roman de Fauvel*, and provides an interesting example of the medieval motet.

The piece demonstrates the medieval fascination with adding upon previous materials *vertically*, that is, by writing music meant to be played simultaneously with other music. The result is a piece with three different texts, one in each of the three parts, all being sung simultaneously. The texts in two of the voices indulge in Biblical and historical references, all the while emphasizing the metaphor of a sneaky fox corrupting the reign of a blind lion, the lion serving as the symbol of monarchy. Lost on modern readers is the likelihood that the foxes in both texts represent an actual person. Enguerran de Marigny, the high counselor to Philip IV of France, was reviled as devious during de Vitry's times. Such political references to contemporary personages certainly lent this piece much of its pleasure in de Vitry's day; today we'll just have to imagine the effect of such subversive gestures. Such criticism of power suggests that by the end of the Middle Ages, the political stability and respect for authority cited earlier in this chapter as central to the politics of the Middle Ages certainly had its critics.

The third of the three parts has a one-word text "neuma," and results from taking a single word of Gregorian Chant. The melody of that chant is repeated several times and is presented using a recurrent rhythmic pattern. Because there is so little text for this third voice, it was usually performed by a musical instrument rather than a singer. The repeated cycles of notes in the third voice have come to be called "the color," while the recurrent rhythmic pattern is called "the talea." Pieces constructed with a voice comprised of a *color* (borrowed, repeating melodic line) and a *talea* (repeated rhythmic pattern) are called *isorhythmic*. In an isorhythmic piece, one voice presents both recurrent rhythmic and melodic material. This strategy for organizing musical materials is intended to lend coherence to complex music. That is, the repeating material helps to orient the listener, and helps the listener to make sense of the otherwise difficult piece. Given that listeners are hearing two different texts sung simultaneously, any effort to make the music coherent was appreciated.

By stacking three highly independent musical lines, juxtaposing similar but different texts on top of one another, and using the most sophisticated structural technique of the day (isorhythms), de Vitry emerges as the most complex composer of his generation. Indeed, authors of his time described his work as "Ars Nova" (New Art) and labled all that preceded him "Ars Antiqua" (Old Art).

Listening Guide

Philippe de Vitry, "Garrit Gallus/In Nova Fert"

[CD1, #5] *(Duration, 1 min. 38 sec.)*

Due to the complexity of this piece, timings do not accompany the text as there are three texts unfolding simultaneously.

The First Voice "Garrit Gallus"

Garrit Gallus flendo dolorose	The cock babbles, lamenting sorrowfully,
Luget quippe Gallorum concio.	for the whole assembly of cocks
Que satrape traditur dolose,	mourns because, while serving vigilantly,
Ex cubino sedens officio	it is trickily betrayed by the satrap.
Atque vulpes, tamquam vispilio	And the fox, like a grave robber,
in Belial vigens astucia	thriving with the astuteness of Belial,
De leonis consensu proprio	rules as a monarch with the consent
Monarshisat, atat angaria	of the lion himself. Ah, what slavery!
Rursus, ecce. Jacob familia	Lo, once again Jacob's family
Pharaone altero fugatur;	is exiled by another Pharaoh.
Non ut olim lude vestigia	Not, as formerly, able to escape
Subintrare potens, lacrimatur.	to the homeland of Judah, they weep.
In deserto fame flagellatur.	Stricken by hunger in the desert,
Adiutoris carens armatura.	lacking the help of arms,
Quamquam clamat, tamens spoliatur,	although they cry out, they are robbed;
Continuo forsan moritura.	perhaps speedily they will die.
O miserum exulum vox dura!	O harsh voice of the wretched exiles;
O Gallorum garritus doloris,	O sorrowful babbling of the cocks,
Cum leonis cecitas obscura	since the dark blindness of the lion
Fraudi paret vulpis proditoris.	submits to the fraud of the traitorous fox.
Eius fastus sustinens erroris	You who suffer the arrogance of his
Insurgito: alias labitur	misdeeds, rise up
Et labetur quod habes honoris,	or what you have of honor is being or
Quod mox in facinis tardis	will be lost, because if avengers are slow
ultoribus itor.	men soon turn to evil doing.

The Second Voice "In nova fert"

In nova fert animus mutatas	My heart is set upon speaking of forms
Dicere formas.	changed into new forms.
Draco nequam quam olim penitus	The evil dragon that renowned Michael once
Mirabilis crucis potencia	utterly defeated by the miraculous power
Debellavit Michael inclitus,	of the Cross,
Mox Absalon munitus gracia,	now endowed with the grade of Absalom,
Mox Ulixis gaudens facundia,	now with the cheerful eloquence of Ulysses,
Mox lupinis dentibus armatus,	now armed with wolfish teeth
Sub Tersitis miles milicia	a soldier in the service of Thersites,
Rursus vivit in vulpem mutatus,	lives again changed into a fox

Cauda cuius, lumine privatus	whose tail the lion deprived
Leo, vulpe imperante, paret.	of sight obeys, while the fox reigns.
Oves suggit pullis saciatus.	He sucks the blood of sheep and is satiated with chickens.
Heu! suggere non cessat et aret	Alas, he does not cease sucking and still thirsts;
Ad nupcias carnibus non caret.	he does not abstain from meats at the wedding feasts.
Ve pullis mox, ve ceco leoni!	Woe now to the chickens, woe to the blind lion!
Coram Christotandem ve draconi.	In the presence of Christ, finally, woe to the dragon.[4]

The 1300s in Europe: The 100 Years War

Just as de Vitry's choice of poetry contains criticism of the politics of the day, the stability that marked so much of the political climate of the Middle Ages was gradually being rocked. The fourteenth century saw the rise of many challenges for society. For one thing, Western Europe was in a state of almost constant war. The Hundred Years War (1338–1453), as it came to be called later, actually lasted more than 100 years and embroiled at one time or another most of the kingdoms of Western Europe. The main fight was between England and France. In 1066 Norman invaders from France conquered England and established a new monarchy under the rule of William the Conqueror. William and the Normans still owned a considerable portion of French-speaking Europe at the time they conquered England. When William became King of England and passed the title to his sons, much of what is now France suddenly fell into English hands. Eventually, French and English claims to the same territories led to more than a century of confusing warfare.

The Black Death

Coupled with the continuous presence of war throughout the century, the Black Death, or bubonic plague, swept in from the East. Merchants who brought goods from the Black Sea accidentally carried with them rats from the Near East. The blood of these rats was infected with the plague. When fleas sucked the blood of the rats and then bit human beings, small amounts of the infected rat blood entered the human victim. Medieval Europeans did not know that fleas carried the disease, but even if they had, they would not have been able to control the spread of fleas. The worst outbreak of the bubonic plague in Western Europe spanned the years 1347–1350. The disease was incurable and untreatable, and it took a terrible toll on its victims. Some historians estimate that one in four Europeans died of the dreaded disease.

The Schism in the Church

Finally, the Christian Church, long the pillar of stability in the Middle Ages, was rocked with scandal. King Philip V of France campaigned successfully to elect a Frenchman to the office of Pope. Rome, the usual home of the Pope, was then controlled by citizens who despised foreigners. They refused to welcome the new Pope, Clement V. The result was a schism between the properly elected Pope, who took up residence in the

---

[4]Translation by Richard Hoppin in *An Anthology of Medieval Music* (New York, W. W. Norton, 1978), 125–126.

Figure 7.10 | Some historians estimate that the ***Black Plague*** killed nearly one in every four Europeans between the years 1347 and 1352. Here we see a depiction of two plague victims, their flesh pocked with large boils. The characteristic wounds symptomatic of Black Plague gave rise to the grim children's song-game, "Ring Around the Rosy." The next time you hear this tune consider its origins.

Ring around the rosy,	The plague wound was red with a dark ring.
A pocket full of posies,	Refers to the flowers of a funeral.
Ashes, ashes,	Possession of the afflicted were all burned.
All fall down.	The plague killed huge numbers of people.

In some places the death toll was so alarming and swift that frightened citizens fled cities in search of a safe haven. This desperation only served to speed the plague to new victims in new cities. First appearing around the Black Sea in 1347, the Black Death originated in China. It reached the port cities of Italy and southern France in December of 1347. Within six months, both nations had been decimated by the hideous illness. (© Bettmann/Corbis)

French city of Avignon, and a rival Pope elected in Rome. At one point during the 1300s, there were three Popes, all claiming legitimacy. Warfare, instability, and confusion resulted.

The Arts in Europe of the 1300s

This political, religious, and social turbulence makes achievements such as de Vitry's all the more remarkable. Indeed the late Middle Ages saw a tremendous flourishing not only in music, but in all the arts. Literature witnessed the creation of Dante's *Divine Comedy* (1307), Du Bus' *Roman de Fauvel* (1310), Boccaccio's *Decameron* (1353), and Chaucer's *Canterbury Tales* (1386). In painting, the Italian Giotto made great strides by producing the first works in the West to render subjects naturalistically. The 1300s witnessed both human strife and artistic triumph.

The superb poet and composer Guillaume de Machaut (1300–1377) expanded upon de Vitry's successes and helped bring the Ars Nova to its zenith. He composed both polyphonic and monophonic secular songs and motets, along with a complete setting of the ordinary of the Mass for four voices, the *Messe de Notre Dame*. Machaut

Figure 7.11 | Giotto di Bondone painted this fresco, *Lamentation,* depicting the mourning of the body of Christ after he was removed from the cross. This fresco was painted in 1305 and suggests the dawn of a new concern for naturalism and visual logic. Note that the figures are presented in perspective against the rocks in the background. Gone are the unrealistic disparities in size among the figures, such as those found in the illustrations for the *Roman de Fauvel.* The details on the faces of Christ's mourners captured the imaginations of future painters, who sought to expand on Giotto's innovations by lending their human subjects individuality and recognizable emotion. (Scala/Art Resource, NY)

capped off 200 years of innovations in the art of music begun by Leonin, continued by Pérotin, advanced by de Vitry, and culminating in the middle 1300s with Machaut.

MUSIC OF THE PEASANTS

So far, all of the medieval music cited in this chapter was created by the educated and social elite. That situation is hardly an accident. In order for a musical work to survive and be studied in the twenty-first century, it had to be written down. The serfs were almost entirely illiterate. Compulsory education for the lower classes in Europe was an idea of the Enlightenment of the late eighteenth century. The music of the peasants was exclusively transmitted orally, as writing was of no value to them. Yet, a few examples of music akin to that created by and for the serfs survive, although exclusively through instances of the wealthy, educated, and powerful writing it down for their own use. Thus we cannot guarantee that what we are hearing was not modified to suit the tastes of the elite. Moreover, it is wildly unlikely that instrumentalists of the Middle Ages made use of musical notation while playing. They certainly improvised their parts on a tune known to all the players. This fact further complicates our relationship with the authentic music of the serfs. Written dance music was very likely written for the purposes of presenting a manuscript copy to an important patron of dance music, usually a member of the nobility. Musicians normally don't make anything physical that can be given as a gift, at least during the ages before recording technologies. Medieval musicians who wanted to give something to their sovereign therefore had to make musical scores, even if the scores were of no actual use for practicing musicians. We call these scores *presentation copies*. Much of the surviving music that may or may not have originated with the peasants exists today in presentation copies made by musicians serving the elite.

Istampita Palamento (CD 1 #6), is an example of medieval dance music. It features no text, and its anonymous composer designed it to be played on instruments. The instruments in use during the Middle Ages are too numerous to mention here. The recording in the anthology features the *psaltery* (similar to the modern zither, a string instrument), the *lute* (a plucked string instrument slightly similar to the modern guitar), a *recorder* (an end-blown fipple flute still in use today), and the *vielle* (a bowed string instrument vaguely like the modern violin).

This particular piece has five sections. The first section is repeated. The second and third sections quote the middle of the first and end the same as one another. The fourth section, like the first, is repeated. The fifth section quotes the entire middle of the fourth, but has its own ending.

Listening Guide

Istampita Palamento
[CD1, #6] *(Duration, 4 min. 43 sec.)*

0.00 PART ONE
0.43 REPEAT OF PART ONE
1.19 PART TWO, features 16 measures quoted from Part One
1.51 PART THREE, features the same quotation of 16 measures and ends exactly like Part Two
2.32 PART FOUR, entirely new material
3.13 REPEAT OF PART FOUR
3.54 PART FIVE, has the same middle as Part Four

Unfortunately for students of medieval music, no two written dance pieces will reveal precisely the same form, making generalizing about form virtually impossible. Dance forms from the Middle Ages until the present generally feature repeats of materials. Dancing to music one has heard before is, after all, easier than dancing to music that constantly changes. In keeping with the need for dance music to maintain some consistency in order for people to dance to it, this piece is entirely in 6/8 meter, with a fast tempo.

Musical Exchange Between the Rich and Poor

The musicians who played dance music may well have come from the lower classes and were willing to play at festivals for both the mighty and the meek. The idea that there is a distinct music of the peasants wholly separate from the nobility may be a projection of modern schisms between such categories as "popular" and "classical" music back into a past where such distinctions have no meaning. The concepts of "popular" and "classical" were entirely unknown during the Middle Ages. While the poorest serfs surely had no access to the court, and therefore were unlikely to hear the music of a medieval sophisticate such as Philippe de Vitry, there were surely servants and attendants present who represented the lower classes. Similarly, the sacred repertory could be heard when serfs attended Mass. Just as the music originating in the upper classes occasionally reached the lower, there was an equal and opposite tendency for music originating in the lower classes to reach the upper. Dance music likely originated with the lower classes, which performed pieces such *as Istampita Palamento* at wedding parties and harvest festivals. The feudal lords surely heard them, and were occasionally taken by their virtue. The same musicians might find their way to court to accompany festivals sponsored by the lord.

THE END OF THE MIDDLE AGES

Historians often link the end of the Middle Ages to the fall of Constantinople in 1452. The Turkish Empire, under the superb leadership of Mohammed II, had long hoped to expand its territory into southeastern Europe, but the last stronghold of the Roman Empire stood in the way. After a masterful siege, the capital of the Eastern Empire fell. The last vestige of the Roman Empire was gone. Turkish troops were soon at the gates of Vienna, and a period of nonstop tension and warfare began between the Christian kingdoms of Austria and Hungary and the Turkish Empire.

Other historians link the end of the Middle Ages with the flourishing of the arts and humanistic enterprises that emerge on the Italian peninsula during the 1400s. Italy had long been a minor player in artistic affairs once the Roman Empire fell. During the1300s, this condition changed with a vengeance as Italy took a leadership role in matters of art. Burgeoning trade with the Middle East brought enormous wealth to Italy. A heated rivalry among Italian nobles flared, as the leaders of the independent city states of Italy strove to increase the wealth and prestige of their cities through the arts and sciences. As conditions in Italy improved, the 1400s saw the dawn of what has come to be known as the Italian Renaissance and, with it, the end of the Middle Ages.

The 1450s also saw the end of the costly Hundred Years War. With peace finally achieved between France and England, the resources of Western Europe could be channeled toward more peaceful pursuits. The main beneficiary of the war was the Duchy of Burgundy. The Dukes of Burgundy, a rich land in the eastern part of what is now France with a capital at Dijon, skillfully switched sides between France and England over the course of the war. Each time, the price of their aid rose, until Burgundy became tremendously rich and powerful. The universities, monasteries, and courts of Burgundy witnessed splendid accomplishments in the arts, and most especially music. As Italy's wealth grew to rival and finally surpass that of Burgundy, Burgundian musicians were attracted south to the courts and chapels of Italy.

Guillaume du Fay

Guillaume du Fay (c. 1400–1474) provides a fine illustration of Burgundy's contribution to music. He was educated in Burgundy and initially served the ducal court at Dijon. By 1420, while du Fay was still a very young man, we know that he came to Italy to serve the powerful Malatesta family in Pesaro. The remainder of his career was spent in the service variously of the Pope in Rome and other Italian nobles in the north of the country. His music demonstrates just how much had changed from the beginning of the so-called Middle Ages to the end. When the story of this period began, virtually no system of notating music existed, and the only texture available to composers was monophony. By the end of the period, their notation system was almost as precise as the main system used today. Polyphony was both invented and endowed with tremendous sophistication.

FIGURE 7.12 | *The cathedral of Santa Maria del Fiore* in Florence, Italy was built during the late Middle Ages. The dome was added in 1436. (George Eastman House)

Representing du Fay's work in the listening anthology is perhaps his most sensational piece, the motet *Nuper rosarem flores* (1436) [CD1 #7]. This piece for voices and brass instruments was composed to celebrate the consecration of the spectacular golden dome built upon the cathedral of Santa Maria del Fiore in Florence, Italy. Like de Vitry's motet of the previous century, this one also uses an isorhythmic structure. The two brass parts play an isorhythmic line with a brief excerpt of Gregorian Chant ("Terribilis est locus iste") serving as the color. Meanwhile, the voices present a Latin poem celebrating Pope Eugene IV and the consecration of the new architectural wonder. The dome of this cathedral is gilt with gold, a row of windows surround the bottom of the dome. When the sun hits the dome, much of the cathedral is bathed in golden light. The city of Florence was justly proud of its wealth, splendid artistic achievement, and traditions of republican government. The dome can be seen as an act that simultaneously gives thanks for the many blessings bestowed on the city while drawing attention to the city's achievements and prosperity.

Just as the architecture of the cathedral simultaneously looks back on the faith of the Middle Ages and forward to the humanistic pride of the Renaissance, the music does so as well. Du Fay's addition of new material upon a structure of old material, the Gregorian Chant, reveals essentially medieval practices. Yet, he coupled this old idea with new ideas, such as the coupling of brasses with voices, and harmony revealing a preference for the new consonances of the third and the sixth. Before du Fay's time, only the fourth, fifth, and octave were considered permissible for simultaneous presentation. In this piece, du Fay uses more thirds and sixths. Burgundian composers, probably emulating the folk practices of their sometimes allies the English, embraced these two intervals as consonant. Their taste for thirds and sixths as consonant intervals remains with us today. With its mingling of the old and new, du Fay's piece serves as a fitting place to end our discussion of musical achievements during the Middle Ages.

Listening Guide

Guillaume du Fay, "Nuper rosarum flores"
[CD1, #7] *(Duration, 7 min. 19 sec.)*

0.00	Nuper rosarum flores	Recently roses bloomed
0.18	Ex dono pontificis	as a gift from the Pope,
0.28	Hieme licet horrida,	although in horrid winter,
0.40	Tibi, virgo coelica,	to you, heavenly Virgin.
0.57	Pie et sancte deditum	Piously and blessedly is dedicated
1.11	**[Instrumental Interlude]**	
1.19	Grandis templum machinae	to you a temple of grand design.
1.31	Condocorarunt perpetim.	May they be perpetual ornaments.
1.42	Hodie vicarius	Today the Vicar
1.50	Jesu Christi et Petri	of Jesus Christ and Peter's
1.59	Successor EUGENIUS	successor, EUGENE,
2.14	Hoc idem amplissimum	this same most ample
2.19	Sacris templum manibus	sacred temple with his hands
2.22	Sanctisque liquoribus	and with holy waters
2.36	Consecrare dignatus est.	he is worthy to consecrate.
2.51	Igitur, alma parens,	Therefore, gracious mother
3.04	Nati tui et filia,	and daughter of your child,
3.17	Virgo decus virginum,	Virgin, decoration of virgins,
3.30	Tuus te FLORENTIAE	your, FLORENCE'S, people
3.39	Devotus orat populus,	devoutly pray with everyone
3.47	Ut qui mente et corpore	with mind and body
3.53	**[Instrumental Interlude]**	
3.59	Mundo quicquam exoravit,	that their prayers may move you.
4.10	Oratione tua	Through your prayer,
4.27	Cruciatus et meritis	your anguish and merits,
5.00	Tui secundum carnem	your second flesh
5.24	Nati domini sui	born of you,
5.44	**[Instrumental Interlude]**	
6.09	Grata beneficia	the benefits of grace
6.22	**[Instrumental Interlude]**	
6.34	Veniamque reatum	and the remission of sin,
6.48	Accipere mereatur.	may the people deserve.
7.01	Amen.	So be it.

Some Questions for Discussion

1 One problem medieval music poses for modern students is the fact that all medieval music was intended for a specific time and place. Those places and times are now mostly gone. What do you think would be the ideal setting for performances of the six pieces discussed in this chapter? Does your choice of an ideal setting change the function or meaning of the piece? Can you think of modern music that makes little sense once it is taken from its original context?

2 The medieval practice of taking an already existing piece of music and adding new material to it, or using part of it in making something new, marks the music of this period as specially the product of the medieval imagination. What are some modern examples of the same processes at work? Here's an example to get the discussion started: In rap music, pre-existing music is often sampled and used as the foundation over which modern musicians add new material. Think of some other examples, then consider whether there is any commonality between these new practices and the medieval mind. After all, many medieval institutions, ideas, and practices are still in use today.

3 In the 1300s, the arts flourished despite terrible troubles. The Black Death, the Hundred Years War, and the Great Schism in the Church failed to derail artistic achievement in the last years of the Middle Ages. What kinds of crises loom on the horizon for the twenty-first century, and what impact do you think they will have for the arts and specifically for music?

C H A P T E R **8**

The Renaissance (1452–1600)

THE WORD "RENAISSANCE"

"Renaissance" is a French word meaning "rebirth." It also refers in both French and English to a period in European history from roughly 1452 until 1600. It can also refer to a period notable for some particularly strong artistic and scientific achievement, or for any other form of excellence formerly absent and now present. The term has come to refer to this period because some later observers of European culture find the achievements of this period superior to those of the Middle Ages. Such conventions of periodization based on modern aesthetic judgments need not trouble us too much one way or another. While the term for the period reflects the positive opinion some more modern scholars hold for the period's achievements, we still have the task of dispassionately examining a few of those achievements.

Interestingly, people alive during this period did not refer to their time as "the Renaissance." The first use of this word to describe the period we are about to examine belongs to the nineteenth-century French historian Jules Michelet. This wide gap between the time itself and the first use of the word might be attributable to the fact that the Renaissance did not actually touch the lives of all, or even most, Europeans. For people living in the eastern half of Europe, the so-called Renaissance touched their lives very little or not at all. Polish aristocrats of the highest rank may have benefited from the intellectual and artistic achievements of Italy and France, but for the peasantry of Eastern Europe who made up the vast majority of the population, nothing changed. Indeed, in Russia, the feudal system of serfdom so closely associated with medieval society would not be abolished until the 1860s. In France, by contrast, the end of feudalism in the 1400s marked a signal moment in the rise of a new era.

Renaissance and the Social Classes

Even in Western Europe, one could easily argue that the Renaissance, with its humanistic idealism, actually touched the lives of comparatively few people in any significant way. Perhaps at the end of this approximately 150-year period, the impact of

FIGURE 8.1 | *Detail of the ceiling of the Camera degli Sposi (1474).* One can argue whether there was or was not a Renaissance that touched the lives of Europeans; however, one cannot argue whether change was afoot within the arts and their place within society during the late 1400s. Among intellectual disciplines, the arts became an increasingly essential part of the lives of the wealthy. In the process, their status changed from craft to fine art. (One need not conclude that this change in status was necessarily a good thing.) Here we see a fresco painted on the ceiling of the Ducal Palace in Mantua. Two of the composers studied later in this chapter, Giaches de Wert and Claudio Monteverdi, worked under this ceiling. Artists such as Andrea Mantegna, who painted this fresco, gained confidence and newfound independence through the advancing status of the arts in Italy. The well proportioned angelic figures are depicted as natural extensions of the human body. The vivid colors and magnificent depiction of the sky in this fresco reflect both an awareness and glorification of the self in harmonious relationship to the universe. The fresco speaks of human beings as social and creative, bound and free, limited and limitless, part of a vast and vibrant nature.

The ideals that inform this fresco informed the musicians of the age as well. Composers sought comparable approaches to achieve naturalness, mastery, and vivid emotion. (© Archivo Iconografico, S.A./Corbis)

the Renaissance was more broadly felt, but for the peasants in Western Europe, change came very slowly.

All this disparity in the ways Europeans experienced or did not experience the Renaissance has led many scholars of medieval culture to argue that there was no Renaissance. They ask how a rebirth of culture could be achieved when the culture was already alive and well. Today many scholars refer to the period from 1452–1600 as "early modernism." This term provides the advantage of admitting that certain priorities central to the medieval imagination had given way to something new, without condemning the Middle Ages and its cultural priorities.

THE ITALIAN RENAISSANCE

While the word is French, the clearest manifestation of the Renaissance took place in Italy. As noted in the previous chapter, Italy emerged as a great commercial and artistic power at the start of the 1400s. As a political entity, however, Italy was fractured into small, rival city states. Italy would not unite as a single nation until 1870. The main disadvantage of Italy's political fragmentation was the problem of foreign invasion. France, Austria, Spain, and the Turkish Empire all made significant incursions into the Italian peninsula during the period from 1450 to 1600. Yet, for all its seeming political weakness, some Italian city states, especially Venice, managed to build powerful political blocks, comprised not only of Italian territory but valuable provinces throughout the Mediterranean region. Venice at one time owned the islands of Crete and Cyprus in the eastern Mediterranean, and used them as bases for trade with ports from Greece to Egypt. They also controlled the entire Dalmatian coast, now a part of the Republic of Croatia. In addition to these valuable properties, Venice held a vast hinterland comprising most of northeastern Italy. Venice, a small city comprised of many tiny islands in the Adriatic Sea, boasted Europe's largest navy and mightiest army of mercenaries. Venice was, in short, a formidable power.

Artistic Rivalry in Italy

The principal advantage of Italy's division into small, independent political entities was a vigorous rivalry among them. Italian merchants vied with one another for most favorable trading partners in the Middle East, Northern Africa, and throughout Europe. The strongest, and wisest thrived, while the weak disappeared. The wealth that poured into Italy fuelled still other rivalries ranging from military adventures (largely fought by hired mercenaries rather than Italians themselves) to lavish displays of artistic patronage. The Italian Renaissance burned brightly in no small degree thanks to the rivalries and hatreds that stirred among Italy's ruling families. The history of European art owes a tremendous debt to the fact that the Borgias, Medicis, Sforzas, Gonzagas, and other Italian families of wealth and power wanted to triumph over one another not only in the marketplace, not merely on the battlefield, but through their magnificently decorated palazzos and cathedrals as well.

HUMANISM

While these economic and political explanations tell part of the story of the Renaissance, there is a philosophical dimension as well. Most historians agree that a spirit of humanism, the belief in the power and importance of human beings and their achievements, also fueled the Renaissance.

The exact nature of humanism is difficult to describe. Some explain it by describing the tremendous activity of leading intellectuals in examining the writings and art-

FIGURE 8.2 | *The Palazzo Ducale in Venice.* Symbol of Venetian power, the ducal palace with its tiled facade and majestic contours serves to this day as evidence of the rivalry among Italian city states during the 1500s. The great cities of Italy all host magnificent architecture from the Renaissance illustrating the mercantile and political might of the region. (© Dennis Marsico/Corbis)

works of antiquity. Certainly a great many manuscripts from the ancient Greeks were translated into Latin, the prevailing language of learned activities in Europe until the 1800s, during this period. How this precisely separates the Renaissance from the Middle Ages, when interest in ancient Greek activity concerned theorists of music enormously, is difficult to say. Scholars of ancient Greece, working in the Renaissance, differed in one interesting way from most (but not all) of their medieval predecessors by using ancient Greek writings as a blueprint for trying to reclaim their civilization, rather than merely maintaining an intellectual and theoretical tradition without actually implementing it. One thing is certain: Renaissance students of ancient Greece owe a tremendous debt to early medieval copyists and scholars such as Boethius for preserving ancient Greek writings.

Humanism and the Sciences

Humanism also implies a philosophical challenge to the medieval imagination's preference for faith. Humanistic inquiry privileges not only artistic achievement, but also scientific achievement. Some scientists working in the Renaissance ran afoul of Church authorities by advancing theories that challenged Church doctrine. The most spectacular of these challenges came from Galileo Galilei who postulated in 1610 that the Earth was not the center of the Universe. He spent a considerable amount of time under house arrest for defying settled matters of faith.

Less spectacular, but earlier examples of scientists challenging received authority can be seen in Giovanni Bardi's research on the migration of birds. Charming folk legends posited that birds simply disappeared during the winter months and flourished during summer months. Bardi, also an important researcher in the field of music, noted the presence of a certain species of bird common in Italy during certain seasons was present in Norway during the seasons of its absence in Italy. Whether at the level of the spectacular as in the case of Galileo or the modest in the case of Bardi, the humanistic fascination with scientific discovery confounded received knowledge.

The Church was not monolithic in its resistance to scientific achievement during this period. After all, many of the men who found their way into positions of authority within the Church were touched by the philosophical doctrines of humanism. Church leaders counted among the patrons of both the sciences and the arts.

A simplistic but potentially useful way to understand the shift from medieval to Renaissance notions about humanism might run this way: Western culture at its most broad can be seen as a swing between two kind of contrasting periods. The Renaissance represents those times when Western society relied on humankind's own power to make sense of an explicable world through powers of observation. By contrast, the Middle Ages can be seen as one of those periods when humankind looked to forces external to itself for answers, even going so far as to imagine itself as buffeted by forces entirely beyond comprehension. Such a broad view carries with it certain dangers of oversimplification, but this method of looking at the history of the West has served some students in forming a clearer understanding of complex cultural shifts.

MUSIC AND HISTORY

Renaissance music picks up where Guillaume du Fay left off. Some scholars have difficulty deciding whether du Fay belongs to the Middle Ages or the Renaissance. This confusion is natural since the boundary between stylistic periods in music will always

FIGURE **8.3** | *Michelangelo's* **David** (1501–1504) stands over thirteen-and-a-half feet tall, and expresses a quality of confidence that seems to entitle Man to accept no other authority but his own genius. Constructed in an age that sought to know the world and the self, this nude champion appears natural and casual, with all his weight supported by his right foot, a foot clearly planted in the physical world. While the composition first emphasizes the glory of the human body, it also expresses conflict. The conflict of the soul imprisoned in the body is expressed in the positioning of the upper body relative to the lower. The upper body and lower body simultaneously express clockwise and counter-clockwise motion. The energy contained in the figure remains only a potential. The figure's stance, seemingly poised to move, yet frozen in marble, expresses the humanist ideal that humankind is both free and limited, at once masterful yet subject to divine laws.

Just as the sculptor strove to express humanist values of naturalness and celebration of the body, musicians did the same. The ideal sonority of the Renaissance was the human voice unaccompanied by any instrument. Words are declaimed in Renaissance vocal music by incorporating rhythms and melodies that approximate normal speech patterns. These melodies are always contained within a tempo and dynamic range that remains relatively constant. The pitches used in any single voice's part are never very high or very low, lending the melodies a naturalness suitable to the voices of the singers.

Through both sculpture, as demonstrated by Michelangelo's *David,* and works of sacred music written during the same century, we see that the ideals of humanism lend themselves to sacred subjects. The human body, either through its physical form or through its voice, serves as the starting point for both humanist sculptors and musicians. (Nimatallah/Art Resource, NY)

be blurry. At the end of this chapter, Claudio Monteverdi will serve as the last Renaissance composer, yet, he will also serve as the first composer discussed in the following chapter on the Baroque era.

Du Fay, a man educated in the affluent Duchy of Burgundy was attracted to Italy by the mounting wealth and power of that region. His musical style is most clearly carried forward by a fellow Burgundian, Johannes Ockeghem (1410–1497). Unlike du Fay, Ockeghem remained in Burgundy into his thirties, when he left to serve the King of France. As the king's most trusted musician, Ockeghem enjoyed a career of considerable importance and influence. He specialized in writing sacred music. His masses were especially influential in the formation of the Renaissance style. He also wrote motets and *chansons* (French for songs). The most important contribution of Ockeghem was his continued emphasis on the newly consonant intervals of the third and the sixth. By creating compelling music emphasizing those intervals as stable, Ockeghem saw to it that the Burgundian style attributed to du Fay would remain the chief style of the new era.

Just as the style of music preferred during the middle 1400s remains fairly stable, the same venues that served medieval music will serve Renaissance music as well. The Church will foster sacred music. The courts of the aristocrats and monarchs will promote achievements in secular music. The peasants will labor in obscurity, dancing to and singing their own music, music that will occasionally attract the attention of the powerful. The humble will serve as an accidental audience for the music of the rich whenever servants (including musical servants, such as singers and instrumentalists) find themselves in the presence of the music of their employers. The idea of the public concert was, as with the Middle Ages, unheard of during the Renaissance. This high degree of stability between the two periods reinforces the arguments of those who prefer to see continuity rather than change during the 1400s.

The Invention of Moveable Type

One historical innovation during this period will have a tremendous impact on the distribution of music, the invention of movable type and the printing press. Johannes Gutenberg, a German inventor, developed a system during the 1440s that made the printing of books radically more practical than it had been previously. In former times, each copy of a book had to be written out by hand. You may recall the beautiful illustrations from the previous chapter of elegant books, such as the *Roman de Fauvel*. The painstaking process of copying books by hand made books both impractical and expensive. On rare occasions medieval copyists would carve entire pages of a book into a single block of wood. This innovation, still time-consuming and expensive, did make printing slightly more practical. Gutenberg's idea was to make small, metal blocks, each printed with a different letter. These blocks could then be placed in a wooden frame to form pages of a book. Ink was applied to the letters, which were then pressed onto paper. This process of movable type (so named because the printer could then remove the letters and move them to the next page) made printing a comparatively efficient process.

In 1501, the printer Ottaviano dei Petrucci (1466–1539) applied this idea to music. He developed small metal blocks, each printed with a note. He made blocks with notes on every space and line of the five-line staff. He also made notes of every rhythmic value. His application of Gutenberg's idea to music made the printing of music a viable industry for the first time in history.

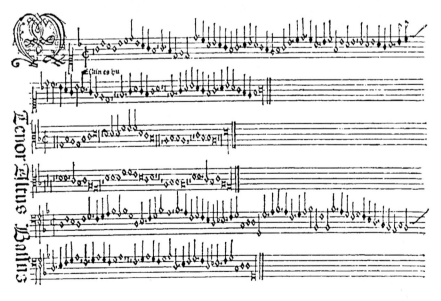

Figure 8.4 | The first music book printed using the Petrucci's movable, musical type was ***Harmoniches musiches odhecaton (1501).*** Note how the individual notes are carved into small pieces of metal. All note types (whole notes, half notes, quarter notes) receive equal spacing. This innovation in printing allowed for the wide distribution of musical scores.

The Protestant Reformation

Another historical development that had an enormous impact on music was the Protestant Reformation. This important complex of events saw the division of Christianity into sects and denominations based upon profoundly held but divergent views on Christian theology. In general, believers who remained constant with the traditions and beliefs of previous centuries are known as Catholics, while the reformers of those traditions and beliefs are called Protestants. Largely a Western European development, this division doesn't take into account the various forms of Christianity practiced in Eastern Europe, such as Greek and Russian Orthodox sects. The Protestant Reformation began during the 1500s, but its effects can still be seen today in the many different churches devoted to different types of Christianity found in every city in America.

Martin Luther (1483–1546), a German priest, announced, through the posting of his 95 theses concerning his objections to what he saw as abuses within the Church, that he wanted to debate an interested opponent. This modest event of 1517 sparked the eventual formation of the Lutheran Church, although Martin Luther himself would not live to see that formation. The Lutheran Church differed with the Catholic Church on several key points of religious doctrine. Some of those differences have been mentioned during the previous chapter in contrasting the Christianity of the Middle Ages with that of the Protestant Reformers.

Among the most specifically *musical* differences brought out by Luther was the tendency for the Catholic Church to rely on professional musicians for the Mass. Luther saw this tendency as an abuse, especially when the congregation was unlearned. He advocated in his *Deudsche Messe* (1526) the use of simple hymns and chorales (four-part harmonizations of hymn tunes) so that the congregation might participate in the worship service more actively. Luther himself was a skillful composer, although his friend Johann Walter (1496–1570) was by far the more prolific musical contributor to Luther's ideal of a participatory sacred music. As Lutheranism moved from an embattled new idea to the dominant Christian sect in much of Northern Europe, aristocratic believers invested in professional performance at Lutheran cathedrals. For his part, Luther was never an enemy of complex church music; only when the congregation was left mystified and unable to comprehend the music did he object.

Calvinism and Music

More radical in his reforms was the Protestant Jean Calvin (1509–1564). Unlike Luther, Calvin opposed the use of music in worship services except when reciting the Psalms (part of the Old Testament of the Bible that may have been intended for singing). Calvin relied on the composer Loys Bourgeois (1510–1560), who wrote monophonic tunes for use in singing psalm texts.

FIGURE 8.5 | *Martin Luther (1483–1546)*, composer and theologian, advocated professional music in worship services when the congregation had sufficient education to justify it. For remote or less well-educated congregations, he advocated participatory pieces such as chorales. (© Austrian Archives/Corbis)

Both Lutheranism and Calvinism benefited from the invention of movable type for music, in publishing their sacred music and distributing it to remote congregations. Lutheran chorales as well as the *Deudsche Messe* were published soon after their composition, while Calvinists benefited from the publication of collections of psalm tunes called "psalters."

The Counter-Reformation

The Catholic Church was not silent in responding musically to the Protestant Reformation. Later in the chapter, we will see the principal figure in the Catholic response to Luther's objections about opaque and incomprehensible music designed for the Mass, Giovanni Pierluigi da Palestrina (1525–1594).

History played a crucial role in the development of music in this and every period. Among the mentioned events and their impact we have seen the skillful diplomacy of the Dukes of Burgundy prompt the flourishing of music within their realm and the eventual embrace of the Burgundian preference for thirds and sixths as consonant intervals. The invention of movable type fostered the codification of these consonances through the mass distribution of music written in this style. The Protestant Reformation brought about innovations in sacred music, and prompted a Catholic response to be discussed later. Finally, the rising prestige of Italy witnessed a vigorous rivalry among Italian ruling families to foster the greatest achievements in the arts within their respective city states. The remainder of this chapter looks at a few examples of sacred and secular music created in Italy (although often by Burgundians) as fuel for this rivalry.

JOSQUIN DES PREZ

Josquin des Prez (1440–1521) fairly represents the outstanding accomplishments in music attributed to the generation after Ockeghem. That generation was packed with talented composers requiring a text configured on this scale to select only one representative from the generation. In terms of quantity of scholarship and performance, Josquin (musicians normally refer to him by his first name) enjoys the most attention today.

Josquin's Career

While Josquin's career poses many questions for scholars, the chronicle of Josquin's career which follows may not interest all students; however, it demonstrates that the most celebrated musician of his age could lead a life that has remained obscure despite centuries of avid study. Students interested in lurid topics such as assassination and plague should resist the temptation to skim over the following chronicle, as both figure into this man's biography.

We aren't sure when or where Josquin was born, although a general consensus chooses 1440 as a date and Burgundian lands (in what is now France) as a location. His early career was devoted to singing, however, the details of where he sang and for how long are not perfectly known. He sang in the court of the powerful Milanese family, the Sforzas, as a young man. We can place him at the Milan Cathedral from 1459 to 1472. When his employer during this period, Duke Galeazzo Maria Sforza of Milan, was assassinated, Josquin began working for Sforza's brother, who was a Cardinal, second in rank to the Pope within the hierarchy of the Catholic Church. Mention of assassination in a music history text may come as a surprise to some, but assassination in Renaissance

Italy was not uncommon. Powerful rivalries between ruling families led to hateful jealousies. One famous composer, Carlo Gesualdo, even boasted of his skill as an assassin. Historians can prove that Gesualdo murdered his wife and her lover, at the very least. Josquin served the Sforza Cardinal until 1494; then we don't quite know where he went. He sang in Rome, but that should come as no surprise for the employee of a Cardinal.

Josquin next resurfaces in France in 1501, where he remained for three years. He may have served King Louis XII, but this too is uncertain. From 1503 to 1504 he lived again in Italy, serving the powerful d'Este family in Ferrara and enjoying a magnificent salary. He left Ferrara suddenly when the first signs of an outbreak of plague reached the city. That plague took the life of one of his most brilliant contemporaries, the composer Jacob Obrecht, another Burgundian living in Italy. Josquin spent the remainder of his life in his home region. By this time, the Kingdom of France had shattered Burgundian power, so Josquin's residence was France. One last note about his career: Josquin dated none of his manuscripts. We have no precise knowledge of when and where his music was written. Perhaps one of the reasons Josquin remains to this day a favorite composer of music scholars centers on the fact that there is so much work to be done in sorting out his comings and goings.

IOSQVINVS PRATENSIS.
(circa 1450—1521.)

FIGURE 8.6 | *Josquin des Prez (1440–1521)* helped establish careful treatment of dissonance, matching the mood of the composition to the mood of the text, and the virtues of voices entering in rhythmic and melodic imitation of one another. (© Bettmann/Corbis)

Josquin's Compositions

As a composer, Josquin excelled in three main genres: masses, motets, and secular chansons. He wrote more motets than anything else. While the musical style of these motets resembles that of Ockeghem in their emphasis on new consonances, Josquin introduced an important innovation: he is credited with taking special care in the way he set texts to music by composing music specially suited to illustrate the meaning and nuance of the words. When musicians talk about music with words, we assume that the words existed before the music was written. We say that a composer "set" a text, that is, the composer created music specially designed to accommodate the words by paying special attention to every syllable stress and dramatic implication. A useful metaphor might be that of a composer of vocal music being a jeweler. The precious stone the jeweler wishes to place within a piece of jewelry represents the words. The setting for that stone, be it a ring or bracelet, is configured to suit the precious stone. That setting is the music the composer writes to accommodate the words. Text setting is an important concept in discussing music with voices. Musicians find it impossible to talk about vocal music without paying attention to the suitability of the setting.

To illustrate Josquin's importance in this area, consider for a moment some of the music we listened to in conjunction with our study of the Middle Ages. In Gregorian Chant, composers wrote music that does not illustrate the meaning of the texts. For medieval composers, this condition would in no way be seen as a defect. Their ideal for setting words was for the music to provide a modest and reverent framework for the words. However, for Josquin and the ruling elite of his time who prided themselves on their interest in humanism, connecting music to words was a highly prized technique. In stark contrast to both Gregorian Chant and Renaissance ideals, Phillippe de Vittry in his motet from the previous chapter set three texts simultaneously. He could reasonably be said to care almost not at all whether listeners understood the words being sung. Josquin, by contrast, strove to set each word so that it could be heard and understood by his audience. Moreover, Josquin scrupulously sought to place accented syllables on strong beats within the meter. This practice typifies the humanistic idea that the human body, in this case as revealed in its voice, should be idealized in music. By capturing the natural flow of declamation, Josquin connects himself to humanistic ideals of celebrating man as natural and worthy of idealizing. Finally, Josquin married the mood of the music to the mood of the text. Somber text was treated to low-lying notes and darker vocal timbres, for example.

Another crucial innovation introduced by Josquin was the use of imitative entrances within a piece. This innovation resulted in Josquin's writing a melody in one vocal part, and then having another voice enter in the next measure singing the same notes the previous voice had just sung. Unlike a full-fledged round, like the song "Row, Row, Row Your Boat," Josquin would not continue with strict imitation for long—just for the first few notes. This technique has come to be called *points of imitation*.

Josquin's masses are more conservative than his motets in their treatment of text. Insofar as the text of "the Mass" is sacred to believers, innovative settings of the words may have seemed inappropriate. Points of imitation, however, are found in virtually all of Josquin's masses. In his masses, Josquin makes up for the rather conservative text setting with the use of imaginative approaches to organization. Like Ockeghem before him, Josquin tried to link the parts of the *mass ordinary* through musical means. His favored method of doing this is called *imitation* or *parody*. For this technique, Josquin would select a popular tune and use it as the basis for each part of the mass ordinary. A famous example is his *L'homme armé Mass*. For this work, Josquin uses the popular

FIGURE 8.7 | *Raphael's Madonna in the Meadow (1505).* Raphael, like Josquin, sought to balance the diverse action of several individuals into a harmonious whole, while preserving the ideals of moderation and balance. The Madonna and children are depicted within two cunningly nested triangles. Complementing the action of the boys on the left, the Madonna's upper torso twists slightly to the right, her extended foot echoing the boys' bare flesh. The activity in the foreground is balanced by the steep landscape on the left.

Josquin and Palestrina after him sought to balance the diverse activity of their several voices toward uniting them in a harmonious whole by emphasizing similar sorts of echoing and balancing. The imitative entrances and carefully handled dissonances capture the spirit of Renaissance aesthetics. (Erich Lessing/Art Resource, NY) tune called "L'homme armé," which is about a brothel, as the basis for each section of the Mass. Many composers of his generation wrote masses using this bawdy tune. Martin Luther would count the use of such profane tunes as one of the abuses within Church music to which he objected. That said, Martin Luther was a great enthusiast of Josquin's music. Luther called him "the master of the notes, while all others are mastered by the notes."

Josquin's Missa Hercules dux Ferrarie

The Josquin Mass represented in our recorded anthology, *Missa Hercules dux Ferrarie* [CD 1, #8], is similarly united, but not by the imitation of a bawdy song. Instead, Josquin uses the vowels in his employer's name, translates them into solfege syllables, and makes a motive from the result to unite all the movements of the Mass. Solfege syllables are names given to musical notes. You may already know these names from the song "Do a Deer" heard in the musical *The Sound of Music*. For those unfamiliar with the song, the solfege syllables are do, re, mi, fa, sol, la, ti, and do again. Please see the Listening Guide for this piece for a chart showing how Josquin derived a musical theme from his employer's name.

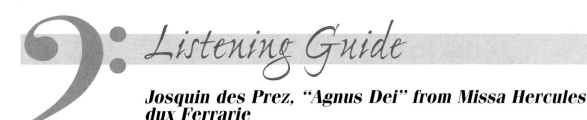

Listening Guide

Josquin des Prez, "Agnus Dei" from Missa Hercules dux Ferrarie

[**CD1**, #8] *(Duration, 5 min. 35 sec.)*

Latin Name:	Ercole dux Ferrarie
Solfege Syllables:	re do re do re fa mi re
Melodic Pitches:	D C D C D F E D

0.00	Agnus Dei,	Lamb of God,
0.19	qui tollis peccata mundi:	who takes away the sins of the world:
0.28	miserere nobis.	have mercy on us.
0.35	Agnus Dei,	Lamb of God,
0.53	qui tollis peccata mundi:	who takes away the sins of the world:
1.00	miserere nobis.	have mercy on us.
1.08	Agnus Dei,	Lamb of God,
1.23	qui tollis peccata mundi:	who takes away the sins of the world:
1.33	dona nobis pacem.	grant us peace.

pause

1.44   *Text is repeated with new points of imitation*

pause

3.35   *Text is repeated again with new points of imitation*

In studying this piece, we must remember that this music was meant for use in the celebration of the Mass. The chapels and cathedrals where it would have been sung were large and resonant. Voices surely sustained long after the singers stopped singing. Moreover, the entire context was a place and time for worship. Presentation of such music in concerts happens today, but with no small loss of original intent and meaning. The clarity of Josquin's writing, with its points of imitation, were helpful in the resonant halls, in that his style gave audiences a rhythmically clear articulation of memorable material in all the voices.

PALESTRINA AND THE MUSIC OF THE COUNTER-REFORMATION

As the Protestant Reformation grew in strength, the Catholic Church found itself facing a crisis. One by one, the nations of Europe abandoned the Church. Northern Germany, the Netherlands, and Scandanavia embraced Lutheranism. Scotland and influential minorities in England, France, and Germany took up Calvinism. The possibility of a pan-European religious rebellion seemed very real by the middle of the 1500s. Wars and furious debates raged throughout Europe. Even among monarchs loyal to Catholicism, allegiance to the Pope was not guaranteed. Spanish and German mercenaries in the service of the Catholic monarch Charles V of Austria sacked Rome in 1527, and revealed the political weakness of the Church's elite during a time of widespread rebellion.

The Council of Trent

In addition to military campaigns designed to protect and extend the power of Catholicism undertaken by that faith's leading monarchs, the Church itself sought an internal reform designed to address many of the complaints voiced by breakaway reformers. Pope Paul III initiated these reforms; his willingness to examine and criticize time-honored doctrines of the Church led to a conference of Catholic leaders, both secular and sacred, at the Italian city of Trent near the Austrian border. This gathering of Catholic leaders is known as the Council of Trent. The council met off and on from 1547 to 1563. Interestingly, Duke Hercule I of Ferrara, to whom Josquin dedicated his Mass, was the presiding figure at the Council of Trent. The members of the council discussed all facets of Catholic doctrine and practice, including the uses of music within religious services.

Many quaint legends have emerged concerning the Council of Trent's discussions of music. Some of these legends suggest that the council contemplated banishing polyphonic music from the Mass, ending the practice of imitation masses using secular songs as their unifying basis, and banning music all together. None of these ideas were seriously considered. Legend also has it that the composer Giovannia Pierluigi da Palestrina (1526–1594) "saved" polyphonic music within the Catholic Church by composing his Pope Marcellus Mass in time for the members of the Council to hear how clearly sacred texts could be set to polyphonic music. Teaching music of this period would be easier if this charming story were true. Unfortunately it isn't. The justly famous *Pope Marcellus Mass* of Palestrina wasn't published until after the Council was disbanded, moreover, no evidence suggests that it was ever performed in Trent. The piece was surely written as a memorial to Pope Marcellus II, who reigned as Pope for only twenty days during 1555 before meeting a most untimely death.

The Pope Marcellus Mass

While the legends about the piece are likely untrue, the *Pope Marcellus Mass* (published in 1567) was an admirably clear example of polyphonic music of the 1500s. The Agnus Dei movement is included in the anthology [CD1 #9]. Interestingly, Palestrina wrote two movements on the same text for this Mass, our anthology contains the first one. An important difference between the two is that the one in our anthology does not include the final text of the Agnus Dei, "Lamb of God, who takes away the sins of the world: grant us peace."

The *Pope Marcellus Mass* represents the prevailing attitudes of musicians during Palestrina's time. For example, he uses great care in handling dissonant intervals between the six voices used for this Mass.

Because people have changed their minds over the centuries concerning which intervals are dissonant and which are consonant, we might revisit the attitude as it existed in the 1500s. The intervals of the unison, fourth, fifth, and octave had been considered consonant since the time of Pythagoras. These remained the consonant intervals throughout the Middle Ages. Late in the Middle Ages, Burgundian and English composers introduced the intervals of the third and the sixth as consonant as well. These intervals so attracted listeners of the 1400s, that their embrace as consonances rapidly became widespread. The twentieth century will find composers attacking the concept of consonance and dissonance as irrelevant, by ending the practice of handling these two kinds of intervals with distinction one from the other. This "liberation of dissonance" is a story for later.

Palestrina always resolves the various seconds and sevenths, the main dissonant intervals along with the *tritone* (an interval formed by reducing a fifth by one half step or increasing a fourth by one half step), that appear during the piece by step on the next strong beat. (For an explanation of steps and half steps, see chapter two.) The effect of this great care is a smooth and untroubled music befitting contemplative worship. Like Josquin, Palestrina takes special pleasure in using thirds and sixths as consonances. At the few pauses in his piece, he constructs musical structures comprised of intervals of the third stacked on top of one another. The resulting chords provide a pleasing, stable sonority befitting moments of repose between lines of text. Like Josquin, Palestrina also takes care to use imitative entrances.

FIGURE 8.8 | The title page of ***Palestrina's First Book of Masses (1554).*** In this frontispiece we see Pope Julius III receiving from a kneeling Palestrina, his first book of masses. Palestrina worked closely with several Popes to implement Church doctrine on music in his works. Note the anvil players in the margin at the top of the page. This scene depicts Pythagoras' discovery of the mathematical relationships of intervals discussed in the chapter on Ancient Music. The revival of imagery related to this event suggests the importance Renaissance intellectuals placed on ancient Greek ideas. (© Bettmann/Corbis)

Giovannia Pierluigi da Palestrina, "Agnus Dei" from Pope Marcellus Mass

[CD1, #9] *(Duration, 4 min. 58 sec.)*

This piece is a setting of the same text as the previous piece in our recorded anthology, except that the composer has omitted the final line of text.

This piece opens with a clear point of imitation. The tenor begins alone by singing a whole note on "D" followed by a half note on "D," a leap up an interval of a fourth to "G," followed by stepwise motion down the scale back to "D." Two beats after the tenor begins this melody, the top-most voice (or "cantus") sings exactly the same notes only an octave higher. The result is a close point of imitation. Two beats after the cantus enters, the bass sings exactly the same melody, only starting on "G," leaping eventually up a fourth to "C," and moving stepwise down the scale to "G" again. This melody in the bass is then imitated four beats later by the altos.

Eventually, all six voices will sing exactly the same opening. The interlocking of these imitative entrances is handled with extreme care by Palestrina, to make sure that the overall effect is calm and graceful. He takes special pleasure in using thirds and sixths as consonances, and balances the diverse imitative activity in all six voices by emphasizing similar sorts of echoing and combinations, uniting them in a harmonious whole.

Musical Theory Concerning Dissonance in Polyphonic Music

Handling dissonance with care was a preoccupation of musical theorists during Palestrina's youth. The theorist and composer Gioseffo Zarlino (1517–1590) was the most famous spokesperson for the delicate handling of dissonance in music. He established rules for both introducing dissonances and resolving them properly. Music majors throughout the West still study his ideas and use vocabulary that he introduced, when discussing how dissonance is handled in polyphonic music. For example, he mentions that when two voices sing a consonance such as a third, a permissible dissonance may result when one of those voices moves by step toward the note of the other singer. The resulting interval between the two would then be a second, a dissonant interval. This move is only allowed, however, provided that the dissonance is then resolved on the next beat, with the voice that moved either returning to its original note, or by joining the other voice in singing the same note. If the dissonance resolves by motion back to the previous note, it is called a *neighbor tone*; if it is resolved by still further stepwise motion away from the original pitch, it is called a *passing tone*. Neighbor and passing tones are, according to Zarlino, permissible uses of dissonance. Palestrina makes creative use of these permissible dissonances. In the following examples, the dissonant pitches are in italics. You can tell for yourself what relationships are dissonant as all consecutive letters of the alphabet (A+B, B+C, C+D and so forth) will represent the interval of the second, a dissonance:

DISSONANT NEIGHBOR TONE IN ITALICS
VOICE ONE: E - *D* – E
VOICE TWO: C - C - C

DISSONANT PASSING TONE IN ITALICS
VOICE ONE: E - *D* - C
VOICE TWO: C - C - C

These two examples are without doubt the simplest possible dissonances Zarlino and Palestrina used. By the end of the century, the taste for dissonance among Italian composers grew enormously. Yet, Palestrina remained the model for sacred music within Catholic nations throughout the remainder of the century. In the field of secular music, however, dissonance treatments would range far afield from Zarlino's rigid ideal.

THE ITALIAN MADRIGAL

During the 1500s, an important genre of secular music rose and flourished in Italy: the *madrigal*. Madrigals are polyphonic compositions for unaccompanied voices. Ideally they feature responsive settings of elegant, secular poetry. During the 1500s, literally thousands of madrigals were composed and published throughout Italy. Madrigals were intended for use by wealthy Italians, who would sing them in their homes. Later in the period, some ruling families in Italy would hire professional singers, but enthusiastic amateurs undertook the majority of madrigal performances. The ideals of humanism brought with them a revival of interest in applying ancient Greek ideas about life and culture to everyday life among the wealthy.

Among the ancient Greek ideas that modern Italians emulated was the goal of making one's own music. You might recall from an earlier chapter that Plato, among others, pitied men who depended on professionals for their music. The madrigal was the Italian application of this ideal. Madrigals were published in "part books" containing the parts for a single singer for many different compositions. Each singer would sing from his or her respective part book, and in that way, an evening might be spent in amiable company, singing and discussing the virtues of the poetry and music. Visitors to Italy during this time admired the ability of wealthy and privileged Italians to make their own music. This situation was a byproduct of humanism, which called for people to be good at many things but specialists in none. Such notions of having many diverse skills was featured in the famous book *The Courtier* (1528) by Baldassare Castiglione. Of musicality in the home, Castiglione wrote "I am not pleased with the Courtier unless he is also a musician, and in addition to his understanding and skill at singing he also possess like skill on various instruments." The ideal of the "Renaissance man" (a person skilled in many things) was surely operative in Italy during the 1500s, and marks a stark contrast to contemporary times when specialization begins in college, if not before.

The History of the Madrigal

The madrigal underwent rapid change during the 1500s. The earlier practitioners of the genre, working between roughly 1530 and 1550, saw the form as primarily a diversion for the wealthy. They set lyric poetry, such as nature scenes. By setting, we still mean that the words existed first and function like the precious stone of the jeweler. The music is created to suit the words, much like a ring is created to show off the diamond. Befitting a form intended for amateur use, the music generally lacked difficult musical features, such as frequent dissonances or wide melodic leaps from note to note. Most singers, amateur and otherwise, consider it more difficult to sing dissonances and wide leaps. Dissonances such as the second, as noted in the previous section in the chapter dealing with pitch relationships, tend to want to resolve to the note below. When you must sing a note and someone else is singing the note immediately below, that tendency toward resolution can make it difficult to hold your ground and stick with your note. Of course, this tendency is conditioned in Westerners and is not inherent in the notes themselves. People from other cultures can find the execution of intervals that we consider dissonant, rather easy. Bulgarian women's choruses, for example, must sing seconds all the time. For them, it is an easily executed interval by virtue of its commonness in the music they sing most.

The second phase of madrigal composition (roughly 1550–1580) saw the influence of literary critic Cardinal Pietro Bembo (1470–1547) inspire composers to include more sophisticated and intricate text and tone relationships, and to select more difficult and subtle poetry. Bembo was a great admirer of the fourteenth-century Italian poet Petrarch. Petrarch's sonnets were set as madrigals many times. These poems included striking images and daring use of language. Bembo successfully helped to popularize the long-dead poet for a new generation of admirers by writing in praise of Petrarch's artistry.

Leading composers of this middle phase for the Italian madrigal include Zarlino's teacher, Adrian Willaert (1490–1562). Willaert had a gift for matching the sonorities of his music to the temperament of Petrarch's poetry. For example, in somber or serious passages, passages that Cardinal Bembo would say possessed "gravitas," Willaert tended to emphasize downward melodic motion and emphasize the lower-pitched voices. He also would slow down the pace of events by using longer durations. The opposite was also true, in passages of lightness (possessing "piacevolezza," to use Bembo's terminology), quick rhythmic values prevail and upward motion and high voices are emphasized.

The final phase of the madrigal as practiced during the 1500s lasted from 1580 until the end of the century. In these works, composers strove to marry their music to the

Figure 8.9 | In the Italian painting *Concert in the Open Air* (from the 1500s), we see four figures singing madrigals from part books. The painter is unknown, but his work emphasizes the naturalness of educated people making their own music, much in the manner called for by Castigleone. Not only are the singers seen in a natural setting, but they provide a visual echo of the clustered flowers in the foreground, the clustered trees in the mid-ground, and the clustered mountains in the distance. (clichè musèe de Bourges)

least change of meaning or tone in the poetry. Extravagant techniques could be used, such as improperly prepared or resolved dissonances to capture painful feelings in the poetry. When poems refer to echoes, some of the singers will echo the melodic lines that the others sing. When the poem refers to mountains, melodies might ascend; by contrast, references to valleys would prompt a melodic descent. References to birds singing would prompt long, tuneful passages. References to melancholy or sadness might prompt a drooping melodic line moving down by half steps. These are a few general practices known collectively as "word painting." Word painting was the great contribution of madrigal composers to the Western tradition. Music to this day often features word painting.

The first of our two examples of late madrigals is by another northern composer (this time from the Netherlands) who emigrated to Italy during the Renaissance: Giaches de Wert (1535–1596). Wert spent most of his career employed in the music-loving city of Mantua, where he worked for the ruling Gonzaga family. His composition "Vezzosi augelli" [CD1 #10] comes from the 1590s and finds him at the height of his game. The text is by the beloved Italian poet Torquato Tasso, whose epic poem *Gerusalemme Liberata* was the rage among upper-class readers.

Listening Guide

Giaches de Wert, "Vezzosi augelli"
[CD1, #10] *(Duration, 2 min. 20 sec.)*

Vezzosi augelli infra le verdi fronde
temprano a prova lascivette note.
Mormora l'aura, e fa le foglie e l'onde
garrir, che variamente ella percote.

Quando taccion gli augelli, alto risponde;
quando cantan gli augei; più lieve scote;
sia caso od arte, or accompagna, ed ora
Alterna i versi lor la musica 'ôra.

ENGLISH TRANSLATION	SETTING (Text painting of words in bold)
0.00 **Graceful birds** among the green branches	high voices only
0.06 Contend by shaping **lascivious notes**.	long melisma
0.13 **The breeze murmurs** and leaves and branches	low voices murmuring on one note
0.18 **stir**, as the breeze variously strikes them.	shaking melody of quick movement up then down then up then down again
0.50 **When the birds are silent**, the wind **answers**;	one voice only/echoes as answers
1.05 When they **sing**, more softly it stirs;	many notes to sing
1.24 Whether by cause or chance, it accompanies,	
1.31 And now breeze and music **alternate verses**.	alternations between all voices

Text Painting

Tasso's poem is full of music. The birds vie with one another as they sing among the branches. The breeze takes its part, either accompanying the birds softly as they sing, or answering their songs. To capture this musical poem through song, Wert employs many imaginative examples of text painting. Notice at the beginning that he holds the lowest voices in reserve, allowing only the high-pitched voices to sing the first two lines when they first appear. The high voices are more suited to emulate the songs of birds, whose cries tend toward the treble rather than the bass. When the lower voices finally enter, they do so singing the words "mormora l'aura" ("the breeze murmurs"). Their rich resonance, singing on only one pitch, creates the very image of murmuring. With their entrance, now the treble birds literally sing to the accompaniment of the murmuring breeze, precisely as the poem describes in line seven. For other imaginative examples of text painting, please follow the listening chart provided.

Claudio Monteverdi

Claudio Monteverdi (1567–1643), like Wert, spent his career during the 1500s in the service of the Gonzaga family at Mantua. Wert was an important influence in the life of the younger Monteverdi. The madrigal on your recordings [CD1 #11] marks an interesting contrast to Wert's "Vezzosi augelli." "Cruda Amarilli" does not deal with pastoral imagery, but with the complaints of a wounded heart. The poem is taken from the play *Il pastor fido* by Giovanni Battista Guarini. This play is made up of a series of speeches, spoken by a chain of unrequited lovers. Each lover loves someone higher than himself or herself in social standing. The problem lies in the fact that the highest-ranking man by social class loves no one, so all the lovers along the chain go on hoping. In the speech set here, the shepherd Mirtillo complains that the object of his love, Amaryllis, does not care for his love and torments him terribly.

Listening Guide

Claudio Monteverdi, "Cruda Amarilli"
[CD1, #11] *(Duration, 2 min. 36 sec.)*

> Cruda Amarilli che col nome ancora
> D'amar, ahi lasso, amaramente insegni.
> Amarilli del candido ligustro,
> Più candida e più bella,
> Ma dell'aspido sordo
> E più sorda e più fera e più fugace.
> Poi che col dir t'offendo
> I mi morò tacendo.

ENGLISH TRANSLATION	SETTING (Text painting of words in bold)
0.00 **Cruel Amaryllis**, who with your name	improperly handled dissonances
0.21 to love, **alas**, bitterly you instruct.	dissonant entrances followed by descending melodic motion illustrating despair

0.57	**Amaryllis, more than the white privet**	no dissonance while praising her
1.11	**more honest and more beautiful,**	
1.17	but deafer than the **asp**	long, snaky melody
1.28	and more vicious and more **elusive**.	quick note values
1.39	Since by speaking I **offend** you,	tritone on strong beat
1.45	**I shall die** in silence.	14 entrances on this text to lend it emphasis through repetition

In comparing his beloved to both a pure, white flower and a deadly snake (the asp), Guarini's hero indulges one of Italian poetry's greatest virtues, the juxtaposition of powerfully opposite sentiments.

In setting such a striking poem to music, Monteverdi shatters the rules for careful dissonance treatment, laid out earlier in the century by Zarlino and so judiciously followed by Palestrina. In the second measure of the piece, on the second syllable of the word "cruel" ("cruda" in Italian) the bass voice leaps to a dissonant pitch, which rubs against the dissonances already heard in the two highest voices. Here are the opening three pitches of all the voices. Pitches with at least one dissonant relationship to another pitch are underlined. Again, consecutive letters of the alphabet are dissonant by virtue of being seconds:

CANTO	D	<u>D</u>	<u>C</u>
ALTO	B	B	<u>A</u>
TENOR	D	G	<u>G</u>
QUINTO	G	G	<u>D</u>
BASS	G	<u>E</u>	<u>B</u>

By the third note of the piece, all voices are singing a dissonant interval in relation to at least one other voice. Monteverdi justified using this degree of dissonance and its improper preparation under the rules of Zarlino by pointing out that the text speaks of cruelty, so why not capture the pathos of the speaker through passionate dissonance. Time and again in this madrigal, Monteverdi used dissonance to accentuate the emotions of the poem. He especially treats the words "ahi" (alas), "amar" (love), and "morò" (death)—all words conveying strong emotions—with dissonances.

Dissonance is not the only tool for text painting in "Cruda Amarilli." Monteverdi sets the word "aspido" (the asp, or poisonous snake) with a long, sinewy melisma. The words for "more elusive" ("più fugace" in Italian) prompt Monteverdi to use shorter, faster rhythmic values befitting text about something being difficult to catch. The listening guide for this piece offers a fuller list of interesting word painting used in this piece.

The Monteverdi-Artusi Controversy

Not everyone interested in the health of the madrigal was pleased with Monteverdi's rule-breaking ways. A theorist named Giovanni Artusi attacked Monteverdi in a pamphlet. In his argument, Artusi dutifully pointed out all of Monteverdi's errors in dissonance usage. For his part, Monteverdi responded by pointing out that Artusi neglected to mention the text anywhere in his argument. For Monteverdi, "the words are mistress to the music." That is, the words take precedence over the tones. Where the words go, so must the music. Monteverdi argued that you cannot logically set powerful juxtapositions of conflicting emotions using the same musical methods you would use to set more innocuous words. Monteverdi concluded his argument by proclaiming that what he was doing should be called "the second practice." In so cutting himself off from tradition, Monteverdi reminds us of de Vitry, who proclaimed his music "ars nova" (the new art) during the 1300s. Every few centuries, reformers emerge to proclaim the old rules finished, and to proclaim the advent of new rules. Monteverdi was such a person. His inspiration surely came from humanism. Humanism trusts the power of humankind to solve problems, create new paths, and foster fresh approaches. It stands in stark contrast to the medieval fascination with tradition and continuity. But such a simplistic comparison of the Middle Ages and the Renaissance seems less than illuminating, for after all, wasn't the reformer de Vitry a man of the Middle Ages? While humanism encouraged change, it cannot be the entire story. Change has been part of the Western tradition since the beginning. Sophisticated audiences sometimes want to be surprised. In moments of this sort, innovation wins favor, and old orders give way to new ones. Monteverdi's audience of northern Italian aristocrats were extremely knowledgeable about music, for after all, many of them sang madrigals for their own pleasure and could be expected to appreciate Monteverdi's daring approach.

Just as Monteverdi announced a new practice, his style changed drastically. By the time he published "Cruda Amarilli" in 1605, he had already altered his approach to the madrigal composition by introducing instruments to support fewer singers. These singers were no longer the enthusiastic amateurs of the Italian upper class, but hired professionals who, like Monteverdi, served the ruling families of Italy. The story of this new style belongs to the next chapter.

THE INVENTION OF OPERA

The word "opera" is the plural of the Latin word "opus" meaning "work" as in a work of art. Opera was called "opera" because people thought of it initially as a string of musical works, one right after another, which taken together, tell a complete story. The plural of "opera," oddly enough, is "opera" but in English, we have come to accept "operas" as the plural.

The rise of opera as a genre may not immediately seem a topic of inherent interest. It should. Opera became by far the most popular form of entertainment in Western Europe from the middle of the 1600s until the rise of cinema in the twentieth century. Europeans of all classes, all educational backgrounds, and all nationalities would embrace opera as an urgent and pleasurable part of their lives. One cannot understand European culture without understanding something about opera. This genre will come up often in all our subsequent chapters.

The Florentine Camerata

Opera was not invented during the Renaissance, strictly speaking, but the seeds of opera are planted by contemporaries of Wert and Monteverdi. The Italian city state of Florence experienced a tremendous concentration of intellectual and artistic talent. Among the pursuits of Florentine intellectuals was the revival of the ancient Greek practice of singing their tragic dramas. An organization devoted to this pursuit emerged known as the Florentine Camerata. This group of likeminded intellectuals and artists began by studying the writings of ancient Greeks on the topic of music and the marriage of music and drama. The linguist and scholar Girolamo Mei (1519–1594) made it his life's work to translate all the Greek material he could locate on the topic of music. Vincenzo Galilei (uncle of the famous astronomer Galileo) wrote a treatise based on Mei's findings that advanced the idea that the madrigal had failed to capture the ideals of ancient Greece. In listening to Monteverdi's "Cruda Amarilli" you may have found it odd that five people are simultaneously reciting the text of a single person's speech. Galilei found this practice absurd and called for writing solo vocal recitations with musical accompaniment such as those Mei found described in Greek manuscripts.

Opera was not the immediate result of Mei and Galilei's efforts. First they persuaded young singers and composers, such as Florence's most-favored singer Giulio Caccini (1545–1618) whose superb voice had captivated the members of the Camerata, to write dramatic solo pieces with instrumental accompaniment. These compositions came to be known as *monody*. In time, Florentine composers set entire dramatic texts in a monodic fashion. The earliest of these dramas was designed for the wedding feast of an important figure in Florentine politics, Ferdinando de' Medici, to a French princess, Catherine of Lorraine. The wedding took place in 1589. As an entertainment for after the wedding and during the intermissions of a spoken play (thus it was called an "intermedi," Italian for "in between"), several members of the Florentine Camerata designed a musical drama on the victory of the god Apollo over Python, a terrible serpent from Greek mythology. Caccini, Jacopo Peri, and Luca Marenzio all contributed music. The poetry was largely by Ottavio Rinuccini, although he had able assistance from Count Bardi (patron of the Camerata) and Laura Guidiccioni, one of the few female members of the Camerata. The success of this entertainment persuaded the Camerata that Galilei had been correct, solo monodies were the ideal means of recapturing the practices of ancient Greece. Eventually the composer Jacopo Peri strung together monodies covering all the speeches of two plays, first *Daphne* (1598) and then *l'Euridice* (1600). While the music for *Daphne* is lost, *l'Euridice* marks the first extant opera. It tells the story of Orpheus, the demi-god of music, and his journey into hell to redeem his wife Euridice, after she was bitten by an asp.

These first operas did not manage to gain widespread fame, however, they did come to the attention of Claudio Monteverdi, who immediately embarked on creating his own opera. That opera informs the beginning of the story of the Baroque Period. Just as the boundary between the Middle Ages and the Renaissance is blurry, with Du Fay straddling both periods, the boundary between the Renaissance and the Baroque period is equally blurry. The first Baroque works, the early operas, clearly owe their existence to the Renaissance fascination with the revival of ancient Greek practices, its humanistic scholarship, and the willingness to attack problems with unorthodox methods.

 ## Some Questions for Discussion

1 Dissonance may be in the ear of the listener. Yet, at various times in history, musicians have had very clear ideas about what constitutes dissonance and what constitutes consonance. An influential dictionary from the middle of the last century defined "dissonance" this way: "any combinations of notes, which on being sounded together produces a painful sensation to the ear." (*Grove's Dictionary of Music and Musicians*, third edition). What do you make of the concept of dissonance? Do seconds, or sevenths, or even tritones produce a *painful* sensation? If they do now, would they still if you listened to them for several minutes every day? Why do you think value judgments and extravagant claims of certain sensations being painful figure so prominently in the way musicians talk about music?

2 Setting text to music is a crucial concern for many Renaissance composers. Is it still? Think about your favorite music with a singer or singers. Can you hear any special connections between the text and the music? Take the song "Somewhere over the Rainbow" from the film *The Wizard of Oz*. The word "over" is set with descending intervals. That doesn't make much sense, but does it mean the setting is wrong? What obligations do you feel composers have in setting words to music?

3 Humanism seems to have impacted the way composers approached music during the 1400s and 1500s. What are some ways that you can connect music to humanism? Is the influence of humanism operative today? Are we in a period of faith and uncertainty, or a period of reliance on human achievement? What about today's music can help you to answer that question?

CHAPTER **9**

The Baroque Period (1600–1750)

BAROQUE MUSIC AND EUROPEAN HISTORY

The Baroque Period is more difficult to grasp than the previous three. The diversity of music created during this period ranges far and wide in terms of styles. Europe was disunited as never before. The individual countries of Europe were busy with the project of inventing for themselves a coherent identity as a nation state. In prior years, the nation was embodied in the monarch. During the 1600s the pressures of war and rivalry made the formation of a national identity beyond the monarch useful in the pursuit of national aims. Meanwhile, their merchant classes were busy inventing capitalism, while their ruling and military classes occupied and ultimately exhausted themselves fighting wars of religion. Still other nations invested in advancing exploration and conquest of the world beyond Europe, projects that were begun during the previous century. Unfortunately for students of music history, these disparate historical trends don't allow us to make easy or sweeping comments about the interaction of music and ideas during this time. Instead, we will have to content ourselves with examining musical works, and making historical connections as they come.

The Formation of Nation States

First, a few words about the large-scale historical trends mentioned above. The formation of nation states may not be clear at first blush. This book has mentioned differences between countries throughout the text. What's the difference between the France of the Middle Ages and the France of the 1600s? Almost everything is different. The lands that now comprise modern France were rarely, if ever, unified under a single ruler before the 1600s. French monarchs held properties, but so did French dukes and counts. The rivalry between Burgundy, a district that now forms a large part of eastern France, and the Kingdom of France during the One Hundred Years' War, typifies the problem for understanding France as a nation before the 1600s. Even today you can meet Burgundians who think of themselves as Burgundian first and French second. Still other Burgundians, delighted with the progress of the European Union, think of themselves as Europeans first and French second. The idea of a nation is exactly that— an idea. Some people conceive nations differently. What France meant once is not what it means now. During the 1600s, powerful monarchs sought to consolidate their power around the idea of a nation. Historians call this idea *absolute monarchy*. To accomplish this form of government, these monarchs emphasized national rivalries with other emerging nations. This period witnessed almost non-stop warfare among the nations of Europe. The effect on music will see genres, such as opera, fragment around national tastes, as people in Europe begin to emphasize their differences along national boundaries. This change will not take effect overnight, but will take root gradually.

Wars of Religion

Wars of religion open the period under examination on a hideous note. The Thirty Years' War was fought mostly on German soil, but every nation from Spain to Poland, from Sweden to Italy, participated at one time or another. The opposing forces were mostly Catholics against Protestants, but as the war dragged on, those boundaries were blurred, as Catholic France sided with Protestant forces in an effort to resist mounting strength in her Catholic rivals, Spain and Austria. National rivalries wound up playing as large a role as religion had when the war began. There were no winners, only losers. The end of this period of war saw Europe more divided than ever along national and religious boundaries. The impact of these wars on music range from the incidental, diminished resources for lavish musical performance, to the central, formation of specific repertories of music meant for worshippers in specific nations.

The Birth of Capitalism

The advent of capitalism can be traced to the exploration and conquest of the rest of the world undertaken by Europeans in the 1500s and largely completed by the end of the1800s. Some parts of the world resisted successfully. Japan, for example, with its powerful military and fanatical opposition to foreign influence, succeeded brilliantly. Remote nations like Afghanistan also held out. The Afghanis successfully defeated attempted invasions by first the British Empire and then the Russian Empire, her remote and rugged terrain coupling with her courageous fighters in this astonishing pair of victories. A few successful resistances aside, most of the planet spent at least some time ruled by Europeans between 1600 and 1900. This European project of conquest would come to be called "imperialism." The principal reason for these conquests was profit. Adventuresome investors dreamed of massive incomes from vast and remote holdings. This served the budding idea of capitalism. Capitalism differs from mercantilism in that mercantilism sees profits earned from the direct activity of the merchant. Capitalism finds investors using capital, that is, their money, to finance other people's labors and activities. These essentially non-participating investors then reap the profits generated through the labor of others. They supply the capital, and someone else supplies the sweat. The Dutch East Indies Company was the first capitalist venture so conceived and duly licensed under those aims. Investors supplied the money for trading ventures to what is now Indonesia. Eventually trading with the inhabitants of Indonesia gave way to simply conquering Indonesia and taking what the company wanted as its own property. The tea plantations and spice harvesting of Indonesia brought tremendous profits to the investors in the company, yet those investors personally harvested no tea or spice.

The impact of capitalism on music manifests itself most clearly in the increasing sense that musicians need something to sell for profit so that investors can finance activities fostered by them. Musicians mostly serve in a mercantile economy. That is, they sell their ability to provide music. Rather than profiting from someone else's labor, musicians' labor is their own. The skills that musicians provide that an investor can exploit for profit include the publication of musical scores that many people will want to play, and the promotion of concerts and operas that enough people will want to hear that they will turn a profit. The effect on music of capitalism's rise will be a drastic increase in professionalism over amateurism. As investors seek to hire the best musicians, musicians will scramble to make themselves attractive in a buyer's market. Plato, with his antipathy toward professionalism, would have wept.

This discussion of historical trends doesn't tell us much about the music itself. We'll check in with these societal trends periodically, as their impact can be more clearly heard in the examples chosen for this chapter.

THE WORD "BAROQUE"

The artistic disunity of this sprawling 150 year period can be summed up partly by the unlikely word that historians have chosen to describe the period: Baroque. The origins of the word come from the Portuguese language. In Portuguese "barroco" refers to a pearl of irregular shape. Today, irregularly shaped pearls are of decidedly diminished value. Briefly during the early 1700s, jewelers developed a passion for them. When this brief fashion ran its course, barroco jewelry was clearly marked as old-fashioned. The term was first applied to art when a French critic, on seeing a newly built cathedral in Italy in what he felt was a decidedly old-fashioned manner, described it as "baroque." Like the jewelry using misshapen pearls, the ornate cathedral was out of fashion by the 1750s when the critic took his swipe. The pejorative stuck, and now it serves as a neutral means of describing this period. There's nothing more or less misshapen about the period, the most remarkable thing about the word "baroque" being used to describe the

FIGURE 9.1 | *Jan Steen. A Family Dinner.* Oil on canvas.

An epithet for an untidy house in the Netherlands has become a "Jan Steen household!" Avoiding any notions of graceful balance, Steen indulged in oblique angles, zigzags, and diagonals to capture the animation at this crowded family gathering. Activities include much more than the simple eating and drinking, that its title might suggest. A mother breastfeeding her child has attracted added attention, the bagpipe player is seated on top of a cabinet, and the bird in its cage is receiving bread from a man on a ladder, dramatically adding to the multiple, chaotic interactions captured. This painting's organization, or seeming lack of it, marks a striking contrast to ideals of the Renaissance. (Rèunion des Musèe Nationaux/Art Resource, NY) period is that such an obscure jab at an unattractive building could serve as the label for 150 years of European art. Language can be a funny thing.

No one word can really capture the diversity of artistic accomplishment during the 1600s and first half of the 1700s. We find works of great piety and works of flamboyant arrogance, works favoring simplicity and works born of extravagant fancies. Some works from the period are brazenly theatrical, maybe even a little shallow in their obvious displays of insincerity. Others scream of their authentic passions and depth of feeling. In painting especially, artists abandoned the graceful balance that informs so much visual work from the Renaissance, in favor of spectacularly dramatic and volatile themes. Generalities fail during this period more so perhaps than any other.

There are, however, a few tried and true generalities that students of music have found useful through the years. Some concern the general attitude of the age toward the goal of the arts. Others have to do with technical developments in music itself.

THE DOCTRINE OF AFFECTIONS

Music historians mostly agree that one aesthetic ideal does help explain the music of the Baroque Period as a recognizably related body of work: the *Doctrine of the Affections*. This idea draws on the notion that the arts should move the emotions. The artist must select a desired affect, an emotional state that his or her work will achieve in the viewer or listener. Confusing emotional messages, such as the striking juxtapositions favored by Renaissance poets like Guarini in *Il pastor fido*, gave way to the evocation of a single, unadulterated emotional state. In short, emotional balance gave way to emotional extravagance.

Most musical works created during this period strive toward a single emotional affect. To achieve something like balance, composers developed genres with multiple movements. That way, individual movements could inspire in listeners a single affect, then subsequent movements could conjure other affects. A movement in music refers to a self-contained part of a musical work comprised of several such parts. We can't reference back to any examples from earlier in the book, except perhaps the masses, because the norm in music before 1600 were compositions comprised of only one movement. Therefore, it will be easier to illustrate this concept with the first excerpt from this chapter, Claudio Monteverdi's opera *Orfeo*.

FIGURE 9.2 | *Gian Lorenzo Bernini, David Slaying Goliath, 1623.* Statue.

The twisted motion of the body and the positioning of feet and hands show an attention to motion, or the dramatic. This composition is a departure from Michelangelo's earlier sculpture of David. (Scala/Art Resource, NY)

MONTEVERDI'S OPERA, *ORFEO*

The legend of Orfeo (or Orpheus) comes from Greek mythology. He was the demi-god of music. He had the power to charm listeners by singing and playing the lyre. Such a personage makes a natural subject for an opera. The first opera that still exists is **L'Euridice**, by Jacopo Peri. Peri was a member of the Florentine Camerata discussed in the previous chapter. Euridice was the wife of Orpheus. Peri's opera was comprised of a series of *monodies*, dramatic vocal works for solo voice and instrumental accompaniment. Taken together, these monodies tell the legend of Orpheus. With this work, opera was born. The humanist ideals of the Florentine Camerata sought the revival of ancient Greek sung drama. They didn't quite achieve that goal, but created something nearly as durable, and more cosmopolitan in its appeal.

The success of Peri's first opera led to many imitations and modifications on his accomplishment. During the first two decades of opera's history, at least a dozen versions of the Orpheus myth were set to music. The most compelling, at least as judged by number of performances, was Claudio Monteverdi's version.

For a text for his opera, Monteverdi turned to the Mantuan poet Alessandro Striggio. The text for an opera is called a *libretto*. The libretto for **Orfeo** spans five acts with a prologue. During the prologue, Music herself addresses the audience. She tells the audience of her power, outlines the story to follow, and requests silence from the audience. Many operas from the 1600s open with allegorical characters addressing the audience directly. That fashion dates from the tragedies of ancient Greece, and reveals the humanistic ideals that inspired the first opera.

FIGURE 9.3 | *Frans Hals. The Clown with the Lute,* 1625. Oil on wood.

The closeness and liveliness imbued in the face of this clown seems to invite the viewer to join in the gaiety of music making already set into motion. No contrasting emotions serve to contradict the singularity of this painting's intended affect. (© www.corbis.com/Corbis)

The first act centers upon the two lovers, Orfeo and Euridice. Nymphs join Euridice in singing of her joy, while shepherds join Orfeo. The act has been described as a meditation on bliss.

The second act begins where the first left off. Orfeo is off celebrating with his friends, the shepherds. They're still happy. A messenger enters with terrible news. Euridice has been bitten by an asp and has died. Now joy turns to anguish as first Orfeo, then the shepherds, pour out their suffering.

Act Three finds Orfeo heading toward Hades, the Greek land of the dead, in order to reclaim his bride. His plan depends on singing so plaintively of his grief that Pluto, king of the dead, will relent and return Euridice to him. On reaching the river Styx, which forms one of four boundaries to Hades, Orfeo finds Caronte, the skeletal boatman who controls the traffic to and from Hades. Orfeo sings and Caronte falls asleep. Orfeo takes Caronte's boat and sets off for Hades.

FIGURE 9.4 | *Claudio Monteverdi (1567–1643).*
(© Bettmann/Corbis)

In Act Four, Orfeo sings before Pluto and his bride Prosperina (daughter to the goddess of fertility). Orfeo's song moves Prosperina to beg her stern husband to allow Euridice to return to the world of the living with Orfeo. The god gives in, on the lone condition that Orfeo refrain from looking at his wife until after they leave Hades. On the way out, Orfeo cannot contain himself and gazes upon Euridice, dooming her forever.

The last act sees Orfeo lamenting his fate once more. In a deviation from the legend, Striggio has the god Apollo descend from Heaven and take Orfeo up to Heaven with him. From heaven Orfeo can gaze upon Euridice's form reflected in the stars. The original myth had Orfeo ripped into pieces by Euridice's wild sisters, the Baccantes.

In our recorded anthology, we have a substantial portion of the second act described above [CD1 #12]. Our excerpt begins with the solemn Messenger bringing her terrible news of Euridice's death. She sings a poignant monody full of anguished dissonances meant to reinforce the urgent emotions of the text. Even if a listener did not know the text, Monteverdi's music captures the affect of sadness and mourning through the music alone. United with its text, this monody provides a clear example of a baroque composer's efforts to move the emotions.

Listening Guide

Claudio Monteverdi, L Orfeo
[CD1, #12] *(Duration, 6 min. 41 sec.)*

Messenger

0.00	In un fiorito prato	In a field of flowers she wandered
0.06	Con l'altre sue compagne	With her other companions,
0.11	Giva cogliendo fiori	Picking flowers
0.18	Per farne una ghirlanda a le sue chiome,	To fashion a garland for her hair,
0.23	Quand' angue insidioso,	When an insidious serpent,
0.27	Ch'era fra l'erbe asconso	Which was hidden in the grass,
0.30	Le punse un piè con velensos dente.	Bit her foot with an evil tooth.
0.39	Ed ecco immantinente	And then, immediately
0.45	Scolorirsi il bel viso e nei suoi lumi	Color fled her fair face, and the light
0.59	Sparir quei lampi, ond'ella al sol fea scorno.	Of her eyes, which shamed the sun, dimmed.
1.08	Allor, noi tutte sbigottite e meste	Then we all, frightened and saddened,

1.16 Le fummo intorno, richiarmar tentando	As by the eternal flame, tended her
1.18 Gli spirti in lei smarriti	With spirits to revive her
1.23 Con l'onda fresca e con possenti carmi;	And with fresh water and potent charms;
1.27 Ma nulla valse, ahi lassa,	But with no effect, alas,
1.35 Ch'ella i languidi lumi alquanto aprendo,	Then she, with languid eyes opening,
1.47 E te chiamando Orfeo,	Called to you, Orfeo,
2.00 Dopo un grave sospiro,	After a grave sigh,
2.09 Spirò fra queste braccia ed io rimasi	She expired in these arms, and I remain
2.15 Pieno il cor di pietade e di spavento.	With a heart full of sorrow and fear.

Shepherd One

2.41 Ahi, caso acerbo!	Alas, bitter chance!
2.46 Ahi, fat'empio e crudele!	Alas, evil and cruel fate!
2.50 Ahi, stelle ingiuriose!	Alas, sorrowful stars!
2.55 Ahi, ciel avaro!	Alas, jealous heaven!

Shepherd Two

3.03 A l'amara novella	At this bitter news
3.06 Rassembra l'infelice un muto sasso	the sorrowful one resembles a mute stone
3.13 Che per troppo dolor non può dolersi.	who, through too much grief, cannot mourn.

Shepherd One

3.19 Ahi, ben avrebbe un cor di tigre o d'orsa	He would have the heart of a tiger or bear
3.27 Chi non sentisse del tuo mal pietade,	who did not pity your misfortune,
3.34 Privo d'ogni tuo ben, misero amante.	Deprived of all goodness, miserable lover.

Orfeo

3.48 Tu sei morta, mia vita, ed io respiro?	You are dead, my life, yet I am breathing?
4.24 Tu sei da me partita	You have parted from me,
4.32 Per mai più non tornare, ed io rimango?	Never to return, yet I remain?
4.51 No, che se i versi alucina cosa ponno,	No, if my verses can do anything at all
5.01 N'andrò sicuro a'più profondi abissi,	I shall descend to the deepest abyss,
5.09 E, inenerito il cor dcl rc de l'ombre,	And, shall move the king of shadow's heart,
5.24 Meco trarrotti a riveder le stelle;	Then bring you up to see the stars again.
5.37 O, se ciò negherammi empio destino,	O, if cruel destiny will not allow this,
5.46 Remarrò teco in compagnia de morte.	I will remain with you in death's company.
6.04 Addio terra, addio cielo e sole, addio.	Goodbye earth, goodbye sky and sun, goodbye.

Chorus
(not included on CD)

Ahi, caso acerbo!	Alas, bitter chance!
Ahi, fat'empio e crudele!	Alas, evil and cruel fate!
Ahi, stelle ingiuriose!	Alas, sorrowful stars!
Ahi, ciel avaro!	Alas, jealous heaven!
Non si fidi uom mortale	Place not your trust, mortal man,
Di ben caduco e frale	In goodness fleeting and frail
Che tosto fugge, e spesso	Which very swiftly escapes
A gran salita il precipizio è presso	For the higher the leap, the greater the fall.

To set this text, Monteverdi employs a musical texture typical of monody. The solo singer is accompanied by only two instruments, the portative organ and the *chitarrone*. The chitarrone is like a lute, but with several additional bass strings. The bass notes performed by the organist's left hand are duplicated on the chitarrone for reinforcement and color. The right hand of the keyboard player freely fills in the chords being outlined note-for-note by the continuous ("continuo") bass ("basso"). Together they lend a solemn timbre to this monody. More generally, this texture of melody (the singer) with an accompaniment of bass instruments captured the imagination of Baroque composers for the entire duration of the period. We call this small group of bass instruments a "basso continuo group." The basso continuo texture can be heard in most of the excerpts on our recorded anthology representing the Baroque period.

One way we might discuss this development is by comparing it to the Renaissance ideal of emphasizing the human voice alone. We linked that tendency among Renaissance composers to the idea of humanism. The Baroque period's new emphasis on voices with instruments stems from their passion for the affects. You might recall that the Florentine Camerata disapproved of using several voices to sing a dramatic speech from Guarini's **Il pastor fido.** Their objection concerned the way this practice deviated from Greek ideals. Through monody—sung melody with instrumental accompaniment—composers of Monteverdi's age could privilege the passion of a single voice urged on by powerful emotions, while still providing the listener with a rich musical texture, including both the soprano melody and the supporting bass notes. In short, these basso continuo instruments round out the texture, provide the harmony, and keep music from returning to the centuries' past practice of monophonic music.

After the Messenger delivers her terrible news, two shepherds, who were only moments earlier celebrating Orfeo's joy, express their lamentations. Much as he had done in his madrigal "Cruda Amarilli," examined in the previous chapter, here Monteverdi employs dissonances between the basso continuo group and the singer, on words like "Ahi" (alas), "l'amara" (bitter), and "misero" (miserable).

This second piece within the series chosen from this opera reinforces that the second act has now become a meditation on sorrow and suffering. This striking contrast between the joy of the previous act and the beginning of this one, against the suffering of these last two monodies, suggests that Monteverdi and his librettist Striggio have not forgotten the virtues of emotional contrast so prized in the Renaissance. Musically and dramatically, **Orfeo** is a transitional work between two periods, periods that have many like qualities to number among their differences.

Like the monody before it, this one for the two shepherds is accompanied by the portative organ and chittarone. It shares also the same mode: aeolian. In time the aeolian mode will evolve into the modern minor mode. Minor, as reported in the earlier section on Musical Fundamentals dealing with pitch, is associated with sadness.

At last, the star of the opera sings on the topic of his grief. The next monody belongs to Orfeo. In it he will pour out his suffering in a florid style full of melismas and melodic ornaments. Melodic ornaments were crucial to singing during the 1600s. Composers were so used to singers presenting ornaments within their melodies, that they would simply leave the ornamental flourishes out of their notation. This practice allowed singers to improvise, that is, make up on the spot what ornaments they would use to present the affect of the work and move the audience's emotions. Differentiating between notes that are ornamental and those that are composed can be a difficult trick, even for professional musicians. Ornaments are small melodic flourishes inserted into the piece. They tend to come before moments of repose, such as those that occur at the end of a line of text. For example, you hear occasionally that Orfeo will sing the same note over and over in rapid succession. He does this especially before the end of a line of poetry. This ornament is called a *"trillo,"* and was a highly prized sound during Monteverdi's time. Quick runs up and down scales are called *"passagio."* These too are ornaments you hear often during the singing of Baroque opera.

Consistent with the monodies before it, Orfeo's monody is also accompanied by the portative organ, but for him a lute is used instead of the chittarone. In addition to plaintive dissonances and opportunities for adding ornaments, Monteverdi indulges in some classic text painting, much in the manner of his madrigals. On the text "deepest abyss," the melody drops to the singer's lowest notes. On "verses" (Orfeo's reference to his own supernaturally powerful songs) the melody becomes more animated and active.

That Monteverdi maintained his old penchant for writing madrigals can be seen in the final movement from Act Two. After Orfeo completes his monody announcing his intention to descend to Hades and win back his wife from the realm of the dead, a chorus of shepherds and shepherdesses sings an unaccompanied madrigal. Opera, you may recall, is named for the plural of "musical work." This opera, typical of the period, contains many small movements set side by side to tell a story. Monteverdi's *Orfeo* contains not only monodies and madrigals, but dance numbers, instrumental interludes, arias (more on this genre later in this chapter), and choruses.

The madrigal material intended for a chorus of six voices has no instrumental accompaniment. This is rather surprising, since Monteverdi had by this time already begun writing instrumental parts to accompany his madrigals written for non-operatic use. For a text, Striggio repeats several lines initially given to one of the shepherds, then closes off the madrigal text with four new lines of poetry. In addition to dissonances on the repeated statements of "ahi" (alas), this madrigal features some very interesting text painting. When the poet speaks of swift escape, the rhythms become quick, just as it was in "Cruda Amarilli" when the text turned to the elusive asp. Most striking of all are the wide melodic leaps on the text *"a gran salita"* ("for the higher the leap").

Taken as a whole, this scene from *Orfeo* can be seen as an important crossroads between two eras. On the one hand, it maintains contact with the ideals of the Renaissance. The humanistic search for a practice comparable to the singing of tragedies in ancient Greece surely stimulated Monteverdi's imagination. While these four short movements all serve as a meditation on sorrow, we must remember that these emotions come quickly on the heels of a long period in the opera of unrestrained joy. Such juxtapositions of powerful emotions were important to the Renaissance imagination. Yet, each individual movement of this opera allows only one striking emotional state, in keeping with the ideals of the Baroque period. Similarly, we find both the Renaissance ideal of the madrigal, and the more modern preference for the monody, side by side in a single scene, even using the same text, as happens when the chorus takes up the text sung previously by the First Shepherd.

Monteverdi's opera *Orfeo* was designed for performance in a small hall in the Palace of the Duke of Mantua. The idea of presenting opera to a paying audience drawn from the general public would not dawn until 1637, when the Teatro San Cassiano opened its doors in Venice. During its earliest decades, opera was an entertainment exclusively for the ruling class. Monteverdi contributed two more successful operas to the repertory. When we return to the subject of opera again later in this chapter, the drawing rooms of wealthy Italians will no longer be the exclusive site of operatic performance. It will have become an international genre attracting the interest of people throughout Western Europe.

MUSIC IN VENICE DURING THE BAROQUE PERIOD

The Concertato Principle

Soon after writing *Orfeo* (1607), Monteverdi received an important new appointment as the music director for the cathedral of St. Mark's in Venice. This cathedral features spectacular architecture, with several layers of balconies radiating outward from the central altar in the shape of a cross. The many fine musicians who worked at this cathedral exploited this multi-layered architecture to tremendous effect. They found that choruses or ensembles of brass players could be stationed in the upper galleries. They would employ these hidden forces suddenly and with striking effect during the celebration of the Mass. Combining forces of diverse timbre, like choruses combined with an ensemble of brasses in the same piece, became a favored strategy of Baroque composers. This practice, called *"the concertato principle"* had its start in Venice. The principle, put simply, calls for composers to combine diverse musical forces toward a common purpose. You may have noticed that in previous periods, composers mostly used one basic timbre, most often human voices, in each piece.

While the origins of the concertato principle can be traced to Venice and the Cathedral of St. Mark's, Monteverdi was not the first to employ the principle at St. Mark's. The list of Monteverdi's predecessors in the position of music director at St. Mark's is illustrious indeed. It includes Adriano Willaert and his student Giosefo Zarlino along with the brilliant Andrea Gabrielli and his nephew Giovanni Gabrielli. This last figure did more to popularize the concertato principle than anyone else. When Monteverdi took up the post, the standards of music making in Venice were equal to or greater than those found anywhere in Europe.

By this time in history, Venetian political power had peaked and begun to decline. The War of the League of Cambrai (1509–1513) saw many of the nations of Europe unite to fight the Venetians. Venice fought England, France, Austria, and the Papal States to a standstill. The following century saw Venice in a state of nearly non-stop warfare to protect her mercantile empire and considerable territory. The strain of this struggle took its toll over time. Finally humbled somewhat on the battlefield, Venetians were unbowed when it came to creating art. The 1600s no longer saw Venice as a major political player, but she remained an important center for the art of music well into the 1700s.

Barbara Strozzi

While there were many famous Venetian musicians working in the first half of the 1600s, none led so interesting a life as Barbara Strozzi (1619–1665?) One could also argue that none was more talented. Strozzi, like most professional female musicians of her age, worked as a singer first. Musical performance was an avenue women could use to express themselves in the art of music, but it came at a social price. Modern readers may find it difficult to believe, but in Western Europe, it was seen as undignified and even morally questionable for a woman to enter a career involving performance and entertainment. The line between prostitution and perfectly innocent pursuits such as music was not very clear before the twentieth century. Upstanding families strongly discouraged their daughters from taking advantage of the very limited opportunities that did exist for women.

Barbara Strozzi was ideally suited to a career in musical performance insofar as her status within society was compromised from birth through no fault of her own. Her father was a Florentine aristocrat who was not married to Strozzi's mother. In past times, children born out of wedlock were called "illegitimate." Children bearing this intolerant and unfair label had few legal rights and a very low social standing. A life in the arts could not damage Strozzi's chances of social advancement, as her birth would not allow for such advancement. Her work as a singer was supplemented by her activities as a courtesan, a hired consort for wealthy men. Her clients ranked among the most celebrated personages of Venetian high society.

These interesting aspects of her life aside, her output as a composer represents a superbly crafted achievement in Venetian music during the middle of the 1600s. Being a singer herself, Strozzi specialized in vocal genres. One emerging genre was the *vocal cantata*. A vocal cantata is a sizable work for small orchestra, chorus, and vocal soloists. Because they were no longer staged after 1685, the dramatic role of the singer is only implied. Sometimes vocal cantatas were intended for religious settings, and took on a devotional tone; other times they were purely secular and intended for performance in a private setting.

We have an example from one of Strozzi's vocal cantatas in our recorded anthology, "Lagrime mie" [CD1 #13]. The poet of the text is unknown, but

FIGURE 9.5 | *Barbara Strozzi (1619–1665?).*
(Erich Lessing/Art Resource, NY)

scholars speculate that the poetry is by Strozzi's father, an avid amateur poet. The poem deals with the poet's remorse at the death of his beloved Lidia. Once again, we find ourselves in the presence of music conveying powerful sorrow.

Listening Guide

Barbara Strozzi, "Lagrime mie"
[CD1, #13] *(Duration, 10 min. 20 sec.)*

0.00 Lagrime mie, à che vi trattenete,	My tears, what holds you in check,
0.40 Perchè non isfogate il fier' dolore,	Why don't you give in to the fierce sorrow,
0.56 Chi mi toglie 'l respiro e opprime il core?	That steals my breath and oppresses my heart.
1:39 Lidia, che tant' adoro,	Lidia, whom I adore,
1.52 Perchè un guardo pietoso, ahimè, mi donò,	Why the pitiful glance, alas, she gives me,
2.04 Il paterno rigor l'impriggionò.	Paternal severity imprisons her.
2.17 Tra due mura rinchiusa	Locked between two walls
2.22 Stà la bella innocente,	Remains the innocent beauty,
2.27 Dove giunger non può raggio di sole,	Where no ray of sunlight shines,
2.37 E quel che più mi duole	And what pains me most

2.41	Ed accresc'il mio mal, tormenti e pene,	And increases my sickness, torment, and pain,
2.53	È che per mia cagione	Is that I caused
2.58	Prova male il mio bene.	My beloved to suffer so.
3.14	E voi lumi dolenti, no piangete!	And you, pained eyes, shed no tears!
3.27	Lagrime mie, à che vi trattenete?	My tears, what holds you in check?
4.29	Lidia, ahimè, veggo mancarmi.	Lidia, alas, I am faltering.
4.32	L'idol mio, che tanto adoro,	My idol, whom I adore,
4.44	Stà colei tra duri marmi	Remains between hard, marble walls
4.47	Per cui spiro e pur non moro.	For her I sigh yet do not die.
5.19	Se la morte m'è gradita,	If for death I am grateful,
5.28	Or che son privo di spene,	Now that I am bereft of hope,
5.33	Dhè, togliatemi la vita	Ah, take my life
5.36	(Ve ne prego) aspre mie pene.	(I beg you) and my bitter sorrow.
6.13	Ma ben m'accorgo, che per tormentarmi	Still I realize, that to torment me
6.24	Maggiormente, la sorte	More powerfully, destiny
6.31	Mi niega anco la morte.	Denies me even death.
6.49	Se dunqu'è vero, o Dio,	It is true then, O God,
7.04	Che sol del pianto mio,	That only for my tears,
7.21	Il rio destino ha sete.	Does wicked destiny thirst.

(last three lines repeated)

7.41	Se dunqu'è vero, o Dio,	It is true then, O God,
7.56	Che sol del pianto mio,	That only for my tears,
8.13	Il rio destino ha sete.	Does wicked destiny thirst.

(first three lines repeated)

8.38	Lagrime mie, à che vi trattenete,	My tears, what holds you in check,
9.16	Perchè non isfogate il fier' dolore,	Why don't you give in to the fierce sorrow,
9.32	Chi mi toglie 'l respiro e opprime il core?	That steals my breath and oppresses my heart

The text of "*Lagrime mie*" resembles Striggio's libretto for *Orfeo* in that it conjures a powerful affect through concentration on a single emotional state. Such emotional meditations on a single affect were not an isolated phenomenon during the 1600s, but comprise its most central feature.

Monteverdi's lamenting monodies from *Orfeo* were surely known to Strozzi, but she does not content herself merely to emulate Monteverdi's style. The opening of the piece is in a style that resembles monody, and surely extends from its roots. We call this style *recitative*, speech-like singing. Recitative remains an important style of composition to this day. It is especially used in opera to convey conversational dialogue. Strozzi's recitative is marked by numerous poignant dissonances befitting the setting of a lament. The first melody sung in the piece begins on the note "E." The note "E" is similarly emphasized in the basso continuo instrument. Yet, after only a single eighth note, the singer moves down a half step to D# and remains there for a quarter note tied to a dotted-eighth note. The extravagant dissonance that results is justified, just as Monteverdi had done when his madrigal "**Cruda Amarilli**" was attacked by Artusi, by the text. The remainder of the vocal line descends lower and lower, arriving at last on a final, jarring D#. Monteverdi may be the model, but Strozzi's daring stands as a singular testament to her superb craft.

After the first three lines of the poem, just when the narrator above begins singing about Lidia, the style of singing changes from recitative to a slightly more tuneful style called *arioso*. Arioso is a cross between the declamatory style of recitative and the lyric style called *aria*. In opera, an aria is a tuneful section in which the singer reflects upon the action that has just taken place. In a cantata, that function of reflection is not necessary. Here, only the tuneful melodic style of an operatic aria is featured. An operatic aria, with its contemplative or reflective function, is discussed later in this chapter. During the arioso section of the piece, florid melismas appear on key words, lending the section a virtuosic quality. The aria style of full-out singing begins with the line *"Lidia, ahime, veggo mancarmi."* When the text returns to the line *"Lagrime mie"* just before the aria section starts, Strozzi brings back the strikingly dissonant music she used at the opening of the piece.

Strozzi's composition manifests many of the elements of Baroque music discussed already. She presents a single, strikingly emotional mood in the piece. She uses the basso continuo texture. In this case, the only instrument accompanying the vocalist is a harpsichord. Performers could, however, use any bass instruments, and any instruments capable of playing chords, that they wished. A portative organ, lute, chittarone, cello, and bass would all suit the music perfectly well. Later in the Baroque period composers will be more demanding and specific in their choices of instruments. Typical of Baroque vocal music, the singer is entitled to sing ornaments. In our recording, you will hear the singer execute a *trillo* (rapid repetition of the same note) on that dissonant D# mentioned above. It's the second note of the vocal part, so you can't miss it.

Castrati

One last important word about the performance of this piece: You may have noticed that the poem deals with a lover's lament over the death of a woman named Lidia. It's safe to assume that the speaker in this case is male (although that point could be debated). Why then do we hear a woman singing this part? Before 1800, a common practice in Italy and other parts of Europe was to castrate boys who could sing particularly well. By executing this painful operation, the boy's voice would never drop to a lower register. They called the men who underwent this procedure *castrati* (singular *castrato*). The castrato voice was treasured above all others. It had the virtue of a boy's high register coupled to a full-grown man's vocal power. Modern performances of castrato parts are usually executed by women, even if the text suggests a man. Otherwise a male falsettist, that is, a man with a particularly well developed falsetto range, must be used. The problem is that falsetto singing is exactly the opposite of castrato singing. Castrati possessed enormously powerful voices, while falsettists are, by definition, thin and quiet voices. The idea of castrating boys with good voices may seem like barbarism today. By 1800 the procedure was illegal in most of Europe. It was never legal in France. The process probably would never have been dreamed up in the first place had women been allowed to appear in public without fear of losing social status. The first castrati sang in churches and cathedrals, not in gender-specific operatic roles. Once the procedure was invented, composers and audiences alike favored hearing the heroic parts in opera sung by castrati.

As mentioned above, the first public opera performance took place in Venice. This signal event in the history of European music marked the last time that Venice has been on the outer edge of changes, both stylistic and social, in music. It does not mark by any means the end of glorious Venetian music.

Instrumental Music

While opera thrived in Venice, we turn our attention now to instrumental music. During the last half of the 1600s, the creation of complex works for instruments without voices occupied many skillful Italian composers. In this area, Venice was not at the forefront of innovation. Arcangelo Corelli (1653–1713) in Rome or Giuseppe Torelli (1658–1709) in Bologna took pride of place as instrumental innovators during the late 1600s. Corelli mastered the solo sonata, in which a basso continuo group accompanies a solo instrumentalist. The texture of these pieces very much resembles the solo cantata for voice by Strozzi. Torelli's wonderful accomplishment was the popularizing of the concerto. In his works, a solo instrumentalist enjoys the support of an ensemble comprised of basso continuo and other instrumentalists. In this generation, Giovanni Legrenzi (1625–1690) was Venice's most celebrated instrumental composer. Legrenzi spent his early career in Ferrara, near Venice. He moved to Venice around 1670 and composed seventeen operas and a large body of concertos in that city. In 1685, he joined the ranks of the great musicians who served as the chief musician at the cathedral of St. Mark's.

Antonio Vivaldi

One of Legrenzi's students, Antonio Vivaldi (1678–1741), provided Venice with its most lavish and celebrated outpouring of instrumental music. Vivaldi excelled in all genres of music, including opera and sacred vocal music. Today, this prolific composer is best known for his concertos.

Figure 9.6 | Antonio Vivaldi (1678–1741).
(© Bettmann/Corbis)

Vivaldi studied both music and theology. In the latter, he attained the position of priest. Uncomfortable with the public duties of the priesthood, Vivaldi received a post more to his liking as instructor of music at an orphanage run by the church in Venice, the Hospital of the Pietà. This orphanage served only the abandoned or orphaned girls of Venice. At its highest importance, there were more than 6000 girls housed there. Insofar as many of the girls were illegitimate or very poor, music was seen as a worthy endeavor for them. A career in music would mean social catastrophe for an upper-class, Venetian girl in good favor with her family. Ironically Venetian audiences had a thirst to hear women singers especially, and thought nothing of paying to hear women instrumentalists as well. Under Vivaldi, the standards of music making among the girls were very high. Venetian music lovers flocked to their concerts, while foreign visitors left behind, in the form of letters home, a written record of lavish praise for the girls' accomplishments.

Vivaldi's most famous composition, the four concertos for solo violin known as "The Four Seasons" (1725), was certainly written for use at the Hospital of the Pietà. Each of the four concertos illustrates, through music, facets of each season. We can hear how Vivaldi achieves this illustration through an example in our recorded anthology. The first movement of the Spring Concerto (*la primavera*) [CD1 #14] contains Vivaldi's pictorial evocation of bird song, a storm, breezes, and a gentle brook.

Before examining the movement's pictorial elements, we need some orientation in the form of the piece. For this movement, Vivaldi uses a formal plan called *ritornello form*. A ritornello form depends on the return of a recognizable musical material. This returning material, or ritornello, lends the movement a structural coherence. Listeners will recognize the returning material. Since music composed prior to the age of recording technology was apt to be heard only once, introducing moments of recognition made excellent sense, and served to orient listeners encountering the piece for the first time. Monteverdi uses ritornello forms throughout the opera ***Orfeo,*** though not during the section discussed earlier. Ritornello form is one of the fine structural achievements of the Baroque Period. It is still very much used today. Popular songs, for example, use a form much like ritornello with their returning chorus. Next time you listen to popular radio or your favorite recent songs, listen to see if there isn't some musical theme, often linked with catchy lyrics, that returns more than once during the song.

Vivaldi was very clear about the images of spring that served as his guide in writing this movement. In order to differentiate between the ritornello and the imagery, Vivaldi consistently let the whole orchestra play the ritornello, while the solo violin emerges out of the orchestra during the springtime imagery. The orchestra for this piece, in keeping with the ideals of the concertato principle, includes a basso continuo group made up of harpsichord, cello, and bass. In addition to these forces, Vivaldi uses an orchestra of strings, including violins, violas, and cellos. Only the basso continuo instruments play throughout the piece.

Antonio Vivaldi, La Primavera, from The Four Seasons (1725)
[CD1, #14] *(Duration, 3 min. 32 sec.)*

First Movement: Allegro

0.00   Tutti (the whole orchestra), first phrase of ritornello, **f,** repeated **p.**

0.07   Second phrase of ritornello, **f,** repeated **p.**

0.31   Birds greet the spring, solo violin plays warbling figures akin to bird song, the orchestra's violins join in.

1.06   Tutti, ritornello, second phrase only, **f.**

1.14   Gentle breezes and a murmuring brook, solo violin with the whole orchestra.

1.38   Tutti, ritornello, second phrase only, **f.**

1.46 Thunder and lightning, the orchestra plays rapid repeated notes in low registers (thunder) while the soloist plays flashy upward scales (lightning).

2.15 Tutti, ritornello in which the storm passes away, made gloomy through the use of the minor mode, second phrase only, **f.**

2.24 Rapid alternation of birds, who have returned after the storm's passing, solo violin joined by orchestra's violins, minor key.

2.43 Tutti, ritornello, first phrase varied to end in the major key, **f.**

2.55 The solo violin plays trills and warbling figures, followed by running passages and scales.

3.12 Final ritornello, tutti, second phrase, **f**, repeated **p.**

The music depicting the storm (see the listening guide) was considered rather scary in its day. Its arrival three-quarters of the way into this movement and the implied dramatic action it is made to serve, provide the movement's musical climax.

After this short movement, Vivaldi wrote two more, intended to follow. The second movement is in the minor mode, and features a very slow tempo to depict a shepherd going to sleep in a flowery meadow, his flock watched over by his dog. The last movement is fast and dance-like, as nymphs and shepherds dance to the sound of pastoral pipes celebrating spring. This format of three movements, opening with a fast movement followed by a slow movement and concluding with a fast dance-like movement, became the standard for many concerto compositions.

The Concerto and Capitalism

Revisiting briefly the historical issues discussed earlier, it might be worthwhile for a moment to consider the relationship of the concerto to the rise of capitalism. The advent of public opera saw money flow into the creation of public spectacles. Many singers, especially the leading castrati, became famous and wealthy. Capitalists found that backing operatic performances could result in profits. Instrumentalists, unfortunately, found themselves laboring in relative obscurity off stage as they accompanied the singers. The concerto can be seen as the genre that brought money and fame to outstanding instrumentalists. Its invention as a genre comes rapidly on the heels of the invention of public operas; moreover, it is simultaneous with the widespread adoption of capitalism as an available means of making money. By creating a compelling genre featuring instrumentalists, there was finally a venture for investors to back financially. Over the later years of the Baroque Period, some outstanding instrumentalists found themselves famous and wealthy—not as wealthy as the leading opera stars, but wealthy nonetheless.

OPERA OUTSIDE ITALY

After the opening of the Teatro San Cassiano in Venice in 1637, only the Italian city of Naples was quick to pick up the passion for public opera. During the following decades, public theaters opened not only in Naples, but in most major Italian cities. The Venetian composer Orazio Benevoli brought opera to Vienna, which led to the swift embrace of Italian opera throughout German-speaking Europe. Grand public theaters, supported either by ticket sales or more commonly by the local aristocracy, opened in Vienna around 1700. England quickly followed Austria and the German states in taking Italian opera to its heart. During the first half of the 1700s, London was home to several professional companies.

Among Western European nations, only France resisted the charms of Italian opera during the Baroque era. In keeping with France's leadership in the crusade to form itself into a modern nation state with an absolute monarch, the French royalty favored indigenous entertainments to Italian imports. What follows is a discussion of the state of opera in the Baroque Period in France, as opposed to the other nations of Europe, and especially England, where Italian opera flourished.

Opera at the Court of Louis XIV

Louis XIV of France ruled with absolute authority from 1643–1715, although during the early years of this period he was a small child who depended on Cardinal Mazarin to manage most affairs of state. Upon achieving the age of majority, Louis XIV exercised tremendous power. He marshalled all the French aristocracy around the idea of the French state. Of course, the king and the state were one in Louis' mind. He even announced publicly "l'état c'est moi" (the state is me). Louis came to be known as "The Sun King," so great was his power and, perhaps, his ego. During his reign, a magnificent palace was constructed at Versailles, a small city outside Paris. This magnifi-

FIGURE 9.7 | *The palace of Versailles* (with its formal gardens, France
The Baroque period is in part characterized by a fondness for large, grandiose structures and the dramatic. Many Baroque artists successfully outdid their predecessors in reflecting the flamboyant expectations of their patrons. Position, power, and wealth were extravagantly displayed in large-scaled, integrated, artistic compositions that were meant to dazzle and overwhelm the spectator. Diverse and widespread, Baroque art took Renaissance clarity of form and recast it into intricate patterns of geometry and fluid movement. Reflected was a complex dualism: pomp and extravagance on one hand, system and calculation on the other. (© Archivo Iconografico, S.A./Corbis)

cent dwelling still stands as a monument to the seventeenth-century dream of absolute monarchy. The palace covers many acres and houses a cathedral, an opera house, and more than 1000 bedrooms. The presence of an opera house within the palace should come as no surprise. For royalty during the Baroque Period, opera served the purposes of propagandizing on their behalf.

Jean-Baptiste Lully

The favorite composer of Louis XIV was an Italian named Giovanni-Baptista Lulli. In order to achieve advancement within the French court, Lulli changed his name to something more French sounding, Jean-Baptiste Lully (1632–1687). Lully began his career as a violinist in the service of the king. He composed dances, as the royal court enjoyed dancing. His endeavors in this regard pleased the king, who eventually granted Lully a virtual dictatorship over music in France. Lully was granted the power to place a stamp on all music published in France; for that service, he was entitled to receive a generous fee. Lully was also allowed to rule on all operatic performances in France. Naturally he ruled against virtually all but his own. This powerful monopoly gave Lully the same sort of absolute power over musical matters that the king sought over political matters. In a sense, Lully enjoyed the king's favor and became a virtual extension of the king's absolute power.

Lully eventually took up the cause of composing operas for Louis XIV, but he did not call them operas. He used the French term *tragèdie-lyrique* (lyric tragedy) instead, in order to distance his works from their Italian counterparts. Lully worked with the librettist Jean-Philippe Quinault. Quinault had a gift for allegories that aggrandized the reign of Louis XIV, thus prompting the king to shower favor upon him and Lully. Quinault understood what the French court wanted from opera. He borrowed on two great French traditions, spoken tragedy and ballet, for inspiration. Unlike Italian opera, French *tragèdie-lyrique* was full of visual spectacle. Lully and Quinault had the wealth of the king behind their productions. There was no question of economizing in order to extend profits, they could spend all that was needed in order to realize their ambitions. Italian opera tends to be modest in its spectacles, although audiences in Rome generally appreciated spectacle more than audiences in Naples or Venice did. Among the spectacular effects that French audiences were treated to at the opera house within Versailles were elaborate

FIGURE 9.8 | Jean-Baptiste Lully (1632–1687).
(© Bettmann/Corbis)

ballet scenes, special effects such as volcanoes and storms at sea, imaginative creatures like sea monsters and mythical beasts, and the occasional appearance of a Greek or Roman god seated upon a floating cloud to gaze down upon the action. Every scene of a *tragèdie-lyrique* required some amount of spectacle. These spectacles have come to be called *divertissements*, diversions within the larger entertainment. Critics of *tragèdie-lyrique* fail to see the point of interrupting the story to admit spectacular effects. These critics misunderstand the tastes and desires of the audience of the day.

In addition to spectacle, *tragèdie-lyrique* emphasized recitative. All the most important scenes are presented in this declamatory vocal style. In this regard, the work of Lully is rather similar to the work of Monteverdi from earlier in the century. Lully used to attend the spoken theater in order to hear the great French actresses of the day perform the sophisticated plays of such giants of French literature as Pierre Corneille (1606–1684) and Jean Racine (1639–1699). He would listen carefully to each inflection of the singer, and then would try to recreate the actresses' rhythm and general melodic outline in his musical versions based on similar stories.

Armide

In our recorded anthology is a dramatic recitative from the *tragèdie-lyrique* **Armide** (1686) [CD1 #15]. This work was written for Louis XIV and the royal court. The action of this work takes place during the Crusades. The titular character Armide is an Islamic sorceress. She has been campaigning against the crusading Renaud. In the previous scene, Renaud scored a victory by freeing his men from Armide's power. Now she has used an enchantment to put Renaud to sleep. She prepares to kill her hated adversary, when suddenly she finds herself unable to do so; his good looks win her over. This important moment in the action is set entirely as recitative. When Armide changes the subject and conjures demons to transform themselves into a friendly breeze to conduct she and her handsome captive away, Lully composes a petit air (little song). This tuneful style of singing was used in *tragèdie-lyrique* for moments of diminished emotional importance.

Jean-Baptiste Lully, Armide, Act II, scene 5, (1686)
[CD1, #15] *(Duration, 7 min. 48 sec.)*

OVERTURE (Orchestral)
0.00 Drum roll.
0.02 Opening section is stately, and in a meter of 2/2.
0.23 Opening section repeated.
0.43 Second, "dance-like" section begins with quick, imitative entrances, in a meter of 6/4, which is felt in two ("**one**-two-three **four**-five-six").
1.11 A stately concluding section reestablishes the opening 2/2meter.
1.33 Section two is repeated.
2.01 Concluding section is repeated.

ACT II, Scene 5, "Enfin il est en ma puissance"

2.30 Orchestral Introduction

ARMIDE (recitative)

3.15	Enfin il est en ma puissance,	Finally he is in my power,
3.23	Ce fatal ennemi, ce superbe vainqueur.	This fatal enemy, this superb warrior.
3.31	Le charme du sommeille livre à ma vengeance;	The charm of sleep opens him to my vengeance;
3.38	Je vais percer son invincible coeur.	I will pierce his invincible heart.
3.45	Par lui tous mes captifs sont sortis d'esclavage;	Through him, all my captives have escaped slavery;
3.49	Qu'il éprouve toute ma rage.	Let him feel all my rage.
3.56	Quel trouble ma saisit? qui me fait hésiter?	What trouble grips me? what makes me hesitate?
4.05	Qu'est-ce qu'en sa faveur le pitié me veut dire?	What does pity want to tell me in his favor?
4.12	Frappons . . . Ciel! qui peut m'arrêter?	Let us strike . . . Heavens! who can stop me?
4.19	Achevons . . . je frémis! vengeons-nous . . . je soupire!	Let us finish . . . I tremble! Let us avenge . . . I sigh!
4.41	Est-ce ainsi que je dois me venger aujourd-hui?	Is it thus that I must avenge myself today?
4.47	Ma colère s'éteint quand j'approche de lui.	My fury is extinguished when I approach him.
4.56	Plus je le voi, plus ma vengeance est vaine;	The more I see him, the more my vengeance is in vain.
5.03	Mon bras tremblant se refuse à haine.	My trembling arm refuses my hate.
5.10	Ah! quelle cruauté de lui ravir le jour!	Ah! What cruelty to deny him the day!
5.18	A ce jeune héros tout cède sur la terre.	To this young hero everything on the earth surrenders.
5.25	Qui croirait qu'il fut né seulement pour la guerre?	Who would believe that he was born only for war?
5.33	Il semble être fait pour l'amour.	He seems to be made for love.
5.42	Ne puis-je me venger à moins qu'il ne périsse?	Could I not avenge myself unless he dies?
5.49	Hé? ne suffit-il pas que l'Amour le punisse?	Hey? Is it not sufficient that love punish him?
5.55	Puisqu'il n'a pu trouver mes yeux assez charmants	Since he could not find my eyes charming enough,
6.01	Qu'il m'aime au moins par mes enchantements.	Let him love me at least through my enchantments.
6.07	Que, s'il se peut, je le haïsse.	Then, if it's possible, I will hate him.

6.13 **Orchestra plays the petit air "Venez, venez" in 3/4 meter.**

6.37	Venez, venez, seconder mes désirs,	Come, come, support my desires,
6.41	Démons, transformez-vous en d'aimables zéphirs.	Demons, transform yourselves into friendly zephyrs.
6.55	Je cède à ce vainqueur, la pitié me surmonte.	I surrender to this conqueror, pity defeats me.
7.00	Cachez ma foiblesse et ma honte	Conceal my foibles and my shame
7.04	Dans les plus reculés déserts.	In the most remote desert.
7.07	Volez, volez, conduisez-nous au bout de l'univers	Fly, fly, conduct us to the end of the universe.

7.15 **Orchestral postlude.**

In listening to this interesting recitative, follow along closely the translation found in the listening guide. Lully was a master of capturing dramatic speech in music. Especially nice is his treatment of Armide's hesitation in killing Renaud. Lully introduces rests in all the natural places, for example, after each hesitation as she goes back and forth between wanting to strike Renaud with her knife and questioning what force stopped her. We learn eventually that love stops her. She finds Renaud irresistible. The scene ends with the petit air *"venez, venez."* Here Lully shifts to a lilting 3/4 meter. For Lully, calling upon demons to transform into friendly zephyrs is less crucial dramatically than Armide's internal struggle over killing or loving Renaud.

Tragèdie-lyrique enjoyed a long history. Jean-Philippe Rameau (1683–1764) sustained the genre well into the eighteenth century. Moreover, Lully's works remained popular with both audiences and the monarchy right up until the time of the French Revolution (begun in 1789).

Unlike Italian opera, *tragèdie-lyriques* were not popular throughout Europe. The expense of producing them, coupled with their allegorical plots celebrating French power, precluded other Europeans from getting to know these works until much later. The ballet music embedded within *tragèdie-lyrique* enjoyed some favor in other lands, but not the dramatic recitatives. Indeed, Italian opera began placing less and less importance on recitative as its history unfolded. Monteverdi's last opera marked one of the last times that an Italian composer would invest so much energy in the creation of recitative. For Italian composers after Monteverdi, the recitative was something hurried through in order to get to the next aria. *Tragèdie-lyrique* maintained its premium on studied, declamatory singing. For lovers of Italian opera, the charms of full-blown lyrical singing prevailed.

The Popularity of Italian Opera Outside Italy

A book conceived on this scale cannot possibly represent all the activity associated with Italian opera outside of Italy. Rather than listing the many outstanding contributors to this genre, let's satisfy ourselves with a few words about the scale of opera's popularity, and then examine one aria by a justly famous composer.

Italian opera was popular. By the beginning of the 1700s opera had seized the imaginations of people throughout Europe (with the exception of France). People of all classes and all backgrounds attended the opera. To be sure, the form had its virulent detractors who objected to the unreality of the dramas, the pretenses of the stars, and the discomfort of jostling with crowds to attend performances. For the majority, however, opera was the centerpiece of civic life during opera season. For religious reasons, opera was not performed in most countries during the weeks immediately before Christmas and Easter. Opera companies also generally took a hiatus in summer. That left the autumn, late winter, and late spring for opera. Wealthy audience members purchased boxes where they could both see the action and be seen by most of the audience. Owners of boxes purchased them for an entire season, therefore, many people went to the same opera for several nights running. One might be led to conclude that they got bored. They did not. Opera houses accommodated numerous amusements in addition to the opera itself. Food and drink were consumed. Conversations were conducted. Most opera houses had casinos in the lobbies where patrons could participate in games of chance. Some boxes even had curtains or shutters that patrons could draw in order to conduct a semi-secret rendezvous. Audience members enjoyed watching their friends and neighbors. Europe gets cold in winter; opera houses were warm. During carnival season, the late winter before Lent begins, people attended the opera in masks, which lent the proceedings a degree of fun. For the poor, the upper most balconies were available at cheap prices. The opera houses of Europe mostly had separate entrances for the cheap seats. These seats were often sold as a block to groups of men who resold them to poorer opera lovers. These men had the responsibility of keeping order in the upper balconies, so that a rain of debris from above would not spoil the fun for the rich below. Audiences of all classes were demonstrative. They didn't sit silently and wait to clap at the appropriate times. They were raucous, wildly cheering favorite singers and heaping ridicule on those in poor voice. Singers strove to keep things interesting by introducing different ornaments each night. Such efforts were appreciated by knowledgeable audience members. In short, going to the opera at the beginning of the eighteenth century was exciting, vibrant, and rich with diverse pleasures.

George Frideric Handel

George Frideric Handel (1685–1759) enjoyed the greatest celebrity among opera composers during the age. Handel was born in Halle in the German States (Germany would not be a unified nation until the late 1800s). His father was a barber, which meant that he not only cut hair but performed surgeries as well. Handel's father opposed his son's attempts to study music. His father pursued a respectable profession and wanted his son to do the same. Handel taught himself to play keyboard instruments on the sly. His progress was so considerable that he found himself playing professionally for the Calvinist Church at age seventeen, accompanying the singing of psalm texts.

FIGURE 9.9 | *George Frideric Handel (1685–1759).* (© Archivo Iconografico, S.A./Corbis)

During this time, he studied music seriously with the composer Zachow. He learned to play the violin. At age eighteen he moved to the large commercial port of Hamburg, where he played violin in a professional opera orchestra. During 1705 he composed three operas for Hamburg. The first of these, ***Almira***, was a great success. He spent the years from 1706 to 1709 in Italy studying opera and writing his own. He scored a tremendous success in Florence with his opera ***Agrappina*** (1707). That opera was performed twenty-seven times, an astonishingly high number for the day. In Italy, Handel met and befriended the leading composers of the times, including Antonio Vivaldi.

Flush with the successes he had won so far, Handel received an important post in 1710 that took him back to Hamburg. He became *Kapellmeister* to the Elector of Hanover. A *Kapellmeister* is the person who leads musical activities for a court or cathedral and sometimes for both. In Italian, they say *maestro da capella* (master of the chapel) to signify the comparable post. Monteverdi and Vivaldi, for example, both served as *maestro da capella* at St. Mark's in Venice—Monteverdi early in the 1600s and Vivaldi from 1710 until his death. The Elector of Hanover was a powerful figure. Electors elected the Holy Roman Emperor, and were themselves high-ranking aristocrats.

Soon after arriving back in Hanover, Handel received permission to visit London, a robust city, bursting with wealth owing to England's vigorous empire building. The musical scene in London could scarcely be rivaled in all the world for its opulence and skill in execution. Handel thrived there, eventually relocating on a permanent basis in 1712 and without the permission of the Elector of Hanover. The Elector of Hanover was heir to the English throne, possibly explaining why he was so lenient in letting Handel remain in London.

Handel's career in London began on a controversial note. His opera **Rinaldo** (1711) was written in Italian, a language little known in London. Handel, however, was so enthusiastic about his chances for success that he wrote the entire opera in two weeks. In an effort to please an audience slightly less familiar with Italian opera, Handel hedged his bet by writing a spectacular part for a distinguished castrato, Nicolo Grimaldi. Grimaldi was so famous on the continent that he went by only one name, "Nicolini." Handel also planned lavish and surprising stage effects, such as releasing wild sparrows in the theater to enhance a pastoral aria about birds, sung by the heroine. On the topic of the wild birds, Joseph Addison, a waggish critic, wrote:

> *There have been so many flights . . . let loose in this opera, that it is feared the house will never get rid of them; and that in other plays they may make their entrance in very wrong and improper scenes . . . besides the inconveniences which the heads of the audience may sometimes suffer from them.*

Despite such criticism, the opera was a fine success, running for a longer-than expected 15 nights to packed houses at the Haymarket Theater, one of London's many public theaters. Controversy marked this debut, however. Some detractors wondered why Londoners would want to listen to music by a German composer, sung in Italian by a fat castrato, with wild birds flying about. No opera, indeed, no music, would ever enjoy universal approval or universal disapproval.

In our recorded anthology, we have an aria from **Rinaldo** called *"cara sposa"* [CD1 #16]. The story of this opera is almost identical to Lully's **Armide**. Rinaldo (the Italian equivalent of the French hero, Renaud from **Armide**) is participating in the First Crusade. He and his troops have the Muslim forces surrounded in Jerusalem. The Muslim leader calls on his lover and ally, the sorceress Armide. She decides that Rinaldo needs to be dealt with in order to sap the Crusaders of their will to fight. For his part Rinaldo prepares for battle by spending some time with his beloved Almirena. Suddenly Armide appears and prepares to battle Rinaldo. He draws his sword, while she conjures a black cloud full of horrible monsters. The cloud envelops both Almirena and Armide; they all disappear, leaving behind two fiendish apparitions who mock Rinaldo before sinking into the ground. Filled with despair, Rinaldo sings his lament.

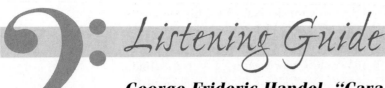

Listening Guide

George Frideric Handel, "Cara Sposa" from Rinaldo
[CD1, #16] *(Duration, 10 min. 23 sec.)*

RINALDO

Cara sposa, amante cara,	Dear betrothed, dear love,
dove sei?	Where are you?
Deh! ritorna a' pianti miei!	Oh! Return at my tears!
Del vostr' Erebo sull'ara,	At your infernal altar,
colla face del mio sdegno	With the fire of my fury
io vi sfido, o spirit rei.	I defy you, o wicked spirits.

A

0.00   Orchestral introduction

0.38   Rinaldo dwells on the opening three lines of poetry, repeating them numerous times. The tempo is slow, and the mood is sorrowful.

4.17   Orchestra brings the **A** section to a close.

B

4.55   Tempo increases to a fast pace for the last three lines of the poem. The orchestra reinforces Rinaldo's indignation.

A

5.19   Orchestral returns to opening material.

5.57   Rinaldo reflects his grief by dwelling once again on the first three lines of poetry.

9.35   Orchestra brings the **A** section to a final close.

This is one of three arias sung by Rinaldo during the first act. Handel felt that it was important for the star to be heard capturing a variety of affects through song. He has a tender aria, a militaristic aria, and this aria featuring both sorrow and outrage. The ideal structure for an Italian opera aria was the *da capo* structure. This structure was invented during the 1600s by Italian composers working in Naples. It was deemed perfect for the purposes of showing off the voice of the singer. The structure is quite simple. The singer begins by singing what we might call an "A" section. A contrasting "B" section follows. Contrast is achieved through a change of mood, often a change of key, and some new affect. Then the performers are instructed to go to the head (*da capo*, in Italian) and repeat the "A" section. The standard practice was for the singer to add numerous melodic ornaments during this repeated "A" section. This practice staved off boredom for the audience, since they had only just heard this "A" section moments before. The pleasure of hearing what great singers would do with a second chance at a passage gripped audiences in fascination, much as modern audiences for jazz never tire of hearing how improvisers will address a standard song. Every night provided different improvised elements.

This particular aria, "cara sposa" exemplifies the *da capo* form. The singer repeats the opening three lines of poetry numerous times. This constitutes the "A" section. The mood throughout this section is sorrowful. The "B" section comprises the last three lines of the poem. Here the tempo increases to a fast pace, the orchestra reinforces the singer's outrage. The entire "B" section requires less than one minute to perform. Rinaldo's rage gives way again to his grief, as the "A" section returns.

The singer in this excerpt is not a castrato, that procedure being mercifully illegal now. Instead, we hear a male falsettist. He sings in the extremely high range with grace and some power. Often women are used to play the hero's role in Baroque Italian opera.

On a larger scale, Handel's opera could be described as a series of recitatives followed by arias. This structure pleased audiences, who paid minimal attention to recitatives, thus providing them time to socialize. This structure stands in stark contrast to French *tragedie-lyrique*, where the recitatives are by far the most interesting parts of the opera, but then the social setting for *tragedie-lyrique* was quite distinct from that of a public opera house in London. Oddly then, *tragedie-lyrique* more closely resembles the ideals of Monteverdi's time, when monody was key, than Italian opera does.

Handel composed more than forty works for the London stage in less than thirty years. His accomplishments always won devoted enthusiasts and heated detractors. As his career in opera ended, he had outlived the style he favored. The English came to prefer English ballad operas, a genre indigenous to their nation and in keeping with the formation of nation states. These works are sung in English, with tuneful songs, and spoken dialogue in place of recitative. As the ballad opera was emerging, Handel sank much of his fortune into a financially troubled opera company, the Royal Academy of Music. He lost much of what he had earned.

HANDEL AND THE RISE OF ORATORIO IN ENGLAND

All during the time that Handel was writing operas for London, he was searching for an alternative form to captivate the British public. The world of opera was risky and expensive. Audiences favored lavish entertainments with spectacular costumes and imaginative stage effects. Those cost money. The best opera singers demanded extravagant fees. Rivals and detractors wanted to see Handel ruined, so even if his operas were expensive and successful, there would be some bad critical reaction designed to damage his reputation. Handel's search for a way out of Italian opera led him to the oratorio.

An *oratorio* is a piece of music that tells a story, much like opera, but unlike opera, these stories are usually religious and meant to be performed without costumes or stage movement. The form comes initially from Italy where composers such as Emilio de' Cavalieri invented oratorio as a substitute for opera during Lent, the weeks immediately prior to Easter, when the secular plots of opera were considered inappropriate. The earliest oratorios were performed in churches, and had as their subjects stories from the Bible. For Christian composers at that time it would have been blasphemous to depict sacred stories on the operatic stage. Therefore, oratorio resisted emulating opera in terms of theatrical presentation; however, they could be very similar in terms of music.

Handel hoped that the oratorio would allow him to escape the field of opera in London. He mounted a large number of them, drawn from stories and myths of the Old Testament and Apocryphal books. Middle-class English music lovers knew these stories well, making staging unnecessary. The text alone could orient the listeners and guide them through the story. By 1737, oratorio composition occupied much of Handel's time. Often Handel dedicated his oratorios to triumphs in the formation of the British State. For example, his first wildly popular oratorio, **Judas Maccabaeus** (1747), was written to celebrate the English victory over an uprising of Scottish Highlanders at

FIGURE 9.10 | *View of the piazza in front of St. Peter's in Rome, designed by Lorenzo Bernini.*

The Piazza exceeds the length of two football fields. The colonnades surrounding it consist of 284 different columns, evenly positioned. The statues of 140 saints, each 19 feet tall, are situated on top of the columns. Clearly, many wealthy church establishments sought to attract and overwhelm parishioners with grandiose, integrated, artistic structures in much the same way powerful aristocrats sought to display their position, wealth, and power.

For large-scale, sacred musical compositions such as the oratorio and cantata, churches borrowed favored secular techniques from the opera. Sacred music composers incorporated both recitatives and arias for vocal soloists, which were accompanied by orchestra. In design then, similar paradoxes are found. Tension and freedom are expressed in the free rhythmic nature of the recitatives, used to propel dramatic text forward. Repose and control are reflected in the meditative interpretations, or sung soliloquies provided by arias. (© Phil Schermeiser/Corbis)

Culloden. While the biblical story and the enforcing of English sovereignty over Scotland through might of arms have nothing to do with one another, Handel understood the importance of connecting his works to the ideal of nation building in order to win favor with the monarchy and the public.

Today, Handel's most celebrated oratorio by far is **Messiah** (1742). Interestingly, this piece was written when Handel was in a state of virtual bankruptcy. He composed this oratorio for a premiere in Dublin, Ireland (then part of the United Kingdom) in an effort to raise revenue quickly. The entire piece was written in fewer than twenty-four days.

The selection of **Messiah** to represent the oratorio is slightly controversial. While it is certainly the most famous oratorio ever written, it is also among the least representative of the typical oratorio. For one thing, the text does not consistently tell a story, although there are narrative sections. Rather, Handel drew from mainly non-narrative passages of the Bible for his libretto. Oratorios more typically contain some dramatic conflict that features something like a beginning, middle, and end. **Messiah** is divided into three parts. The first deals loosely with Old Testament prophecies of the coming of a messiah. The second describes the suffering and death of Jesus, followed by the spread of his teachings. The final section offers a meditation on faith.

In our anthology are two selections from *Messiah*. The first is a choral recitative [CD1 #17]. This text is narrative as it tells the story of an angel appearing before shepherds tending their flocks.

Listening Guide

George Frideric Handel, "There were Shepherds" and "Glory to God" chorus from "Messiah" (1742)

[CD1, #17] *(Duration, 1 min. 06 sec.)*

The highlighted text represents natural syllable and word stresses. Begin by reading the text out loud, paying close attention to the normal pitch inflections, stresses, and pauses, before you listen to Handel's melodic setting, with his close attention to pitch, rhythm, and pause. A description of the setting appears in the right-hand column.

(TEXT)	(MUSIC)
Recitative parts 1–3 on CD	

Part 1:

0.00 There were **shep**herds abiding in the **field,** keeping watch over their **flock** by **night**.

Words or syllables indicated by **bold type** are normally emphasized in speech, and are therefore musically accented by higher and lower pitches, rhythms, and pauses. The pipe organ serves as continuo, providing occasional chords for this portion of narrative vocal recitative.

Part 2:

0.14 And **lo!** the angel of the Lord came upon them, and the **glory** of the Lord shone round about them; **and they were so afraid.** (full cadence)

Handel incorporates the Renaissance principle of "word-painting," by utilizing the high orchestral strings to illustrate through music the beating of an angel's wings, and to invoke the image of a halo.

Part 3:

0.33 And the angel said unto **them:** "**Fear** not, for be**hold,** I bring you good **tid**ings of great joy which shall be to **all people.** (full cadence)

Part three of the recitative is accompanied once again by the continuo.

For unto **you** is born this **day,** in the city of **David,** a Savior, which is **Christ,** the **Lord.** (full cadence)

(Not included on CD)

Part 4:

And **sud**denly there was with the **angel,** a **multitude** of the heavenly host: praising **God, and saying:** (full cadence)

The word-painting heard in part two, is reinforced by more orchestral strings to capture the dramatic image of many angels.

CHORUS

The choir interrupts the recitative, taking on the dramatic role of the multitude of angels by singing the angelic message. In addition, Handel musically indicates both heavenly and earthly realms with his selection of voice types and rhythms. The angelic text, "Glory to God! Glory to God in the highest!" is sung by the high voices of the choir in an excited and animated rhythm. For the words "and peace on earth," the lower voices of the choir are heard, utilizing a much slower, or peaceful rhythm. The imagery is reinforced by repetition of these text lines.

With a simple change of texture from homophony to imitation for the words "good will toward men," the role of the choir is changed to represent the entire congregation, and by extension, all of Christendom. The intent here is to poignantly reflect the message and its meaning being passed from one member of the community to another.

A unique dramatic effect is captured with dynamics at the conclusion of this choral number. Handel asks the orchestra to gradually fade away, as the Shepherds' angelic vision dissipates.

The second excerpt from *Messiah* in our recorded anthology is by far the most famous section of the oratorio, the "Hallelujah Chorus." [CD1 #18] Its title indicates that the choir is gathered, here, to express thanks or praise to God.

Listening Guide

George Frideric Handel, Hallelujah Chorus from "Messiah" (1742)
[CD1, #18] *(Duration, 3 min. 48 sec.)*

This popular choral number concludes Part II of **Messiah**. At the beginning, Handel introduces the words, "Hallelujah! Hallelujah!" and the passage "For the Lord God omnipotent reigneth" in homophonic texture, but with distinct melodic phrases that are repeated for emphasis. When the introduction is concluded, Handel employs the phrases as "subjects" in a double-fugue. Juxtaposed, each melodic subject is repeatedly passed to other voices. This polyphony soon returns to a homophonic treatment of the words "The Kingdom of this world is become the Kingdom of our Lord and of His Christ." Imitation is incorporated for "and He shall reign for ever and ever," soon giving way to an antiphonal call-and-response between low and high voices respectively, for the text, "King of Kings, and Lord of Lords"—countered by "for ever, Hallelujah!" Throughout, orchestral instruments double the vocal parts, as all musical participants symbolize a community united in praising God.

(TEXT)

0.00   Hallelujah, Hallelujah!
0.26   For the Lord God omnipotent reigneth. Hallelujah!
0.50   Double-fugue
1.17   The Kingdom of this world is become the kingdom of our Lord and of His Christ.
1.38   And He shall reign for ever and ever,
2.02   King of Kings for ever and ever, Hallelujah!
2.22   And Lord of Lords for ever and ever.
2.43   Last three lines repeated.

Because King George II of England was so moved by this choral tribute paid to the "King of Kings" at the first London performance of *Messiah,* he stood to show his respect. The whole audience rose to their feet as well, as loyal subjects would never sit in the presence of their standing monarch. Consequently, it has become tradition for the audience to stand during the performance of the Hallelujah Chorus.

J.S. BACH

Johann Sebastian Bach (1685–1750) has risen today as the central figure of the Baroque era. His music enjoys international interest far greater today than ever existed while he was alive. He occupies an unusual place in history for such a revered figure. So far in this historical survey, we have devoted most of our attention to innovators and composers who introduced new concepts, forms, genres, and ideals to the art of music. J. S. Bach was not primarily an innovator. His accomplishment resides in his capacity to synthesize the innovations of the previous decades. He created outstanding music, but did not intend that music to overturn the practices of the past through innovation. Yet there are innovations embedded in his output. He synthesized stylistic traits from Italian, French, and German music, all the while helping to codify the system we call *tonality*.

Bach's Early Career

Bach entered a life of music for the same reason that most young men entered into their profession: his family had long been associated with professional music making. In times of economic uncertainty for the lower classes, sons generally took up their fathers' professions in order to benefit from the father's position and rank within the profession. When Bach took up the profession of music, it was generally regarded more as a craft than an art. The way people think about art has changed over the centuries. Today we mainly value the singularity of the artistic temperament, and tend to exaggerate the creative aspects of artistic activity such as musical composition. We subscribe to the myth of pure creativity and imagine the creative people around us to be wholly given over to their imaginations. In Bach's time, composers were seen more often as providing a useful service. Indeed, musicians employed at the courts of aristocrats and monarchs were regarded as servants; their creativity was seen more as the application of useful knowledge in making something of value. Little distinction was made between composers and other craftsmen, such as furniture makers. If a chair needs to be made, then you hire someone who can make one. Similarly, if the court needs a new concerto to listen to after a festive dinner, you find someone who makes concertos. Bach seems to have thrived within this understanding. He was a superb craftsman in his own mind. Later centuries would remake him into something more, or at the very least something different.

FIGURE 9.11 | *J.S. Bach (1685–1750).*
(© Bettmann/Corbis)

Because of this craftsman-like quality to Bach's output, the immediate circumstances of his employment determined to a large degree the sorts of pieces he composed at various times during his career. The first stop in his professional career was the small city of Arnstadt, where he served as organist and choirmaster at the Lutheran cathedral from 1703 to 1707. Most of his compositions from this period were for organ, as befits a church organist. The image of the humble craftsman doesn't always fit Bach perfectly during his youth. He was given a four-week leave to visit northern Germany to hear the brilliant church organist Dietrich Buxtehude (1637–1707), then much revered and in the twilight of a fine career. Instead of visiting for four weeks, Bach remained for four months, leaving the cathedral without an organist. Still other times, Bach was censured by the church's leaders for confusing the congregation with overly ambitious music. These moments from his early biography suggest that Bach's craftsman-like self conception sometimes gave over to an ego capable of disappointing his masters when called upon to serve some higher good known only to Bach himself.

Bach's next position was identical in duties to his first, but now in the city of Mühlhausen. He remained there only briefly, but did distinguish his appointment by writing his first choral works for the Lutheran service. From 1708 to 1717 Bach was rewarded for his increasing virtuosity in playing the organ with a position as court organist to the Elector at Weimar. In this capacity, Bach perfected his craft in composing for the organ by making a serious study of Italian instrumental work. Vivaldi occupied his greatest attention, as Bach even recomposed Vivaldi concertos for the organ. After nine years in Weimar, Bach became weary of his duties and sought to leave. His employer, the Elector, was not legally obliged to let Bach depart. Bach wanted to leave so badly that he apparently offended his aristocratic employer, who made Bach spend one month in prison before letting him depart for employment elsewhere. This anecdotal evidence of Bach's extreme stubbornness again lends nuance and color to our view of him as the simple craftsman.

The Brandenburg Concertos

From Weimar, Bach moved to the very small city of Anhalt-Cöthen, where he served as court musician to a patron infatuated with music. From 1717 to 1723, Bach created some of his best-loved instrumental music. Our first selection by Bach [CD2 #1] in the recorded anthology dates from this period of his career. We can gain a glimpse of the quality of musicians Bach hired and worked with in Anhalt-Cöthen, through the fine concertos he wrote for them. The most celebrated of these concertos are the six Brandenburg Concertos. While they were surely written for use at the court of Anhalt-Cöthen, they are named for the margrave of Brandenburg, to whom Bach sent copies of all six concertos.

The Brandenburg Concerto No. 2 is represented in our anthology [CD2 #1]. This piece, unlike the Vivaldi concerto discussed earlier in this chapter, requires many solo instrumentalists, rather than just one. Therefore we call it a *concerto grosso* (large concerto). *Concerti grossi* divide the ensemble into solo and ripieno players. The soloists can change in number and instruments from *concerto grosso* to *concerto grosso*. This particular *concerto grosso* requires a solo oboe, recorder (an end-blown fipple flute), trumpet (actually a piccolo trumpet is used because of the very high register required for this piece), and violin. These four soloists are accompanied by the usual basso continuo group, plus a small string orchestra. The form of the piece is a *ritornello* form, very much like the one used by Vivaldi. The main differences are that the solo sections will have several different instruments featured, and the material in the solo sections sounds thematically related to the main theme of the *ritornello*.

In this concerto movement, Bach employs a very important motivic technique called "*Fortspinnung*" (forward spinning). The idea here is that the melody seems almost endless. Just as one instrument's melodic phrase is coming to an end, another instrument enters with a fresh melodic idea. The result is a seemingly breathless unfolding of melody that never allows the focus of the listener to stray. This idea of binding a piece together through not only the *ritornello* form (which presents the listener periodically with familiar material) but also through a seamless melody, distinguishes Bach's style from that of his contemporaries.

Johann Sebastian Bach, Brandenburg Concerto Number 2
[CD2, #1] *(Duration, 5 min. 2 sec.)*

First Movement: Allegro

0.00 Tutti—Recorder, Oboe, and Violin soloists double the orchestral strings playing the ritornello theme, while the solo trumpet reinforces the thematic eighth-note pulse and ends on an ornamental trill.

0.19 Solo Violin (with basso continuo group)
0.25 Tutti—first part of ritornello
0.31 Soloists—Oboe and Violin
0.35 Tutti—middle portion of ritornello
0.40 Soloists—Recorder and Oboe
0.46 Tutti—middle portion of ritornello
0.50 Soloists—Trumpet and Recorder
0.56 Tutti—last two thirds of ritornello with Trumpet ornamentations
1.11 Soloists—Trumpet and Violin play fast notes while Recorder and Oboe reinforce the eighth-note pulse.
1.16 Tutti—middle portion of ritornello with Trumpet trill
1.21 Soloists—Trumpet initiates an imitative dialogue with Oboe, while the Recorder and Violin play fast notes with orchestral strings (a chain suspension occurs)
1.34 Tutti—final portion of ritornello
1.38 Soloists—fragments of ritornello are freely passed from one instrument to another
1.50 Tutti—middle portion of ritornello
1.55 Soloists—imitative dialogue
2.00 Tutti—middle portion of ritornello

2.05   Soloists—imitative dialogue
2.20   Tutti—first two thirds of ritornello
2.30   Soloists – Recorder and Violin begin, Oboe and then Trumpet join in later
2.51   Tutti—large portion of ritornello, in new key
3.01   Soloists—imitative dialogue
3.14   Soloists—chain suspension
3.22   Tutti—last two thirds of ritornello
3.31   Soloists—imitative dialogue
4.15   Tutti—concluding portion of ritornello, ending with a cadence
4.19   Tutti—whole ritornello played with varied orchestration
4.29   Soloists—imitative dialogue
4.49   Final Tutti—concluding portion of ritornello, ending with a cadence

Bach in Leipzig

The last stop in Bach's career took him, in 1723, from tiny Anhalt-Cöthen to the huge city of Leipzig, where he became the music director to the city's two Lutheran cathedrals and the St. Thomas Choir College. His duties at the college required Bach to teach the boys who sang the soprano and alto parts in church. Because Bach's duties now centered on the Lutheran church, the craftsman Bach turned to composing mostly sacred music. The genres that occupied him most during this time were *cantatas* (multi-movement devotional works for voices and small orchestra for use in the Lutheran service) and settings of the gospels.

Given Bach's enormous reputation today, it's interesting that he was not Leipzig's first choice for his final position. The job was first offered to the fine composer, Georg Philipp Telemann (1681–1767). When Telemann refused to accept the position, it was then offered to Christoph Graupner (1683–1760), a composer who today has fallen into obscurity. Not only was Bach the third choice for the position in Leipzig, but the city fathers of Leipzig were aware of Bach's history of insubordination at Arnstadt and Weimar. The contract they drew up for him to sign reflects their anxiety about this quiet craftsman's willingness to defy authority. For example, recognizing Bach's past tendency to stray from his place of employment for overly long periods, the town council placed this clause in Bach's contract: "That I should not quit the town without leave from the burgomaster in office." At least now the town council would have fair warning were Bach to try and stray. Leipzig was home to a major university with a superb musical establishment. Recognizing that Bach was both studious and inclined to lose interest in his duties after a period of years, this clause was placed in his contract: "And [I shall] take no office under the University without the consent of their worships [the town council]." The contract contains many other pledges of loyalty and agreements to respond to the changing needs of his employers. While Bach benefited mightily from his time in Leipzig, this contract would at times become much more of a burden than a pleasure to him.

In our anthology of recorded music is an example of Bach's handling of text from the gospels, in this case the gospel according to Matthew [CD 2 #2]. Bach set the gospel writer Matthew's version of the final week of the life of Jesus and the aftermath of his resurrection for use at a Good Friday observance in 1727. The work is monumental in scope, requiring nearly three hours to perform. Our excerpt is very short indeed, a mere handful of minutes. The excerpt concerns the crucifixion of Jesus, the central event of Good Friday. The alto soloist sings in a style more akin to *arioso* than

Johann Sebastian Bach, "Ach Golgatha" from Saint Matthew Passion

[CD2, #2] *(Duration, 1 min. 35 sec.)*

TEXT, from "The Gospel According To Matthew"

Arioso

0.00	Ach Golgatha, unselges Golgatha!	Ah Golgatha, unhappy Golgatha!
0.12	Der Herr der Herrlichkeit	It was there that the lord of glory
0.18	muß schimpflich hier verderben,	was hideously rejected,
0.24	Der Segen und das Heil der Welt	The blessed savior of the world
0.32	Wird als ein Fluch und Kreuz gestellt.	Here hangs upon the accursed cross.
0.38	Der Schöpfer Himmels und der Erden	The creation of heaven and earth
0.48	Soll Erd und Luft entzogen werden.	On thee must perish from earth and air.
0.57	Die Unshuld muß hier shuldig sterben,	Innocent and guilty must die,
1.07	Das gehet meiner Seele nah;	How this agony effects my soul;
1.19	Ach Golgatha, unselges Golgatha!	Ah Golgatha, unhappy Golgatha!

Though the supporting instruments' (oboe, pizzicato cellos, and continuo) four-note theme changes slightly with each repetition, over the unvarying pulsation of the continuo, the single relentless motive serves to maintain the painful effects of the crucifixion expressed in the text. Without breaking the mood, Bach utilizes the alto voice to text-paint such words as "Himmel" (heaven) and "Luft" (air) with high notes, and "Erde" (earth) to a low note. He uses dissonance for the more agonizing images expressed by such words as "verderben" (perish), "Krent" (cross), and "sterben" (die). In spite of everything, this aria conclusively culminates on a major chord (consonance), reflecting a resolute, unquestioning or "resolved" Christian faith and optimistic response.

recitative, that is, fusion of the declamatory style of recitative with the more lyrical style of the aria. In Bach's time this part would have been sung by a skillful boy, but today often a woman takes the part. The alto is joined by an obligato part for double reed. The four-note theme played by the supporting instrument changes slightly with each repetition, allowing more dissonance for the more painful images in the text, but culminating on a sweet consonance. Bach ends this poignant passage about the martyrdom of Christ on a major chord, in order to emphasize the optimistic aspects of Christian theology. The four-note accompanimental theme also serves to maintain the ideal of affects; by having a single relentless motive the affect remains consistent throughout the excerpt. The text refers to Golgatha, the hill in Jerusalem on which Jesus died.

While Bach's settings of the gospels contain many such *arioso*-like passages, they also contain many arias, choruses in the manner of Handel, and clear examples of recitative. In this variety of material, they resemble both opera and oratorio. Unlike opera, they deal with sacred texts. Unlike oratorio they do not tell a single dramatic narrative.

Late in his life, Bach became increasingly disenchanted with his employers at Leipzig. He gradually cut back on his composition of sacred vocal music. His last works seem to reflect projects dear to him. In 1747 he began a project that he did not live to

Johann Sebastian Bach, Fugue, Contrapunctus III, from *The Art of the Fugue*

[CD2, #3] *(Duration, 2 min. 18 sec.)*

Four Part Fugue:

0.00   Subject is presented in tenor voice alone

0.08   Subject enters in alto, as tenor moves to a chromatic countersubject

0.15   Subject in soprano, alto moves to the countersubject
0.26   Subject in bass, countersubject in soprano
0.33   First episode
0.41   Subject, in soprano, is presented in varied form by use of passing tones and syncopation
0.47   Second episode
0.51   Subject in bass, varied form
0.58   Third episode
1.03   Subject in tenor, varied form
1.10   Fourth episode
1.17   Subject in soprano, original or unvaried form
1.24   Fifth episode
1.31   Subject, in bass (original), begins a series of subject entries that are not separated by episodes
1.53   Subject's final unvaried statement is in the tenor
1.59   Last six measures serve to bring the fugue to an end

For the readers of this book who possess the ability to interpret musical notation, or for those who have developed fairly advanced listening skills, you will observe that the **subject**, in the exposition, is first presented in the **tonic** or home key of **d minor**. The next **subject** entrance (in the alto voice) is in the **dominant**, or five scale-degrees higher. As a result, the second entrance is called the **answer**, a term that designates "statement and response." The third and fourth entrances in the exposition continue to alternate—tonic, then dominant. Though the fugue is based on a single principal theme, the harmonic polarity between tonic and dominant established from the beginning reflects a Baroque fondness for contrast and the dramatic.

finish, a series of fugues of graduated complexity called ***The Art of the Fugue.*** He wanted to leave this piece as a monument to posterity on the craft of writing in this form. By 1747, new currents were stirring in Europe, currents that would render Bach old fashioned. Those currents are the topic of the next chapter. For the purposes of this chapter, we need only mention that the fugue, as a form, had fallen on hard times before Bach died. Fearing that the subtleties and values of this form might be lost, Bach hoped ***The Art of the Fugue*** would illustrate its worth to future generations. Imagining that the piece would mainly serve purposes of study rather than performance, Bach did not designate what instruments should play the fugues found in his collection. Included in our recorded anthology is the third fugue from this collection. [CD 2 #3]. For a detailed description of the fugue as a form, see Chapter Five.

As mentioned above, J.S. Bach outlived the style in which he composed. New currents in musical taste emerged during the 1720s, first in Italy and eventually throughout the continent. Bach's music fell into disuse, although a few keyboard works would remain in publication. The nineteenth century would reclaim Bach as a major figure. That story is not a matter for the next chapter, but for the one after that.

The Bach name did not decline with the death of J.S. Bach, however. Bach had a large family, and his sons carried on the family's tradition of professional music making. Most notable among his sons was Carl Philipp Emanual Bach, who served the King of Prussia and took his place as a most interesting innovator in the history of composition. C.P.E. Bach's impassioned playing at the keyboard is seen as a harbinger of musical romanticism. Johann Christian Bach also became quite famous. He composed concertos for his patrons in London and became an important innovator in that field. The accomplishments of the sons reflect back on the influence of the father. J.S. Bach provided brilliant examples of the potential of baroque music.

Some Questions for Discussion

1 Humanism is a concept most closely linked with music of the Renaissance. Is there anything humanistic about any of the music discussed in this chapter? Can we really single out one particular period in the history of a human endeavor as humanistic?

2 Changes in economic organization led to changes in musical practice during the baroque period. How would you describe the modern economic situation and how might you use it to explain changes in the way musicians make their livings today? Do you know any musicians? Perhaps you could ask them about how they make a living. Is our current economic situation ideal for artists? Does it have an impact on the way art is made?

3 French opera doesn't sound like Italian opera during the Baroque period. Can you think of any examples of national differences in seemingly similar kinds of music today? Do nations still have distinct ways of making music? If so, why do you think that is? If not, what is different about today compared to the time of Lully or Handel? Do nations matter in the same way today that they did then? Do they mean the same things? What role does music play in the manufacturing of our modern sense of nations?

4 The Doctrine of Affections calls for composers to try and move the emotions of their audience. When you hear sad music, do you actually become sad? Or do you remember what it might be like to be sad? Or do you find yourself admiring the power of the music to sound sad without becoming at all sad yourself? This baroque idea that music moves the emotions seems a natural one, but as students of music and society, we might benefit from analyzing how music actually affects our emotions.

CHAPTER | **10**

The Classical Period (1750-1825)

*A*s mentioned previously, the Baroque period declined extremely gradually. This situation was no doubt facilitated by the period's amorphous nature, which saw many styles and musical priorities in simultaneous play. The next period covered in this book, the Classical period, was comparatively homogenous. By looking at one of the earliest examples of music born of what might be understood as the classical sensibility, we might see the font from which many of the prevailing stylistic ideals flowed.

THE RISE OF THE GALLANT STYLE

Naples, Italy had long been one of the most important centers of activity in the field of opera. During the 1720s, a young composer emerged in Naples who captured the imagination the many Europeans of his generation. Today, this composer's name is not widely known, but in his time, the name of Giovanni Battista Pergolesi was uttered with respect from Naples to London, and even in the center of opposition to Italian opera, Paris.

Giovanni Battista Pergolesi

Giovanni Battista Pergolesi (1710–1736) lived an extremely brief life. Though he died at age 26, he lived long enough to energize tremendously important changes in Italian opera. When Pergolesi began composing, Neapolitan opera (opera originating in Naples) had become an important part of the life of the city. Citizens of all classes attended one of Naples' seven public opera houses almost every night during the early autumn and the period between Christmas and Lent (roughly January and most of February). These were the high seasons for opera. The opera houses of Naples were the center not only of the people's entertainment, but their entire social lives.

The style of Neapolitan opera centered on a strict format of recitative passages (in which the action of the opera advances) and periods of reflection upon the action, called *arias*. The arias constituted the most important part of the opera for enthusiasts of the genre. Like the aria from Handel's *Rinaldo*, discussed in the previous chapter, Neapolitan arias were usually in an ABA, or *da capo*, form. The repeat of the "A" material afforded the singer an opportunity to improvise new, spectacular ornaments. The recitative sections were accompanied most often by basso continuo instruments only. However, when particularly important or dramatic action unfolded during the recitative, composers used the whole orchestra. These were called "accompanied recitatives," an odd name considering that all recitatives are accompanied.

Just as the format of the opera was strictly conceived around alternating recitatives and arias, so the dramas were also increasingly formulaic. The playwrights Apostolo Zeno and his student Metastasio were the main architects of the format for operatic dramas. Their work received so much praise for its elevated language and superb use of simile and metaphor that audiences objected when the texts of lesser authors were used. Moreover, the plays of Zeno and Metastasio presented composers with ready-made *libretti* (the plural of *libretto*, meaning the text of an opera) as their characters were forever excusing themselves from the action to utter soliloquies reflecting on the previous action.

Essentially, Metastasio wrote semi-historical love stories. Invariably the action revolved around a pair of lovers who were, due to circumstances beyond their control, parted from one another. Often tyrannical fathers served as the impediment to the lovers' happy union. In other instances nature interfered, such as when storms at sea would cause one or the other lover to be shipwrecked for some period. Villains might abduct one or the other lover for variety, although this happens only rarely. The plays of this period reinforce the idea that human beings are incapable of accomplishing anything without divine intervention, thus the happy endings usually happen without the lovers doing much beyond remaining faithful to one another. A mythological deity, an unexpected benefactor, a benevolent monarch, or sometimes a piece of dumb luck would see the lovers into one another's arms. In this way, the plays of Baroque opera differ radically from the humanistic ideals of the Renaissance, where human merit counted for so much. In addition to the tale of the lovers, Metastasian dramas presented each member of the couple with a sidekick, most often a servant. The servants were usually in love too, thus providing a comic mirroring of the main couple. Thus an evening at the opera around 1720 provided audiences with some drama and some comedy. This mishmash of entertainments did not necessarily please everyone.

Intermezzos

Pergolesi's first innovation boils down to his objecting to the presence of comic characters amidst the serious stories. He felt they distracted from the action. He also felt that they weren't really all that funny. Most good comedy is set in contemporary times and concern relevant situations. The dramas for operas avoided contemporary situations in order not to look like they might be criticizing any living person in power. To solve the problem of comic characters distracting the audience from the action, and solving the difficulty of finding real humor amid antiquated sidekicks, Pergolesi began writing *intermezzos*. These were short operas intended for performance between the acts of the main opera. By jettisoning the comic characters, the effect of the serious opera wasn't shattered by comic intrusions. Moreover, by giving the comic characters their own short show, Pergolesi could take advantage of the inherently funnier possibilities of contemporary settings.

The music Pergolesi wrote for his intermezzos never strove for the lofty heights of his serious operas. He wanted his intermezzos to be performed by good comedians rather than great singers. Toward this end, he adopted a tuneful and simple musical style in the arias of his intermezzos. Little did he know, those tuneful and simple arias would give rise to a new style of music.

La serva padrona

In our recorded anthologies is an aria from Pergolesi's most celebrated intermezzo, *La serva padrona* (the servant girl as mistress) of 1733, called "A Serpina, penserete." [CD2 #4] Before turning to this aria alone, let's summarize the plot of the opera. There are only three characters. Such a small cast is typical of intermezzos. All the characters are drawn from the commedia dell'arte, an Italian type of improvised street theater based on stock characters. Commedia dell'arte featured a large body of stock characters who by their dress and manners conjured instant associations in audiences. These well-known characters include Pulcinello, the lovelorn clown; Arlecchino, a mischievous character; and Dr. Uberto, a pompous and stupid man with lots of money and an eye for young girls. The closest thing to commedia dell'arte we have today in this country are the stock characters of *Saturday Night Live*. The moment audiences see Marty Culp and Bobbi Moughan-Culp (the middle school music teachers), Gemini's Twin, the grotesque Mr. Peepers, or Mango; they can instantly tap into prior knowledge about those characters, thus saving the actor a lengthy process of introduction. Stock characters remain vital to contemporary comedy, from Pergolesi's time through today. In *La serva padrona*, Pergolesi calls on three stock characters: Dr. Uberto, a mute clown named Vespone, and Serpina (a sneaky and quick-witted servant girl). The plot finds Dr. Uberto enjoying the service of both Vespone and Serpina. He is rich and stupid, yet Serpina would like to marry him in order to get at his money. All indications suggest that Dr. Uberto will never marry so far beneath his station in life. Serpina conspires to win Dr. Uberto through a trick. She invents a fictional suitor for herself, a Bulgarian captain. The sneaky Serpina tells Dr. Uberto that, since the doctor does not find her attractive, she must reluctantly leave his service to marry the Bulgarian. Dr. Uberto is heartbroken at losing so pretty a girl from his company, and proposes marriage to her at last. This extraordinarily simple plot line doesn't hint at the real pleasures of the opera. The actors would have to carry the day, hamming up their roles and acting perfectly ridiculous.

The aria in our recorded anthology shows Serpina hatching her plot. Unlike so many arias in serious operas, this one advances the action by showing the audience Serpina's manipulation of the stupid doctor. There are two contrasting kinds of music in this aria. The first, or "A" section, finds Serpina pretending to be heartbroken at having to leave the service of Dr. Uberto. Pergolesi's orchestra affords the singer a chance for broad comic acting, as loud musical sniffles in the violins punctuate the section. Pergolesi achieves these sniffles by having the violins play the same note over and over at the end of phrases. You can hear two of them in the first few bars of the orchestral introduction. The second, or "B," section is in a quicker tempo. Here Serpina addresses the audience only in an aside. She describes her sense that her plan to make Dr. Uberto jealous of her fictitious Bulgarian captain is working. Throughout the aria, the A and B sections alternate lending the entire movement a form of ABABA followed by a *da capo* sign resulting in a repeat of both A and B sections one last time. *Da capo* literally means "to the head" in Italian. It instructs performers to return to the beginning of a piece and play it again until instructed by the mark "fine," meaning "end," to stop.

More interesting than this rather conventional da capo structure is the melodic style of the aria. Inventing a pleasingly simple melodic style was Pergolesi's greatest innovation. The opening phrase is made up of two tiny melodic figures. The last of these is repeated, lending the phrase a pleasing ABB structure. The notes of this melody are mostly related by step. Here is the simple melody that opens the aria.

A Ser - pi - na   pen - se - re - te,   pen - se - re - te,   qual-che

FIGURE 10.1

Notice that most of the melody moves by step in a simple scalar fashion. Only the jump from F to B flat constitutes an intervalic leap, that is, a move greater than a step. Stepwise motion is very easy to sing, just like singing a scale. The simplicity of this tune is also enforced by the narrow range. The entire melodic phrase is contained within the interval of the perfect fifth. Again, singers in intermezzos were chosen for being good comic actors first and good singers second. Pergolesi's style accommodates that situation.

Listening Guide

Giovanni Battista Pergolesi, La Serva Padrona
[CD2, #4] *(Duration, 5 min. 30 sec.)*

0.00 **Orchestral Introduction**—Loud musical sniffles in the violins punctuate the section.

FIRST "A" SECTION

0.17 A Serpina penserete, penserete
0.27 qualche volta e qualche di,
0.33 e direte, e direte:
0.40 ah! poverina, ah! poverina,
0.49 cara, cara untempo, untempo
1.00 ella mi fu, ella mi fu.

FIRST "B" SECTION

1.07 (Ei mi par che già pian piano
1.10 s'incomincia a intenerir,
1.14 s'incomincia, si, già pian piano, si
1.17 s'incomincia a intenerir.)

REPEAT FIRST "A" AND "B" SECTIONS

1.25 (FIRST "A" SECTION)
2.09 (FIRST "B" SECTION)

LAST "A" SECTION

2.29 S'io poi fui impertinente,
2.35 impertinente
2.40 mi perdoni, mi perdoni;

(to Dr. Uberto)

Ah, Serpina, you will remember, you will remember
now and then, now and then,
and you will say, and you will say:
Ah! Poor girl, Ah! Poor girl,
so dear, so dear at one time, at one time
she was to me, she was to me.

(to the audience)

(He now seems to be a little less puffed up
out of sorts, so I'll keep it up,
out of sorts, yes, and less puffed up, yes
out of sorts, so I'll keep it up.)

(to Dr. Uberto)

If at times I was impertinent,
impertinent
forgive me, forgive me;

2.46   malamente mi guidai,   Sadly that's my nature,
2.54   lo vedo sì, lo vedo sì.   I was wrong, yes, I was wrong.

DA CAPO SIGN—Instructs the performers to return to the beginning and play it again until instructed
           by the mark *fine*, meaning "end," to stop.
3.16   REPEAT Orchestral Introduction
3.34   REPEAT FIRST "A" SECTION
4.24   REPEAT FIRST "B" SECTION (The "repeat" sign at the end of this section, once again directs the
           performers to return to the first "A" Section.)
4.43 REPEAT FIRST "A" SECTION

Pergolesi's humble little intermezzo captured the imagination of music lovers. His simple style, built around the needs of amateur singers, became the rage. People found his style unpretentious and extremely innovative. That it also accommodated comic performances from his actors only added to the luster of his ideas. His popularity grew so tremendous that when he died suddenly in the prime of his life, theater owners and publishers bribed newspapers not to print obituaries for him. Composition students from the Naples Conservatory were hired to write music under the name of Pergolesi and in his style in order to perpetuate the idea that he was alive and composing. Soon, traveling troops of singer/actors were performing *La serva padrona* throughout Europe.

These troops eventually reached Paris in 1752, a city that had always despised Italian opera. Much of the French public was swept up by the charms of Pergolesi's simple style. This style came to be known as the "gallant style." Gallantry seems the perfect concept to apply to Pergolesi, for gallantry sets aside its own needs in order to accommodate the needs of another. A gallant person opens the door for someone else, is never overly competitive, and certainly doesn't burden others with complaints. The dramatic style of the Baroque period, like Dr. Uberto, is puffed up with its own pathos and emotion. The gallant style is detached and anxious to please. The Baroque style looks inward to the emotions; the gallant style looks outward to society.

THE ENLIGHTENMENT

Among the legion of admirers for Pergolesi's style was the French philosopher Jean-Jacques Rousseau. Pergolesi's style so inspired this enlightenment era philosopher that Rousseau took up pen and paper and composed an opera of his own, *Le Devin du village* (The Village Fortuneteller). No one should be surprised that Rousseau composed his little opera in 1752, the same year he heard *La serva padrona*. Rousseau not only favored the gallant style in his own compositions, but he also railed in pamphlets and in his philosophical writing against all music that failed to conform to its contours.

Rousseau's philosophical grounds for favoring the pleasing and simple style of Pergolesi boil down to two contentions. First, music should be natural. In order to be natural, music must embrace the dictates of nature and favor an easy singability. The human voice being natural, music should sound well when sung. Second, music is the product of genius, but genius only triumphs when it submits itself to the norms of taste. For Rousseau, taste was not a matter of personal opinion. Instead, taste existed as the common property of all persons of wisdom and breeding. Today, we often find that appeals to the concept of taste are designed to end discussions about art. You may have witnessed or even participated in a dialogue about art that ran more or less this way:

FIGURE 10.2 | *Jean-Jacques Rousseau (1712–1778)*, philosopher. In his *Dictionary of Music* (1767), Rousseau defined "taste" as follows "Genius creates, but taste selects: and a too abundant genius is often in want of a severe censor to prevent it from abusing its valuable riches. One can do great things without taste, but it is taste that makes them interesting." In defining "composers" Rousseau gives this clear endorsement of the role of nature in forming music: "Whatever efforts we may make, whatever acquisitions we may have, we must still be born to the art [of composition], otherwise our works can never mount above the insipid. It is with the composer as it is with the poet. Nature herself must have formed him so." Such endorsements of taste and nature typify Enlightenment writing on music. (Translations of Rousseau from *Music in the Western World: A History in Documents,* Piero Weiss and Richard Taruskin, editors.) (© Archivo Iconografico, S.A./Corbis)

FIRST STUDENT
I really liked Handel's *Rinaldo*. The composer captured the affect perfectly.

SECOND STUDENT
Gee, I hated it. It was boring, just like most of the music discussed in this book.

FIRST STUDENT
Maybe boring isn't a property of the piece, but a property of you. A property which you project onto everything you contact.

SECOND STUDENT
Hey, lay off me, man. When I tell you I think Handel's *Rinaldo* is boring, it's just a matter of a taste. Go ahead and like it if you want, you can't argue about such things. It's personal.

FIRST STUDENT
You're right. I guess that ends this dialogue.

Okay, maybe you haven't witnessed exactly this dialogue, but one like it. Substitute a contemporary film for Handel's *Rinaldo* and adjust the argument accordingly then maybe the whole thing will look a little more familiar. The important point is this, today discussions of taste are almost seen as impolite and certainly fruitless. Everyone has his or her own taste and everyone should "lay off" before attacking the taste of others.

Eighteenth-Century Taste

In Rousseau's day, the previous dialogue (or one like it) would never have happened. People certainly disagreed about what they liked or didn't like, but not nearly so much as they do today. More importantly, taste was not something to which everyone was equally entitled. Taste was shared throughout the community and existed independent of what individuals thought about it one way or another. The secret to having good taste was not a matter of going off by oneself and searching one's feelings for an answer about the relative value of an artwork. Instead, the individual looked to others for guidance, especially those with a fine education or high standing within the society.

Getting back to Rousseau's two points, we see that naturalness and genius tempered by taste provided the philosophical underpinnings for a rational claim for the superiority of one musical creation to another. To Rousseau's generation, the music of J.S. Bach, discussed in the previous chapter, was needlessly complex and therefore unnatural. It failed to meet Rousseau's standard. Moreover, it had fallen out of favor with well-educated and influential people, therefore it could not be said to have been tempered by taste. No one argued that J.S. Bach wasn't a genius, only that his genius was too much in the service of his personal, and by then old-fashioned, ideas about good music. Now you can understand why the word "baroque," meaning misshapen and unnatural, came to be applied to so much wonderful music created between 1600 and 1750. It was a term of derision invented by people who shared Rousseau's view.

Classicism and the Gallant Style

By contrast to the pejorative term "Baroque," the music of Rousseau's time came to be called *classical*. This term by definition implies a model of excellence to be emulated. Curiously, the term "classical" would not be used to describe music until the middle of the 1800s and then for unexpected reasons. In Rousseau's own time, the term *gallant style* prevailed as a descriptor for music of the late 1700s.

Philosophical appeals to naturalness came to be the watchword of the late eighteenth century. Taken together, such appeals have come to be associated with Enlightenment. The project of Enlightenment in the West (Asian cultures have very different notions about this important term) is configured around the questioning of powerful institutions (such as the church and the monarchy) on natural grounds. For example, the Enlightenment philosophers such as Rousseau saw man as possessing natural rights.

Figure 10.3 | ***Thomas Jefferson, Monticello, Charlottesville, Virginia (1770–1800).*** The simplicity, grace, and rational formal plan seen in Thomas Jefferson's home, Monticello, reflect analogous classical attitudes of the ancient Greeks. Note the similarity between this classical home and the formal symmetry and grace of the Parthenon in Athens (Figure 6.4). Equally striking is the similar concern in the classical imagination for symmetry and grace in music. (© David Muench/Corbis)

The American Declaration of Independence articulates these rights as "life, liberty, and the pursuit of happiness." Thomas Jefferson, the author of the Declaration of Independence, was a great admirer of Jean-Jacques Rousseau and the Enlightenment.

The articulation of natural rights flew in the face of monarchical systems built on the idea of divine privilege. The late eighteenth century saw two important revolutions topple monarchical authority, first in America, where colonists escaped the rule of King George III of England, and later, when the rabble in Paris led by Enlightenment intellectuals shattered the once unquestioned power of the French monarchy. The church came under similar attack, as a general skepticism attracted a large percentage of the educated classes in Western Europe. For some of those who remained adherents of Christianity, they imagined the Christian god as a benign watchmaker who put the world in motion and then left it to run on its own. This image of the divine suited Enlightenment era believers, and struck them as far more natural than previous conceptions of God.

The Enlightenment's impact on music was enormous. From the transformation of the social role of music to the rationale for making it, everything was touched by the ideas of the age. Up to this point in the book, most all of the composers we have discussed worked either for the princes of the church or of the state. Only Pergolesi worked largely independently from one of those institutions, because he could compose operas for the public. Even the opera specialist Handel depended at times on the support of the British monarchy. By the end of this chapter, we will see this rigid relationship between the composer and the powerful personages of his or her time broken, as artists begin to serve themselves to the extent they can. The consequences of the Enlightenment for music in particular, and culture in general, are still playing out in the West, and we will examine them again and again in subsequent chapters.

FIGURE 10.4 | *Christoph Willibald Gluck* (1714–1787)
(© Austrian Archives/Corbis)

OPERA REFORM

One of the most interesting applications of the ideals of naturalness in music was Gluck's opera reform. During the 1760s, Christoph Willibald Gluck (1714–1787) sought to transform opera, the most popular genre of music in Europe by far. His transformations were both dramatic—and here he enjoyed the able support of librettist Raniero de Calzabigi (1714–1795)—and musical. Their project marks an important difference between Baroque opera and classical opera. While the operas of Naples described earlier in this chapter privileged formulaic plots, Gluck and Calzibigi hoped to create operas in which the structure of the opera was determined by the needs of the drama. In this regard their efforts resemble the ideals of the Renaissance, when Monteverdi declared poetry the mistress of the music. Indeed for their first reform opera, Gluck and Calzabigi returned to those bygone days when opera was born out of humanist ideals; they took the story of Orfeo and his poor wife Euridice as their topic. That story has inspired so many composers in the early days of opera.

By returning to their pet theme, Gluck and Calzabigi align themselves with the initial intentions of opera and reject opera's more recent history.

The scene in our recorded anthology presents the moment in act two of *Orfeo ed Euridice* (1762) when the grief-stricken Orpheus attempts to enter Hades, the realm of the dead. [CD2 #5] For a full account of the plot of Orpheus, see pages 117–118 of the previous chapter. The structure of the scene is a mixture of diverse types of music, rather than a succession of recitatives and arias.

Listening Guide

Christoph Willibald Gluck, Orfeo ed Euridice, Act II (1762)
[CD2, #5] *(Duration, 11 min. 03 sec.)*

	ACTION	GLUCK'S MUSICAL TREATMENT	TEXT	TRANSLATION
0.00	A group of Fire Demons guard the gates of Hades.	No singing; instead, the Fire Demons dance a ballet.		
1.05	Early on, Orpheus appears and hides as he watches the demons and summons his courage.	When Orpheus is first seen, we hear a harp. According to legend, Orpheus played the lyre, a harp-like instrument.		
			(CHORUS OF FIRE DEMONS)	
1.15	The Fire Demons sing a warning about their miserable realm.	The chorus presents a rhythmically insistent tune.	Chi mai dell'Erebros Fralle caligini Sull'orme d'Ercelo E di Piritoo Conduce il pi`e?	Who from Erebros through the smokes in the shadow of Hercules and of Peirithous would conduct himself on foot?
1.32	The Fire Demons dance furiously.	A lively, fast-paced music in the orchestra only supports their ballet.		
2.09	The Fire Demons sing on about Hades. The text mentions Cerberus, the three-headed dog who helps guard the gates of Hades.	Each time Cerberus is mentioned, three loud, bark-like chords are played in the orchestra. The insistent choral material is built on the same rhythm as before.	D'orror l'ingombrino Le fiere Euminidi, E lo spavention Gli urli di Cerbero, Se un dio non `e.	Horror would block him by the fiery Eumenides, and he would be frightened by the barks of Cerberus, unless he were a god

ACTION	GLUCK'S MUSICAL TREATMENT	TEXT	TRANSLATION
3.17 The Fire Demons resume dancing.	A short, gloomy instrumental section unfolds.		
		(ORPHEUS)	
4.23 Orpheus addresses the Fire Demons and begs them to take pity on him so that he might enter the forbidden realm of Hades.	The harp plays a gallant accompaniment as Orpheus (a castrato) sings a pleasing melody made up of short, natural phrases.	Deh, placatevi con me, Furie, Larve, Ombre sdegnose!	Please, be gentle with me, Furies, Spirits, scornful Shades!
		(CHORUS OF FIRE DEMONS)	
4.40 Throughout the above, the Fire Demons refuse.	The chorus sings "no" periodically.	No! No!	No! No!
		(ORPHEUS)	
4.48 Orpheus' magic power to move through music wins out. The Fire Demons gradually give in.	The above continues, but slowly the chorus gets quieter before their cries of "no" become hesitant.	Vi renda almen pietose Il imo barbaro dolor!	May it render you full of pity my wild sadness!

In this scene, we see a classic reform approach to operatic structure. The Italian ideal of arias as moments of reflection gives way to the more natural notion that arias advance the action. There is no *da capo* structure for this scene as Gluck felt that nature does not allow for such repetitive structures in a dramatic work. The French ideal of using ballet and other diversions in *tragèdie-lyrique* sees such pleasures serve the plot rather than serving themselves as interruptions to the story. Ballet material only happens in places when an opportunity to introduce dancing into the opera occurs as the result of the plot. The chorus lends a pleasing variety to the musical forces available to Gluck. That the chorus sings during Orpheus' aria represents a supreme triumph of the natural needs of the drama over formulaic approaches to opera. Finally, the orchestra is pivotal to the scene, as it takes on the voice of Cerberus (a fierce, three-headed dog that guards the entrance to Hades), paints the gloomy scene, and provides the harp of Orpheus. Opera orchestras in all the earlier scenes we have studied have nowhere near so vital a role as they play in this reform opera.

Gluck's approach, favoring dramatic unity over operatic formula, would never catch on completely. Formulaic serious operas were simply too popular to fall completely out of favor. However, he did manage to persuade many people in his own time and among subsequent generations to look for ways to increase the realism and naturalness of opera. His efforts mark one of the clearest applications of reason, a hallmark of Enlightenment philosophy, to the art of music.

THE RISE OF THE SYMPHONY

One of the most important developments in the history of Western instrumental music was the emergence of the symphony. The symphony is a genre usually exemplifying the following characteristics: instruments only, multi-movements, lofty musical ambitions, and an abstract subject matter. There are many exceptions to all of the characteristics just mentioned. Sometimes composers use singers in symphonies; Beethoven, Mendelssohn, and Mahler all did at times. Some symphonies are in a single long movement. The Finnish composer Jean Sibelius wrote one. Some symphonies are intentionally trivial rather than ambitious—Mozart's father, Leopold wrote a "toy" symphony requiring the use of all manner of toy instruments—while still others use concrete story lines rather than an abstract subject. In the next chapter, we'll see Hector Berlioz telling a story through purely instrumental sound in a symphony. Despite all these exceptions, the symphony still basically exemplifies the characteristics listed above.

Franz Joseph Haydn (1732–1809) is traditionally called "the father of the symphony." Such titles aren't particularly interesting, and this one also happens to be false, if fatherhood entitles one to the claim of being first. The earliest symphonies were written by Italian composers as overtures for their operas. An *overture* is a piece of instrumental music that comes before a dramatic work such as an opera. Italian opera audiences were noisy, with so many people arriving happy to see one another. Modern standards of concert etiquette requiring the audience to be both sober and silent were unknown before the nineteenth century. If a composer wanted the beginning of his opera to be heard, he learned that an overture gave the audience fair warning that the opera was about to start. To help ensure this function of the overture, composers typically began overtures with several loud chords called *hammerstrokes*. Composers such as Nicolò Jomelli (1714–1774) began writing multi-movement overtures to their operas in order to provide first a loud and fast movement, then a slow and quiet one, and finally a spirited and fast one. This formula gave even the most boisterous crowd ample time to settle into the evening's entertainment.

Giovanni Sammartini and Johann Wenzel Stamitz

In the important Italian city of Milan, the composer Giovanni Sammartini (1700–1775) began organizing performances of symphonies by themselves; thus, works once meant to introduce operas became a separate, independent musical genre. This practice of performing only symphonies was an especially good idea during Lent and Advent, periods of the church calendar leading into important feasts, when opera was banned. Sammartini oversaw what was known as an *academia* of enthusiasts for instrumental music. Many members of the *academia*, or music-loving society, were members of the nobility. In time, the Milanese taste for symphonic performances independent of opera spilled into the parts of the year when opera wasn't banned. Moreover, Sammartini began writing symphonies meant to stand alone, and not as overtures to operas. Thus the symphony was born, and if one must identify a father of the symphony, probably best to choose Sammartini.

Sammartini's symphonies were generally quite short, and usually included only string instruments. The composer probably most closely associated with the rise of the symphony into an important international genre was Johann Wenzel Stamitz (1717–1757). Stamitz played violin in the court orchestra at Mannheim, where he eventually took up leadership of the orchestra. The Elector at Mannheim was Duke Karl Theodore, who wanted to establish within his lands an enlightened monarchy. Toward that purpose he built institutes for the study of language and science, along with a fine salon for the performance of symphonies. The middle-class merchants of the town were allowed to visit the salon and admire not only the Duke's orchestra, but the Duke and his aristocratic guests as well. Generally the aristocrats played whist, a forerunner to the modern card game bridge, while the middle-class visitors stood behind velveteen ropes. The orchestra would have been located in a corner, never on a stage. Eyewitness accounts of visitors to symphony concerts at Mannheim are far more apt to mention the Duke and his guests rather than the orchestra.

One visitor who did much more than mention the orchestra was the independently wealthy Englishman, Charles Burney. Burney was more interested in music than observing the habits of aristocrats as they played cards. He published two volumes chronicling his musical travels through Europe. On one occasion he remarked that the Mannheim orchestra was like "an army of generals. Each player as suited to managing an entire campaign as to fight one." He marveled at the discipline of the group and the superb compositional craft of Stamitz. Stamitz' fame as an organizer of instrumental performance grew so great that during Lent each year, Stamitz took some of the best players with him to Paris to present public concerts in that city. In doing so he inspired French musicians to achieve still greater heights of discipline and craft.

The success of Sammartini and Stamitz lies in their ability to persuade subsequent generations to nurture the symphony as a genre. Their hard work has inspired generations of musicians, so much so that the symphony is still with us today.

FRANZ JOSEPH HAYDN

Franz Joseph Haydn did much more than compose symphonies, although if that's all he had done it might have been enough to solidify his fame for centuries to come. Haydn composed more than 110 symphonies during his long life. He also composed in all the other important genres of his age: concertos, operas, masses, oratorios, keyboard sonatas, and more. He invented the genre of the string quartet. He also found time to compose more than one hundred pieces for a now defunct string instrument called the "baryton." That was the favorite instrument of his most important employer, the Prince Nicholas Esterházy.

Haydn's prolific output cannot merely be attributed to his long life. He was the consummate Enlightenment era composer. He had a function in society: to make music for the important occasions in the life of his employer the prince. He had a keen knowledge of the taste of his day, and was abundantly capable of employing the prevailing styles to the edification of the society around him. That may not sound like high praise, but it should. Along the way he also managed to introduce innovations (such as inventing entire genres of music) and increase the sum of human pleasure. By the end of his illustrious career, he established himself as an independent musician no longer beholden to the wishes of an employer. The social importance of this last accomplishment cannot be overstated.

Haydn's early days are not well documented. He came from humble origins. We do know that he was educated at the St. Stephen's Choir School in Vienna, a school much like the one J.S. Bach taught at in Leipzig earlier in the century. At the school, Haydn first learned to sing in the church choir. After his voice changed during adolescence, he learned to play musical instruments in order to serve in the church's orchestra. After reaching a certain age, he was dismissed from the student orchestra. He made his living playing string instruments in various orchestras in Vienna. After a brief stint in the service of a Hungarian count named von Morzin, Haydn joined the service of Prince Paul Anton Esterházy.

Prince Esterházy was one of the wealthiest men in the Austro-Hungarian Empire. The empire had its capital in Vienna. The emperor, or in the case of much the eighteenth century, the empress did not have reliable nor total authority over the empire. The individual aristocrats reserved considerable independence. The Esterházy family had huge land holdings in what is now Hungary. The revenues from the farms, mines, and harvesting of other natural resources made the Esterházy family extremely wealthy and influential.

Prince Paul Anton Esterházy did not enjoy the services of Haydn for long. His death in 1762, one year after Haydn joined the Esterházy's service, resulted in his brother Nicholas' ascendancy to the position of prince. From 1762 until 1766, the prince spent much of his time in Vienna while a new country house was being built. When it was completed in 1766, the Esterházys, along with Haydn, moved into the country house called Esterháza. The house was a small version of the palace at Versailles pictured in the previous chapter. Like Versailles, Esterháza contained an opera house and a large salon for music making. Prince Nicholas Esterházy was a tremendous devotee of music. The two men would be in almost daily contact, as Haydn was expected to wait each morning to receive instructions from

FIGURE 10.5 | *Franz Joseph Haydn (1732–1809).* (© Gianni Dagli Orti/Corbis)

the prince concerning his musical requirements for the day. The prince played the baryton, mentioned above. He expected Haydn to write pieces for Haydn and the prince to play together. The prince often expected musical entertainment after dinner, especially when many of the nearly 100 guestrooms at Esterháza were occupied

Haydn's Service at Esterháza

When he first entered the service of the Esterházys, Haydn found that the family had only a small number of musicians in their employ. Year by year, Haydn persuaded the prince to hire more musicians. Eventually there was a small orchestra, which could be expanded on special occasions by drawing upon the other servants who could play instruments. Haydn's symphonies were not written for an orchestra made up entirely of professionals. Instead Haydn depended on various huntsmen and grooms to play brass instruments, while the other members of the orchestra might also serve as valets, footmen, and servants of every description. Haydn instructed the less skillful in how to play their instruments better.

In addition to after-dinner concerts, the prince also liked to use the household's opera stage from time to time. Haydn composed nearly forty operas for use in Esterháza. Professional singers were employed, and Haydn was expected to keep them in good voice through coaching.

Haydn was an extremely busy man during his years at Esterháza. In any given week, he might organize three chamber music gatherings with the prince, three evening concerts, a special mass for Sunday, and an opera. The prince much preferred to hear new music rather than old, thus compounding Haydn's burden. He had to do much composing while preparing performances.

Haydn's contract finds him serving much like a trusted personal servant to the prince. He had certain authority over the discipline and training of the other musicians. He received certain privileges, for example, he was allowed to eat at a table with the most trusted servants: the head butler and cook, the chief huntsman, the manager of the estate's large sheep ranch, the personal valet to the prince, and so forth. Haydn could also travel with the household to Vienna whenever the prince elected to take up residence in the capital. Haydn relished his time in Vienna as the prince did very little entertaining there, thus lessening Haydn's duties considerably. Haydn had free time to meet with friends. Among his Viennese friends was Wolfgang Amadeus Mozart after 1780. Together with two other friends, Haydn and Mozart played together in a string quartet from 1780 until roughly 1790.

The principal disadvantage of the contract between Haydn and Esterházy was the fact that the prince owned all of Haydn's compositions. Haydn could not seek publication, or benefit financially in any way from his mounting international popularity. Of lesser impact but still stifling at times for Haydn was the fact that the contract would not allow him to travel on his own without the prince's permission, and permission almost never came. Haydn was stuck in a relatively remote part of the empire for most of the year. Sometimes his diaries and letters reveal that he ached to visit Vienna with its lively musical scene. Unfortunately, he could only go when the prince went, which wasn't nearly often enough to suit Haydn.

Haydn's Symphony No. 56

In our recorded anthology there is a relatively obscure but quite interesting example of Haydn's music, the first movement of the Symphony No. 56. [CD2 #6] This piece was composed at Esterháza for the purposes of entertaining the prince and large number of guests during hunting season. Every autumn, the prince staged many hunts for the sporting pleasure of his friends and fellow aristocrats. After the hunt, an outdoor banquet was served, weather permitting. Then the orchestra would assemble in the out-of-doors to entertain with a symphony. Haydn composed several symphonies for such occasions. As befits a piece written for the out-of-doors, this symphony requires several brass instruments as well as double reed instruments. These instruments are joined by the usual body of strings and a basso continuo group. As mentioned before, the brass players likely came from the hunting establishment of the prince's estate. Huntsmen were generally versed in playing the horn in order to call to the hounds. A large sheep ranch surrounded Esterháza, so Haydn likely enjoyed the service of some of the shepherds to play the double-reed instruments. Since ancient times, double-reed instruments have been associated with shepherds and other folk with pastoral occupations. Some of the string players were likely professionals, while a few were servants of one description or another. Because Haydn wasn't writing for an orchestra entirely comprised of professionals, he made many compromises in his musical style. This symphony is spirited, however, suggesting that Haydn did his best to instruct his less accomplished players.

The symphony expresses a happy confidence. The orchestra at Esterháza existed not only because the prince liked music. The orchestra was intended to confirm the

FIGURE 10.6 | *Esterháza Palace.* Haydn spent most of his life working for the Esterházy princes at this palace in what is now Hungary. Again clarity and symmetry inform both the architecture and formal gardens of this magnificent example of 18th century architecture. (© Vittoriano Rastellii/Corbis)

rational order that the prince sought to manifest all around him. It was a glorious adornment in the life of the enlightened ruler, a pleasure he gladly shared with his friends and servants. For the most part, the symphonies of Haydn written during his years of service all confirm the prince's power as justly held. Modern readers may imagine that life under a monarch, even a supposedly enlightened one, would have been galling. Not so for Haydn's time, there were no plots of revolution circulating at Esterháza. The symphony, like the beautiful house and well tended grounds, confirmed the power of the prince, and marked the willing submission of those around him.

SONATA FORM

The form of this movement is Haydn's favorite, sonata form. This important form is much discussed in Chapter Five. However, we must review its essential features here as well. When composers have no text to set, there is a problem of how to organize abstract musical material in a pleasing way. Baroque composers like Vivaldi and Bach favored the ritornello form, its recurrent material serving to orient the listener's attention as recognizable material periodically returns. Another favored Baroque form was the fugue. The texture of equal voices presenting a fabric of polyphonic entrances captured the Baroque imagination.

The gallant style has no use whatsoever for the fugue. The premium placed by Rousseau and others on natural melody led them to favor a homophonic texture. With a homophonic texture, the melody is easier to fixate upon, since there is never more than one important melody presented at a time.

The *ritornello* form continued to inspire Haydn's generation, although they mainly reserved it for the concerto. Both the *ritornello* forms in the previous chapter by Vivaldi and Bach are concertos as well.

The sonata form emphasizes a harmonic arrangement as much as a dispensation of melodies. The essential harmonic scheme of the sonata sees a move from tonic to a polar key (usually the dominant) during the first large section of the piece. Next, a period of harmonic instability unfolds, often featuring modulations resulting in fleeting arrivals of different keys. Then the tonic returns and remains in place until the end of the work. This harmonic plan has many advantages. For one thing, it resembles certain effective narrative formulas. For example, stories about journeys feature an opening at home (tonic), a move to someplace else (the polar key, usually dominant), adventures (harmonic instability), and a return home again (tonic). Musical theorists of Haydn's day, such as Augustus Kollmann, were no more specific in describing sonata form than this. They called it a harmonic plan formed by moving from tonic to dominant to instability to tonic again.

Within this seemingly simple framework, an infinite variety of specific outcomes exist. The flexibility of sonata form is also one of its great advantages.

In actual practice, there are often other distinguishing features to sonata form. Haydn often found it useful to match the four harmonic sections described above with certain motivic practices. For example, in many of his sonata forms there is a characteristic theme or themes associated first with the section in tonic, then a contrasting theme or themes that arrive along with the polar key. Most of the time, Haydn introduces development upon the themes of these two sections during the period of harmonic instability.

The idea of musical development takes some getting used to before it becomes easy to hear. What typically happens is that tunes from earlier in the piece are repeated, sometimes in fragmented ways. They invariably appear in different keys and sometimes in different modes. For example, in this symphony, themes from earlier in the piece return in the minor mode, whereas their original appearance was in the major mode. This idea of musical development will dominate our discussion of the Beethoven symphonic movement later in this chapter, so we'll save further description for that piece. Suffice it to say that Haydn, Beethoven's teacher, taught his student much about how to develop material. The last section of the harmonic plan sees the theme (the one associated with the tonic key at the beginning of the form) return when the tonic key returns. Just to ensure that the listener realizes that the harmonic journey of sonata form is over, Haydn brings back the theme or themes associated with the polar key, but presents them now in the tonic key. More often than not, a *coda*, or musical tail, rounds off the form with some rousing presentation of the first theme of the piece, still in the tonic key.

While Kollmann and other music theorists of Haydn's own time saw the sonata form as having four essential parts clarified by their harmonic function, later theorists saw the sonata form as having three parts clarified by their motivic function. Carl Czerny, a student of Beethoven who wrote mainly during the 1830s, was just such a theorist. He collapsed parts one and two of Kollmann's plan into a single section and called it the "exposition," because this section exposes its listeners to the main thematic ideas of the piece. The period of harmonic instability he called the "development," because virtually all composers developed themes from the exposition during this part of the form. The return to tonic Czerny called the "recapitulation," because it recalled the opening thematic material. Our listening guide anachronistically favors Czerny's description of sonata form from the 1830s, rather than the four-part descriptions dating from Haydn's lifetime.

Returning to the specific topic of Haydn's Symphony No. 56, this cheerful piece seems ideally suited to its intended context. After a day of hunting and an evening of feasting, this piece was played under the stars for the prince, his guests, and the other servants. Its happy optimism seems to confirm the idea that the prince is a good man whose enlightened rule is both just and natural. No brooding, no hidden anxiety sneaks into Haydn's work. He was for several decades the willing servant of a social order he considered beyond question. The writer E.T.A. Hoffmann described Haydn as "before the fall." Haydn provides a final respite for music before the more turbulent career of Beethoven and the brooding work of the Romantics.

Listening Guide

Joseph Haydn, Symphony Number 56, in C Major (1774)
[CD2, #6] *(Duration, 5 min. 16 sec.)*

First Movement: Allegro di molto
Sonata Form, 3/4 meter

EXPOSITION

0.00 **First Theme:** A descending arpeggio on the tonic triad opens the movement. This is followed immediately by a short, lyric tune also in tonic. Spirited fanfares with dotted rhythms make up the rest of the section and lead to the next.

0.16 First theme and spirited fanfares are restated though slightly altered.

0.32 **Bridge:** The polar key in this case is the dominant. It arrives with a new theme played at a fortissimo dynamic level. The melody is confident and the overall effect is busy. This section culminates in a quiet arrival on a long note.

1.00 **Second Theme:** A new theme, still in the polar key appears, played very softly by strings only.

1.18 **Cadence Theme:** Still in the polar key, the double reeds and brasses rejoin the strings at a loud dynamic, as the exposition is brought to a close with yet another new theme. [Though Haydn indicates a repeat of the exposition in his score (the "classical" rationale for this repetition is found under Sonata Form, in Chapter Five of this book), orchestras nowadays often consider them optional. In this recorded anthology, the performers go directly into the development section.]

DEVELOPMENT

1.54 All the themes from the first section of the exposition return, although all of them are now shortened and mostly in the minor mode. They tumble in one after another rapidly as the harmony modulates.

2.36 The confident bridge theme from the second section of the exposition returns, only now in a new minor key.

2.58 The quiet second theme, played initially only by the strings in the third section of the exposition, returns. Initially it's in a new key, but it eventually reaches the dominant, serving as "retransition" to the recapitulation.

RECAPITULATION

3.11 **First Theme:** The material of the first section of the exposition returns with very few alterations.

3.27 First theme and spirited fanfares are restated, though slightly altered.

3.50 **Bridge:** The confident theme from the exposition returns, but now in the tonic key.

4.18 **Second Theme:** The quiet theme initially presented only by the strings returns, only now in the tonic key and with the melody played by an oboe instead of a violin.

4.35 **Cadence Theme:** The same theme that brought the exposition to a close returns, only now in the tonic key.

CODA

4.52 The confident bridge theme returns in an altered version and still in the tonic key.

5.04 The fanfare motive with the dotted rhythms is played one time in the tonic key.

As in most Classical period symphonies, there are three movements that follow: a second "slow movement," a "minuet and trio movement" as the third, and a light-hearted, fast movement to conclude. Each movement is self-contained, introducing new thematic material that is explored in different ways and resolved by the end. All movements provide interesting contrasts of themes, tempos, meters, forms, moods, and so forth, to each other.

HAYDN'S CAREER AFTER 1790

In 1790, Prince Nicholas I Esterházy died. Haydn served him during his entire reign as prince. Now his son Nicholas II took the position of prince. Understandably, given that he grew up in a household where music was constantly being made, the young prince was little interested in music. He kept Haydn and an elderly violin virtuoso his father had employed on as nominal servants, but they were both free to leave Esterháza on their own business. Moreover, all the music that Haydn would write from this point forward belonged to Haydn alone.

Haydn immediately took up residence in Vienna. There he composed for many aristocrats, who were only too pleased to receive the services of Haydn for an evening. He also took students, among them was Ludwig van Beethoven.

Haydn made two important journeys to England under the auspices of the concert promoter Johann Piter Salomon. These two journeys were hugely successful, both financially and artistically. Haydn drew unbridled satisfaction from the fame he enjoyed in the British capital. In a letter to Prince Nicholas II, he bragged about having to take a larger suite of rooms at his hotel in order to accommodate all the visiting aristocrats, diplomats, and influential personages. Haydn may have labored happily while a servant to the Esterházy family, but he relished his emancipation when it came. Haydn's career marks a turning point in the social status of the composer. The growth of cities in the late eighteenth century, along with a growing middle class, afforded composers an opportunity to make their living by promoting public concerts rather than always suiting the taste of an aristocrat.

In addition to twelve new symphonies written in the most modern and formidable style, Haydn composed oratorios for his London audience. That genre had remained a favorite in England since Handel's time. Haydn was awarded honorary degrees at Cambridge and Oxford, an enthusiastic journalist called him the Shakespeare of music (high praise indeed in England), and professional musicians presented thoroughly polished performances of his most complex and challenging pieces. Haydn had come a long way from waiting each morning to learn whether or not the prince wanted a new chamber work for baryton that day, from sitting to meals with the high-ranking servants, and tailoring his pieces to the limitations of an orchestra of huntsmen and valets. A new era was dawning when composers of talent could become their own kind of aristocracy, chosen not by birth but by accomplishment. The Enlightenment, with its notions of Man's inalienable rights, was changing the landscape of music making, and Haydn paved the way for a host of others.

WOLFGANG AMADEUS MOZART

Wolfgang Amadeus Mozart (1756–1791) was never so fortunate as Haydn. While Haydn enjoyed steady employment until such time as he could strike out on his own, Mozart sought satisfactory steady employment but never found it. Their ends illustrate the danger of striking out on one's own as a composer without a proper reputation and network of support. Haydn lived in luxury during his final years, years that saw him reach his seventies. Mozart died penniless in his thirties. His final resting place was an unmarked pauper's grave shared by other destitute residents of Vienna who had met their end. The Enlightenment, something more talked about than actual in the eighteenth century as far as most people were concerned, never came to his rescue. Just as the renaissance touched comparatively few lives, the Enlightenment was too often active only in the imaginations of philosophers and artists.

The beginning of Mozart's story would hardly suggest such a sad ending. His father, Leopold Mozart, was a professional composer in the employment of the Archbishop of Salzburg. Although Leopold never rose above the rank of assistant director of the chapel, he had a modest reputation as both an accomplished composer and author of a treatise on violin playing. The young Mozart showed prodigious talent at a young age, so much so that Leopold placed his own career on hold in order to foster his son's remarkable abilities.

Mozart's Youthful Compositions

One facet of Mozart's career has reached near mythic status. That facet concerns his youthful output as a composer. He produced his earliest compositions at an almost unbelievably early age. By age ten he had produced works

Figure 10.7 | *Wolfgang Amadeus Mozart (1756–1791).* (© Bettmann/Corbis)

in many of the leading genres of the day. He was talented in the extreme to be sure, however, his youthful works are not masterpieces. Most of the music for which Mozart is famous today was written during Mozart's maturity. The point here is not to claim that Mozart was not a child prodigy, only that we must guard against the temptation of romanticizing his youthful exploits and in the process denigrating his mature successes.

From 1762 until 1771, Mozart spent the vast majority of his time performing. He mostly played keyboard instruments. His father and sister traveled with him. The family would typically visit a city, sometimes at the invitation of a local music lover with wealth and position. Once there, they would entertain in the homes of the aristocracy. Compositions, mostly by the young Mozart, were presented along with improvisations. Mozart had an unbelievably facile imagination. He could improvise variations on popular aria melodies on the spot. Such displays of musicality led some admirers to view Mozart as a scientific curiosity. Daines Barrington, a Fellow at the Royal Society (a scientific academy in London), wrote precisely such an account to his fellow scientists after observing the young Mozart perform:

> SIR,
>
> *If I was to send you a well attested account of a boy who measured seven feet in height, when he was not more than eight years of age, it might be considered as not undeserving the notice of the Royal Society.*
>
> *The instance which I now desire you will communicate to that learned body, of as early an exertion of most extraordinary musical talents, seems perhaps equally to claim their attention.*[1]

During his youthful tours, Mozart composed in most every major genre. He wrote his first symphony at age eight. He wrote an oratorio at age eleven and a first opera at age twelve. While these childhood creations are seldom performed today except as curiosities, they reflect a high degree of understanding of the prevailing musical styles and tastes of his time. In addition to native talent, Mozart had a full-time teacher of the first rank in his father. Mozart makes a wonderful case study for those interested in the old "nature versus nurture" debate, because he provides ample arguments on both sides. Friends of nature argue that a person's abilities, intellect, moral character, and work ethic are innate. We are each, according to this logic, born the way we will be. Friends of nurture look to the environment to explain a person's abilities, intellect, moral character, and work ethic.

Mozart in Salzburg

By 1774 the Mozart family returned to Salzburg so that Leopold could resume his professional duties. Child prodigies could make a good living during the eighteenth century. When Mozart reached the age of eighteen, his charm as a child had long worn off. By 1771 his act was no longer widely attractive. The time had come for Mozart to settle into a steady career. He began by joining his father in the service of the Archbishop of Salzburg. Mozart was miserable in his duties. Salzburg was a musical backwater by this time. Mozart complained bitterly of the Archbishop's lack of taste and about the slovenly standards of the musicians around him. Finally sick at heart at the prospect of remaining a minor figure in a minor city, Mozart embarked on a journey designed to secure a new position for himself. His mother traveled with him in 1777.

---

[1]*Music in the Western World: A History in Documents*, Piero Weiss and Richard Taruskin, editors (New York: Schirmer, 1984): 308.

They visited several courts in Germany, including the Bavarian court at Munich and the Court of the Elector of Mannheim. Mozart was well received at each place, but no offers of employment came his way.

What galls modern students of music history is how the aristocrats of the day could miss Mozart's obvious talent. What such students misunderstand is the crucial role of taste in Mozart's day. What Rousseau wrote in his dictionary of 1767 held true as Mozart sought a job: genius must be tempered by taste. Mozart's music by this time had become complex and artful. He could affect the simplicity of the gallant style when he wanted to; it's just that he didn't want to often enough. Perhaps more devastating was Mozart's quick and irreverent wit. He indulged his scatological sense of humor too much and made jibes at men of standing too freely. Moreover, he drank, and sometimes to excess. Enlightenment era aristocrats didn't want to have irreverent musicians in their permanent employ. A brief visit by Mozart to entertain for several evenings, even for several weeks, was welcome enough; but a permanent presence might foster dissatisfaction among the other servants or cause an unexpected affront to a distinguished visitor. Mozart did not end his days in an unmarked grave because everyone loved him and wanted to help him. As often as his manners, his mature music was subjected to criticism for being too complex, too artful, and out of touch with the propriety dictated by good taste.

The journey Mozart undertook to secure a permanent job finally took him to Paris. He hoped that the French would take a more sophisticated view and welcome his talents. They did, but not as a permanent employee of any aristocrat. His public concerts were well attended, but no offers appeared asking him to remain. To compound Mozart's disappointment and frustration at rejection in two countries, his mother died in Paris.

Mozart returned to Salzburg in 1778 a beaten man. He had bragged that he would not return when he left. Now he had to eat crow in front of the slovenly musicians of Salzburg whom he so despised. After nearly three years in the service of the Archbishop, Mozart defied his father's advice and set out on his own to Vienna in the hope of making a living as a free composer.

MOZART IN VIENNA

Had Mozart managed his money prudently in Vienna, he could have been quite comfortable and even wealthy. Vienna was full of aristocrats and music lovers. Commissions for new works came at a steady clip. All during his years in Vienna, Mozart hoped to secure steady employment. That never happened. Some historians claim that secret machinations and plots were designed to deprive Mozart of a post suitable to his talents. There were no plots. Mozart undermined his own suitability through the same bad habits that had frustrated him before, plus some new ones. He and his wife, Constanza had extravagant tastes. They spent more than he made. Debts mounted, and with them heavy interest.

All was not grim for Mozart in Vienna. He excelled in two genres and enjoyed tremendous celebrity and broad public support. While Mozart contributed importantly in every genre of music, his operas and piano concertos find him at his best.

Mozart's Piano Concertos

Mozart was a piano virtuoso. He wrote his concertos for his own use in public concerts. Often Mozart's piano concertos appeared initially in what are called "subscription concerts." These concerts provided a way for free composers to make a living. Mozart would contact a theater owner and book a night for the performance. Then he would contract a small orchestra suitable to his purposes. In both cases, the theater owner and the orchestra members knew that the show would only take place if enough tickets could be sold in advance of the performance. Mozart would advertise that he had written a new concerto and perhaps a symphony, which would be performed at the upcoming subscription concert. If enough people became interested and they bought tickets, the concert would happen. Often wealthy patrons would underwrite the event. Such patrons would provide the lion's share of the money in exchange for the event being dedicated to their good graces.

Subscription concerts often provided the general public with their first access to orchestral music outside the opera. Regularly scheduled public concerts, that is, concerts to which the general public had access, became a regular feature of the civic life of more and more European cities over the course of the 1700s. Milan hosted outdoor, public concerts of symphonic music sporadically, starting in the 1750s. Paris had the *concerts spirituels* starting in the 1750s as well. These concerts were also outdoor affairs, but unlike the Milanese equivalent, they were presented on a regular basis every Lent. London played host to a variety of concert presentations, although always scheduled on an irregular basis. Amsterdam witnessed fewer concerts than London, but like London the burgeoning middle class in Amsterdam could support a lively concert life. Vienna benefited from the activities of men like Mozart, who organized concerts on a subscription basis. The large, professional symphony orchestras resident in a particular city that we find in large and medium-sized cities all across North America and Europe today were unknown during the eighteenth century. The first professional orchestra specializing in purely instrumental music that still exists today was the Leipzig Gewandhaus Orchestra. It was founded in the nineteenth century, rather than during the Classical period. Yet the robust concert life of large cities of the 1700s paved the way for the formation of such professional organizations.

The Mozart piece representing his work with subscription concerts in our anthology is the finale of the Piano Concerto No. 17. Concertos in the 1780s were typically comprised of three movements. The first usually used some kind of *ritornello* form, although some composers adopted ideas from sonata form and employed them during first movements. The second movement was usually slow and lyrical. These movements often drew upon operatic arias for their inspiration. The finales of concertos were often in rondo form, although in this case, we find an excellent example of theme and variations. The general mood of finales was spirited and happy.

The finale in our anthology [CD2 #7] certainly exudes spirit and happiness. The form of this movement, as mentioned above, is a theme and variations. This musical form is discussed in Chapter Five. A quick review of the form indicates that theme and variations must open with the statement of some memorable theme. Then the composer would write varied versions of the theme, called "variations." Variations come in all shapes and sizes. A number of common practices in writing variations include changing the mode of the theme from major to minor or minor to major, adding a few notes to the theme in order to change its details but not its general contour, fragmenting the theme by using only a few of its notes, changing the accompaniment of the theme, and changing the instrumentation of the theme. In this movement, Mozart uses several of these typical approaches to writing variations. This particular movement has five variations and a coda.

Wolfgang Amadeus Mozart, Piano Concerto Number 17 in G, K453 (1784)

[CD2, #7] *(Duration, 7 min. 49 sec.)*

Third Movement, Theme and Variations Form

Theme:

0.00 **a**

0.11 **a** (repeat)

0.23 **b**

0.35 **b** (repeat)

     The orchestra presents a cheerful theme in G major, comprised of mostly quarter notes, with little adornment so that listeners can focus on it. (The variations will make more sense to listeners if they have a good grasp of the theme.) This theme is divided into two phrases of equal length, each of them repeated. Its form may be indicated ‖: **a** :‖: **b** :‖. Of particular interest is an imitative dialogue that takes place between the violins and cellos at the beginning of the **b** section. Mozart sustains this call-and-answer throughout all of the following variations.

Variation One:

0.47 **a1**

0.59 **a1** (repeat)

1.11 **b1**

1.23 **b1** (repeat)

     The piano soloist makes its first appearance. This variation is quiet, with the orchestra presenting only light support for the piano. The piano's version of the theme depends on the variation technique of adding notes to it. Notice how the piano plays extra notes in between the notes of the theme, as it proceeds with eighth-note rhythms, which move twice as fast as the quarter notes heard earlier. Both **a** and **b** phrases are repeated verbatim. The dialogue in the **b** section this time takes place between the solo piano and orchestra.

Variation Two:

1.35 **a2**

1.46 **a2'** (This type of indication reflects that the "repeat" has been altered slightly.)

1.58 **b2**

2.10 **b2'**

     With triplet-eighth notes, the piano plays many more notes than before, making the theme sound much more brilliant. In addition, Mozart treats the repeats of each phrase differently, by varying them slightly. As the orchestra plays the theme throughout, the piano first plays fast notes in the upper pitch register with the right hand. On each repeat, the fast runs are played in a lower pitch register by the left hand. Essentially, the pianist begins a new dialogue, in addition to sustaining the first. Listen for the pianist's right, then left hand communicate with the orchestra in the **b** section. This variation constitutes an example of changing the accompaniment as well as the theme.

Variation Three:

2.21 **a3**

2.34 **a3'**

2.47 **b3**

3.01 **b3'**

The woodwind section of the orchestra appears to pick up on the additional dialogue introduced by the piano in the previous variation, for this variation opens with first the flute, then the oboe, next the bassoon, and finally the flute again, playing a varied portion of the theme with added notes. Again, this becomes a variation within a variation as the repeats are altered each time. On each repeat, the piano solo responds to the woodwinds. This variation utilizes an embellished version of the theme that is passed back and forth between the woodwinds and the pianist. Not only does Mozart add notes to the theme, but he also indulges in changing the instrumentation.

Variation Four:

3.13 **a4**

3.27 **a4'**

4.40 **b4**

4.54 **b4'**

There is a change to the minor mode. This more subdued version of the theme is presented at a quiet dynamic level, first by the string instruments and then by the piano on each repeat. Throughout, the use of syncopation adds to this variation's mysterious quality. The theme's original cheerfulness is gone, as the variation ends with the strings and piano, in turn, presenting another minor-mode version of it.

Variation Five:

4.07 **a5**

4.20 **a5'**

4.32 **b5**

4.45 **b5'**

The orchestra abruptly changes the mood with a striding march-like treatment of the theme in the major mode. The piano does not try to compete with the orchestra on the returns. Instead, the pianist plays an unaltered version of the original theme as the orchestra provides a march-like accompaniment. At the end of this variation, the tempo slows. The piano plays a transitional passage that leads into the concluding coda section.

4.58 **Transitional Passage**

5.21 **Coda:**

The Coda is much faster than the ending of the previous variation. Most of the coda finds the theme missing altogether in favor of a brand new theme. At the end of the coda, the original theme returns in a highly fragmented form.

This piano concerto's concluding movement provides light-hearted entertainment for the audience, and is composed in such a way as to leave them smiling and feeling happy.

Audiences in Mozart's day delighted at his ability to play the piano. His concertos for piano were a major attraction for his subscription concerts. In addition to playing concertos such as the one in our anthology and described in the Listening Guide, Mozart often improvised at his concerts. He often asked the audience to suggest favorite melodies so that he might spontaneously create varied versions of their favorite themes.

MOZART AND OPERA

In addition to concertos, symphonies, and periods of improvisation Mozart often included arias excerpted from his operas on his subscription concerts. His operas were usually very popular. Audiences enjoyed hearing favorite arias in concert settings. A little vocal music among the instrumental works also lent the evening a happy variety. Concerts in Mozart's time often lasted three and four hours. Audience members from that time had long attention spans compared to audiences today. Moreover, the code of audience conduct was different then. Now it's really considered rude to talk, eat, drink, or walk about at a concert. Many concert organizers will simply ask rude patrons to leave. This was not so in Mozart's time, as the definition of what constituted rude conduct differed then. Perhaps that explains why audiences expected Mozart and other organizers of subscription concerts to present so much varied music.

Mozart began his career as an opera composer at an extremely early age. His most youthful works really are more interesting oddities than important parts of the repertory. In 1780, while concocting his strategy for leaving Salzburg, Mozart composed his serious opera *Idomeneo* for the purposes of using it to make a splash in Vienna when he arrived. This opera reflects Mozart's relative isolation, as many of the pre-reform qualities that Gluck objected to are present in the work. Mozart was a fast learner and he quickly adapted his style to the more progressive conceptions of opera prevalent during his life.

His first unqualified hit in Vienna was *Abduction from the Seraglio* (1782), a *Singspiel*. Singspiels are a kind of German opera in which spoken dialogue is used instead of recitative. Gluck drew the idea of using an important and centrally engaged orchestra in his reform operas from the traditions of Singspiel. *Abduction from the Seraglio* was performed frequently, and earned Mozart a handsome income.

In his mature operas, Mozart exercised his irreverent wit. More than once his irreverent approach placed him in trouble. In his Singspiel *The Magic Flute* (1791), Mozart revealed secrets of the initiation rites of the Freemasons, a secret society committed to universal brotherhood to which Mozart belonged. Angry over this betrayal of their fiercely guarded secrets, the Freemasons expelled Mozart from their ranks. This was a bitter blow late in Mozart's life, as he was by then in the habit of borrowing money from his brother Masons, and most particularly Michael Puchberg, a high-ranking Mason. With his expulsion from the society, that road to generous loans was closed to him. For his opera *The Marriage of Figaro* (1786), Mozart used a banned book as the basis for the libretto. That book belittled the aristocracy. Opera was subjected to careful censorship all over Europe. How Mozart felt he could mount an expensive production of an opera based on a banned book suggests either the heights of his audacity, or the depths of his inability to understand the world and its ways. That opera was mounted with very little success in the Imperial capital of Vienna, but the provincial city of Prague threw its arms wide and embraced Mozart's creation. Anything that annoyed the empire interested the Czechs living in Prague. Mozart may have been lucky to find favor in Prague, or perhaps he sensed the quality of his work and trusted in it to see him through difficult times. Whatever the case, Mozart rewarded Prague's fascination with his opera by composing a "Prague" symphony (his 38th and possibly most complex) as well as writing his opera *Don Giovanni* (1787) specifically for a premiere in Prague.

Don Giovanni

Don Giovanni, the opera represented in our recorded anthology, is sufficiently bizarre that Mozart did not know whether to call it a serious opera or a comic one. To end the confusion, he coined a new genre called the *dramma giacoso* (jocular drama). *Don Giovanni* tells the story of the notorious womanizer Don Juan as he travels about seducing women indiscriminately. This darkly humorous subject appealed to Mozart's penchant for black comedy. As the opera begins, a country girl is enjoying her wedding day and her union with a simple country boy. Don Giovanni, traveling with his servant Leporello, spies the happy wedding party and conceives the cruel idea of seducing the bride on her wedding day. Black comedy relishes nasty situations, which are at once horrible and hilarious in their audacity. Eventually Don Giovanni's past catches up to him through the appearance of Donna Elvira. This steadfast woman was seduced as a young girl. Since then she has pursued Don Giovanni toward the purpose of forcing him to marry her. The aria in our recorded anthology deals with Leporello, Don Giovanni's servant, doing the Don's dirty work. [CD2 #8] Having been found by Donna Elvira, the Don now wishes to escape, so he leaves Leporello to talk to the outraged Donna Elvira. Leporello produces a large book that contains a catalogue of the Don's seductions. What follows is the famous "catalogue aria."

Listening Guide

Wolfgang Amadeus Mozart, "Madamina" from Don Giovanni, Act I, scene V (1787)
[CD2, #8] *(Duration, 5 min. 41 sec.)*

Aria is in AB or binary (two-part) form.

A	**LEPORELLO (TEXT)**	**TRANSLATION**	**MUSICAL TREATMENT**
0.00	Madamina,	Madamina,	Allegro; light-hearted.
0.04	Il catalogo è questo	This is the catalog	
0.06	Delle belle che amò il padron mio;	of the beauties who my patron loved;	
0.09	Un catalogo egli è che ho fatt'io;	it is a catalog that I made myself,	
0.13	Osservate, leggete con me!	Observe, read with me!	
0.23	In Italia seicento e queranta,	In Italy, six hundred and forty,	Staccato notes in
0.29	in Almagna due cento e trent'una,	in Germany two hundred and thirty-one,	orchestra sound
0.34	Cento in Francia, in Turchia novant'una	in Germany, two hundred and thirty-one,	like giggles.
0.37	Ma in Ispagna son già mille e tre.	in Spain there are 1003.	Longer notes

A	LEPORELLO (TEXT)	TRANSLATION	MUSICAL TREATMENT
0.54	V'han fra queste contadine,	There are countesses, baronesses,	Shorter notes
0.57	Cameriere, cittadine,	chamber maids, city girls,	
1.00	V'han contesse, baronesse,	there are countesses, baronesses	
1.02	Marchesane, principesse,	marchionesses, princesses,	
1.04	E v'han donne d'ogni grado,	there are women of every rank,	
1.07	D'ogni forma, d'ogni erà.	of every shape, and every age	
1.11	In Italia seicento e queranta, ecc.	In Italy, six hundred and forty, etc.	Descending notes imitate laughter.
1.26			—Slowdown and longer notes
1.44			—Staccato notes that sound like giggles
2.00			Cadences
B			
2.05	Nella bionda egli ha l'usuanza	In a blonde he usually	Andante con moto;
2.14	Di lodar la gentilezza,	praises her gentility,	in a meter of 3/4.
2.25	Nella bruna la costanza	in a brunette her constancy,	Flourish of sneering notes
2.35	Nella bianca la dolcezza;	in a gray hair her sweetness;	Elegant melodic phrase
2.47	Vuol d'inverno la grassotta,	in the winter the plump,	
2.52	Vuol d'estate la magrotta,	in the summer the slender,	
2.57	E' la grande maestosa;	the large one is majestic;	Crescendo; the melody slowly rises to a high sustained note.
3.20	La piccina è ognor vezzosa.	the small one is charming	Playful notes
3.41	Della vecchie fa conquista	He conquers the old	Elegant melodic phrase.
3.51	Pel piacer di porle in lista;	for the pleasure of adding her to the list;	
4.01	Ma passion predominant	but his predominant passion	Soft, quick notes that sound like whispers
4.07	È la giovin principiante;	is the young beginner;	Dotted rhythms
4.11	Non si picca se sia ricca,	He is not the least bothered if she's rich,	and trills
4.16	Se sia brutta, se sia bella,	if she's ugly, if she's pretty,	
4.21	Se sia ricca, brutta, se sia bella;	if she's righ, ugly, or pretty,	
4.26	Purchè porti la gonnella:	so long as she wears a skirt;	Melodic phrases sound warm and tender.
4.37	Voi sapete quel che fa.	You know what it is he does.	
4.54	Purchè porti la gonnella, ecc.:	so long as she wears a skirt, etc.	
5.33			Final cadences

FIGURE 10.8 | *Costume designs for the characters Don Giovanni and Zerlina*. This is an early engraving depicting Don Giovanni and Zerlina as presented in Mozart's opera. Seduction is not a recent invention. In the 18th century much literature, both fictional and non-fictional, dotes on the subject. Among aristocrats seduction was often portrayed as a fashionable art, a preoccupation, and a source of frolicsome comedy.

The text of this opera, like most of the late operas of Mozart, was written by Lorenzo Da Ponte. Together, Mozart and Da Ponte created several operas that remain the bedrock repertory of many professional companies around the world. The text found in the Listening Guide reveals a sardonic wit. On the one hand, the exploits of the wicked Don are admirable in their outrageous indifference to standards of decency; they may even be a little funny. On the other hand, his womanizing is a terrible affront to moral standards. More sly sex jokes find their way into the aria. For example, the Italian word "costanza" used to praise the most excellent quality of brunettes is very similar to Mozart's wife's name, Constanza, herself a brunette. When you listen to the aria, note how Mozart celebrates his wife's name with long, dramatic notes. The seduction of 1003 Spanish women plays upon the eighteenth-century notion that Spanish women are all irresistible, a ribald notion held by womanizers of the time.

In addition to relishing the presence of his wife among the seduced, Mozart's musical setting also lends insight into the flamboyant character of Leporello. This weary servant has a gift for melodramatics. Mozart indulges the singer who plays Leporello by giving him ample opportunity for melodramatic mugging, such as when he sings the words "la piccina" ("the small one") over and over again.

All the characters in this opera have distinctive ways of revealing their character through music. Donna Elvira, to whom Leporello addresses his aria, the steadfast woman who seeks restitution for the wrong the Don has done her, reveals her character in the scene prior to this aria by singing resolute melodies full of wide leaps expressing strength and indignation. The Don's music always has a mocking and disingenuous quality. Leporello often gets to ridicule his boss by singing immediately after him, using the same rhythms and a silly impression of the Don's melodic line. Such fabulous details of musical character are what modern opera lovers use to elevate Mozart to a position of supreme importance within the opera repertory.

The formal plan of Leporello's aria reflects to a modest degree the influence of opera reform. This is not a *da capo* structure, but rather a simple AB or binary (two-part) form. The A section coincides with Leporello listing the Don's conquests. At the words "nella bruna" ("in a brunette") the tempo slows. This latter section is more concerned with describing the Don's differing attitudes toward his various conquests. Mozart employed a pleasing array of diverse strategies for lending form to operatic arias.

MOZART'S DEATH

While Mozart never managed to find steady employment sufficient to support his remarkably extravagant tastes, he was never without income. His poor business decisions based on borrowing more than he made led him into crushing debt. As the years went by, his income decreased. As a touring novelty act with his father and sister, Mozart was able to make a fine living as a child; but once he started shaving, it was no longer possible to sell him as a child prodigy. An unhappy period in Salzburg followed. At the end of his life, perhaps his charm was wearing thin again. Audiences are fickle, and favor novelty. Commissions came less frequently and were less lucrative. His drinking mounted along with his debts. He finally died of a general physical collapse at the prime of his life.

After Mozart died, Vienna mourned as word spread. The music-loving Prince Lichnowsky believed that Mozart's ghost haunted Vienna. The city should have embraced such a superbly talented musician, but it did not. The Prince vowed that the city would never again despise its best and brightest musicians. He led a group of wealthy music lovers in supporting the career of another supremely talented composer who called Vienna home, Ludwig van Beethoven. Lichnowsky wanted no more Mozarts on Vienna's conscience. When an economic depression hit Vienna in 1809, Beethoven looked for steady employment elsewhere. Prince Lichnowsky intervened. He raised an annual stipend for Beethoven with the one requirement for receiving the money being that Beethoven remain in the city of Vienna. So Mozart's sad death opened the door for still greater respect and admiration for fine composers of subsequent generations.

After Mozart died, both his sister and his wife strove to control his legacy. His sister, Nannerl, fostered the view that Mozart was a savant. That means that he was supremely gifted in one aspect of life (music) but totally naïve in all others. She argued that her brother's fall was the product of no one giving him good advice or helping him get along in a world he could not understand.

This perspective on Mozart was hotly contested by his widow, Constanza. For one thing, it was insulting to her to claim that her husband did not know what he was doing. Constanza argued that Mozart was too tough minded, too singular in his methods. He would not, in short, compromise with the taste of the day, nor would he suffer insults from the idiots who inherited positions of privilege. According to his wife, Mozart was far from naïve—he was an uncompromising genius who had to suffer for his superiority to other men.

Whatever case is true (and one might even favor a middling approach between these extremes), students of music's history must wrestle with the death of Mozart. This so-called enlightened period made the author of works of tremendous beauty suffer and die in wretched poverty. Whether he was the casualty of his own naivete or a casualty of his own uncompromising nature, whether he was the victim of capitalism's new economy of supply and demand or a victim of the period's over-refined notion of taste, Mozart died penniless in an unmarked grave. His music failed to save him.

LUDWIG VAN BEETHOVEN

We conclude this chapter with a figure who fits comfortably into two periods. Ludwig van Beethoven (1770–1827) inherited the ideals of Classicism and helped to chart the vague boundaries of musical Romanticism. His career reveals the limitations of two ways of approaching the study of music history. On the one hand, his career (much like that of Monteverdi) refuses to sit nicely into one or another style period. The result should be a healthy measure of skepticism for the whole idea of style periods. On the other hand, his career underscores the dangers of focusing on individual heroic figures in the arts rather than looking at all that transpired in a particular time and place. His career manifests a gradual stylistic transition, but in doing so makes it appear that he made the transition somehow alone. He didn't. Like J.S. Bach, Beethoven was interested in all that transpired around him. Yet his way of synthesizing the musical developments of his age into compelling pieces may set him apart.

The question of whether Beethoven best serves the Classical or Romantic ideals invites a certain interrogation. The German musicologist Friedrich Blume has argued in an interesting book on the subject that Classicism and Romanticism are not two stylistic periods, but two sensibilities. The former favors clarity of formal plan, modesty through acquiescence to taste, and naturalness through simplicity and grace. The latter favors unbounded emotion, the terror and awe of the sublime, and the artist at free disposal of his or her most personal passions. Armed with this understanding, we can safely say that Classicism does not disappear from European music nor does Romanticism ever perfectly supplant it. These two distinct sensibilities, so Blume argues, may reside in a single movement of a single piece as striking contrasts to one another. Mozart, for example, was called a Romantic before anyone else, yet no one would exclude him as a central figure in the development of the Classical ideals of naturalness and formal clarity. Beethoven too can strike us as serving both styles, once we set aside the notion that Classicism and Romanticism in music exclude one another.

Beethoven's Youth

Beethoven came from a musical family. His father sang in the chapel of the Archbishop Elector of Cologne, Maximilian Franz, in the city of Bonn in western Germany. Beethoven's father was by all accounts a brutal man who pushed his talented son in the direction of music. His father was Beethoven's first teacher, although the younger Beethoven little loved or respected his father. He would eventually have to sue his father for custody over his brothers when Beethoven's father lost his position owing to drunkenness. Beethoven kept a daily diary; however, there is no entry marking his father's passing or making any mention of special feelings one way or the other over the news. Biographers interested in psychology would come

FIGURE 10.9 | *Ludwig Van Beethoven (1770–1827).*
(© Archivo Iconografico, S.A./Corbis)

to link his bad feelings toward his father to a general tendency in Beethoven to disrespect authority of all kinds.

This tendency in Beethoven to disrespect authority ran to his political leanings. Beethoven lived in Bonn, a city near the frontier between Germany and France, and was nineteen years old when the French Revolution unfolded. Beethoven hung on every scrap of news he could get from France. His sympathies lay entirely with the revolutionaries. He hoped that the Revolution would eventually spill over the borders of France and would lead to a pan-European revolution in which all those who ruled by privilege of birth would be toppled in favor of a democratic system in which the governors served at the pleasure of the governed.

Beethoven began playing music professionally as a very young man. He played organ and later harpsichord in the orchestra of the Elector. At the suggestion of one of the Elector's close friends, the Count Waldstein, Beethoven was sent to Vienna to study music with Mozart. The year was 1787, and Mozart was composing *Don Giovanni*, Beethoven made the fourteen-day journey from Bonn to Vienna by stagecoach. Mozart heard him play his own composition on the fortepiano. Legend has it that Mozart said "Watch this young man closely, he will make a great noise some day." That legendary quotation speaks as much of Mozart's wit as of Beethoven's talent. Watching a composer may not be as complimentary as listening to him, moreover, "a great noise" can be either a compliment or an insult, depending on how one feels about noise. Mozart did not take Beethoven as a student. The young composer returned to Bonn with only debts to show for the Elector's troubles.

Beethoven in Vienna

Five years later and with considerably more musical polish after years of professional work and additional study, Beethoven was sent once more to Vienna, only this time to study with Franz Joseph Haydn. Haydn recognized Beethoven's talent, but he was an indifferent teacher. Beethoven, for his part, had become more interested in dancing masters and purchasing fashionable wigs rather than attending to his studies. Both Haydn and Beethoven became disenchanted with one another. Haydn did not take his best student to London with him, something that would have been expected. Beethoven did not dedicate his first published works to his teacher. They were string quartets, a genre Haydn had popularized. Tradition dictated that Beethoven pay his teacher that honor.

The last straw came when Haydn, finally tired of loaning his student money, wrote to the Archbishop Elector of Cologne (Beethoven's employer) to inform him that Beethoven needed a larger stipend in order to live in Vienna. He sent along some of Beethoven's recent compositions, which Beethoven had brought to lessons with Haydn as illustrations of his progress. The Elector's reply to Haydn's letter was withering. He informed Haydn that Beethoven had badly misrepresented the stipend he was receiving from the Elector, more importantly, all the pieces Haydn sent were already known in Bonn before Beethoven ever left for Vienna. The Elector concludes by asking that Beethoven return home immediately, since he obviously wasn't making any progress in Vienna. Haydn felt humiliated. Unlike Beethoven, he respected personages of authority and hated to look the fool in front of the Elector. Beethoven had been lying to Haydn, and that ended good relations between them.

Beethoven rounded out his education by studying counterpoint with the organist Georg Albrechtsburger and vocal writing with the opera specialist Antonio Salieri. He then went about the business of composing and playing the piano for a living.

FIGURE 10.10 | Eugene Delacroix, *Liberty Leading the People* (1830). Delacoix captures dramatic moments with a brilliant sense of detail, but his painting does not so much present the viewer with visual evidence of how things happened as much as he captures the emotion and hope of the moment. The charge of the bare-chested Lady Liberty followed by a motley group of armed citizens depicted in this famous painting speaks more of the democratic spirit of the upstart citizenry than of any particular event from the French Revolution. Note the revolutionary flag of France prominently unfurled in the painting. This symbol was unmistakably linked to the Revolution. The three colors of the flag represent the revolutionary ideals of patriotism, purity, and liberty. (© Bettmann/Corbis)

Today, scholars generally agree that Beethoven's career falls into three distinct periods. The early period (1794–1802) was Beethoven's least remarkable. He labored in the prevailing style of the day by emphasizing formal clarity and the modesty of a certain taste-bound naturalness. The influence of Haydn is felt powerfully during this period, for like his old teacher, Beethoven favored melodies ripe with developmental potential. He lacked Mozart's facility with memorable melody. During the early period, Beethoven enjoyed the increasing support of aristocratic music lovers, including the Prince Karl von Lichnowsky and Count Ferdinand von Waldstein, both mentioned previously. Along with these two generous patrons, Beethoven was supported by the Baron van Swieten and Prince Lobkowitz. All of these men enjoyed dedications from Beethoven, and rightly so. Their generosity was enormous. The Prince von Lichnowsky even allowed Beethoven to live in a room in one of his palaces in Vienna. While Beethoven repaid these men with dedications, he did not admire them. In his diaries he called them "the princely rabble." Beethoven wrote during this time before his fame that, "there are many princes, counts, and barons; but only one Beethoven." Beethoven was politically and philosophically committed to the democratic notion that an individual's actual accomplishments mattered more than inherited privileges.

BEETHOVEN'S "HEROIC" PERIOD

Unlike the early period, Beethoven's middle period (1802–1816) is markedly distinct from the prevailing tastes of the day. Scholars often refer to this as Beethoven's "heroic" period. His style is marked by greater striving for forceful expressive means and a general expansion of the scope and emotional weight of such forms as the sonata and such genres as the symphony.

In addition to the generous support of music-loving aristocrats, Beethoven made his living by publishing his works and promoting them through subscription concerts, where he also played piano. He also earned money by occasionally playing piano in the homes of aristocrats, although that activity was more typical of his early period. Unlike his old teacher Haydn, Beethoven did not hold a regular post serving anyone after he terminated his relationship with Maximilian Franz. Indeed, Beethoven was supposed to return to Bonn. He was only sent to Vienna to perfect his craft in order to turn it to the Elector's service. Beethoven ignored the Elector's requests that he return. Later, Napoleon Bonaparte, the protector of the French Revolution and eventual emperor of

FIGURE 10.11 | Baron Antoine-Jean Gros, ***Napoleon in the Pesthouse at Jafra*** (1804). As an official painter for Napoleon, Gros sought to aggrandize the accomplishments of the emperor. Here we do not see the emperor winning his trademark victories through audacity and courage, but visiting the sick and dying. Note the genuine feeling Napoleon has for the afflicted as he touches the sores of a patient. Napoleon is made to look both heroic and caring. Even in the midst of his bloodiest campaigns, Napoleon surely had his admirers. (Rèunion des Musèe Nationaux/Art Resource, NY)

FIGURE 10.12 | Francisco Goya, *The Third of May, 1808* (1814) The Spanish painter Goya chronicles a historical event in this famous painting. On May 3, 1808, Napoleon's army executed hundreds of Spanish citizens in Madrid. Despite the obvious plea for mercy by the man in white holding his arms up, the soldiers cruelly take aim. Goya underscores the martyrdom of the Spanish people by creating a clear parallel between the man's outstretched arms and the image of Christ on the cross. Spain fought tirelessly against Napoleon's armies, and the Spaniard Goya naturally has a contrasting opinion of the French emperor to that held by Baron Gros. (© Archivo Iconografico, S.A./Corbis)

France, dissolved the Holy Roman Empire and with it the position of Elector, since they elected the Emperor.

Just as Beethoven mistreated his first employer, he also mistreated his many publishers. Beethoven was in the habit of selling exclusive publication rights to more than one publisher. He felt that by the time the deceit was discovered and the slow wheels of justice had ground their course, the deception would have paid off financially. By a fluke, Beethoven enjoyed considerable legal privilege in the Austro-Hungarian courts. He had a letter of introduction from Count Waldstein that called him "Ludwig von Beethoven" rather than van Beethoven. This made him seem like an aristocrat. In the Austro-Hungarian Empire, aristocrats were entitled to have their legal business heard in a court where the judge was an aristocrat and where commoners, such as music publishers, suffered a real disadvantage in pressing cases against aristocrats.

While Beethoven could be unscrupulous, ungenerous, and disloyal, he compensated by being supremely talented. Before examining a piece from his heroic period, we should look at the psychological underpinnings of his new style. One could say that a figure with such a profound contempt for authority might make an ideal candidate for the development of an audacious and striving musical style. While that may be true, there were still other forces at work in Beethoven's life. Beethoven was losing his hearing. His deafness was a source of formidable anxiety for Beethoven. In a letter to his brothers now known as "The Heiligenstadt Testament," Beethoven expresses his feelings about his mounting deafness. He begins by blaming a new misanthropy evident in his conduct on fear of his condition being detected. He lived in unforgiving times when deafness would doom a musical career. Spending time with friends and strangers placed him at risk of exposing his bad hearing to their notice. He complains of incompetent doctors selling him false hope. Between 1799 and 1802 when Beethoven wrote the Heiligenstadt Testament, he underwent a primitive version of electroshock therapy and took doses of mercury, a terrible toxin once believed to possess curative powers. Eventually Beethoven turns to the topic of suicide. His life had become so unbearable, he confessed to his brothers, that he often thought of ending his wretched life. "Only art, only art held me back," he wrote. "For how could I end my life before I had said to the world all that I had to say?" In contrast to his tough and unscrupulous business dealings, Beethoven's generosity lay in his certainty that he had something valuable to share with the world.

For many critics, the middle period begins for Beethoven with his Piano Sonata No. 17 in D minor, which has come to be known as "The Tempest." This dramatic piece features an oddly shaped sonata form including the insertion of a strange, recitative-like section at the end of the development. This section, drawing on operatic ideals but obviously with no singer, draws the listener's attention to the plaintive melody, which seems to cry out against a cruel fate. Composed at roughly the same time as The Heiligenstadt Testament, this sonata reflects the growing tendency among nineteenth-century composers to reflect their personal feelings and biographical details in their music. One can learn little or nothing about Haydn as a person by listening to his Symphony No. 56. Good taste dictated that the piece be configured for the purposes of Prince Esterhàzy, not Haydn. That's not to say that Haydn wasn't perfectly glad to compose for the Prince's purposes, only that Beethoven's tendency to reflect his own concerns rather than that of his audience marks a distinction that underscores the singularity of Beethoven's middle period.

Beethoven admired Napoleon Bonaparte. Napoleon was born on the remote French island of Corsica. He joined the army and eventually became a corporal in the artillery corps. After the French Revolution in 1789, many European monarchies felt that if the revolutionaries weren't punished and a king put on the throne in France, commoners may get the idea that monarchs could be toppled through violence, a notion filled with ominous portents for monarchs everywhere. England, Austria, and Prussia entered into an agreement that they would all attack France at once toward the purpose of restoring the monarchy in France. As a huge Austrian army neared the French border, a comparatively small and disorganized French force looked ripe for destruction. Napoleon was there and in command of artillery. Up to that time, artillery was seen as useful only in laying siege to fortifications. They had only a minimal role in land battles between armies. As the larger Austrian force approached, Napoleon conceived of the radical idea of aiming artillery pieces at the advancing Austrian infantry. That day, military strategy changed dramatically. The Austrian army was put to rout. The English and Prussians cancelled their invasion plans, and Napoleon earned the title "defender of the Revolution."

Beethoven watched Napoleon's career with interest. Rather than waiting for their enemies to regroup and reorganize for another invasion, the French went on the attack. Napoleon won a string of crushing victories over the monarchies of Europe. Beethoven and other admirers hoped this meant that the French Revolution would be exported across Europe. This did not happen. Instead, Napoleon declared himself Emperor of

France. Beethoven saw this as a betrayal of the ideals of democracy. Beethoven had just written his third and by far most ambitious symphony. He had dedicated the work to Napoleon, quite an irreverent move for a citizen of Austria, a nation at war with Napoleon. When he learned of Napoleon's coronation, Beethoven violently scribbled over the name of his dedicatee with an ink pen. Beethoven's third symphony was rededicated to an anonymous hero and is now known by the Italian word for heroic, "eroica."

Beethoven's third symphony embodies the most striving ideals of the time. The piece is huge in scope, with individual movements as long in duration as entire four-movement symphonies by Mozart or Haydn. The emotional weight of the work lies not only in its celebration of the ideal of heroism and struggle, but in the music itself. In this piece Beethoven indulges in extremes of dynamic contrast, rhythmic complexity, insistent dissonance, and sophistication of formal plan. While this symphony is unquestionably part of the symphonic repertory today, at its first appearance many listeners were baffled by it. Critics found it outside the bounds of good taste and simply too full of Beethoven's strivings for singularity and originality. Today those concepts are honored in the arts, but in the enlightened era, taste triumphed over such things, and demanded a more modest approach clearly in the service of the public's sense of what good music should sound like. A sample from one contemporary critic will lend us a sense of how someone versed in the ideals of taste would object to this piece:

> *If Beethoven continues on his present path both he and the public will be the sufferers. His music could soon reach the point where one would derive no pleasure from it, but rather would leave the concert hall with an unpleasant feeling of fatigue from having been crushed by a mass of unconnected and overloaded ideas and continuing tumult by all the instruments.*[2]

In our recorded anthology, we have the first movement of this most difficult symphony [CD2 #9]. Among the many idiosyncratic features of this piece is its vast size. The first movement lasts nearly thirty minutes by itself. The form is sonata, but that form had never been conceived on such a vast scale previously. The exposition section comprises 155 measures, the development section a titanic 245 measures, the recapitulation 154 measures, and the coda sprawls over a gigantic 135 measures. No larger single movement of any piece was ever composed before this piece. For the purpose of comparison, Haydn's Symphony No. 56 spans 271 measures for the entire sonata movement.

Beyond its scope, the piece is informed by a daring and striving sensibility. It opens with hammerstrokes, a sort of homage to the origins of the genre. Returning to the origins of a genre was a common maneuver for reformers, you may recall that Gluck returned to the first story ever told through opera when he embarked on his opera reform.

After the hammerstrokes, a simple triadic theme appears; however, the simplicity of this theme is belied when suddenly the non-harmonic tone of C# is introduced in a melody grounded in E-flat major. This sore note serves as a source of anxiety within the symphony, as though the heroic melody were marred by a single, glaring flaw. In the recapitulation, Beethoven will change this theme on its second and all subsequent appearances by omitting the problematic C#. After the lengthy struggles of the development section, the heroic theme seems to emerge changed, even improved, for having been through the struggle.

The huge development section contains many unusual features. At one point, Beethoven introduces an entire fugue exposition. He passes through far-flung keys dis-

---

[2]Ibid, 329

tantly removed from the tonic E-flat. For example, a new theme appears within the development section in the remote key of E minor. E-flat major and E minor have very few notes in common.

At various points within the exposition section and the development section, Beethoven introduces biting dissonances and vigorous rhythms that work at cross purposes with the prevailing triple meter. These moments are called *hemiolas*, moments when triple-meter pieces start to sound as though they are in a duple meter. More important than the name is the emotional impact of these biting *hemiolas*. They create considerable instability.

At the climax of the development just before the return of the tonic key and the arrival of the recapitulation, Beethoven has one lone horn enter with the heroic theme in the tonic key while all the other instruments play the dominant key. It's as though the horn player has become overwhelmed by the atmosphere of anticipation and has jumped into the recapitulation early.

The coda functions as a second development section as Beethoven continues the process of modulation and reconfiguration of his theme. It ends in tonic on a suitably enthusiastic and optimistic tone befitting a symphony about heroism.

Taken together, all these innovations mark the ideals of Beethoven's heroic period. With his gestures to the history of the genre, his evolving theme, his use of dissonance and hemiola, his unlikely moves like rooting a fugue or a new theme into the development, his having the horn player enter the recapitulation early, and his huge coda full of developmental material, Beethoven points to himself as an individual creator. These techniques mark Beethoven's singularity and originality. He throws a gauntlet at the feet of tradition and defies his critics to resist the appeal of musical heroism. Critics resisted at first, but today, Beethoven has few detractors among the ranks of professional musicians. Yet, as thoughtful students of music's history, we must note how many of these techniques have their roots in the traditions of the symphony that Beethoven sought to serve. Moreover, Beethoven did not invent originality, and in striving for it he strives to join those who came before him. The pages of this book are full of the names of small-scale and large-scale originators of one sort or another. There lies the problem of achieving real originality.

Ludwig van Beethoven, Symphony Number 3, in E♭ Major, Op. 55 (1803)

[CD2, #9] *(Duration, 14 min. 44 sec.)*

First Movement: Allegro con brio
Sonata Form, 3/4 meter

EXPOSITION

0.00   Two loud chords serve as Beethoven's homage to the origins of the symphony when they were used to signal opera audiences to be quiet.

0.03   **First Theme:** A theme built of an ascending then descending E-flat major triad (made up of three notes), but ending on the sore note of C#, appears in the cellos. This heroic theme is repeated in turn by other members of the orchestra.

Violoncello

0.28   The first of many hemiolas (sections when duple meter breaks out in the midst of a triple-meter piece) appears. These halting rhythmic patterns serve as an obstacle to the flowing triple-meter, and serve as a motive for "conflict" or "struggle."

0.42   Orchestra plays the first theme at a forte dynamic level.

0.52   A three-note, descending motive appears as a sort of fragmentation of the heroic first theme, which features both a three-note ascending and a three-note descending melody.

1.07   **Bridge:** Energy builds toward the arrival of the polar (or dominant) key of B-flat major.

1.37   **Second Theme:** The key of B-flat arrives along with a piano dynamic marking and a new calmer theme first heard in the woodwinds. This second, "calmer" theme does not last very long.

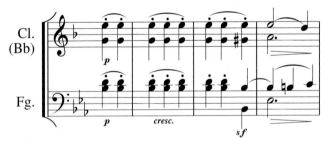

2.01   **Cadence Material:** Energy begins to build to more dissonance, hemiolas, and loudly accented chords combining with fragments of the first theme. After this thematic battle reaches its peak and the exposition nears the end, this "closing" material seems transitional as it begins to wander, and becomes more and more inconclusive. [Beethoven directs performers to repeat the entire exposition in his score, excluding only the initial two loud chords commanding the audience's attention. Regardless, the orchestra in this recorded anthology moves directly into the development section.]

DEVELOPMENT

3.30   Elements of the three-note motive reappear in a quickly modulating harmony.

3.45   The heroic first theme returns in the minor mode. Tension builds as the theme in minor is reinforced by more and more instruments.

4.35　The three-note motive returns in the woodwinds.

4.55　An imitative fugato (only the opening exposition of a fugue) appears, first in the violas, then answered in rapid succession by the violins and cellos.

5.10　Hemiolas appear along with loud, accented chords in the entire orchestra. This section culminates with the arrival of repeated chords made up of dissonant pitches.

5.53　E minor chords are emphasized through repetition, first loudly then decreasing in volume.

5.59　A new and mysterious theme appears in the far-flung key of E minor. This theme is related to the first theme, but has a sufficiently distinct character to call it new.

6.20　The heroic first theme returns first in the cellos and basses, then in the entire orchestra, at a loud dynamic level.

6.47　The new theme appears again.

7.09　The heroic first theme returns in a contrapuntal texture achieved by having the theme appear first in the bassoon, then the clarinet, then the oboe and flute. Each entrance creates an overlap with the one before it.

7.46　**Retransition:** The dynamic level decreases gradually until only the violins are playing two dissonant notes that want to resolve to E-flat major, the tonic of the piece.

8.23　Suddenly a lone horn enters two bars early with the heroic theme in tonic. This rubs against the violins and creates even more urgency to resolve back to tonic.

RECAPITULATION

8.28　**First Theme:** The first, heroic theme appears first in the cellos. The repeats of this theme are re-orchestrated.

8.41　The horn plays the heroic theme but omits the sore C#.

8.51　The flute answers playing the heroic theme as the horn.

9.03　Energy builds until the entire orchestra plays the heroic theme with no sore C#.

9.30　The three-note motive returns in the woodwinds and again at a quiet dynamic level.

9.46　**Bridge:** Energy builds toward the arrival of the polar key.

10.17　**Second Theme:** No polar key arrives; instead the second theme appears in the tonic of E-flat major.

10.43　**Cadence Material:** Energy builds much in the fashion as the exposition with hemiolas and loud chords. Its ending remains inclusive, and leads directly into the coda.

CODA

12.00 The heroic theme appears in the unlikely key of C major. The violins play a new, sprightly counter-melody.

12.25 The new theme, heard first in the development section, appears and is developed.

12.54 A long, slow crescendo unfolds.

13.28 The dynamic level suddenly becomes quiet. The heroic theme appears in the horn. The violins play a new, rhythmically vigorous counter-melody comprised of quiet scales.

13.58 The entire orchestra hammers home the heroic theme at a loud dynamic level as the movement is brought to a rousing end.

Beethoven's Third Symphony, typical of symphonies of the 1800s is in four movements. The second movement is a funeral march, the third movement minuet was displaced by a livelier scherzo, and the last is based on a set of variations with fugally developed episodes and coda. Beethoven utilized classical forms in each movement to propel his themes forward, as one often appears to unfold out of another. In addition, there is motivic consistency between the movements, which creates a psychological progression from beginning to end. Beethoven freed existing forms to achieve non-classical ends.

Other crucial works Beethoven wrote during his middle period include his beloved fifth symphony with its meditation on fate, the heroic opera *Fidelio*, his pastoral sixth symphony, and his last three piano concertos. Throughout this period, Beethoven's fame grew and grew. He would always have detractors who found his music too striving, too far outside the bounds of taste. But he also enjoyed many influential supporters and a generously sized public, not only in Vienna but throughout Western Europe.

THE LATE PERIOD

Toward the latter years of his life, Beethoven became increasingly isolated and irascible. His deafness was likely the product of a congenital defect, incurable and progressive. He had occasional moments when he could hear a little, but he found these periods more agony than anything, as the ringing and popping in his ears that coincided with these surceases of deafness drove him to distraction. His general health also started to fail. He spent long periods without leaving his home.

Beethoven never married; he may never have even loved anyone except in the most abstract fashion. When his brother died, he sued his sister-in-law for custody of his nephew, and won. The relationship was unfortunate. Beethoven wanted greatness from his nephew, who felt crushed under the weight of his uncle's alarming expectations. A suicide attempt followed. After that, Beethoven took little or no pleasure from contact with his extended family.

Beethoven's late style (1816–1827) is marked by a renewed concern for a variety of formal plans. A certain serenity finds its way into his music. The impatient and heroic striving of the middle period gives way to eccentric and meditative pieces. He wrote some outstanding examples of the fugue, theme and variations, and sonata form during his late period. These pieces demonstrate Beethoven's attempt to surprise himself rather than engage the contemporary audience, with whom he had less and less contact. For many enthusiasts of Beethoven's music, his late string quartets and piano sonatas rank among his very best works. These observers admire the audacity of formal plans and the strangeness, ranging from the bleak to the serene, of his expressions.

Our recorded anthology contains a much-celebrated work from late in Beethoven's career, the first movement of his op. 110 piano sonata [CD2, #10]. In this piece, we can hear the heroic striving of the third symphony give way to greater subtlety, as this piano sonata reflects an inner quest rather than strivings for massive social change. Typical of his late works, this piece features a blurring of Classical structural lines throughout. The contrasting themes are not introduced as conflicting material that need to be repeated, developed, and resolved by the end of the movement. Instead, they are invitations to contemplation. Once the heroic journey commences, there is no looking back. Without repeating the exposition, the development section, which simply repeats the opening motive in different keys, is made to inspire the listener to deeper and deeper thought. This movement consists of yearnings, which appear to transcend worldly matters, and of questions that remain unanswered. His Eroica Symphony seems full of confident certainty; the opus 110 piano sonata seems ready to embrace unfulfilled yearnings for answers to questions so vague that each listener will enter into a personal, subjective relationship with the work. This situation marks the goal of the absolute autonomous artwork. Invented as a byproduct of Enlightenment, instrumental works on vague subjects allow the individual listener space for personal rumination.

Listening Guide

Ludwig van Beethoven, Piano Sonata Number 31, in A♭ Major, Op. 110 (1822)

[CD2, #10] *(Duration, 7 min. 12 sec.)*

**First Movement: Moderato cantabile molto expressivo
("Moderate tempo, songlike, highly expressive")
Sonata Form, 4/4 meter**

EXPOSITION

0.00   **First Theme:** Commencing as part of a four-measure introduction, the first theme initiates a melodic motive that enters on the note C or "Mi" (the third of the tonic A♭ Major chord), and develops into the lengthy melodic line which continues into the exposition. Its meditative quality sounds almost improvised as it freely progresses at first to a fermata (literally, "to hold," a "cessation of counting") on a trill, in the concluding measure of the introduction. Brief ornamental flurries complete the measure and link the introduction to the exposition. A pulse in the pianist's left hand accompaniment is heard, reinforcing the meter and moving the contemplative first theme on its way, continuing upwards to a climax that takes place three-quarters of the way through its lengthy line.

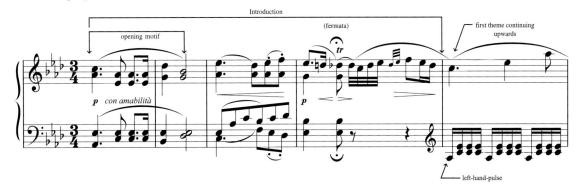

0.46 **Bridge:** This highly original material consists entirely of fluffy arpeggios, which introduce entirely new tone colors, as they effortlessly move to the second theme in the dominant key.

1.09 **Second Theme:** This new theme is a little more assertive than the first, but remains rather gentle in character. Like the first theme, it progresses to a climax three-quarters of the way through its phrase.

1.55 **Cadence Material:** Descending scales sound as though they will bring the exposition to a close, but the melodic line appears to lose steam as it is extended and begins to wander, eventually progressing to chords in a minor key, which seem to question.

[Beethoven does not indicate a repeat of the exposition!. Instead, he moves directly into the development section.]

DEVELOPMENT

2.25 The themes of the exposition are not developed in the usual way. Rather, the opening motive is simply repeated eight times, as it continually modulates in a descending sequence. On the eighth repeat, a trill once again halts the rhythmic motion. Its resolution leads directly into the recapitulation, which begins with the same "opening" motive just repeated.

RECAPITULATION

3.19   **First Theme:** The first theme appears in the tonic key of A♭, now initially accompanied by arpeggio patterns derived from the bridge. The pulse in the pianist's left-hand accompaniment returns just before this theme reaches its climax.

4.08   **Bridge:** These arpeggios do not lead to the dominant this time, and they are interrupted by another series of questioning chords just prior to the return of the second theme.

4.27   **Second Theme:** This theme is now in the tonic key. As it progresses to its climax, the piano left-hand accompaniment adds a series of trills, while the melody in the right hand is decorated by grace notes (notes played quickly before the principal melodic notes, which serve to embellish).

5.29   **Cadence Material:** Descending notes once again sound as though they will bring the section to a close. Again, they soon begin wandering and eventually arrive on more questioning chords. This time, these chords lead directly into a coda section.

6.26   **Coda:** The coda material sounds even freer than the cadence material just heard, as though it is being improvised. Fast note patterns are soon slowed by longer note durations. The movement is brought to a close on the tonic A♭ Major chord, with the melodic line left hanging in midair on the note C or "Mi" once again.

The second movement is a very fast scherzo in F minor, with an even quicker trio section that is jolted by syncopations. The last movement begins with a slow introduction that is full of instrumental recitatives, which lead into fugues and other decidedly emotional "arioso" melodies. The piece ends with flashy A♭ Major arpeggios moving from high to low notes on the piano and back. Essentially, formal structures are blurred to such a degree in this movement that Beethoven appears on the verge of abandoning them entirely.

The Symphony No. 9 provides Beethoven's most optimistic statement from the late years of his career. Written in 1824, this piece requires not only a large symphony orchestra but also a chorus and vocal soloists. These singers participate only in the finale, when they sing a text by Beethoven's favorite writer, the arch-romantic Friedrich Schiller. The overall aim of this finale is a rousing musical call for universal brotherhood. For Beethoven, the symphony changed in terms of its seriousness and social purpose from the days when his teacher Haydn was writing symphonies. Beethoven viewed the symphony as a means of communicating something profound to his times and to posterity. He didn't write symphonies on demand for social occasions, as his teacher had done. The effect of this different attitude toward the genre is that Haydn composed more than 100 symphonies. In a career of comparable duration, Beethoven wrote only nine. Beethoven's more weighty approach had a ripple effect on later composers, as subsequent composers approached the symphony with trepidation, as though Beethoven were looking over their shoulders to make sure they undertook the enterprise of writing a symphony with sufficient seriousness of purpose.

Another reason for the change in Beethoven's attitude is that he did not have to write many symphonies in order to make a handsome living. Haydn may or may not have seen the potential for the symphony as a conduit of profound ideas, but the trajectory of his career would not allow that attitude. He wrote symphonies for a living, not to communicate weighty ideas to posterity.

Among Beethoven's admirers for his strange, late period was the brilliant German author E.T.A. Hoffmann (1776–1822). While Hoffmann did not live to hear the ninth symphony, he was very much inspired by the previous eight. Hoffmann attributed to

Beethoven the power to open the portal to the sublime for the music lover. The concept of the sublime was important to intellectuals of Beethoven's generation. The sublime was born of an experience comprised of terror and awe in which the observer emerges clarified as an individual for having had such an intense experience. Rugged landscapes, wild places, powerful emotional sensations, and overwhelming experiences achieved through the arts were the normal path to sublime experience. On the topic of Beethoven's instrumental music, E.T.A. Hoffmann wrote "Beethoven's music sets in motion the levers of fear, of awe, of horror, of suffering, and awakens just that infinite longing which is the essence of Romanticism. He is accordingly a completely Romantic composer." That Romanticism, born as it is of infinite longing, provides the subject of our next chapter.

 Some Questions for Discussion

1 What is the difference between Rousseau's conception of taste and the way the concept is used today? Can you identify any contemporary uses of the concept of the taste as Rousseau conceived it? What has changed since Rousseau's time to explain the transformation of taste?

2 The law of supply and demand had a different impact on each of the main composers presented in this chapter: Haydn, Mozart, and Beethoven. Describe the impact of supply and demand on their careers and their music. How does the law of supply and demand function today? Have new technologies changed the way composers and musicians are impacted by supply and demand?

3 Beethoven had a keen sense of the value of heroes in society. Was Beethoven a hero? If not, why not? If yes, in what way? What about Haydn and Mozart—do they fit your definition of a hero?

4 The absolute, autonomous artwork emerges out of the Enlightenment at roughly the same time as the ideal of democracy. Is there anything democratic about musical works with no fixed story, no clear meaning?

CHAPTER

11

Romanticism (1820–1900)

ROMANTIC SENSIBILITY

Romanticism may be one of the most difficult words to define referring to a stylistic period in music. One way to think about it stems from the reductive model of understanding history described in previous chapters. Expressive acts, such as the creation of musical works, reveal a general cultural tendency among people of seeing themselves either as rational and essentially in control of their situation, or buffeted by unseen and uncontrollable forces. The Classical Period clearly falls within the rational side of this duality, with its premium on balance and simplicity and absorption of Enlightenment rhetoric. The Romantic Period celebrates the irrational forces of intuition, fantasy, and indefinite feelings of longing and nostalgia.

While this reduction of human history into periods adhering to a simple duality is wildly imprecise, it offers certain advantages for shaping an understanding of artistic style periods. Another simplistic but nonetheless useful method of developing a sense of Romanticism lies in looking upon it as the natural expression of post-Enlightenment ideals. The Enlightenment taught that man is rational and can understand the world by observing it keenly. When the basic tool of understanding is located in each person's head, subjective experience triumphs over appeals to some objective or external means of understanding. The Enlightenment's conception of taste tried to be objective through appeals to nature. Yet there isn't anything particularly objective about the way Rousseau wrote about taste. There's nothing, in short, more natural about Pergolesi's music than about J.S. Bach's music. Human beings constructed both, and both exemplify characteristics that will please some people and not others.

The objection to Rousseau's appeal to naturalness in his preference for Pergolesi over Bach in the previous paragraph might best be called an appeal to the *subjective* rather than the *objective*. Romantics slowly allowed subjectivity to replace appeals to objectivity, setting aside for the moment whether objective appeals truly are objective. According to this logic, the location of meaning is in the individual's head, in his or her own subjective responses. The Romantics drew the logic for trusting subjectivity from the same source as Rousseau drew the logic of genius submitting to taste, from the Enlightenment, with its locating the meaning of experiences in human rationality and its power to make sense of the world.

Romanticism is the product of new privileged authority for subjectivity and the power of the individual to reason for himself or herself. Romanticism rejects the idea that some kind of taste, held in common by all right-thinking people, should govern genius. Indeed, Romanticism puts all its faith in the intuition and subjectivity of self-styled geniuses. Rousseau argued that taste must regulate genius; the romantics will argue that genius is everything in the creation of art.

Romanticism versus Classicism

A final way to think about Romanticism for purposes of this introduction was mentioned in the previous chapter. This approach asks us to think of Romanticism and Classicism as two simultaneously operative, rival sensibilities. As mentioned in the previous chapter, Friedrich Blume argued that Romanticism and Classicism are not consecutive stylistic periods, but sensibilities that may be present within a single piece or even within a single movement. The Classical sensibility favors formal clarity and emotional restraint, while the Romantic sensibility strives for singular and unfettered creativity that plunges into the realms of idealism and fantasy.

The main debate between Romanticism and Classicism centers on genius and taste. Interestingly, there may not be such a thing as "genius" and there may be no such thing as "taste." A genius may simply be someone who is good at something in the eyes of someone else. Taste may be not so much a word as a linguistic technology designed to enforce the will of the more powerful upon the less powerful, a simple means of silencing a minority on matters of art. This argument between Romanticism and Classicism, between genius and taste, may be an argument between rival misunderstandings regarding human creativity and the ways by which we evaluate it. While most in the field of music would disagree with this notion, serious students must at least temporarily entertain the possibility that neither genius nor taste mean what we conventionally think they mean.

ROMANTICISM APPLIED TO MUSIC

Whatever take on Romanticism appeals to each reader, the word first appeared in a dictionary in 1803 when a French linguist defined it as "a certain inexpressible something." Soon after that, the writer E.T.A. Hoffmann applied it to music by describing Mozart as a Romantic, especially in his opera *Don Giovanni*. Hoffmann was taken with the singularity of Mozart's genius and his willingness to defy convention in expressing powerful emotional states. Later Hoffmann applied the term to Beethoven, his favorite composer. What Hoffmann loved about Beethoven's music was its power to transport the listener to the sublime, that realm of experience where the subjective individual is clarified for having faced awe-inspiring and even terrible forces and returned from the experience whole.

Put another way, Beethoven's instrumental music—as understood by Hoffmann—clarifies our individuality. Like a vast chasm or some other awesome and inspirational natural place, Beethoven's music reveals powers that could overwhelm the individual; yet, those powers do not destroy us. We leave the experience clarified for having experienced the sublime. Time and again Romantics will privilege the individual as both creator and as consumer of creations. At first this strategy of privileging the individual

FIGURE 11.3 | Joseph Mallord William Turner, *Fishing Boats Entering Calois Harbor, 1802.* Painting. (Copyright The Frick Collection, New York)

THE FIRST GENERATION OF ROMANTICS 1815–1835

If you had asked the leading composers of the 1820s and 1830s if they fancied themselves "Romantics," few would have said "yes." The music of Mozart, Haydn, and Beethoven was still performed far and wide. These composers were held up as "classics" or models of excellence to be emulated. Each of the younger composers discussed in this section of the book admired and sought to emulate, the older composers; what aspects they admired most depended on each composer's subjective sense of what was valuable about the Classical period. Together, they devoted themselves to all forms and genres, but a certain specialization crept into their work. Mozart, Haydn, and Beethoven all composed in every important genre. The composers discussed below specialized more, although even in that there is some disagreement among them. Franz Schubert composed in every genre, while Frédéric Chopin wrote almost exclusively for the solo piano. Vincenzo Bellini's non-operatic works can be counted on one hand, while defining the genre of Hector Berlioz' creations is almost always problematic.

What these men accomplished as a group is the establishment of feeling and sentiment at the center of music. Their works strive in distinct ways to permit the listener to examine inexpressible longings, nostalgia, searching, and all manner of other individualistic and subjective pursuits.

FRANZ SCHUBERT

Franz Schubert, like the romantic poet John Keats, lived an extremely short life. Born in 1797, the son of an Austrian schoolteacher, Schubert died at the age of 31 through complications from syphilis, a sexually transmitted disease that was incurable before the discovery of penicillin. During his brief life, Schubert was little known outside the city of Vienna. Perhaps his untimely death lent him an air of tragedy, thus inspiring the Romantics of subsequent generations to dote on his legacy. In truth, Schubert never allowed his personal misfortune to interfere with his creativity. Although he knew that he would die young from roughly the age of 22, the last nine years of his life were almost unbelievably productive.

Like Haydn, Schubert was educated at the Imperial Singing School. Initially he sang in the chorus of St. Stephen's Cathedral in Vienna. By the time his voice changed, he had learned to play several musical instruments, including the piano, and had a thorough knowledge of musical theory and composition. After leaving the service of the church, Schubert took a six-month course to become a teacher like his father. His first teaching appointment placed him as an assistant teacher where his father was headmaster, in a little village outside Vienna. Schubert was miserable. He had lived in Vienna amidst the splendid musical life of that city since his early childhood. He longed to return, and did so against his father's advice.

Life in Vienna for Schubert was full of excitement. He led a hand-to-mouth existence; the business of publishing musical compositions was not especially lucrative for an unknown, young composer. Some biographers claim that Schubert used the ample money he made unwisely by supporting friends within a Bohemian community of young artists. Schubert supplemented his income as a composer by performing. He and several friends would prepare evening entertainments for the large class of wealthy Viennese music lovers who could not afford to hire a musical staff on a permanent basis. After Austria's defeats in the Napoleonic Wars, the economy of the country was a muddle. Gone were the days when every aristocrat could afford a large staff of artisans and artists. But the wealthy could certainly afford to hire Schubert and a few friends to come over for an evening of piano works, art songs, and chamber music. These musical evenings came to be known as "Schubertiads."

Schubert excelled in the genre of the art song. Before looking more closely at the area where he achieved his greatest fame, a few words about his total output are in order. Schubert was slightly frustrated by his efforts at composing symphonies and operas. His symphonies were often composed without a specific commission. Therefore he some-

FIGURE 11.4 | *Franz Schubert (1797–1828)*
(© Archivo Iconografico, S.A./Corbis)

FIGURE 11.5 | Moritz von Schwind, *A Schubertiad at the home of Joseph von Spaun,* sepia drawing. Here we see depicted a Schubertiad. Schubert is pictured at the piano wearing glasses. Next to him is the singer Vogl, no doubt performing a *Lied* by Schubert for the edification of the well-dressed audience. (© Archivo Iconografico, S.A./Corbis)

times devoted long hours to composing a piece that yielded him no income. His early symphonies were written while he was a student at the Singing School, and were performed by the student orchestra. His later symphonies were heard very infrequently. For example, some had only one subscription concert performance during his life. His most famous symphony, the "Unfinished," was not performed at all during his lifetime. It had its premiere in 1865, thirty-seven years after his death. As a symphonist, Schubert emphasized lyricism. His melodies are memorable and easy to sing, and reflect his fascination with the song genre. Unlike Beethoven or Haydn, Schubert avoided short, motific melodies ideal for development.

Schubert's operas were seldom produced during his life and are almost never performed today. He favored the Singspiel, a type of German opera that enjoyed a second-class status compared to the more lavishly supported Italian opera.

Schubert created outstanding examples in almost every major genre. He wrote masses, string quartets, solo piano music, a handful of concertos, and chamber works of every description. This eclectic approach and his prolific output link him more closely to Mozart and Haydn as a composer than to the composers of later years who tended to specialize and worked more slowly.

THE ART SONG

The piece in our recorded anthology to represent Schubert was easily one of his most successful in a commercial sense, having sold several thousand copies of its score. The piece is an art song, or "Lied" to use the German term. Schubert's Lieder remain in the repertory of almost every singer. He composed more than 600 of them during his brief life, an unbelievable degree of productivity for a man who died at age 31. This particular song dates from very early in his career, when he was only 17 years old. The song takes its text from Goethe, a brilliant German poet who despised Schubert's Lieder. Goethe held old-fashioned notions about Lieder. He remembered the days when the German Lied was a genre for enthusiastic amateurs. During the 1700s, professional singers sang opera or worked for the church. Lieder were the common property of amateurs and composers wrote them according to this social function. Schubert's Lieder are designed for his professional friends and, while amateurs can sing them, their artistic ambitions and intricate melodies benefit from professional attention. Goethe regretted the professionalizing of the Lied. He saw Schubert as a menace to taste. In general, Romantics will favor professionalism. This theme will rise up several times during this chapter.

Gretchen Am Spinnrade

Schubert's song "Gretchen am Spinnrade" [CD2 #11] presents a text from Goethe's epic drama *Faust*. This drama tells the story of a medieval doctor named Faust who finds himself late in life full of regrets and unease. He claims that he would trade his immortal soul for a moment's pure contentment. Suddenly Mephistopheles, the agent of Satan, appears and volunteers to help Faust realize this exchange. Mephistopheles begins his quest to find Faust a moment of pure contentment by transporting him to his youth and the company of a girl he loved named Gretchen. In the drama, Gretchen sings a song while spinning wool, of her excitement on meeting Faust and kissing him. Schubert's song is his realization of what Gretchen sang as she spun. The title "Gretchen am Spinnrade" translated "Gretchen at the Spinning Wheel."

One of Goethe's many complaints about this song was leveled at the important use of the piano to illustrate the scene. In the 1700s, the accompaniments for songs were considered optional. They never contained important musical information. In this song, Schubert creates an onomatopoetic illustration of the spinning wheel in the piano

Listening Guide

Franz Schubert, Gretchen am Spinnrade
[CD2, #11] *(Duration, 3 min. 43 sec.)*

FIRST STROPHE

0.00	Meine Ruh' ist hin,	My peace is gone,
0.06	Mein Herz ist schwer;	My heart is heavy;
0.10	Ich finde sie nimmer	I'll never find peace
0.14	Und nimmermehr.	And never again.
0.22	Wo ich ihn nicht hab'	Where he is not
0.26	Ist mir das Grab,	Is a grave for me,
0.29	Die ganze Welt	The entire world
0.33	Ist mir vergällt.	Is bitter to me.
0.37	Mein armer Kopf	My poor head
0.40	Ist mir verrückt,	Is disorienting me,
0.44	Mein armer Sinn	My poor sense
0.47	Ist mir zerstückt.	Is torn for me.

SETTING

The spinning-wheel figure can be heard throughout in the piano part. This section begins in D minor and ends in C major.

SECOND STROPHE

0.54	Meine Ruh' ist hin,	My peace is gone,	The second strophe begins identically to the first.
0.58	Mein Herz ist schwer;	My heart is heavy;	
1.01	Ich finde sie nimmer	I'll never find peace	
1.05	Und nimmermehr.	And never again.	

1.13	Nach ihm nur schau' ich	For him only I look	
1.18	Zum Fenster hinaus,	out the window,	
1.21	Nach ihm nur geh'ich	To him only I go	
1.25	Aus dem Haus.	Out of the house.	

1.28	Sein hoher Gang,	His high step,	F major prevails as the text turns to the happy subject of Faust's attractive qualities.
1.32	Sein' edle Gestalt,	His lofty bearing,	
1.35	Seines Mundes Lächeln,	His smiling lips,	
1.38	Seiner Augen Gewalt,	His strong eyes,	

1.42	Und seiner Rede	And his word's	The spinning figure stops on the last line of this group of four lines. The high G on "kiss" is the highest note in the piece so far.
1.46	Zauberfluß,	magic flow,	
1.50	Sein Händedruck,	His hand's touch,	
1.53	Und, ach, sein Kuß!	And, ah, his kiss!	

THIRD STROPHE

2.06	Meine Ruh' ist hin,	My peace is gone,	After three tries, the spinning resumes.
2.18	Mein Herz ist schwer;	My heart is heavy;	
2.22	Ich finde sie nimmer	I'll never find peace	
2.28	Und nimmermehr.	and never again.	

2.35	Mein Busen drängt sich	My spirit seeks him	With this line, the rest of this section emphasizes chromatic motion in the voice suggesting Gretchen's longing.
2.38	Nach ihm hin;	Near and away;	
2.41	Ach, dürft' ich fassen	Ah, if I could touch him	
2.45	Und halten ihn	And hold him	

2.48	Und Kilssen ihn,	And kiss him,	Schubert has the singer repeat the last two lines of this section several times as Gretchen loses herself in the thought of his kisses.
2.51	So wie ich wollt',	As much as I want,	
2.55	An seinen Küssen	In his kisses	
2.58	Vergehen sollt'!	I would lose myself!	

3.26	Meine Ruh' ist hin.	My peace is gone.	The song ends as it began.

part with its swirling *ostinato* (a musical phrase that is repeated persistently). Schubert is so faithful to this *ostinato* pattern illustrating the spinning wheel, that he breaks the pattern only once when Gretchen sings "and, oh, his kiss!" Here the spinning stops. In order to restart a spinning wheel, you must make three pulls forward to get the tension in all the strands of wool and then it can resume spinning. Listen for when the singer sings "und, ach, sein Kuss!" and you will hear three attempts to get the pattern started in the piano again before the spinning music resumes.

Goethe also disliked the form of this song. Songs in the 1700s were almost always strophic. In a strophic setting the same music would be recycled to set different text. Schubert introduces modifications in the music so that it will better illustrate the changing mood of Gretchen as she sings. Worse, as far as Goethe was concerned, is Schubert's marking of each modified strophe with a repetition of the line: "my peace is gone, my heart is heavy; I'll never find peace, and never again." Goethe, the poet, certainly could have repeated this line at the start of each strophe had he wanted to, but he didn't want to. The idea of Schubert changing his poem to suit his musical ideas struck Goethe as insupportable.

The quarrel between Goethe and Schubert illustrates an important reversal in the history of text set to music. You may recall Monteverdi defending himself by proclaiming that words were the mistress to the music, when Artusi challenged him during the first years of the 1600s. Now Schubert, the romantic and self-styled genius, no longer submits to the poet, but goes so far as to change the poem to suit the musical form. Later in the chapter we'll find a composer finally doing away with the poet altogether and composing his own words.

In the listening guide for this song, you will find a description of the many admirable features of Schubert's setting. While Goethe complained, and while Schubert's ideas seem out of step with those of Monteverdi, audiences have embraced Schubert's approach to text setting, which could be extraordinarily sensitive to the words.

As mentioned before, Schubert composed more than 600 songs, all of comparable artistry to this early one. His contribution to the song literature revolutionized the genre. Gone was the amateurism that Goethe so valued. In its place is a genre for professionals with demanding accompanimental parts that contribute to the overall effect. In order to preserve some connection to the roots of the Lied, Schubert affects what scholars call "*volkstummlichkeit.*" This German word might be translated as "folk voice-ness." In musical terms, it comes down to thoroughly professionalized music that strives to sound like folk song. In "Gretchen am Spinnrade," Schubert affects the simplicity of a folk song with a strophic structure; however, each strophe explores musical difficulties suitable really for professionals. In the second, for example, the operatic treatment of the line concerning his kiss departs from the folkloric ideal of the Lied in earlier days. In the third strophe, the wandering and chromatic vocal line expressive of Gretchen's longing strays from the simplicity prized in folk song. The next generation will sustain the thorough professionalization of the Lieder manifested in Schubert's work.

BEL CANTO OPERA

The first half of the 1800s in Italian opera was dominated by the style known as "*bel canto.*" This Italian phrase means "beautiful singing." The name sums up the principal goal of Italian opera composers and audiences during this period. Try though Gluck did to reform opera in the previous century, by the 1810s a certain ritualized formula emerged again in the construction of operas, and audiences loved it.

Gioachino Rossini

Gioachino Rossini (1792–1868) popularized the style of bel canto opera and invented most of the formulas for composing operas during the first thirty years of the 1800s. His first sensational hit as an opera composer came at the youthful age of 21 with the serious opera *Tancredi* (1813). In this opera, Rossini introduced a formal plan for the opening of an opera called an *introduzzione*. In swift succession a good *introduzzione* orients the audience as to where and when the opera is set and what the crucial stakes are within the drama. A principal character is also introduced in the process. This formula, which features details not worth mentioning here, was so successful that many subsequent composers imitated Rossini's procedure. Indeed, most everything that Rossini did was copied by others until eventually a "Code Rossini" appeared. This so-called code was comprised of all the successful structures, formulas, and practices associated with Rossini's marvelous career as a bel canto composer.

Rossini's comic operas are his best loved today. He had a special gift for musical farce. *The Barber of Seville* (1816) was a flop at its debut in Rome, but soon became one of the most beloved and frequently performed operas in the entire repertory.

Here is a partial list of stylistic features, priorities, forms, and circumstances that Rossini popularized in opera in addition to the *introduzzione*.

1. He made the bel canto style the dominant style throughout Italian opera. This style emphasized the singer above all. The orchestra sinks to supporting status whenever an aria begins. The style places a premium on florid vocal display, often characterized by long melismas before cadence points.

FIGURE 11.6 | *Gioachino Rossini (1792–1868)*
(© Corbis)

2. The formal plan for the aria was based on an important tempo change, part way through the aria. Today scholars call Rossini's approach the "two-tempo aria." This form opens with a *scena*, a section of recitative that advances the action. Next comes the *tempo primo*. During this first tempo, there is usually a move from tonic to a polar key (most often the dominant). Sometimes a transitional *scena* occurs. With or without this *scena*, the next move for the aria is to a new tempo. This next section is called the *tempo di mezzo*, or middle tempo. This section is often slower, contrasts in emotion with the *tempo primo*, and often sees a modulation to the mediant, or flat third scale degree. The "two-tempo aria" ends with a rousing *cabaletta*, a section that caps off the form through the return of the tonic. The *cabaletta* is often in a faster tempo. You may have noticed that the two-tempo aria has three tempi, making the label a misnomer.

3. Stock situations often arise in Rossini's operas. For example, in serious operas, just when things seem hopeless for the heroine, she will sing a *preghiera* scene in which she prays for divine intervention. In both comic and serious operas, Rossini often included a Grand Scene of Stupefaction. These are moments when the characters are stunned by some revelation. The music becomes clipped and the tempo extremely slow as the audience is allowed to relish the complete bewilderment of the characters.

4. Placing instruments on stage to form a *banda* was a favorite device of Rossini's. Subsequent Italian composers would search for any dramatic excuse to place instrumentalists on stage.

During the 1820s, Rossini's fame took him to Paris where he managed the *Theatre Italienne*, a state-supported opera company designed to provide Parisians with the option of enjoying Italian opera. In 1830 after a whirlwind career spanning less than twenty years, Rossini retired at the height of his fame. He and his wife devoted themselves to good food, and died very rich and very fat after nearly forty years of living off the revenues generated from Rossini's operas. Before leaving too clear an impression that Rossini was always happy, we must note that his health was faltering during the last decades of his life. He found himself embroiled in a nasty lawsuit with the French government as he tried to recover a stipend promised him by King Charles X in exchange for residing in Paris. Unfortunately for Rossini, Charles X was deposed, and his promised stipend lost. That said, there were always monies coming into Rossini's coffers, as Rossini's music has never fallen out of favor, possibly because he had the good sense to retire before tastes changed.

VINCENZO BELLINI

When Rossini retired, Italian opera lovers were suddenly bereft of new operas worthy of their homage. The young composer Vincenzo Bellini (1801–1835) emerged in southern Italy just as Rossini was contemplating his departure from the limelight. Bellini, like Schubert, died young and for similar reasons. Yet during his very short career, he enjoyed one success after another. His ten operas, all of them serious, were all hits initially. Part of the credit for this situation must go to Giuditta Pasta, the soprano for whom he wrote his operas. They provided Europe with an astoundingly effective collaboration. Eventually they were married.

FIGURE 11.7 | *Vincenzo Bellini (1801–1835)*
(© Hulton-Deutsch Collection/Corbis)

Norma

Bellini created the title role of his opera *Norma* (1831) for his future wife. Opera lovers rank it among the best roles in the entire history of opera. The most famous aria from *Norma*, "Casta diva" [CD3 #1], is in our recorded anthology of music. This aria provides a clear example of the bel canto style with its dramatic, florid, and astonishing vocal line. It also provides us a glimpse of the two-tempo form popularized by Rossini.

The story of *Norma*, like that of many fine operas, revolves around complications in love. The opera is set in ancient Gaul, the region of Western Europe that's now France. As the opera begins, the Romans have occupied Gaul by force; and the local Druids (nature worshipping residents of Gaul) are unhappy about it. Norma is the high priestess of the Druids. In that role, she must serve as the human intermediary between the Druidic gods and the people. Her position also requires her to be a virgin. Unbeknownst to her people, she is not a virgin. She bore two sons. Worse still, the father is the Roman proconsul. Unfortunately for Norma, she loves this Roman still, but the proconsul no longer loves her. Instead, he loves Norma's best friend, Adalgisa. The section of the opera on our recordings begins as the Druids are awaiting word from Norma before they rise up and kill the invading Romans. Horrified that her people will murder the man she loves and the father of her children, Norma tries to buy time. The Druids have amassed at the temple, and Norma speaks to them in an effort to temper their zeal for revenge against the invaders. In asides to the audience, Norma reveals her essential dilemma. She wants to perform her duty to her people while still protecting the father of her sons.

The scene is a textbook two-tempo aria and a masterful application of the ideals of bel canto opera. Florid and melismatic vocal material proliferates in Norma's part. The orchestra serves as a clearly subservient support for her line. This resulting homophonic texture typifies the bel canto style. From the Code Rossini, Bellini takes the formal plan of the scene. The principal advantage of the two-tempo aria is the opportunity for emotional contrast. Each tempo area (*tempo primo, tempo di mezzo,* and *cabaleta*) allows the singer to embrace a distinct affect. Another element of the Code Rossini is a *banda,* a group of instrumentalists who appear on stage. As the Druids march into the temple, the *banda* accompanies them, as on-stage instrumentalists form part of the action. Limitation of time on the CDs only allows for inclusion of tempo primo.

In addition to Bellini, we must acknowledge the contribution of two other artists to this scene: Felice Romani and Giuditta Pasta. Romani created the libretto for *Norma.* It ranks among the best loved of all romantic libretti. The dramatic situation, doomed as it is from Norma's point of view, provides the opera lover with a delicious sense of looming catastrophe. In this scene, for example, we can see beautifully illustrated through the text how trapped Norma has become. Pasta was the first Norma. Her superb voice inspired Bellini to create one of the most famous roles in the history of opera. Eventually Bellini and Pasta were married. Surveys of music history before the advent of recording technology generally neglect the performers, as their performances died with them. At least in a role like Norma, which was designed for a particular singer, we have some indication of Pasta's formidable talents. The part is both exacting in its technical difficulty and full of opportunities for a great singer to luxuriate in the beauty of her voice. After all, audiences primarily attended the opera in order to hear their favorite stars.

Listening Guide

Vincenzo Bellini, "Casta diva" from Norma, Act I, scene 4 (1831)

[CD3, #1] *(Duration, 6 min. 22 sec.)*

INTRODUCTION (Andante sostenuto, "Moderately slow and sustained"): The orchestra presents a short introduction. In this introduction the flute plays the melody that will initially be assigned to Norma. Note how slowly this melody unfolds. That slow quality illustrates Norma's hope that time itself might stop so that she might reconcile her conflict between patriotism and love.

TEMPO PRIMO: Here Norma enters and sings the text translated below. She calls upon the Goddess of the Woodlands to temper the Druid warriors and make them patient. As this section continues, Norma is eventually joined by the chorus, which sings quietly along with the supporting accompaniment in the orchestra. Note too that toward the end of this section, Norma's part becomes increasingly virtuosic, with long melismas at cadences and long-held high notes.

NORMA

1.13	Casta Diva, che inargenti	Chaste Goddess, who coats with silver
1.43	Queste sacre antiche piante,	These sacred, ancient plants,
2.05	A noi volgi il bel sembiante;	Turn your beautiful face toward us;
2.42	Senza pube e senza vel!	Without clouds and without veil!

2.53 *Chorus joins with supporting accompaniment.*

3.54	Tempra, o Diva, tu de' cori ardenti	Temper, oh Goddess, all these ardent hearts
4.21	Tempra ancora lo zelo audace,	Temper too their audacious zeal,
2.43	Spargi in terra, ah, quella pace,	Spread over the earth, ah, that peace,
5.16	Che regnar tu fai nel ciel.	That you make reign in the heavens.

(Not included on CD)
SCENA: Here the *banda* plays as the Druid army marches into the temple. Then Norma resumes her address to the crowd, concluding that they are to wait for her voice to give the signal for the massacre of the Roman invaders. Typical of a scena, the chorus provides an important contribution. The scena is the section ideally suited to advancing the action. In this case, the chorus growls for the blood of the Romans and specifically mentions the Proconsul, Norma's former lover and the father of her two sons. Norma's hopelessly conflicted situation is further clarified in the final aside that she sings in recitative. Notice that lines in parentheses are asides, audible only to the audience and not the characters who share the stage with the speaker.

NORMA

Fine al rito; e il sacro bosco	The rite is finished; let the sacred woods
Sia disgombro dai profani.	Be cleared of the profane ones.
Quando il Nume irato e fosco,	When the irate and brooding God,
Chiegga il sangue dei Romani,	Demands the blood of the Romans,
Dal Druidico delubro	From the Druidic Temple
La mia voce tuonerà.	My voice will sound.

CHORUS

Tuoni; e un sol del popol empio	Let it sound; and not one of the impious folk
Non isfugga alguisto scempio;	Shall escape our just cruelty;
E primier da noi percosso	And first for our vengeance
Il Proconsole cadrà.	The Proconsul will fall.

NORMA

Cadrà . . . punirlo io posso . . .	He will fall . . . punish him I can . . .
(Ma punirlo il cor non sa.)	(But punishing him my heart does not know how.)

TEMPO DI MEZZO: As the tempo changes to a faster clip, Norma continues revealing her inmost thoughts to the audience and not to the other characters on the stage. She sings of her ongoing love for the Proconsul and of her hope that he will return to her. Meanwhile, the chorus punctuates her reflections with complaints of how their long-dreamt about day of vengeance drags. The impatience of the chorus for violence juxtaposes nicely with Norma's confused and frenzied hopes for lost love restored.

NORMA

(Ah! bello a me ritorna	(Ah! Love return to me
Del fido amor primiero:	My faithful first love:

E contro il mondo intiero	And against the entire world
Difesa a te sarò.	I shall defend you.
Ah! bello a me ritorna	Ah! Love return to me
Del raggio tuo sereno;	The serenity of your look;
E vita nel tuo seno	And living in your arms
E patria e cielo avrò).	I'll possess both homeland and heaven.)

CHORUS

Sei lento, si, sei lento,	How slowly, yes, how slowly,
O giorno di vendetta;	This day of vengeance;
Ma irato il Dio t'affretta	But the irate God hurries you
Che il Tebro condannò.	Who the Tiber condemned.

CABALETA: This last section sees not so much an abrupt tempo change as a quickening of the former tempo. The chorus continues to sing, but they introduce no new text. The quickening pace brings the aria to a rousing close.

NORMA

(Ah! riedi ancora	(Ah! Return again
Qual eri allora	To what you were then
Quando, ah quando il cor	When, ah, when my heart
Ti dicdi allora.)	I gave to you.)

Norma continues throughout the opera to hope that her lover will return to her. He doesn't. He suggests that he be allowed to take their sons to Rome to raise them as Romans. She refuses. She contemplates killing her children to hide her crimes against her people and against her oath to the Druid gods. She can't do it. In the end, her crimes are exposed. The Druids sentence her to die for her dishonesty and duplicity. The Proconsul is captured. As Norma is burned to death, the Proconsul realizes her virtue and throws himself onto the fire with her.

Italian Opera after Bellini

As mentioned above, Bellini died young. With his death and Rossini's retirement, enthusiasts for Italian opera feared that the bright light of the bel canto style might be extinguished. Initially Gaetano Donizetti (1797–1848) stepped into the breach. While his operas were failures as often as they were commercial successes, he did manage to keep the bel canto style going into the second generation of the Romantic period. Donizetti's works that win the most frequent productions today are his comic opera *Don Pasquale* (1843) and his tragic opera *Lucia di Lammermoor*, based on a hugely popular novel by the Scottish writer Sir Walter Scott. This latter opera tells the horrific tale of a young girl forced to marry against her will, resulting in her murdering her husband on their wedding night. Donizetti's work is heavily indebted to the innovations of Rossini. However, all the bel canto composers owe some debt to Mozart, who did so much to clarify individual characters through music and who capitalized on so many structural innovations introduced by Gluck. Like all of the first generation Romantics, bel canto composers extended many strong features of the classical style into their own time.

FRÉDÉRIC CHOPIN

Just as Bellini specialized in composing operas, Chopin specialized in composing for the piano. This situation reflects the fact that Chopin was himself a superb pianist. All of Chopin's works include a piano and with the exception of a few songs, the piano is either the only instrument or the central instrument in every piece.

Chopin's Career

Frédéric Chopin (1810–1849) was born in Poland to a Polish mother and a French father. His father taught French to the children of Polish aristocrats, while his mother was a lady-in-waiting to a Polish countess. As a very young man, Chopin showed enormous talent for the piano. He was frequently picked up from his family's modest home by the carriages of the wealthy and powerful in Warsaw in order to entertain at their palaces.

The 1820s were a difficult time for Poland. Poland formed a reluctant part of the Russian Empire, a situation that pleased very few Poles. In entertaining both Russian and Polish aristocrats living in Warsaw, Chopin initially seemed unconcerned with the affairs of his homeland. However, when he moved to Vienna to seek his fame as a pianist in that great musical city, he wept for fear that he would never return to his beloved home.

FIGURE 11.8 | Eugène Delacroix, *Portrait of Chopin,* painting. The brilliant romantic painter Delacroix captures something of Chopin's dreamy and introverted nature in this portrait. Delacroix seems to capture his subject's commitment to his own subjectivity. (© Archivo Iconografico, S.A./Corbis)

Initially Vienna welcomed Chopin with open arms. Among the pieces he presented during his visits were works based on Polish national dances such as the Polonaise and Mazurka. These works struck Viennese audiences as attractively novel, the national dances of central and eastern Europe having seldom been invoked in so-called high art music. However, soon after Chopin arrived in Vienna, a war broke out between Poland and Russia. The Austrian Empire possessed many lands that were, like Poland, Slavic in language and ethnicity. The Austrians sided with the Russians in the hope that this revolution would be squelched before it spread to other Slavic lands. Suddenly, a visiting Polish pianist playing works with a distinctly Slavic character was no longer seen as an attractive novelty, but as a menace. Chopin began working to move to Paris, as the French were nominally allied with Poland in their struggle for independence. If Chopin wasn't particularly interested in the politics of his homeland when he was young and entertaining the aristocracy, the politics of his homeland became interesting in him. Once in Paris, he composed his *Revolutionary Etude*, reflecting his anger at the Russian occupation of his native land.

Once in Paris, Chopin gravitated toward a highly literate and accomplished circle of friends while seeking out aristocratic, or at the very least wealthy, music lovers to support his art. Among Chopin's friends were the brilliant pianist and composer Franz Liszt and the accomplished novelist George Sand. Through these connections and others, Chopin made his living playing the piano in private salons, publishing his works for the piano, and teaching young women of unremarkable talents but high social standing.

Chopin could be a reluctant public figure. Since his youth in Warsaw, he was used to interacting with aristocrats. He maintained their airs, and was irritable and distant. Since childhood he had a weak constitution that left him bed-ridden for weeks at a time. In adulthood he tended toward hypochondria. These idiosyncrasies endeared him to the Parisian elite, who relished Chopin's eccentricities and aristocratic bearing.

Chopin's Music

His music reflects in some interesting ways his introverted and singular temperament. The Romantics took great pleasure in using the arts as a forum for self-revelation. The novelist George Sand, the pen name of Aurora Dudevant, who found life in the world of literature easier to negotiate with a man's name, lived with Chopin for a number of years. She recorded the following description of his work habits, which captures his exacting nature and minute quest to make his spontaneous musicality live in his compositions:

> *His creation was spontaneous and miraculous. He found it without seeking it, without foreseeing it. It came on his piano suddenly, complete, sublime, or it sang in his head during a walk, and he was impatient to play it to himself. But then began the most heart-rending labor I ever saw. It was a series of efforts, or irresolutions, and of frettings to seize again certain details of the theme he had heard; what he had conceived as a whole he analyzed too much when wishing to write it, and his regret at not finding it again, in his opinion, clearly defined, threw him into a kind of despair. He shut himself up for whole days, weeping, walking, breaking his pens, repeating and altering a bar a hundred times, writing and erasing it as many times, and recommencing the next day with a minute and desperate perseverance. He spent six weeks over a single page to write it at last as he had noted it down in the very first.*[1]

Imagine if Haydn, while working at the Esterháza Palace, worked in this fashion. If the Prince had not simply dismissed him, we can at least imagine that Haydn would not have written over 100 symphonies, along with dozens of works in every other major musical genre, for Haydn in the 1700s, like so many composers before him, served a master other than himself. Chopin was his own master in a certain sense. He could afford to dote on the tiniest details of his pieces, even though the process caused him pain. For Romantics after Chopin, the path was paved toward a career of self-indulgence, if we want to place a dark spin on the Romantic imagination, or on the pursuit of perfect self-expression (to take a more positive approach).

George Sand's description of Chopin's habits jibes with the pieces themselves. Chopin was something of a perfectionist whose works, at their best, sound spontaneous, yet which reveal minute craft and attention to the smallest detail. Given these tendencies, Chopin wisely specialized in miniature forms. Most of his output is comprised of single-movement compositions of relatively short duration. Many of his favorite genres were new in the 1800s; others were miniature genres that achieved their greatest popularity during Chopin's time. Among his favorite genres were the nocturne, Polonaise, Mazurka, impromptu, ballade, etude, waltz, and prelude.

---

[1]*Music in the Western World: A History in Documents*, Piero Weiss and Richard Taruskin, editors (New York: Schirmer, 1984): 370.

The Nocturne

The piece in our recorded anthology to reflect Chopin's work is a nocturne [CD3 #2]. The nocturne genre was developed by the Irishman, John Field. The goal of the genre centers on the evocation of moods and feelings associated with the night. Chopin composed twenty-one nocturnes, making it one his most favored genres. The attraction of the genre partly stems from the fact that there is no preconceived formal plan associated with the genre. While sonatas usually open with sonata form, or fugues reveal by definition a particular form, the nocturne had no such history. Chopin, and indeed many Romantics, wanted to illustrate their individual creativity in their work. The Romantics favored spontaneity in creativity, seeing it as superior to the taste-bound calculations of their classical predecessors. One way to appear spontaneous in musical composition is to resist obvious formal planning. Each of Chopin's nocturnes has a distinct structure, but there is one general principle governing them all: once presented, most material returns but always with important details altered. We mustn't confuse this with theme and variations. Chopin's methods aren't nearly so rigid as to permit the presentation of a single theme followed by variations. There might be as many as six segments, each receiving one or more varied restatement. For Chopin, variations on ideas are a way to reflect his spontaneous, seemingly improvised methods.

Chopin's nocturnes are remembered by their key, in this case F# major, rather than by their number. The Nocturne in F# major exemplifies a structure on both the small and large scale that reflects Chopin's concern with variation. The overall form of the piece is A-A1-B-C-A2-coda. The reason for placing numbers after the returns of A is simple: each return is sufficiently different that some recognition of that difference is required in describing the form. Within each A section, there is also small-scale variation. The piece begins with a two-measure phrase. The phrase features a two-note ascent, followed by a rapid descent to a low, repeated note. This melody is accompanied by attractive chords in the left-hand part. This essential shape, a two-note ascent followed by a rapid descent to repeated low notes, is presented four times. Each time, Chopin adds more notes, changes the repeated low note, and adds rhythmic complexity to each restatement. The result is not only variation at the large scale through varied restatements of the entire A section, but variation at a smaller scale with varied restatements of a two-measure phrase within each A section. One could even say that the B section itself isn't much different from a variation on the A section. The B section opens with a haunting four-measure motive that begins with ascending material, reaches a high note, and repeats that high note several times, only to fall back quickly with a rapid descending pattern. This phrase is almost a perfect opposite of the phrase that opens the A section.

The minute detail of these variations conjures to mind George Sand's description of Chopin at the piano, weeping to recall the details he heard in his head and struggling one hundred times to write them down. Chopin was a perfectionist aiming to please his most exacting audience, himself.

In terms of melody, you may notice that Chopin's florid and intricate melodies have much in common with Bellini's *bel canto* melodies. This similarity has been observed by many and seems intentional. *Bel canto* opera was much beloved in Chopin's time, it isn't any wonder that the pianist emulated it in his compositions.

Among the many pleasures Chopin's music afforded the elegant music lovers of Paris' exclusive salons, surely the indescribable longing expressed in his music takes pride of place. Through his compositions, Chopin had a gift for breathing life into the Romantic ideal of giving oneself over to inward feelings and longings.

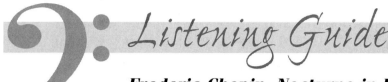

Frederic Chopin, Nocturne in F-sharp

[CD3, #2] *(Duration, 3 min. 24 sec.)*

FORM: **A-A1-B-C-A2-coda**

0.00 **A**   The piece begins with a two-measure phrase. The phrase features a two-note ascent, followed by a rapid descent to a low, repeated note. The melody is accompanied by chords in the left-hand part. This two-measure pattern is presented four times. Each time, Chopin adds more notes, changes the repeated low note, and adds rhythmic complexity to each restatement.

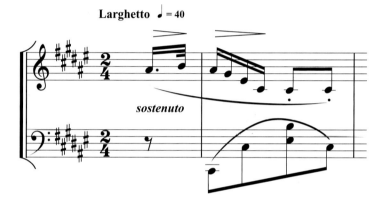

0.31 **A1**   Varied restatement of the entire A section.

1.06 **B**   Opens with a haunting four-measure motive that begins with ascending material, reaches a high note, and repeats that high note several times, only to fall back quickly with a rapid descending pattern, This phrase is almost a perfect opposite of the phrase that opens the A section.

1.38 **C**   Chopin indicates that the tempo of this section should move twice as fast as the opening tempo. The two-note ascent motive in dotted rhythm heard at the beginning is repeated throughout this section. As the motive surges passionately up and down with harmonic turns, this section may be heard as a quasi-development.

2.1? **A2**   The A section is varied again. Its return in the first tempo, coming just after the previous section, may have the affect of a recapitulation.

2.55 **Coda** Falling from a high-note, right-hand arpeggios bring this nocturne ("night piece") to a dreamy, meditative close.

Few may find this interesting anymore, but this lovely piece was included in a most unlikely film, *Dracula's Daughter* (1936). This impressive sequel to the original *Dracula* (1931) starring Bela Lugosi finds the infamous count's daughter hopeful that her father's death will liberate her from the unholy appetites of vampirism. She plays this nocturne at the piano as she dreams of release from her curse, but all the while her evil servant reminds her of the old ways, and points out that the music speaks not of release, but of unfulfilled longing for release. The servant proves correct, and Dracula's daughter leaves the piano to stalk another victim. Why filmmakers a century later would use this piece as the perfect expression of unful-filled longing for release from one's troubles speaks to Chopin's persuasive power as a Romantic artist versed in the expression of longings.

HECTOR BERLIOZ

Our last stop in this brief tour through the first generation of Romanticism keeps us in Paris, where Hector Berlioz lived. Born the son of a surgeon in rural France, Berlioz moved to Paris in order to study medicine. Once in the capital, Berlioz was soon seduced away from his medical studies to pursue music as a career, despite having shown very little aptitude in the field up to that time. His parents were understandably horrified at this bizarre change of career plan. They disowned him. Berlioz, ever confident in his instincts, persisted. His first move was an attempt to gain admission into France's greatest school of music, the Paris Conservatoire. François-Joseph Fétis, one of the faculty members present at Berlioz' interview for admission, recalled the scene this way:

FIGURE 11.9 | *Hector Berlioz (1803–1869)*
(© Hulton-Deutsch Collection/Corbis)

I remember one day (about twelve years ago) when I was a member of the examining jury for the composition classes at the Conservatory. Among the students who brought examples of their work was a young man who seemed quite bored with the whole proceeding. He showed me some monstrosity that he believed to be double-counterpoint: it was nothing but a tissue of harmonic horrors. I made a few corrections and explained the reasons for them to the young man in question. His sole response was to inform me that he held all studies in great contempt, and that he considered them completely useless to a man of genius.[2]

Hector Berlioz (1803–1869) holds a reputation as something of a maverick. No rule or tradition could stop him if he felt his way was better. Why a young man who held studies in contempt would want to attend a school illustrates the irony of Berlioz' career. On the one hand, he felt satisfied with his own way and reluctant to change in order to please anyone else; on the other hand, he worked hard at his craft, and took musical studies seriously. While his first attempt to enroll at the Conservatoire failed, his later effort did not. Once a student, he longed to win the school's most prestigious prize, the Prix de Rome. This prize was established under Napoleon and entitled the winner to live in Rome at the French government's expense for two years. On returning to Paris, a gala "concert envoi" entirely made up of the winner's compositions would be performed by the finest musicians available. Berlioz entered the competition five times before finally winning. On the four unsuccessful attempts, he sought to please himself by putting himself at the free disposal of his vivid and unorthodox musical imagination.

[2]*Berlioz Fantastic Symphony*, Edward T. Cone, editor (New York: Norton, 1971): 216.

Finally, on the fifth try, he tempered his willful musical personality sufficiently to please the jury. In winning the prize, his status as a composer of note became incontestable. His parents even forgave him his rash career change. Berlioz was a maverick, who also managed on occasion to please both himself and the larger world around him.

Unlike the other composers discussed in this section, Berlioz was never quite able to make his living entirely as a composer. He worked also as a musical journalist. In that role, he could campaign for his uncompromisingly romantic vision of what music should be.

His compositional output is comparatively sparse. His works tend to be large, sometimes even mammoth in their scope. Some of them are quite impractical to execute. For example, his opera *Les Troyens*, based on Virgil's *Aeneid*, sprawls over five acts. After Act two, a generation passes, and all the characters from the first two acts are dead. In order to stage this work, two complete casts of stars are required. More impractical was his vision for the orchestra. He felt that the modern symphony orchestra should be comprised of hundreds of musicians, thus drastically increasing the expense for concert promoters. Not only would he have increased enormously the number of players on all the usual orchestral instruments, but he would have added all manner of exotic instruments seldom mentioned by other composers, let alone actively used.

Symphonie Fantastique

Berlioz' compositional style tends toward the flamboyant. Among his most striking choices were the subjects about which he chose to compose. Unlike composers of the past, Berlioz believed that instrumental music benefited from telling a specific story. We call this sort of storytelling piece *programmatic music*. The example in our recorded anthology representing Berlioz is taken from his most famous programmatic work, the *Symphonie Fantastique* [CD3 #3].

Berlioz composed his *Symphonie Fantastique* while he was a student at the Paris Conservatoire. The symphony is in five movements. For the purposes of audience members understanding his intentions, Berlioz wrote a literary text to accompany and explain his symphony. The story is taken from the life of a young musician. Berlioz probably saw the young artist as an extension of himself. Here is Berlioz' program for the symphony:

> 1. **Reveries and Passions**: The author imagines that a young musician, afflicted with that moral disease that a well-known writer calls the *vague des passions*, sees for the first time a woman who embodies all the charms of the ideal being he has imagined in his dreams, and he falls desperately in love with her. Through an odd whim, whenever the beloved image appears before the mind's eye of the artist, it is linked with a musical thought whose character, passionate but at the same time noble and shy, he finds similar to the one he attributes to his beloved.

This melodic image and the model it reflects pursue him incessantly like a double *idée fixe*. That is the reason for the constant appearance, in every [movement] of the symphony, of the melody that begins the first Allegro. The passage from this state of melancholy reverie, interrupted by a few fits of groundless joy, to one of frenzied passion, with its movements of fury, of jealousy, its return of tenderness, its tears, its religious consolations—this is the subject of the first movement.

2. **A Ball**: The artist finds himself in the most varied situations—in the midst of the tumult of a party, in the peaceful contemplation of the beauties of nature; but everywhere, in town, in the country, the beloved image appears before him and disturbs his peace of mind.

3. **Scene in the Country**: Finding himself one evening in the country, he hears in the distance two shepherds piping a *ranz des vaches* in dialogue. The pastoral duet, the scenery, the quiet rustling of the trees gently brushed by the wind, the hopes he has recently found some reason to entertain—all concur in affording his heart an unaccustomed calm, and in giving a more cheerful color to his ideas. He reflects upon his isolation; he hopes that his loneliness will soon be over.—But what if she were deceiving him!—This mingling of hope and fear, these ideas of happiness disturbed by black presentiments, form the subject of the Adagio. At the end, one of the shepherds again takes up the *ranz des vaches*; the other no longer replies.—Distant sound of thunder—loneliness—silence.

4. **March to the Scaffold**: Convinced that his love is unappreciated, the artist poisons himself with opium. The dose of the narcotic, too weak to kill him, plunges him into a sleep accompanied by the most horrible visions. He dreams that he has killed his beloved, that he is condemned and led to the scaffold, and that he is witnessing his own execution. The procession moves forward to the sounds of a march that is now somber and fierce, now brilliant and solemn, in which the muffled noise of heavy steps gives way without transition to the noisiest clamor. At the end of the march the first four measures of the *idée fixe* reappear, like a last thought of love interrupted by the fatal blow.

5. **Dream of a Witches' Sabbath**: He sees himself at the Sabbath, in the midst of a frightful troop of ghosts, sorcerers, monsters of every kind, come

FIGURE 11.10 | Francisco de Goya y Lucientes, ***Witches' Sabbath.*** Painting. Goya's painting may perhaps mirror the frightful crowd of ghosts, sorcerers, and monsters, that which Berlioz imagines in the fifth movement of his *Symphonie Fantastique*, Dream of a Witches' Sabbath. (© Archivo Iconografico, S.A./Corbis)

FIGURE 11.11 | Albrecht *Dürer, **The Four Horsemen of the Apocalypse. c. 1497.*** Woodcut. *Dürer's* work reflects tensions present in northern Europe at the end of the fifteenth, and early sixteenth centuries. Like many German artists of his time, he replicates medieval preoccupations with fear and death. Although similar concerns are expressed throughout human history, Hector Berlioz later romanticized them with a unique use of the widely known Gregorian chant, ***Dies Irae*** ("Day of Wrath"), in the fifth movement of his ***Symphonie Fantastique* (1830).** While heroically exploring multiple macabre arenas traditionally taboo, the climactic announcement of the chant by trumpets, sounding over a witches' motive previously established, creates an apocalyptic landscape similar to *Dürer's.* (© Bettmann/Corbis)

together for his funeral. Strange noises, groans, bursts of laughter, distant cries which other cries seem to answer. The beloved melody appears again, but it has lost its character of nobility and shyness; it is more than a dance tune, mean, trivial, and grotesque: it is she, coming to join the Sabbath.—A roar of joy at her arrival.—She takes part in the devilish orgy.—Funeral knell, burlesque parody of the *Dies irae*, Sabbath round-dance. The Sabbath round and the *Dies irae* combined.[3]

In this fantastical story, Berlioz draws upon some basic Romantic preoccupations. The idea of a love so desperate that it consumes the artist reveals a complete lack of the sort of moderation that classicism valued. The fascination with mysterious forces of death captured the imagination of innumerable Romantic artists. Similarly, nature as an entry to the sublime and source of calming reassurance also served the Romantic imagination well.

Some aspects of the story, however, are completely personal to Berlioz. Some, for example, feel that the composition of this symphony was influenced by Berlioz' then

FIGURE 11.12 | Harriet Smithson
(© Hulton-Deutsch Collection/Corbis)

unrequited love for the Irish Shakespearean actress Harriet Smithson. Indeed, Berlioz was infatuated with her at the time he was working on this piece. Later, the two were married, had a son, and finally divorced due to Berlioz' chronic unfaithfulness. The transformation of the idealized beloved into melody for this piece was a brilliant stroke. Many subsequent composers would take up this idea by assigning melodies to represent everything in their programmatic music, from characters to places to emotional states. Berlioz' use of the *idée fixe* in every movement of the symphony helps lend some musical coherence to the symphony as a whole. After its initial appearance in the first movement, this sprawling theme reappears as a waltz melody in the second movement, part of a *ranz des vaches* (cattle herd's song) in the third, a mocking snip before the guillotine strikes in the fourth, and a grotesque basis for a Sabbath dance in the fifth. The fifth movement is in our recorded anthology.

Listening Guide

Hector Berlioz, Symphonie Fantastique
[CD3, #3] *(Duration, 9 min. 41 sec.)*

Dream of a Witches' Sabbath

INTRODUCTION:

PROGRAM	MUSIC
0.00 The musician finds himself at a Witches' Sabbath, in the midst of a frightful crowd of ghosts, sorcerers, and all kinds of monsters, come to bury him.	Low strings introduce an ascending witches motive. Orchestral effects generate a rather scary, macabre landscape.

0.25 Unearthly sounds, groans, shrieks of laughter, distant cries echoed by others.	Trumpets and horns echo one another with distorted calls.
0.44	Opening sections repeat.
1.18 The melody of his beloved is heard, but it has lost its character of nobleness and timidity. It is she who comes to the Sabbath!	The first portion of the *idée* fixe. It is heard, though by two E-flat clarinets (the piccolo members of the clarinet family).

1.25 There is a roar of joy at her arrival. She joins in the devilish orgies.

There is a boisterous orchestral response to Harriet Smithson's theme (the idée fixe) before the E-flat clarinets present it, this time in its entirety (distorted).

2.01

The orchestra crescendos and the witches' motive is restated.

2:14

The orchestra quiets down with a descending transitional passage. (The implication is that their meeting is coming to order for the mass to begin.)

2.53 The funeral knell,

Three sets of funeral bells are heard. The witches' motive is also present, indicating (if there were still any remaining questions) that this is a black mass taking place.

3.19 burlesque of the *Dies irae.*
—The *Dies irae* ("Day of Wrath") is one of the gravest Georgian chants. It was frequently heard in Catholic Requiem Masses throughout France. The meaning of this chant as a token of death was unmistakable to Berlioz's audience.

Tubas and bassoons play the chant boldly in a fixed meter.

3.41

Horns and trombones play a faster version.

3.51

Woodwinds play the chant faster still.

3.57

The three versions above are all repeated twice.

4.55

Afterwards, there is a transitional passage that crescendos and develops the upward witches' motive

5.13 A macabre witches' round-dance begins.

The upward witches' motive serves as the subject for a free fugue. The fugue entries overlap one another, in stretto.

5.41

There is a short episode before three more entrances of the subject are heard in stretto again.

6.17	After a second brief episode, consisting of a loud, accented rhythmic motive, derived from the subject, the music dies down.
6.57 The *Dies irae* and sabbath round dance are combined.	Fragments of the *Dies irae* are heard in the distance.
7.12	Over a drum roll, a long transition builds as it steadily brings these gigantic forces head-on.
7:31	Several dissonances are heard, as these bodies cannot harmoniously coexist.
7.48	The witches' motive is heard in the low strings.
7.57	The trumpets present the *Dies irae* exultantly, in a high register over the witches' motive on the bottom.
8.22	The witches' motive is played by the string instrumentalists' striking the wooden part of their bows against their strings to create a frenzied, macabre effect.
9.03	A portion of the *Dies irae* is the only theme heard.
9.11	Grand cadences conclude this movement, and thus the entire symphony.

Berlioz' *Symphonie Fantastique* persuaded many subsequent Romantic composers to embrace the ideals of programmatic music. Program music had existed before. Baroque composers like Heinrich Biber, classical composers like Carl Ditters von Dittersdorf, and even Beethoven (in his *Symphony No. 6*) had created purely instrumental pieces configured to tell a story or conjure specific images. What made Berlioz' efforts along this line so persuasive were the vividness of his musical imagination, his journalistic polemics on behalf of his ideas, and the conviction with which he persisted.

THE SECOND GENERATION OF ROMANTICS

Dividing the 1800s into three distinct generations is by no means the only or even the most efficient way of telling the story of Romanticism. What the composers who flourished in the 1840s and 1850s inherited was a difficult situation. The first generation of Romantic composers took time to rediscover past music and to celebrate it through performances. J.S. Bach and G.F. Handel were two figures whose scores had lain dormant and unperformed for many decades. During the 1830s, Felix Mendelssohn in Berlin, and others in London and Paris, began reviving old works. The resulting fascination with the history of music led to an explosion of interest with past music among audiences. The term "Classical," itself a term of honor, came to be applied to older music in an effort to hold it up as the model of excellence. For composers working in the middle part of the 1800s, they suddenly found themselves competing for attention with all the great music of the past that was then under excavation. This competition placed tremendous pressure on new composers to either share the prevailing fascination with the past and do it honor through their work, or to strike out in ever more innovative directions and embrace the future. We'll begin this section by looking at two composer/conductors who chose different paths in crafting a relationship with the past.

Felix Mendelssohn and Franz Liszt

Felix Mendelssohn (1809–1847) took part in the revival of Bach's music in Berlin during the 1830s and 1840s. As an enthusiast of older music, Mendelssohn felt that concerts should have an educational function. He would lecture from the stage before the antique works of Bach or Handel were performed. Mendelssohn conducted the Leipzig Gewandhaus Orchestra, the oldest professional symphony orchestra in continuous operation in the history of the West.

Mendelssohn's compositional education was undertaken, with strict interest in the formal plans and ambitions of the 1700s, by the conservative musician Carl Zelter. Mendelssohn's own compositions reflect this conservatism. He favored antique genres like the oratorio. Even his more fanciful works, like the concert overtures, exemplify textbook application of sonata form.

Franz Liszt (1811–1886), by all accounts, was the most technically gifted pianist of his age. His on-stage personality was flamboyant. Eyewitness accounts of his performances attest that the sensation he created was so singular and forceful that a few women would faint at most all of his concerts. Armed with an otherworldly appearance and theatrical bearing, he would concentrate on establishing the ethos of the great artist from the moment he walked onto the stage. Once he reached the piano, he would remove his red satin-lined cape with an extravagant flourish, and drape it at the feet of the piano. He allowed patrons and supporters to sit on stage with him so that they could be closer to the great artist whom they supported financially, but also to model the appropriate level of awe for his unparalleled talents for the remainder of the audience in the more distant seats. Liszt's abilities as a musician and entertainer took him to the far reaches of Europe. He performed from Turkey to Ireland, from Portugal to Russia.

As a composer, Liszt distanced himself from the revivalist movement that honored older works. His piano compositions tend to be showy and technical. Some are programmatic, while others move in ethereal realms of pure emotion. All of them are a terrible chore for pianists to play. He had a formidable talent that few can hope to emulate when executing his pieces.

FIGURE 11.13 | *Felix Mendelssohn (1809–1847)*
(© Bettmann/Corbis)

By the middle of the 1840s, Liszt's interest in sensational concertizing waned. He abruptly turned his attention to the orchestra. Acknowledging the accomplishments of long-ago masters had no fascination for him. His orchestral works are as flamboyant as his piano pieces. All of them are programmatic, although the specificity of his programs never approached that of Berlioz.

As a conductor, Liszt also held the post of leading the Leipzig Gewandhaus Orchestra. He favored newer music, and shunned the learned practices of his predecessor Mendelssohn.

Mendelssohn and Liszt share a common generation and even for a time a common profession as orchestral conductors. They do not share a common sense of their relationship to the past. Mendelssohn is associated with revivalist tendencies, while Liszt's name became associated with the phrase "Music of the Future."

ROBERT SCHUMANN

The most influential composer of the mid-century was Robert Schumann (1810–1856). Schumann's influence not only stemmed from his work as a composer, but from his work as an important journalist as well.

Schumann was the son of a bookseller. Unfortunately, Schumann's father died when he was very young. Schumann's mother wanted her son to study law, which he did for two years, yet all the while his thoughts ran toward the piano. When he was expelled from the university for his failure to attend classes, his mother feared the worst. Madness ran in his father's side of the family. Sometimes the incurable mental affliction skipped generations, but Schumann's mother felt that a career in the arts would overstimulate her son's already fragile psyche. Unable to dissuade her son's ambition to pursue a career in music, she secured a most stern and disciplined teacher for her son, the famous Friedrich Wieck. At the time when Schumann began studying with Wieck, his teacher was already embarked on advancing his daughter Clara's career as a pianist. Wieck had no sons, so he poured his ambitions onto his daughter. For her part, Clara Wieck excelled in the role of protégé, and became one of Europe's most celebrated pianists. Interestingly, Clara Wieck turned out to be the much finer pianist than Robert Schumann. This situation partly stems from Schumann receiving a crippling injury to his hand as a result of overpracticing while wearing a contraption of his own design intended to strengthen his third and fourth fingers.

Once Schumann's career as a pianist was over, he turned toward journalism and composition. As a journalist, he co-founded the paper *Neue Zeitschrift für Musik*. This paper is still being published. Schumann's reviews often took the form

FIGURE 11.14 | *Robert Schumann (1810–1856)*
(© Bettmann/Corbis)

of dialogues between characters who served as advocates for different facets of Romanticism. Eusebius was Schumann's studious and introverted side, while the character Florestan nearly burst with a fiery enthusiasm for all that was new and wonderful. These two characters were joined by Master Raro, a pedant who reflected the conservatism of Friedrich Wieck. Wieck's daughter Clara, whom Schumann would eventually marry, is represented by the elegant Chiarina. Readers delighted in Schumann's fanciful discourses about the latest trends in music.

As a composer, Schumann initially favored the piano. He composed a large volume of solo piano music during the last half of the 1830s and early 1840s. Sometimes he would attribute works or name pieces after the fictional characters of his writing. In our recorded anthology of music, we have one of Schumann piano works, a movement from a collection called *Fantasiestücke* (Fantasy Pieces) [CD2 #12]. This movement is called "Aufschwung," or "Soaring." The piece exemplifies a clarity of form befitting a Romantic working in the aftermath of the new revivalist interests of his age. Yet, the clarity of the form obscures a larger ambiguity. The key of the piece is also wonderfully ambiguous. The tension caused by ambiguity energizes much of Schumann's best work.

FIGURE 11.15 | *Clara Wieck-Schumann (1819–1896)*
(© Michael Nicholson/Corbis)

The form of the piece is ABACABA, or rondo. However, elements of the A section are developed in the C section, making it seem as much like a development section as an independent thematic area. This rondo is further complicated by the superimposition of the basic elements of sonata form. The first grouping of ABA opens in the tonic key of f minor (or at least so it seems), then moves to the polar key of D-flat Major. This polar key is rather minimal, as D-flat Major has only a tangential relationship to f minor. The C section is tonally unstable, much like a development section. When the A section returns, tonic returns with it and remains in place until the end of the piece, just like the recapitulation of a sonata form. The result is a hybrid form that is at once a rondo and a sonata. Some call this a *sonata-rondo*.

In addition to the hybrid form, the piece has a hybrid tonic. The initial A section appears to be in A-flat Major, yet the stormy material and occasional leading tones in the key of f minor suggest otherwise. Only in the final bars of the piece does Schumann unequivocally side with f minor. This hybrid tonic mirrors the hybrid form nicely.

While the title of the piece, "soaring," suggests a program, Schumann differed from Berlioz and Liszt concerning the value of specific programs in instrumental music. His work more closely resembles Chopin's in that regard. Like the nocturne, this piece's title gives the listener a general idea regarding what the piece is about, but the details must come from the fantasies of each individual listener.

Listening Guide

Robert Schumann, Fantasiestucke ("Fantasy Pieces")
[CD2, #12] *(Duration, 2 min. 52 sec.)*

Aufschwung ("Soaring")

SONATA-RONDO FORM (ABACABA)

(Exposition)

A

0.00   The initial A section begins with forceful chords and appears to be in A-flat Major, yet the stormy material and occasional leading tones in the key of f minor suggest otherwise. In fact, the first grouping of ABA opens in the tonic key of f minor (or at least so it seems), and then moves to the hybrid tonic key of D-flat Major. This polar key is rather unusual as D-flat Major has only a tangential relationship to f minor.

B

0.17   Lighter, fanciful flurries of notes in the key of D-flat Major contrast the opening material and add extra-musical poetic images.

A

0.46   The opening A material returns.

(Development)

C

1.00   Elements of the A section are developed in the C section, making it tonally unstable, much like a development section as an independent thematic area.

1.55   Re-transition material is based on the forceful chord motive used to begin section A. Continually modulating with each repetition of the motive, this transitional material heightens the anticipation for the recapitulation and the forceful chords to come back to the tonic key.

(Recapitulation)

A

2.06   The tonic returns and remains in place until the end of the piece, just like the recapitulation of a sonata form.

B

2.14   Lighter, fanciful flurries return.

A

2.41   The final return of the opening A material. Only in the final bars of the piece does Schumann unequivocally side with f minor. This hybrid tonic mirrors the hybrid form nicely.

ROBERT AND CLARA SCHUMANN

By the end of the 1830s, Clara Wieck and Robert Schumann were in love. When Schumann asked the permission of Clara's father to marry Clara, he declined. Wieck felt that Robert Schumann was too dreamy and unreliable. He drank, allowed himself to be seen with Clara in public places without the benefit of a chaperone, and had mental illness running in the male side of his family. In the Kingdom of Saxony at that time, a woman needed her father's permission before she could legally marry. France had no such law, so Robert proposed that Clara come with him to Paris. She refused, choosing instead to sue to have her father found incompetent to make her choice. The trial was a clumsy affair. The mental illness that had taken Schumann's father's life had now seen his older brother die a miserable death in an asylum. In an effort to avoid losing the trial, a delay was secured. Robert was instructed not to be seen with Clara unless when in the company of a chaperone. For his part, Robert convinced an important friend to grant him an honorary doctorate in music so that he might return to court "Herr Doktor Schumann."

During this anxious time of near total separation, Schumann composed. He wrote dozens of songs in a very short time. One scholar, looking at the trajectory of Schumann's career, has argued in the pages of *The Scientific American* that Schumann was likely a manic-depressive. During his manic periods, he was hyper-productive and impossibly happy. During his depressed periods, he could scarcely work at all. The tremen-

FIGURE 11.16 | *Robert and Clara Schumann* (© Bettmann/Corbis)

dous output of songs during the year while he waited the completion of their trial lends important evidence to this posthumous diagnosis of the mental illness that would eventually kill Schumann, as it had previously done his male relatives.

Waldesgesprach

In our recorded anthology, we have a song dating from this manic period in Schumann's creativity called "*Waldesgesprach*" (Forest Conversation) [CD3 #4]. The song provides an interesting opportunity to examine more thoroughly the Romantic Period's fascination with the macabre. Joseph Freiherr von Eichendorff, one of Schumann's favorite poets, penned the poem, which participates in a long tradition of supernatural dialogues. In this case, a young man meets a beautiful woman while traveling through a forest. He decides to aid her, although his intentions may not be entirely honorable. Both the poem and Schumann's setting of it strongly hint that the young man has plans for this young woman. She turns out to be a supernatural being, in this case the Lorelei, a terrible witch cursed for having taken her life over unrequited love, and now condemned to seduce men and to lead them to their ruin. Like many of the classical monsters of old movies—the wolfman, the vampire, the hapless Frankenstein's monster—the Lorelei is a reluctant villain. She acts not out of her own choices, but as a curse brought upon her. The song as a whole was not so much meant to impress adults with its details, but to warn young men to beware strange women. In an era without such basic drugs as penicillin, a sexually transmitted disease meant almost certain death (both Schubert and Bellini, among the composers studied so far in this chapter, suffered this fate). So the fascination with such oddly childish matters as the Lorelei had a real purpose in the 1800s as a warning to stay on the path of the straight and narrow. In this regard, the poem resembles a fairy tale with a clear moral: Don't talk to strange women who are alone in the woods after dark.

As you listen, note the cheerful piano introduction and postlude. It's as if Schumann wants us to realize that *he* realizes that this small story is not a weighty tragedy to be taken too seriously. Not all macabre subjects in Romantic music were meant to be taken too seriously. Just as Berlioz is having fun with the Witches' Sabbath in his *Symphonie Fantastique*, Schumann lets us know, through his charming piano introduction and coda, that he's aware of the fairy-tale quality of the poem. This opening and closing material adopts the calm innocence of childhood, for after all, fairy tales such as this are meant as warnings to children.

Listening Guide

Robert Schumann, Waldesgesprach ("Forest Conversation")
[CD3, #4] *(Duration, 2 min. 15 sec.)*

	TEXT	TRANSLATION	MUSICAL TREATMENT
0.00			Piano introduction captures the calm innocence of childhood.

Young Man

0.06	Es ist schon spät, es wird schon kalt	It is already late, it is already cold,	Lower pitches used in melody. Music sets up a chain of dominant to tonic resolutions. On the word "heim" (home) the music ends with a dominant to half-step away irresolution.
0.11	Was reist du einsam durch den Wald?,	Why are you riding alone in the woods?	
0.15	Der Wald ist lang, du bist allein	The woods are large, you are alone,	
0.19	Du schöne Braut! Ich führ dich heim!	You lovely bride! I'll lead you home!	

Lorelei

0.26	"Gross ist der Männer Trug und List	"Great is the deceit and cunning of men,	Higher pitches used in melody. Descending chromatic scale in the piano sounds gloomy
0.34	Vor Schmerz mein Herz gebrochen ist.	From pain my heart is broken	
0.41	Wohl irrt das Waldhorn her und hin,	The hunting horn sounds here and there,	
0.47	O flieh! Du weisst nicht, wer ich bin."	Oh flee! You do not know who I am.	

Young Man

0.56	So reich geschmückt ist Ross und Weib	So richly dressed is steed and lady,	Return to lower melodic pitches.
1.01	So wunderschön der junge Leib,	So wonderful is your young body,	
1.09	Jetzt kenn ich dich—Gott steh mir bei!	Now I know you—God be with me	Piano plays chords and the vocal line switches from lyrically melodic to declamatory and speech-like.
1.12	Du bist die Hexe Lorelei.	You are the witch Lorelei	

Lorelei

1.22	"Du kennst mich wohl—von hohem Stein Rhine;	"You know me well—from a high rock	Higher pitched, lyrical melody over descending chromatic material in the piano.
1.36	Es ist schon spät, es wird schon kalt,	It is already late, it is already cold,	
1.44	Kommst nimmermehr aus diesem Wald!"	You will never depart these woods Again!"	
1.55			Coda returns music back to the calm innocence of childhood.

Some excellent text-tone relationships can be found in Schumann's setting of this poem. When the young man speaks at the beginning, Schumann sets up a chain of dominant-to-tonic resolutions. We call such *progressions*, the circle of fifths. In tonal music, the chord built upon the note a perfect fifth above the tonic creates an expectation in the listener that the chord built on tonic will follow. After traveling through the circle of fifths for several measures, and thus creating a strong sense of homeward motion, Schumann plays a trick rooted in the hidden meaning within the text. On the word "heim" (home), Schumann suddenly breaks the circle of fifths and clearly doesn't go home musically by ending with a dominant to half-step away irresolution. In this way Schumann points to the insincerity of the young man. He's going to take her somewhere, but the music tells us that somewhere isn't home.

When the Lorelei sings, Schumann uses the descending chromatic scale in the piano. This figure strongly disrupts any sense of tonal center. What better way to present a character who is appearing differently than she is? Moreover, descending chromatic material tends to be gloomy. We'll encounter a very gloomy piece in the next chapter where descending chromatic material is put to excellent use.

Another very nice touch is the evocation of recitative when the young man finally recognizes the Lorelei. The piano plays chords, and the vocal line switches from lyrically melodic to declamatory and speech-like. This change lends the young man's realization a realistic urgency that contrasts nicely with his glibly tuneful material at the opening of the song.

In general, when the female character speaks, the melody becomes higher in pitch and when the male character speaks the melody becomes lower in pitch. This device helps the listener to understand that the "Forest Conversation" is actually a conversation. Only one singer performs this piece, so that one person must play both the male and female parts. Schumann helps by relating high and low pitch levels to the female and male characters.

Robert and Clara's Marriage

Robert and Clara won their suit against Friedrich Wieck. Their case was helped enormously when a former servant agreed to testify that Wieck could be violent. Outraged that the topic had changed from Schumann's fitness as a husband to his own temper as a father, Wieck attempted to throttle Schumann in the courtroom. Clara won, as the magistrate found Wieck incompetent to choose on his daughter's behalf.

Before they married, Clara already had an important career as a pianist, and had composed several pieces. After their marriage, Clara's career faltered for a time. They had a large family—eight children in all. Robert did little to help at home. Worse, he insisted Clara not practice the piano while he was composing. This restriction had a terrible effect on Clara's ability to continue her career. Robert did encourage her work as a composer, but only intermittently. Clara's marriage to Robert served as a hiatus in her otherwise brilliant career. She was far the superior pianist, even before Robert injured his hand. She outlived Robert by forty years and during that time played an important role in the musical life of Germany.

Clara Wieck Schumann's Music

The Fugitive Piece No. 1 represents Clara Schumann (1819–1896) the composer within our recorded anthology of music [CD2 #13]. This work, not surprisingly given Clara Schumann's important career as a performer, is for solo piano. The formal plan of the piece is simple: ABA, or ternary form. The great delight of the piece lies in how the suave material in all the sections is almost wholly unpredictable. Short phrases, mostly two bars in duration, follow one upon the other. Her wonderful application of small-scale variation makes each phrase sound at once familiar, yet totally unpredictable. If you doubt this contention, try humming along with the melody after listening to the piece once. The task is very difficult, as each phrase contains unexpected changes. The contrasting B section is faster and louder than the A section, yet on closer inspection it closely resembles the A section in the generally unpredictable variations on the small-scale and in the melodic contour. Both the melody in the A section and the B section begin with rhythmically hesitant, ascending material.

The title of the work stems not only from the tendency in Romantic poetry to refer to certain ethereal works as "fugitive," but from this unpredictable small-scale variation and unexpected motion that makes up so much of the piece. Clara Schumann's piece seems to skitter by like a thought that can't quite be formed into words before it evaporates into nothing. Such Romantic fancies inform the work of both she and her husband. They strove to express the inexpressible in their instrumental works, never providing the listener with more than a vague gesture toward the possibility that some literal meaning might reside within the work. In this regard, they are both very different from their fellow exemplar of mid-century Romanticism, Franz Liszt. The schism between literal depiction through music and the expression of the inexpressible would widen as the century unfolded, especially in Germany.

Clara Schumann possessed complete command of the romantic style at mid-century. The only regret her career affords is that she produced comparatively little music. Motherhood and life with an exacting husband took their toll, but the prejudices of society as a whole took theirs as well. In the 1800s, artistic achievement was still very much coded as a male domain. Philosophers argued that women's capacity to bear children made them little inclined to more artificial modes of creation, such as art. Others developed even more preposterous rationalizations for excluding women from conser-

Clara Schumann, Fugitive Piece No. 1
[CD2, #13] *(Duration, 2 min. 22 sec.)*

TERNARY FORM (ABA)

A

0.00 Beginning with rhythmically hesitant, ascending material, short phrases, mostly two bars each, follow one upon the other in small-scale variation.

B

0.42 The contrasting B section is faster and louder than the A section. Nonetheless, it closely resembles the A section in the generally unpredictable variations on the small scale and in the melodic contour. Both sections begin with rhythmically hesitant, ascending material.

A

1.28 The rhythmically hesitant, ascending material of the A section immediately follows a series of harmonic turns that bring the B section to a close. The small-scale variations and melodic contours of this A section sound as a distant reminder of the opening, bringing this character piece to a close.

vatory study of music or from enjoying the support available for artists during their formative years. Clara Schumann's accomplishments in music were only possible because she came from the middle class. Had she been born to a higher social standing, so public a career in the arts would have had a catastrophic influence on her reputation. Barbara Strozzi in the 1600s was a courtesan. The link between women entertainers and artists with the sullied world of courtesans still loomed in the European imagination of the 1800s, even though in actual fact very few such women existed. Old stereotypes die slowly and rarely completely.

Clara Schumann was not the only accomplished female composer of the 1800s. Felix Mendelssohn's sister Fanny was a quite prolific composer. Unfortunately, few of her works were published, and her career was distinctly discouraged by both her brother and her husband. They did not mind that she composed, but they did not want her to become a public figure. The Mendelssohns were a wealthy family. As a member of the upper class, Fanny Mendelssohn (once married she became Fanny Hensel) had to play out her life of composition in obscurity from the public eye.

THE THIRD GENERATION ROMANTICS

Robert Schumann came to a sad end. Like his older brother, he collapsed into incurable mental illness. In 1853 he had himself placed in an asylum so that his wife and children could remember him in good health and be spared the pain of his decline. Shortly before this event, he had begun fostering the career of a young protege, Johannes Brahms (1833–1897). Like Robert and Clara Schumann, Brahms was both a pianist and a composer. When Robert's health failed him, Brahms faithfully visited him in the asylum and took reports back to Clara. Clara Schumann and Brahms became great, lifelong friends.

FIGURE 11.17 | *Johannes Brahms (1833–1897)*
(© Bettmann/Corbis)

Johannes Brahms

Brahms carried forward the traditions of Romanticism advocated by Robert and Clara Schumann. Like them, he favored instrumental music without a definite subject. He also took seriously the burden of living up to the challenge of music's past. Rather than striving for some new way, he engaged the older forms established in the previous century. As a result, much of his output as a composer falls into the instrumental genres of symphony, concerto, solo piano music, and instrumental chamber music. Within these instrumental works, Brahms was perfectly content to employ the formal designs that had been established by the past Viennese Masters: sonata, rondo, theme and variations, binary, and ternary. When he composed for voices, the art song as imagined by Franz Schubert captured his fancy. Other times he wrote for chorus, for he made his living as a choral conductor. At a time when most composers were abandoning the past or distancing themselves from it, Brahms maintained the links between late Romanticism and its origins in the music of the Classical period.

Brahms' most interesting innovation was the constant use of variation. His best pieces demonstrate a beautiful coherence, as most melodies within the piece, no matter how large, relate back to the initial melody through some sort of imaginative variation. Theorists of a later age would call his approach *developing variations.* This term reflects that his works seem to begin doing what we normally think of us as development almost from the first measure forward.

Brahms marks the most conservative and classical extreme of late Romanticism. His efforts were not typical of the years following 1860. Two new and progressive forces dominated much of the musical landscape: Music of the Future and nationalism. A terrible quarrel broke out between advocates of Music of the Future and those who preferred to look back with nostalgia on better days gone by. Their fight seems strange from the vantage point of later years. The controversy indicates that by 1860 Romanticism had moved from being an urgent expression of larger cultural forces, and had become on the one hand unwholesomely nostalgic and on the other hand absorbed in a cult advocating art for art's sake that verged on confusing art for religion. While this may sound like criticism, some of the most enduring works of the Western concert tradition date from this period of Romanticism's peculiar and beautiful decline.

MUSIC OF THE FUTURE

The term "Music of the Future" was coined by the second editor of Robert Schumann's journal the *Neue Zeitschrift für Musik*, Franz Brendel. While this man succeeded Schumann as editor, he did not share many of Schumann's prejudices. In a review of the *Symphonie Fantastique,* for example, Schumann found fault with the overly specific program, arguing that it curtailed the romantic impulse to explore one's individual feelings while listening to music. By contrast, Brendel hailed Berlioz as part of a triumvirate of composers whose work pointed the way to the future of important music. Brendel specifically cited Berlioz' program as the strong point in the conception of the symphony. Joining Berlioz in Brendel's advocates of Music of the Future was Franz Liszt and the youthful Richard Wagner (1813–1883). While Berlioz specialized in unusually configured programmatic pieces for orchestra, and Liszt specialized first in piano music and later programmatic orchestral music, Wagner devoted himself almost exclusively to opera. What the three shared in common was a commitment to the fusion of music with other arts, most usually literature.

RICHARD WAGNER

Richard Wagner was the son of a police inspector in the large German city of Dresden. In his youth, Wagner attended the opera. Through his education, however, a career as a writer seemed most likely. Upon graduation from the Leipzig University, he took up a career conducting operas for a small touring company. Little by little he composed his own operas. At first they were highly derivative of other composers; for example, his youthful *Liebesverbot* (Forbidden Love) owes much to the style of Bellini. By the 1850s, however, he had established a more personal style as he consciously distanced himself from the conventions of opera. Eventually, he would no longer refer to his creations as operas, but as "music dramas." The distinction was very important to Wagner. Opera comes from the plural of opus, meaning "work" in Latin. From the beginning, operas were a complex of smaller works that, when performed together, told a story. Wagner did not want his music dramas to be divisible into discreet sections. For one thing, such divisions broke the illusion of an alternate reality on the stage that Wagner was striving for. He wanted to craft works of such integrity and power that society itself would be reshaped by them. Far-flung as this ambition may seem to modern readers, the most amazing thing is that he nearly succeeded.

FIGURE 11.18 | *Richard Wagner (1813–1883)*
(© Bettmann/Corbis)

Wagner's Music Dramas

The crucial features of Wagner's music dramas that distinguish them from other sung spectacles run as follows:

1. Seamlessness, or endless melody, as Wagner called it, was the ideal of music unfolding almost without stops or pauses. Wagner felt that this approach increased the likelihood that listeners would not drift out of rapport with his creations.
2. Leitmotifs were his principal means of connecting the music to the drama. Leitmotifs are musi-

cal motives that Wagner would consistently associate with a person, place, or thing within the drama. He crafted an entire network of such motifs to serve as signposts for the listener in apprehending any hidden meanings, foreshadowing passages, or duplicity within the drama.

3. Wagner coined the term *Gesamtkunstwerk* (total artwork) as a way of expressing his ideal of fusing all the arts at their highest perfection, so that the whole of this fusion would be greater than the sum of its parts. Toward this end, he wrote his own librettos in order to ensure to his own satisfaction the quality of the text he would set to music. He also sought to hire the finest performers and the most gifted stage designers to aid in his dream of a perfect alternate reality on the stage. Wagner even managed to convince the young King of Bavaria to finance the creation of an opera house intended solely for the performance of his works, thus ensuring that even the architecture would be in sympathy with his plans.

4. Wagner instituted a revolution in harmonic practice by utilizing what we now call linear chromatic harmony. While this is a rather technical aspect of his work, we can hear its impact. Instead of imagining his works in terms of chords, Wagner allowed chords to materialize out of the unfolding of individual and highly independent melodic lines. That might sound like simple polyphony. It is polyphony, but it isn't simple. Instead, Wagner emphasizes the constant use of pitches outside the tonic scale, often moving by half-step along the chromatic scale. The effect of this technical innovation is a yearning sensation in his music that suggests an urgent but frustrated search for stability. Audiences in Wagner's time dearly loved this style of harmony. They found these frustrated strivings extremely beautiful. Many composers after Wagner adopted this style.

5. Wagner's music dramas tend to be gigantic in their conception. His works tend to be far longer than a typical *bel canto* opera. Moreover, the orchestra he utilized is huge in comparison with the modest forces required for Bellini's *Norma*. In keeping with the huge orchestral forces, the men and women who sing Wagner's music dramas must have extremely powerful voices. No singers in the history of opera have excelled in singing both *bel canto* roles, which always require flexible voices of extreme grace, and Wagnerian roles, which require great power and stamina.

THE RING OF THE NIBELUNG

Wagner's most ambitious project comprised a series of four music dramas called *Das Ring des Nibelung* (The Ring of the Nibelung—The Nibelungs are a race of dwarves). This massive composition has to be performed over the course of an entire week in order to give the singers time to rest between works. The story of this mammoth creation covers the twilight of the old German gods and the dawn of the world dominated by men. German mythology asserts that Wotan was the king of the gods and the god of binding agreements. In the ancient world, when there were no courts to appeal to for justice, keeping one's word was important to the orderly conduct of society. By always keeping his word, Wotan finds that being king of the gods is of little value. He lacks freedom. Frustrated, he spends his time admiring mortal heroes and siring children with mortal mothers, much to the consternation of his wife, Fricka, goddess of marital vows. Wotan's fascination with mortals will ultimately be his undoing, for one day a hero will come who knows no fear. That hero, so a prophecy tells, will bring the end of the gods. *Der Ring des Nibelung* (*The Ring*, for short) tells the story of the idle gods, the coming of the hero, and the destruction of the old order.

Background

In our recorded anthology, we have the conclusion of the second of the four music dramas comprising *The Ring*. Before discussing that scene in particular, we'll need some background in the story.

Das Rhinegold

The first music drama, *Das Rhinegold* (The Rhine Gold), begins on the floor of the Rhine River. There, a group of nymphs called Rhine Maidens sing as they lazily guard the river's cache of magic gold. They are joined by Alberich (an evil dwarf), who tries to catch one of the Rhine Maidens in order to make love to her. They elude his grasp and tease him cruelly. Finally in despair, Alberich steals the gold, renounces love, and forges an all-powerful ring that will allow him to rule the world. Fans of J.R.R. Tolkein's *The Lord of the Rings* can see here the source material for his evil Lord Sauron.

The action moves to the lofty peaks overlooking the Rhine. Here we find the gods as they bargain with two giants who happen to be brothers. These giants have built a palace in the sky for the gods. In exchange, Wotan has promised them whatever they wish. They demand the goddess Freia. Humiliated to lose one of their own into the custody of giants, the gods lament Wotan's powerlessness, but he cannot break his binding agreement with the giants. As the giants depart, Loge (the embodiment of fire) enters. He tells the gods that they are fools. While they've been bargaining with the giants, Alberich has forged an all-powerful ring. Loge persuades Wotan to join him on a journey to Nibelheim, the subterranean home of Alberich.

Once in Nibelheim, Wotan and Loge discover that Alberich has enslaved his fellow dwarves, forced his hapless brother to make him a magic helmet allowing him to take the shape of any creature, and has begun preparations for the conquest of the world. Fortunately for the gods, Loge tricks Alberich and captures him. Wotan and Loge leave Nibelheim with the gold, the magic helmet, and most importantly, the all-powerful ring.

The first music drama concludes with the gods giving the giants the gold, ring, and helmet in exchange for Freia's freedom. In keeping with the overall theme of *The Ring*, the power represented by possession of the ring turns brother against brother, and one giant slays the other in order to possess the ring. The work concludes with the gods parading into their new palace in the sky. As they ascend to their new home, Loge ridicules their vanity and shortsightedness.

Das Rhinegold powerfully reflects Wagner's ideal of seamlessness. There are absolutely no breaks in the music for its entire two and one half-hour performance time. Even when the action moves from the high mountains to Alberich's subterranean lair, the music continues. Wagner felt that his mythological plot required the absolute absorption of his audience. Breaks would shatter the illusion and allow the audience to reflect upon themselves rather than his creation.

Reforms in the Presentation of Opera

At the *Festspielhaus*, the opera house created exclusively for the presentation of Wagner's work, Wagner instituted many reforms in the presentation of opera. Previously in this book, you have read that audiences at Italian operas enjoyed considerable latitude in terms of acceptable behavior. Food and drink were served, and people could either watch the opera, or watch one another. The most expensive seats were those not with the best view of the stage, but those that offered the rest of the audience the best view of the seat's occupant. People wanted to see other people and be seen at the opera, which was conceived as a social event almost as much as an art form. Wagner, who tried to distance his work from opera, detested such split interest. His opera house had seats fixed to the floor and oriented toward the stage. The boxes with poor views of the stage but excellent views of the audience don't exist. Food and drink, even conversation, were all strictly forbidden. As a final blow to audience freedom, the lights were turned out on the audience during the performance, making people-watching almost impossible. Today, these reforms are the norm world-wide at operatic performances. Critics of Wagner's reforms argued that he was unwisely elevating art to a near-religious status. Such critics made up a clear minority of opera lovers, as Wagner's work soared in popularity. This borderline worship of art is one of the strangest and most interesting features of late Romanticism. We see its vestiges still in the codes of conduct intended for audiences, not only of the opera, but most concerts of classical music these days.

Die Walküre

The second music drama of *The Ring* is called *Die Walküre* (The Valkyrie). Many know it by the justly famous "Ride of the Valkyrie," which opens the second act. Most Wagner enthusiasts feel it is the strongest music drama of *The Ring*.

The story of this second opera is complicated, but a brief recounting of it is necessary here, since our recorded anthology represents Wagner with the finale of this interesting work. *Die Walküre* begins with a storm. A lone man flees for his life. He takes refuge in a home built around a giant tree. The man is Siegmund, and unbeknownst to him, he is the son of Wotan and a mortal woman. There's much more this man does not know. First, he has taken refuge in the home of one of his pursuers. Second, the wife of his pursuer is his twin sister, separated from him at birth. Complicating matters, Siegmund falls in love with his sister, Sieglinde, at first sight. Their love is instant and mutual. One can scarcely blame them for falling in love, as they are unaware of their familial relationship. One should also refrain from thinking Wagner prurient for including an incest theme in his music drama, as that theme is in the mythology itself. When Sieglinde's husband, Hunding, returns home, he is surprised to find the enemy he was hunting under his own roof. Laws of hospitality force Hunding to tolerate Siegmund's presence, but he vows that in the morning, he will kill Siegmund if his enemy is still there. Sieglinde puts a sleeping drug into Hunding's mead so that the two lovers can talk. During their discussion they tell of their sad lives. Shared suffering confirms their bonds of love. When their stories link and they realize that they are brother and sister, Wagner has Nature herself bless their union as gentle spring breezes blow open the door and the fragrances of the forest confirm the rightness of their love. The lovers decide to flee together. Sieglinde tells how an old man, who fits Wotan's description perfectly, came and plunged a sword into the trunk of the tree around which Hunding built his house. The old man prophesied that only a superb warrior could remove the sword. Siegmund pulls the sword out of the trunk and rushes off together with Sieglinde, his lover/sister.

Act Two

Act two opens with the famous "Ride of the Valkyrie," as nine daughters by Wotan and the Earth elemental (Erde) collect fallen heroes of a battle to take to the palace of the gods, where they might feast with Wotan, who loves mortal heroes. Wotan appears and praises his son, Siegmund. Fricka, Wotan's wife and goddess of matrimonial vows, appears and condemns the incestuous twins Siegmund and Sieglinde. She reminds Wotan of his binding agreement with her to punish those who defile the vows of marriage. Wotan hates to do it, but he orders the Valkyrie, and especially his favorite Brünnhilde, not to help Siegmund. Fricka is satisfied.

ACT THREE

Act three finds Hunding and his men closing in on the fugitive lovers. Brünnhilde elects to defy her father and protect Siegmund from harm. Brünnhilde loves her father and feels that she is doing his true will. Fricka is outraged, and Wotan cannot placate her. He allows the sword he left for his son to shatter in battle. Hunding kills the heroic Siegmund. Disgusted at this turn of events, Wotan kills Hunding. Fricka, oddly concerned with marital vows previously, does not complain when the husband she championed dies. She plainly wanted Siegmund punished as a way of punishing her unfaithful husband. (Wagner's treatment of Fricka is unflattering in the extreme, perhaps owing to the fact that he had divorced once and married his friend's wife, suggesting that his own attitudes toward marital vows were ambivalent at best.) Brünnhilde helps Sieglinde to escape. In the next music drama, we will learn that Sieglinde was pregnant with her brother's child at the time.

WOTAN'S FAREWELL

The music drama ends with Wotan punishing his wayward, yet most beloved daughter, Brünnhilde. He knows he must punish her because she defied his orders and nearly caused him to break his word to his wife to protect marital vows. Yet Wotan cannot kill Brünnhilde. Instead he deprives her of her immortal status, places her into a magical sleep, and surrounds her sleeping place with magic fire. Only a hero who knows no fear can pass through the magic fire, kiss Brünnhilde, and claim her for his wife. The third music drama will deal with the son of Siegmund and Sieglinde, a man named Siegfried, who will walk through the flames and kiss the Valkyrie.

In our recorded anthology is Wotan's farewell to his beloved daughter [CD3 #6]. Poor Wotan may be king of the gods, but just as in the previous music drama, his many binding agreements conspire against his acting in the service of his will. Wagner's text illustrates the great importance Romantics placed on individual freedom. This is not a superficial observation. The 1800s would give rise to fledgling democracies in Europe. Democracy is the natural political expression of a philosophy of individual determination. Wagner, contrary to the harsh picture some paint of him, was a great advocate of democracy in Germany. He even hoped that his music dramas would serve the cause of democracy. Wotan as ruler in a monarchical system, even when well intentioned, fails. With his inevitable fall, the divine power of the gods gives way to the rule of mortals, just as Wagner hoped the divine right of monarchs would give way to democracy. When Loge ridicules the gods at the end of *Das Rheingold*, it is really Wagner ridiculing the foolishness of the old order that placed power in the hands of the undeserving.

Leitmotifs

All of the characteristics of Wagner's music dramas are represented in the conclusion to *Die Walküre*. The characteristic we'll emphasize here is the technique of leitmotifs. In this scene several elements of the plot are central. Wagner creates an individual leitmotif for each of these central elements: sleep, farewell, magic fire, Siegfried (the as yet unborn hero who will free Brünnhilde and marry her), love, binding agreements, and Loge (the fire elemental). Sleep is rather obvious, as that's what Brünnhilde is doing throughout this scene. Farewell is what Wotan is saying. The magic fire is started during this scene after Wotan calls on Loge to start it. The binding agreement motive, a gloomy descending scale in the low brass instruments, appears only once and illustrates Wotan's total lack of freedom to do as he wishes. Love, a crucial motive throughout *The Ring*, illustrates Wotan's enormous love for his favorite daughter. Finally and most interestingly we hear the motive for Siegfried, a character who hasn't been born

Listening Guide

Richard Wagner, Das Ring des Nibelung (The Ring of the Nibelung), second music drama, Die Walküre (The Valkyrie), 1856

[CD3, #5] *(Duration, 10 min. 54 sec.)*

Wotan's Farewell (to his beloved daughter, Brünnhilde)

(Moved and enraptured, Brünnhilde sinks on the breast of Wotan, her holds her in a long embrace; then she throws back her head again, and, still embracing him, gazes into his eyes with emotion and awe.)

TEXT	TRANSLATION	LEITMOTIF
WOTAN		SLEEP
0.00 Der Augen leuchtendes Paar,	That bright pair of eyes,	
0.19 das oft ich lächelnd gekost,	That oft' I caressed with smiles	
0.31 Wenn Kampfes-Lust	when battle lust	
0.34 ein Kuss dir lohnte,	won you a kiss	
0.39 wenn kindisch lallend	when childish talk	
0.42 der Helden Lob	of heroic deeds	
0.44 von holden Lippen dir floss:	flowed from thy dear lips:	
0.53 dieser Augen strahlendes Paar,	that radiant pair of eyes	
1.05 das oft im Sturmmir geglänzt,	that oft' in storms gazed at me	
1.16 wenn Hoffnungssehnen	when hopeful longing	
1.22 das Herz mir sengte,	blazed in my heart,	
1.26 nach Weltenwonne	with worldly delight	
1.28 mein Wensch verlangte	my desires longed	
1.30 aus wild webendem Bangen:	while wild fears gathered:	
1.34 zum letztenmal	for the last time	
		FAREWELL
1.47 letz' es mich heut	let them cheer me	
1.52 mit des Lebewohles	with a last	
1.59 letztem Kuss!	farewell kiss!	
2.09 Dem glücklichern Manne	For a happier man	LOVE
2.16 glänze sein Stern;	let them shine like a star;	
2.23 dem unseligen Ew'gen	For the unhappy immortal	
2.36 muss es scheidend sich schliessen!	they must close on departing!	

2.49   (He takes her head in both hands.)

3.00 Denn so—kehrt	So thus—in parting
3.05 der Gott sich dir ab:	the god from you:
3.17 so küsst er die Gottheit von dir.	So he kisses your godhood from you.

3.37   (He kisses her long on the eyes, and with these chosed
          she sinks back softly into his arms, unconscious. He carries
          her gently to a low mossy mound, and

4.24	lays her there beneath the broad, spreading pine tree which overshadows it. He gazes at her and closes her helmet; his eyes then rest on the form of the sleeper, which he completely covers with the great steel shield of the Valkyries. Having done so, he moves slowly away, turning	SLEEP
6.34	to take one more sorrowful look. Then he strides with solemn resolve to the middle of the stage, and points his sword toward a large rock.)	BINDING AGREEMENT

6.41	Loge hör!	Loge listen!	LOGE
6.46	Lausche hieher!	Attend to me!	
6.49	Wie zuerst ich dich fand	Just as I first found you	
6.51	als feurige Glut,	a flickering flame,	
6.53	wie dann einst du mir schwandest	as once I lost you	
6.56	als schweifende Lohe:	an untamed flame:	
6.57	wie ich dich band,	as I joined with you,	
6.57	bann ich dich heut!	now I summon you!	
7.01	Herauf, wabernde Lohe,	Arise magic fire,	
7.12	umlodre mir feurig den Fels!	surround this rock for me!	

(He strikes the rock three times with his spear during the following.)

7.20	Loge! Loge! Hieher!	Loge! Loge! Attend!

7.34	(A gleam of fire issues from the stone and gradually becomes a fiery glow; then flicker-ing flames break forth. Soon wild, flickering flames surround Wotan, who, with his spear, directs the sea of fire to encircle the rock. It spreads toward the background, so that the mountain is surrounded by flame.)	MAGIC FIRE

8.34	Wer meines Speeres	Whoever fears my spear
8.40	Spitze fürchtet,	point,
8.49	durchschreite das Feuer nie!	that person shall not cross this fire!

(He stretches out his spear as a ban, looks sorrowfully back at Brünnhilde, then moves slowly away, turning his head for a farewell gaze. Finally he disappears through the fire. The curtain falls.)

MAGIC FIRE+
SLEEP+SIEGFRIED
(THE HERO)

yet). With the appearance of this motive, Wagner demonstrates that leitmotifs are not merely a matter of having the orchestra play the motive corresponding to what is transpiring on stage at each moment, but that their use is a technique capable of foreshadowing events, revealing hidden meaning, and even illustrating the unspoken aspects of the drama. The listening guide supporting this piece will point out where the various leitmotifs occur, and provide some insight into Wagner's use of this important technique.

The conclusion of this music drama sees Wagner combining three leitmotifs simultaneously. Magic Fire and Sleep refer to what is happening on stage. The Siegfried motive refers to what will happen in the future. The third music drama is titled *Siegfried* and tells of his wresting the ring from the giant and freeing Brünnhilde from the rock where she sleeps. The final music drama, *Götterdammerung* (Twilight of the Gods) depicts the fall of the gods through both the heroism and treachery of mortals.

The conclusion of *Die Walküre* comprises Wotan's last truly important moment. When we see him next, Siegfried will defy him and shatter his spear, as evidence of his total lack of fear for the law of the gods. This scene is poignant in the context of the complete work. Brünnhilde and Wotan have a relationship of genuine love during this music drama. Seeing the king of the gods so reduced that he must punish his beloved daughter for doing what she thought he would truly want indicates the near overturn of an entire order. Wagner wants that order overturned, yet he can marshal some fine music to capture the sentiment of the moment. By having Wotan summon Loge, however, Wagner reminds us of the conclusion of the previous music drama, when Loge ridiculed the ineffectual gods as they paraded into their hard-won palace. At the end of this music drama, although he is called up, Loge does not appear. The king of gods no longer rates a personal appearance for the fire elemental.

WAGNER'S INFLUENCE

The technique of leitmotifs has become increasingly influential. Not only do opera composers take up this technique, but film composers as well. Many readers may be familiar with the *Star Wars* films. The scores for these films by John Williams are laced throughout with leitmotifs. Next time you watch one, listen for the various motives and note their recurrences at similar dramatic moments. One example might be helpful. You may know the Imperial March, first heard in *The Empire Strikes Back*. That tune is heard in a very quiet and tender variation for solo harp as Darth Vader dies in his son's arms at the end of *The Return of the Jedi*. In the most recent film, *Attack of the Clones*, we hear a tortured version of the Imperial March as Annakin Skywalker (the future Darth Vader) tells the story of hating the Sand People and killing all of them. While no empire exists yet in the story, its leitmotif appears at this point in Williams' score to illustrate an ominous foreshadowing. Comparing *The Ring* to *Star Wars* is not uncommon on the part of commentators familiar with both. They are both *Gesamtkunstwerks* intended to create an alternate reality for the audience that flows from the combined efforts of artists working in many fields. Williams is only one of hundreds of composers influenced by Wagner's idea. Yet we must also acknowledge the influence of Berlioz, whose *idée fixe* began The Music of the Future's fascination with melodies associated with a person, place, or thing being used to tell a story through music.

The influence Wagner and his music had on the musical world is almost impossible to overstate, and extends far beyond film music. His harmonic language proved irresistible, as most composers adopted at least a watered-down version of linear chromatic harmony. Even Brahms, the principal enemy of Music of the Future, composed with linear chromatic harmony at times. Wagner's idea of *Gesamtkunstwerk* extended influence beyond the walls of opera houses, as filmmakers of the next century would look to his ideas. The technique of leitmotif captured the imagination of innumerable composers and can still be found today, especially in Hollywood. Wagner's celebration of art and almost unbridled enthusiasm for art's power filled a void of meaning for an increasingly world-weary and skeptical European upper class, many of whom pledged their devotion to his art and ideas.

ITALIAN OPERA AFTER 1850

Giuseppe Verdi

While the music drama dominates the story of opera in Germany after 1850, Italian composers continued to produce new works in this most favored genre. The third-generation figure who carried the torch for Italian opera was Giuseppe Verdi (1813–1901). Verdi's career began with his composing works unmistakably in the *bel canto* style. In 1850 he began to make an important transition with works such as *Il Trovatore* (The Troubadour, 1850) and *La Traviata* (1851). These works see the breakdown of *bel canto* ideals. First, they have more flexible and dramatic structures. Second, beautiful singing still happens in them, but a new emotional weight is placed on the drama. Characters develop and reveal sophisticated shadings of motivation in a way little explored in earlier *bel canto* works.

Like Rossini before him, Verdi retired at the height of his popularity. He had just completed new operas commissioned by the French, British, and Russian governments, along with a new piece commissioned by the city of Boston (*Un Ballo in Maschera*, The Masked Ball). These prestigious commissions from foreign governments confirmed that Verdi had established himself as an international figure of tremendous importance.

The journalist, composer, and librettist Arrigo Boito had always seemed like a critic of Verdi's work. However, after Verdi retired, Boito revealed that his criticisms of Verdi were meant to inspire the man's greatest efforts. He claimed to care more for Verdi than anyone else, caring for him even enough to criticize him. Boito made it his ambition to lure Verdi out of retirement. Knowing of Verdi's fondness for Shakespeare, Boito crafted a superb libretto based on Shakespeare's play *Othello*. The libretto was structured in a most difficult and dramatic fashion. No arias (where singers step out of the action to talk to the audience) appear except when Shakespeare allowed them. At age 74, Verdi agreed to compose an opera using Boito's libretto. The result is a clear and imaginative departure from anything before in Italian opera: a perfectly seamless and dramatic work vivified by supremely dramatic music. The sensational success of Verdi's *Otello* prompted one final collaboration between Boito and Verdi, this time on an opera based on a character who

FIGURE 11.19 | *Giuseppe Verdi (1813–1901)*
(© Stefano Bianchi/Corbis)

appeared in more than one Shakespeare play, Falstaff. When *Falstaff* had its debut, Verdi was 80 years old. Boito then left him in peace to enjoy his retirement.

NATIONALISM

Our final stop in this historical survey of Western concert music during the Romantic Period takes us away from Western Europe for the first time. The 1800s saw the romantic style take root in many countries, not just Germany, Austria, France, and Italy. As the economic boom of the Industrial Revolution reached the far-flung nations of Europe's periphery, nations such as Norway and Russia saw their middle classes grow in number and power. The middle class enjoyed leisure time sufficient to warrant an indigenous arts community in every land. Meanwhile, these nations emulated the mighty powers of Western Europe by fashioning a more keen sense of themselves as nation states.

Nationalism in Music

We could profitably use any of several emerging nations as a case study for the purposes of understanding musical nationalism. Smetana and Dvorak in Czech-speaking parts of the Austrian Empire, Grieg in Norway, Enesco in Romania, Nielson in Denmark, Sibelius in Finland all offer worthy examples of musical nationalism. Russia, however, in terms of scope and international importance, lends us the most sweeping case of musical nationalism in the 1800s.

Russian music has not been mentioned in this book so far, mainly because what music that was created in Russia before the 1830s failed to gain attention outside of Russia. The reasons for this situation are complicated and many. Most crucial is the preference of the Russian ruling class for the art of Western Europe. Even in terms of language, the Russian aristocracy looked west by favoring the French language over Russian.

When Russia defeated Napoleon, accomplishing something that Spain, Austria, Prussia, and England had all failed to do, suddenly this remote and little-understood nation took its place as a major player in the politics of Europe. In order to capitalize on this new position of respect and importance, the Russian Empire needed to hasten its transition from a feudal nation to a modern nation state. The seeds of this transition were sewn in the seventeenth and eighteenth centuries, but the bulk of the work needed to be done in the decades after Russia's victory over Napoleon. What Russia lacked most centrally in forming a modern nation was a robust middle class that was educated and able to form the bureaucracy required to keep the military and economic transformation of Russia on track. Urbanization in Russia unfolded quickly as literate peasants were relocated to the cities. This new middle class had leisure time sufficient to support bourgeois arts such as opera and concert music. The first artistic fruit of Russia's transformation was literary. Alexander Pushkin began writing in the Russian language for the new Russian middle class. Initially he emphasized recognizably Russian themes that were familiar to peasants and bureaucrats alike. His literary versions of Russian fairy tales sold well and paved the way for one of the greatest literary flourishings of any land in any century, as Russians proved to be voracious and eventually quite sophisticated readers. That the transition was achieved through folk tales indicates the role that nationalism plays in the arts. Nationalists empower their country by creating art that speaks to the people of their particular nation by invoking indigenous elements. In the case of Pushkin, fairy tales peculiar to the Russian language and culture served as the indigenous element drawn from Russian culture to popularize high art.

Mikhail Glinka

Music's closest equivalent to Pushkin was Mikhail Glinka (1804–1857). Glinka was born into a wealthy and powerful family. This situation enabled him to indulge his interests as he saw fit. One interest was music, which he studied with indifferent discipline. Despite at best an informal education, Glinka produced the first widely popular operas in the Russian language, *A Life for the Tsar* and *Ruslan and Lyudmila*. The first of these tells a patriotic story from Russian history; and the latter tells the story of a fairy tale written as literature by Pushkin. In both cases Glinka drew upon stories unique to his country. In addition to the stories, Glinka introduced Russian folk songs into both operas. These folk songs lent his operas a characteristically Russian sound that appealed to the relatively new Russian middle class.

Glinka laid out a blueprint for effective use of Russian musical idioms in classical music. When using Russian folk material, Glinka did not develop that material in the usual Germanic way. Instead he would change the background, the orchestration, or accompanimental figures, while allowing the borrowed Russian material to maintain

Figure **11.20 |** *Mikhail Glinka (1804–1857)*
(© Michael Nicholson/Corbis)

its native character. This technique, which scholars sometimes call the *changing background* technique, enabled the borrowed material to remain recognizable to the audience.

Each subsequent generation of Russian nationalist composers held Glinka in high respect, even as they attempted to improve on his methods. Alexander Dargomyzhsky (1813–1869) worked on adapting operatic style to the idiosyncrasies of the Russian language. Nikolai Rimsky-Korsakov (1844–1908) strove to inject life in the changing background technique through ever-increasingly more imaginative orchestration. Modest Mussorgsky (1839–1881) sought to distance Russian music from Western models through his distinct and flamboyantly individual musical style. Mili Balakirev (1837–1910) expanded the range of Russian idioms available for use by nationalistic composers by creating large anthologies of folk tunes gathered from throughout the empire. Pyotr Ilyich Chaikovsky (1840–1893)—the more familiar, Western, spelling of his name is Peter Ilyich Tchaikovsky—explored a plaintive and emotional style reminiscent of the volatile Russian temperament, and in the process crafted many pieces that remain beloved by audiences around the world to this day. While Chaikovsky did not share the goal of distancing Russian music from the West, he did compose several clearly nationalistic works: his second and third symphonies based on regional folk songs, the famous *1812 Overture*, the tone poem *March Slav*, and operas based on nationalistic literature.

NIKOLAI RIMSKY-KORSAKOV

Russian nationalism is represented in our recorded anthology by a short orchestral excerpt from an opera by Nikolai Rimsky-Korsakov [CD3 #6]. His career as a composer

FIGURE 11.21 | *Nikolai Rimsky-Korsakov (1844–1908)*
(© Bettmann/Corbis)

began in an unusual fashion. His family had been associated with the Imperial Russian Navy. He was preparing to depart on an officer-training voyage, when he met Mili Balakirev at a party. Balakirev heard Rimsky-Korsakov play some youthful compositions on the piano. Balakirev praised the largely untrained sixteen-year-old composer and encouraged him to write a symphony. During his voyage, he completed his first symphony, despite the fact that he did not know even the most rudimentary lessons about harmony. The piece was performed in St. Petersburg to a generally favorable response. Balakirev, who took seriously the role of recruiting new nationalist composers, was elated. Little by little Rimsky-Korsakov's interest in commanding a ship gave way to composition. At age 25 he was appointed to the faculty of the relatively new St. Petersburg Conservatory. A man of his limited training would never have been hired as a music professor in Western Europe. Russia's newness as a nation where western-style composition was prized allowed for such unlikely events. In his interesting autobiography, *My Musical Life*, the young professor admits that he was never more than a page ahead of his first students. Rimsky-Korsakov took his studies sufficiently seriously that he was soon regarded as an important teacher. He wrote a textbook on orchestration—the art of composing for instruments—and even attracted a host of brilliant students.

Rimsky-Korsakov's works are almost all in a nationalist vein. The features that make them nationalistic include: quoting Russian folk songs, borrowing idiomatic Russian dance rhythms, composing operas on distinctly Russian themes (such as Russian historical events, important Russian literature, or Russian fairy tales), and attaching obviously Russian programs to instrumental works. Even when Rimsky-Korsakov was not quoting a folk song, his melodic style tends to sound like Russian folk songs. The point of all this quoting and drawing from clearly Russian materials was the empowerment of the Russian people through the manufacture of cultural artifacts which ennoble and aggrandize the collective experiences and accomplishments of a particular nation. In short, Rimsky-Korsakov's means, as well as his aims, were in sympathy with a nationalist agenda.

The Tale of Tsar Saltan, of His Son, the Glorious and Mighty Knight, Prince Saltanovitch, and of the Swan Princess

The short piece in our anthology reflecting Rimsky-Korsakov's style is taken from one of his fairy tale operas. This one is based on a work that Pushkin had earlier published in a literary version back in the 1830s. The opera boasts, without doubt, the longest and perhaps most absurd title in the long history of opera: *The Tale of Tsar Saltan, of His Son, the Glorious and Mighty Knight, Prince Saltanovitch, and of the Swan Princess*. The opera tells the story of how a young girl went from being a peasant

Listening Guide

Rimsky-Korsakov, "Farewell and Departure of the Tsar" from *The Tale of Tsar Saltan, of His Son, the Glorious and Mighty Knight, Prince Saltanovitch, and of the Swan Princess*

[CD3, #6] *(Duration, 4 min. 07 sec.)*

Ternary Form (ABA), with introduction and coda

0.00   **INTRODUCTION**: a solo trumpet presents a short martial fanfare accompanied only by a snare drum. Rimsky-Korsakov is much loved by orchestral percussion players because he made such frequent and interesting use of percussion instruments. This piece, for example, requires the presence of four percussionists, more than Beethoven ever used.

0.09   **A SECTION**: A light and simple march unfolds in the key of G Major. Initially Rimsky-Korsakov leaves the string instruments out of the orchestration simulating a small wind band's bright texture. A four-bar theme is presented first in the flute. On its next appearance, Rimsky-Korsakov varies the orchestration and places the melody in the piccolo. Roughly every four measures throughout the A Section, Rimsky-Korsakov alters the orchestration lending the work (with very little in the way of motific development) an air of constant change and interest. Initiating musical interest through orchestration is a specialty of nationalist composers in the 1800s. Just as the A Section is about to end, the theme heard initially first in the flute and then in the piccolo is played one last time by the entire orchestra, bringing the section to a climactic close.

1.25   **B SECTION**: The new section begins with a key change to E-flat Major, a key fairly far removed from G Major reflecting that this piece was written late in the century when unlikely modulations were more normal. Immediately a solo horn presents a more broad and dignified theme. This eight-measure theme is immediately answered by the violins, which repeat the melody first heard in the horn. In this section too, orchestrational changes generate most of the musical interest.

2.50   **A1 SECTION**: The repeat of the A section is not literal, that is, Rimsky-Korsakov does not simply present a *da capo* structure. It contains, not surprisingly, different orchestrations from the first A Section. The first surprise is that the return of the initial march theme appears in the unexpected dynamic level of pianissimo. The piccolo carries the tune, but the supporting material is changed from the first appearance in the A Section. This constitutes a good example of Glinka's changing background technique. The key, however, is the expected tonic, G Major. After several similarly altered statements of the march theme, the section ends as quietly as it began.

3.31   **CODA**: The coda is made up thematically of snatches of the march theme. It ends very quietly with a pianissimo scale in the flute. This quiet ending might seem anti-climactic, but we must remember that this piece comes out of an opera. The small fairy-tale army has left the city. It makes sense that their march should fade away.

to being the wife of the Tsar, how she and her young son suffered, and how they were eventually restored to power. Rimsky-Korsakov filled his score with folk songs presented in delightful orchestrations befitting the whimsical plot. In a prologue, the heroine and her sisters are singing as they sew. The three wicked sisters sing in praise of laziness. Then they turn to the subject of what each would do were they to become the wife of the Tsar. The wicked ones brag of silly and materialistic ambitions, but the heroine sings of how she would bear the Tsar a glorious son. Suddenly, the Tsar appears. He has overheard everything and immediately asks for the heroine's hand in marriage. The first act begins with the Tsar leaving the capital to fight a war. The music in our anthology [CD3 #6] is the orchestral work that depicts the Tsar and his troops marching out of their fairy tale kingdom.

The structure of this fairy tale march is ternary (ABA) with a short introduction at the beginning and coda at the end. Throughout this piece, orchestration (the art of employing instruments in an orchestral work) figures prominent among the piece's charms.

Certainly one could find more profound examples of Russian nationalist music, but the fairy-tale quality of this piece typifies a quite large amount of nationalist work. The piece also has the added advantage of showing the extreme importance placed on orchestration in Russian nationalist music. Finally, the changing background technique so crucial to the early days of Russian nationalism is still present.

CONCLUSION

Today, much of the music that professional musicians working in the field of Western concert music perform was composed during the Romantic Period. Concepts like programmatic music, nationalism, and the expression of infinite longing appealed to a large number of people, including much of the middle class. While the audience for this music has shrunk per capita, it remains a robust part of Western culture. The general trend to privilege the individual genius, without worrying about such strictures against individualism as taste or royal patronage, resulted in an interesting fragmentation of styles. Today, many people still hold generally Romantic notions about art and the artist. They see art as serving only itself; put another way, it serves the artist's need to express himself or herself rather than appeal to society in general. This liberalizing tendency had both happy and unwelcome consequences for the relationship between the artist and society, consequences that will mostly play out in the following century.

 Some Questions for Discussion

1 Now that you've read the chapters and listened to the music of both the Classical and Romantic periods, discuss them in terms of Blume's theory that Classicism and Romanticism are two sensibilities rather than periods. Is there anything Classical about the pieces presented in this chapter? Is there anything Romantic about any of the pieces in the last chapter? Are some genres of music better suited than others to these respective sensibilities?

2 Many Romantics found that telling stories through music was a good idea. How do you feel about the conflict between absolute (music with no particular story) and programmatic (music with a story) instrumental music? Do you find it helpful to know Berlioz' plot when listening to the fifth movement of the *Symphonie Fantastique*? If you didn't know the story of, say, Rimsky-Korsakov's march or Berlioz' symphony, would the pieces still make sense? How do these works compare to the piano pieces of Chopin, Robert Schumann, and Clara Schumann in your mind? Do you tell yourself stories as you listen to music? What are the intrinsic values of programmatic and absolute music?

3 Democracy rises in Europe about the same time as Romanticism. That doesn't mean that democracy takes a lasting control in very many places, only that many Europeans came to admire it. Can you find some connection between the Enlightenment's insistence that the individual's capacity for rationality is where meaning exists, and the nearly simultaneous rise of both Romanticism and democracy? Do the two concepts gain anything from one another? Some argue that absolute music is democratic, in that the audience, like an electorate, needs leadership; yet an important part of functioning in both a democracy and an audience for absolute music is allowing the individual to choose the value and meaning of candidates and artists. Does this parallel between music and democracy seem convincing to you?

CHAPTER 12

Concert Music 1900–1945

TWENTIETH-CENTURY DEVELOPMENTS

The previous century saw more change come to music more quickly than in any previous century. New technologies, exploding populations, and cultural fragmentation of every sort conspire to make the last century very difficult to generalize about. With that in mind, the twentieth century will be divided into four chapters. The first two will each take roughly half the century and examine concert music using the end of World War Two as a line of demarcation. That cataclysmic event for the West saw important shifts in the social positioning of concert music, along with crucial changes in stylistic priorities. The next chapter will deal with the emergence and development of Jazz, America's most influential contribution to Western classical music. The final chapter will look at the post-modern sensibility emergent at the end of the century. All the chapters in this book contain over-simplifications. This situation is a necessary evil in order to tell a coherent story about the past. These chapters will be no different; indeed, they may suffer even more. More than half the human beings who have ever lived in the West lived during the twentieth century, making the century a fecund period for musical creativity.

Modernism and Traditionalism

The early twentieth century witnessed drastic social change, the development of new technologies, and the exaggeration of key tendencies of the dynamic Romantic period. Taken together, these changes, developments, and exaggerated continuations led to a mounting fragmentation of Western concert music. Understanding these processes must begin with an examination of what the twentieth century inherited from the nineteenth century.

The historicism described in the previous chapter, that is, the tendency on the part of musicians and audiences to enjoy music from the past and to hone their historical awareness of music created a generation or more earlier, continues and increases in the twentieth century. With each passing generation after 1800, the volume of antique music that occupied the stages of Europe and North America increased. Among the effects this historicism had on music was a trend toward fostering newness and innovation in contemporary music in order to distance it from historical music. The pressure to compete with audience nostalgia forced composers to carve out a niche for themselves. This desire for newness came to be known as modernism. Not all artists who billed themselves as modernists were necessarily doing anything particularly new. The term served as an accurate descriptor in some cases, and in others as a marketing tool designed to prompt audiences to apply new aesthetic criteria to the new work, and to resist the nostalgic temptation to compare the new work to older works of time-honored reputation.

New Technologies

After 1900 technologies emerged to facilitate audience nostalgia in unprecedented ways. First, recording technology made it possible for music lovers to shun concerts that did not present familiar music, since familiar music was readily available through recordings. The automobile similarly fostered such selective spectatorship as potential audience members no longer needed to remain close to home in order to hear the music that interested them. They could instead seek out only those like-minded music lovers in the vicinity and hear together only the music they already knew they liked. Unfortunately for contemporary composers, audiences often prefer familiar music to unfamiliar music. In Europe, cheap rail travel had an even greater impact than the automobile. Taken together, recording technology and inexpensive travel increased the strain between the audience and the modern composer.

Today, many music lovers favor recordings over live experiences, moreover, the internet makes it possible to indulge almost exclusively in the music an individual likes best, making encounters with whatever live music happens to be performed in the community unlikely in the extreme. These tendencies in Western technological advance serve the ongoing project of the Enlightenment with its premium on individual discernment. The unexpected consequence of technologies allowing for almost perfect discernment is a coming apart of certain aspects of the social fabric. With so many people able to indulge individual tastes, few common experiences of live music take place. Interestingly, while common experiences of live music by a large segment of an area's population have become relatively rare, common experiences of recorded music have become much more common. While the days are gone when a healthy cross-section of a city's population would see and hear the same opera, millions of people might own the same compact disk or watch the same musical event on television.

The Rise of Popular Music

Another key difference for composers after 1900 is the competition of commercial and popular music. The technologies mentioned in the previous paragraph serve the purposes of commercial and popular music far more efficiently than they serve concert music. The result has been a gradual marginalization of concert music over the course of the twentieth century. The rise of popular music stems not only from technological advances but from social change as well. As the population of urban centers increased, waves of immigrants moved into the city from the country or from other countries where economic times were bad. The wealthy citizens of cities found the presence of new immigrants and the poor at concerts and operas distasteful. Over the course of the 1800s, barriers were put in place to keep the poor and immigrants out of so-called "high art" events. Patrons engaged in a sacralization of culture, to borrow a term from the distinguished historian Lawrence Levine. *Sacralization* refers to making cultural events seem like sacred events. In the previous chapter, this process was already begun. Wagner's turning out the lights on the audience and fixing chairs in a position oriented toward the stage were practices associated with sacralization. They made the social aspects of going to the opera secondary to the silent worship of the opera itself. Such changes, along with increased ticket prices and other attitudinal impediments, drove a wedge between classes in matters of culture.

The lower classes once attended operas regularly; by the end of the 1800s they did not. Naturally, the lower classes didn't take things lying down. They still enjoyed the arts; it's just that the arts they created and enjoyed came to be regarded differently from the lofty arts this book describes. The label "popular" came to describe music designed for consumption by great numbers of people. The originators of the term probably meant it as a pejorative, a way of elevating the high arts and denigrating art of lesser complexity. Whether a work was actually popular in any numerical sense of the word didn't matter. The label was meant in part to clarify the art of the poor and the middle class.

Soon the upper classes embraced popular culture in equal measure with the classical arts. The pressure felt in art forms such as concert music became even more intense. Now their audiences, regardless of class, were slimmer by virtue of pressure from the past in the form of antique art and from the present through so-called popular art. Today in the age of relatively inexpensive education at even the highest levels, enthusiasts of concert music are apt to come from any class or background.

Music and Musicians in Society

Finally, the patronage system almost completely collapsed for contemporary music. The old aristocracy had given way to a new entrepreneurial class that lacked a tradition of artistic patronage. The churches of the West had long ago faltered as patrons for the arts by the time 1900 rolls around. During the 1900s, in an effort to remain relevant to the largest number of people possible, most churches embraced popular styles in their services. Moreover, the universities that would become a major source of support for modern art would not take up that role on a wide scale until after 1945.

The general faltering of all concert music as an important part of many people's lives in the West arose as an unexpected consequence of so many supporters of music preferring antique music over contemporary music, starting in the 1930s. Not only do contemporary composers have difficulty attracting powerful music-making institutions to their cause, but also those institutions have witnessed a widespread decline of per capita interest in all concert music. No artistic repertory has managed to remain a robust and dynamic part of any culture for very long after it was created. Advocates of antique music who do not support contemporary music must understand that their favorite works inevitably become gradually less relevant to the culture as a whole. The schism between contemporary and antique music hurts both in the long run.

In addition to the above factors, a mounting anxiety was gripping European and American cities as the twentieth century dawned. As cities swelled, people found formerly familiar places filled with strangers. The second industrial revolution saw smokestacks proliferate on the skyline as they belched coal smoke. The effect of growth and alienation naturally influenced artists. An age of anxiety, as social and technological progress began to unleash unexpected and undesired consequences, marks a stark contrast to the more utopian ideals that informed the first Industrial Revolution of the late eighteenth and early nineteenth centuries.

FIGURE 12.1 | Kazimir Malevich, ***Dynamic Suprematism,*** 1915. Oil on canvas. Like composers, many painters began exploring radical new techniques and ideals. In Malevich's radical path of abstraction, he utilized basic geometric forms in pure colors that seemed to float against a white background. The interactions among the shapes, colors, and their effect in space, appeared to stress feeling over any objective meaning. Such artists may have inspired Albert Einstein's revolutionary view of the universe, for his mathematical theory of relativity permanently changed perspective on the interactions of mass and energy through time and space. (Tate Gallery, London/Art Resource, NY)

While the above may sound like doom and gloom for modernists, the artists themselves extended the advantages of their relative lack of support by indulging in an even greater degree of individualism unchecked by some external taste. What starts around 1900 as a trickle of unbridled experimentation would soon rage into a mighty cataract. This almost libertine sense of personal empowerment felt by artists working in the early 1900s lends the period an aura of real excitement. While the attitude that fuels the radical spirit is clearly a Romantic one rooted in the previous century, the stylistic innovations of the early 1900s make this one of the clearer stylistic breaking points in the history of music.

AUSTRIA AND GERMANY BEFORE WORLD WAR ONE

While not the first of the stylistic breaks with the previous century, nor the most radical, the rise of atonal music in Austria and Germany affords us a very clear example of how music in the twentieth century would differ from previous eras. Tonality had been used more or less exclusively in European music since 1700. As a system of organizing pitches, tonality is ideally suited to create a sense of anticipation and arrival, a supremely goal-oriented approach to pitch in music. The system also has a profound impact on how the listener experiences time in music. With Wagner's use of linear counterpoint and chromaticism, tonality started to break up. Audiences in Europe were passionate about chromaticism. They adored the sense of longing and anguish it fostered. After Wagner's death, Richard Strauss (1864–1949) continued to hold the affection of upper-class Germans and Austrians, first through his chromatic and programmatic orchestral works and later through his music dramas. He was the heir to the Music of the Future, and he carried it into the new century.

In his music drama *Salome* (1905), Richard Strauss told the decadent story of a deranged young girl, step-daughter to King Herod, who insists on having John the Baptist's head on a silver platter when he refuses to love her from his prison cell. In a climax that is at once gruesome and disturbing, Salome receives her prize from her stepfather and proceeds to kiss the severed head. Appalled by her conduct, King Herod orders his troops to crush her to death with their shields. The music Strauss created for this piece tested the last vestiges of tonality, for while it is tonal, the tonal language is so thoroughly saturated with chromaticism that few could hear the vestigial tonal implications. This work won Strauss a tremendous success and showed the way for younger musicians to introduce even greater shocks into their compositions, not only in terms of tonality but in terms of shocking Victorian values by wallowing in the darker aspects of the human mind.

The success of *Salome* coincided with the publication of Sigmund Freud's ideas about psychoanalysis. Freud theorized a three-part structure to the human mind. He postulated the existence of the Id, the manifestation of all the seething desires and transgressive thoughts that human beings are capable of but seldom show. Its antithesis according to Freud is the Super-ego, that part of the mind that serves to restrain the individual from acting exclusively out of selfish interests and in the exclusive pursuit of pleasures. Finally, the Ego served Freud as the embodiment of the whole mind. During the late 1800s, Europe experienced an almost unprecedented degree of moral rigidity. Historians name this phenomenon after the ultra-prim English monarch, Queen Victoria, calling it the "Victorian Age." Victorian morality struck Freud as featuring an overactive Super-ego. He theorized that many neuroses stemmed from repressive Victorian ideals. The success of works such as *Salome* suggests that audiences were thirsty for art that allowed the Id center stage.

ATONALITY

Arnold Schoenberg

While Richard Wagner and Richard Strauss were maverick in their approach to tonality, it was a young Jewish composer named Arnold Schoenberg (1874–1951) who would take the full fatal step of abandoning tonality altogether. Interestingly, Schoenberg did not consider himself a maverick at all. He admired the traditions of German and Austrian music and wanted to contribute to that tradition, not overturn it. In examining the works of Johannes Brahms, Schoenberg felt that the motive, and not tonality, was holding music together and lending it coherence. Armed with this belief, he composed the first atonal piece in 1909. In lieu of a tonal center, he used recurrent motivic material to bind his musical ideas together into a coherent structure.

Atonality refers to the absence of a pitch hierarchy that makes one note any more important than another within a given piece. All pitches achieve essential equality. In tonality, we have a tonic pitch around which all the other pitches are oriented. One important implication of atonality is that the dissonant intervals all enjoy use without any special preparation and no special resolution.

FIGURE 12.2 | *Arnold Schoenberg (1874–1951)* (© Bettman/Corbis)

Essentially, the questions of dissonance and consonance that had occupied the attention of Western musicians since at least the time of Pythagoras were no longer operative. In tonal music, and modal music even before that, all dissonances had to be prepared and resolved specially, and some dissonances avoided all together. Schoenberg adopted the phrase "the liberation of dissonance" as the rallying cry for his new approach. While his phrase sounds like revolutionary talk, Schoenberg intended no revolution. He was merely building on the accomplishments of composers adept in the ways of chromaticism.

Expressionism

At the same time that Schoenberg was introducing atonal music, an important movement in the arts in Germany was hitting its stride: Expressionism. Expressionism refers to art that seeks the expression of pure emotional states liberated from all repression. Expressionist art explores dark, previously hidden emotions or pure and ecstatic emotional states once thought out of bounds as a subject for art. Music had long operated in the realm of pure emotion, so it looked to literature in order to ground it within the expressionist movement.

FIGURE 12.3 | Edvard Munch, *Anxiety.* 1894. Expressionists pressed Romantic fervor to its ultimate conclusion by exploring an inner world of reality as described by Sigmund Freud. It included extreme subconscious emotions such as insanity, nightmarish images, and hysteria. Centered in Northern Europe, expressionists were often concerned with social protest, as they sought to capture the anguish of the poor and oppressed and the horrors of war for common people. This painting by Edvard Munch portrays a colorless world. The water appears as a stagnant, deadly reflecting pond, which does not harbor any life. The figures emerge as walking zombies, their eyes mirroring the inner lifelessness of the pond. Many composers, who pressed forward with music that was increasingly emotional and complex, shared Munch's views and wanted to make art that called for positive action in the face of emotionally troubled times. Schoenberg set twenty-one of Albert Giraud's expressionist poems, filled with Freudian imagery, in his song cycle, *Pierrot lunaire* (1912). Pierrot is the eternal figure of the sad clown; his obsession with the moon, his amorous frustrations, his neurotic aspirations, his pranks and adventures are presented in the characteristically heightened manner of the expressionists.
(© Burnstein Collection/Corbis - © 2003 The Munch Museum/The Munch-Ellingsen Group/Artists Rights Society (ARS), NY)

PIERROT LUNAIRE

The piece representing Schoenberg's atonal music is taken from a collection of expressionistic songs called *Pierrot Lunaire* (Moonstruck Pierrot). The poems by Albert Giraud center around a little love-lorn clown from the *Commedia dell'arte* named Pierrot. In a series of poems, some with Pierrot as protagonist and some without, Giraud explored the hidden desires and fears of the Id. The song in our anthology [CD 3 #9] is the eighth from Schoenberg's collection, "Nacht" (Night). The text serves as a parody of the nocturne, as it creates an anxious and terrible metaphor for the night as a time when giant black moths blot out the sun's rays.

Romantic evocations of the night in poetry take many forms. We can easily imagine poetry describing the night sky as the dark cloak of a prince, the stars as tiny pinpoints of light passing through the cloak's coarse fabric. Variations on this basic

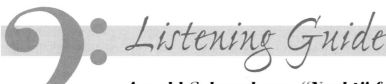

Listening Guide

Arnold Schoenberg, "Nacht" from Pierrot Lunaire
[CD3, #9] *(Duration, 2 min. 10 sec.)*

	TEXT	TRANSLATION	MUSICAL TREATMENT
0.00			*Low, sustained notes in the piano, then cello and bass clarinet present the three-note, "unifying" motive and paint a bleak landscape.*
0.22	Finstre, schwarze, Riesenfalter	Gloomy, black moths	
0.30	Töteten der Sonne Glanz.	Kill the sun's rays	
0.38	Ein geschlossnes Zauberbuch	Like a closed magic book,	
0.48	Ruht der Horizont—verschwiegen	Broods the horizon-in silence.	*Tempo slows and instruments move to silence.*
1.02	Aus dem Qualm verlorner Tiefen	Like mists from deep recesses	*Tempo increases, and the instruments become more active.*
1.07	Steigt ein Duft, Erinnrung mordend!	Rise up fragrances murdering memory!	
1.12	Finstre, schwarze Riesenfalter	Gloomy, black moths	*Low notes played fortissimo block out the voice.*
1.18	Töteten der Sonne Glanz.	Kill the sun's rays.	
1.29	Und vom Himmel erdenwärts	And from heaven earthwards	*Tempo slows and instruments play softly.*
1.33	Senken sich mit schweren Schwingen	Downward sink with somber wings	*Piano line descends.*
1.38	Unsichtbar die Ungetüme	Invisible monsters	*Instruments gradually get softer.*
1.43	Auf die Manschenherzen nieder	To prey upon the hearts of men.	
1.52	Finstre, schwarze Riesenfalter . . .	Gloomy, black moths.	*Instruments create extremely dark, sustained textures. The cello and bass clarinet curtail this scene with an accent on their last note, suggesting the poetic music has fallen "prey" to the "invisible monsters" as well.*

poetic theme are limitless. This poem confronts poetic tradition and explores a disturbing image by requiring the reader to imagine a sky so filled with black moths that the sun's rays are not merely unable to reach the earth, but they are killed. Expressionist poets stamped the traditional poetic themes with their dark vision as though finally able to write the poetry of the Id. Images of fragrances murdering memory and invisible monsters preying on the hearts of men reinforce the poem's pessimistic sensibility. Expressionism gave voice to the mounting anxiety of Western Europe in the face of industrialization.

Sprechstimme

Such a poem as Giraud's required a new kind of musical setting. Schoenberg obliged us with a setting of the utmost originality. First, the singer does not sing in the usual sense, but declaims the text using a technique called *Sprechstimme* (speaking voice). Yet, Schoenberg asks the singer to speak on pitches, creating a spoken melody quite unlike recitative. Whenever we speak, there is a pitch. We tend to rise in pitch when asking a question. A monotone speaker is so called because he or she speaks on only one (mono) pitch (tone). Schoenberg calls for a wonderfully modulated pitch language that typifies the old-fashioned melodramatic acting styles popular early in the twentieth century.

Instrumentation

The instrumentation of this song is also odd. Schoenberg reinforces the usual accompanimental instrument, the piano, with two bass-clef instruments: the cello and bass clarinet. This combination will inevitably lend the song a dark tone, as the ensemble features more bass instruments than anything else.

Unifying Motive

In this piece, Schoenberg allows free rein to his theory that motives, and not tonal centers, hold pieces together. The piece has no tonal center and is, in fact, atonal. In order to impart his work with some coherence, Schoenberg presents a three-note motive at the beginning of the piece using some of the lowest notes of the piano. This three-note motive appears in every measure of the piece in one form or another. Initially it's made up of the notes E-natural, G, and E-flat; put another way, there is one note a minor third above the first, and another note a half-step below. This combination of a minor third and half-step serves as the motive. In some parts of the piece, Schoenberg allows one of the three notes of the motive to appear an octave higher or lower than where the listener expects it. This lends the piece some variety, but is really nothing more than a very simple variation on the original motive. We call this "octave displacement." Other variations on the motive found in this piece include "retrograde," or presenting the motive backwards by first rising a major third then dropping a minor third instead of first rising a minor third then dropping a major third to the half-step below the first note. Sometimes Schoenberg "inverts" the motive. In inversion he reverses all the steps, so the motive first falls a minor third, then rises a major third, arriving on a note now one half-step higher than the first. He also presents retrograde-inversions, or presentations of the motive upside down and backwards. Here is a chart of the developmental techniques found in this seminal atonal work.

THE MOTIVE:
      E   G   E-flat

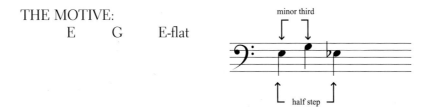

RETROGRADE:
     E-flat   G   E

INVERSION:
     E   C#   E#

RETROGRADE-INVERSION:
     E#   C#   E

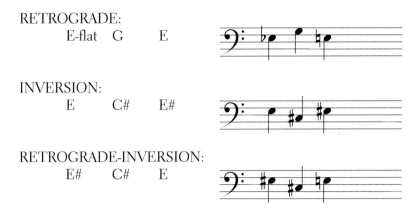

Schoenberg also transposes all of these variations. He can start any of these variations on any of the twelve pitches of the chromatic scale. Add to these transpositions the idea of octave displacement, and you can see that Schoenberg had many options at his disposal. Yet, if you sit at a piano and play these three-note motives, you'll find that they all sound very much alike. In this way, Schoenberg felt he was continuing a good and worthy tradition in German music. While his music is not tonal, it is built upon the idea of motivic variation, and therefore is linked to the work of Brahms and others before him. Thus, atonal music might seem like a radical departure from the past, but its inventor believed it was an obvious extension of accomplishments achieved during the 1800s.

Schoenberg's contention, that atonal music was both inevitable and logical, gains strength when we consider that Charles Ives (1874–1954) in America and Béla Bartók (1881–1945) in Hungary both wrote atonal pieces within a year of Schoenberg doing so, and in both cases without either man knowing about Schoenberg's accomplishment.

Schoenberg's *Pierrot Lunaire*, for all of its interesting innovations, was well received in its day. Schoenberg attracted a cohort of outstanding students in the years prior to the First World War. Among his most outstanding students were Alban Berg and Anton Webern. Along with his students, Schoenberg fostered atonality and found it well suited to the setting of expressionist texts. After the war, he and his students found the public in Austria and Germany more resistant to their atonal music, but that story will be told later in the chapter.

MUSIC IN PARIS BEFORE THE FIRST WORLD WAR

While the late 1800s in Germany saw chromaticism and the music drama holding center stage, in France different and perhaps more radical steps were being taken. The composers Erik Satie (1866–1925) and Claude Debussy (1862–1918) were in the process of embracing individual styles that challenged honored traditions of music from the previous two centuries.

ERIK SATIE

Erik Satie was an eccentric by any standard. Among his many eccentricities he disliked traveling in vehicles. As a result, he was often late and found it difficult to keep jobs. At the time of his death, he owned fifty identical umbrellas and a large number of identical red velvet suits. He drank to excess and had a wily sense of humor that

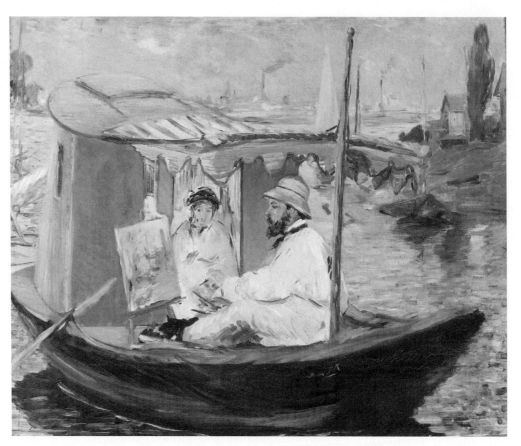

Figure 12.4 | Edouard Manet, ***Monet Working on His Boat, Argenteuil.*** 1874. France was fertile ground for artistic innovation during the late nineteenth century. Edouard Manet served as a role model for many younger artists in this trend toward innovation. Preferring to work in the open air, Manet depicts a simple scene from everyday life. The technique used blends pastel colors into recognizable forms. The extremities are intentionally left vague, as the expressed interest was in the impression of a subject rather than its specific content. French Impressionists alleged that preconceived mental notions developed from personal experiences tend to influence one's perceptions, and reasoned that particulars were automatically filled in anyway—that observations took place in the mind, not its portal, the eye. (Scala/Art Resource, NY)

he indulged in print on numerous occasions. As an illustration of his eccentricity, here is a brief excerpt from his writing. After working in near total obscurity from the 1880s until 1913, he found some belated interest in his work stemming from recent performances of his pieces in Paris by the Spanish pianist Ricardo Viñes. Asked to write something about his work habits, Satie produced this brief and totally fictitious document:

> *The Musician's Day*
>
> *An artist must organize his life.*
>   *Here is the exact timetable of my daily activities:*
>   *Get up: 7:18 am; be inspired: 10:23 to 11:47 am. I take lunch at 12:11 pm and leave the table at 12:14 pm.*

Healthy horse-riding, out in my grounds: 1:19 to 2:53 pm. More inspiration: 3:12 pm to 4:07 pm.

Various activities (fencing, reflection, immobility, visits, contemplation, swimming, etc. . . .): 4:21 to 6:47.

Dinner is served at 7:16 and ends at 7:20 pm. Then come symphonic readings, out loud: 8:09 to 9:59 pm.

I go to bed regularly at 10:37 pm. Once a week (on Tuesdays) I wake up with a start at 3:19 am.

I eat only white foodstuffs: eggs, sugar, scraped bones; fat from dead animals; veal, salt, coconuts, chicken cooked in white water; mouldy fruit, rice, turnips, camphorated sausage, things like spaghetti, cheese (white), cotton salad and certain fish (minus their skins).

I boil my wine and drink it cold mixed with fuchsia juice. I have a good appetite, but never talk while eating, for fear of strangling myself.

I breathe carefully (a little at a time). I very rarely dance. When I walk, I hold my sides and look rigidly behind me.

Serious in appearance, if I laugh it is not on purpose. I always apologize about it nicely.

My sleep is deep, but I keep one eye open. My bed is round, with a hole cut out to let my head through. Once every hour, a servant takes my temperature and gives me another.

I have long subscribed to a fashion magazine. I wear a white bonnet, white stockings, and a white waistcoat.

My doctor has always told me to smoke. Part of his advice runs:
—Smoke away, my dear chap: if you don't, someone else will.[1]

Satie's sense of humor extended to some of his musical compositions as well. From 1913 to 1915 he wrote a large volume of pieces with outlandish titles such *Three Pieces in the Form of a Pear* (interestingly, this set is made up of more than three pieces), *Dehydrated Embryos*, and the *Bureaucratic Sonata*. While these humorous pieces brought Satie a measure of fame, his more important work was done earlier. In compositions dating as early as the 1880s, he created music that opposed the prevailing trends in Romantic music, most particularly the giganticism that resulted in mammoth works such as Wagner's *Ring*. Satie's early pieces are humble in scope, avoiding any possibility of the listener fantasizing about a Beethovenian hero genius creating them, and generally pointing the way to a radical simplicity. A work of this sort appears in our recorded anthology, [CD3 #7].

Gnossienne No. 1

Satie's *Gnossienne No. 1* (1890) eschews the cult of virtuosity that had taken hold of the Romantic imagination. With a modest amount of practice, a first-year piano student could execute this piece. The piece also has no bar lines. Satie had very neat handwriting. He felt that bar lines were superfluous since medieval music didn't have them and his music was clear and specific enough without them. The harmony of this piece is extremely simple and very unlike the chromatic developments that so occupied German composers since the rise of Wagner. The harmony is so simple, in fact, that it uses exactly three chords in the accompaniment of its exotic, f-minor melody.

---

[1] *The Writings of Erik Satie*, Nigel Wilkins, ed and tr. (London: Eulenburg, 1980): 59.

FIGURE 12.5 | *Erik Satie (1866–1925)*
(© Bettmann/Corbis)

One of three chords used in the piece, the tonic of f minor, appears almost all of the time. Using only one chord almost all of the time lends the music a static and calm quality ideal for a piece that rejects everything that Wagner and the late Romantics embraced, including their fascination with restless longing.

The formal plan of this piece is very repetitive: A A B B C C B B A¹ B B C C B B. Within each of these short sections, Satie uses considerable small-scale repetition. For example, the first two short phrases of each A section begins exactly the same way. Note too that a distinct sameness exists in all the sections. A, B, and C are all accompanied by exactly the same pattern in the left hand. Please notice that only one section is modified in the formal outline above. The third and final appearance of the A material, or A¹, has two tiny features that distinguish it from the other two appearances. One small-scale repetition in the melody is omitted and one of the very few chord changes in the piece that is found in the earlier two appearances of the A section is omitted. Otherwise, all the repeats above are exact. Just as he justified his non-use of bar lines by looking at medieval music, he justified repetitious formal plans by looking to medieval models as well. Satie claimed to have been born in the wrong time, preferring the Middle Ages of his imagination to the sprawl of modernity.

Satie's style models his irreverence for the excesses of late Romanticism. While late Romantic music was often huge and serious, his is brief and irreverent. While the Romantics loved complexity, Satie favored simplicity. While the Romantics sought variation, Satie avoided it for the most part. Romanticism often aligns itself with luxury through excess. Satie aligns himself with austerity through lack. His music may provide the clearest break with the past of any studied in this book.

Listening Guide

Erik Satie, Gnossienne No. 1 (1890)
[CD3, #7] *(Duration, 3 min. 20 sec.)*

Tempo: Lent (slow)
Tonality: F minor (only three chords used)
Form: A A B B C C B B A¹ B B C C B B (no bar lines)

0.00 **A**   Two short phrases begin each A section on the tonic chord, F minor. Note too, sections A, B, and C are all accompanied by exactly the same pattern in the left hand of the piano.

0.23 **A**   Excluding the A1 section which appears later, this repeat, like all the others, is exact.

0.45 **B**   Begins with grace notes (a quick note just preceding the main note) accentuating the IV chord, B♭ minor, found four scale-steps higher than the tonic.

0.54 **B**   Repeat

1.03 **C**   The melodic line in this C section first rises then slowly descends.

1.17 **C**   Repeat

1.30 **B**   Return of B material

1.39 **B**   Repeat

1.49 **A1**   This final appearance of the A material, or A¹, has two tiny features that distinguish it from the other two appearances. One small-scale repetition in the melody is omitted and one of the very few chord changes in the piece that is found in the earlier two appearances of the A section is omitted.

2.09 **B**   Return of B material

2.18 **B**   Repeat

2.28 **C**   Return of C material

2.42 **C**   Repeat

2.56 **B**   Return of B material

3.05 **B**   Repeat

CLAUDE DEBUSSY

Claude Debussy counted Erik Satie among his closest friends. Debussy claims to have learned much from Satie, even going so far as claiming that the old eccentric saved him from a career of imitating Wagner. Sometimes Satie could be a difficult friend to keep since he very much resented that Debussy became much more famous than he did. Debussy's fame rests on his forward-looking style.

FIGURE 12.6 | *Claude Debussy (1862–1918)*
(© Bettmann/Corbis)

Debussy, like many French composers, was educated at the Paris Conservatoire. Like Berlioz before him, he won the Prix de Rome. When Debussy returned to Paris after two years in Italy, he was thoroughly disgusted with his prestigious victory. He found everything about his time in Italy insufferable. Oddly, his letters home are full of complaints about such unusual things as the architecture of the villa where he was housed being too ornate. "I had difficulty sleeping amidst so much Baroque ornamentation," he complained. Irritable and sensitive, Debussy declined the Concert Envoi, the last stage of the prize, wherein his compositions would have received a gala debut. He had always been a difficult and fussy student at the Conservatoire. Earlier in his career as a music student he would argue endlessly with his teachers. One of his fellow students was so impressed with one of these arguments that he rushed home and wrote it down. Here is some of what he recorded of Debussy's argument with the professor Ernest Guiraud.

DEBUSSY: [I have] no faith in the supremacy of the major scale. The tonal scale must be enriched by other scales. Nor am I misled by equal temperament. Rhythms are stifling. Rhythms cannot be contained within bars. Music is neither major nor minor. The mode is that which one happens to choose at the moment.

(Debussy then played a series of chords at the piano.)
GUIRAUD: What's that?
DEBUSSY: Incomplete chords, floating. One can travel and leave by any door.
GUIRAUD: But when I play this [he plays a dominant-seventh sonority] it has to resolve.
DEBUSSY: I don't see that it should. Why?
GUIRAUD: I'm not saying that what you do isn't beautiful, but it's theoretically absurd.
DEBUSSY: There is no theory. You merely have to listen. Pleasure is the law.[2]

Debussy's last statement gets to the heart of the matter: "Pleasure is the law." Since the time of the ancient Greeks, music in the West has been governed by rules. These rules, as you've surely noticed by now, change from age to age and lead to fierce debates; but the suggestion that individual pleasure has replaced discipline and order marks the climax of the Romantic rebellion.

Debussy's music may not always live up to his radical rhetoric, however, he did accomplish a large number of attractive audacities. He allowed himself to be influenced by widely varying materials. For example, after the Paris Exhibition of 1889 (a sort of World's Fair for which the Eiffel Tower was built), Debussy allowed his style to embrace ideas he borrowed from Indonesia and Russia. Music from both of these lands was performed at the exhibition. Debussy was impressed by the examples he heard of Indonesian classical music performed by a gamelan orchestra. The *gamelan* is an

---

[2]*Music in the Western World: a History in Documents*, Piero Weiss and Richard Taruskin, eds. (New York: Schirmer, 1985): 417–418.

orchestra mainly constituted of tuned gongs and chimes. Debussy adopted a scale used by the visiting gamelan. This scale is made up of five pitches instead of the usual seven comprising the Western major and minor scales. In keeping with his contention that major and minor must be enriched by other scales, Debussy frequently inserted passages of pentatonic (five-note scale) material into his works. These passages disrupt the rules of Western music and introduce an exotic and hauntingly unstable quality into his pieces. Debussy was equally taken with the "whole-tone scale." This scale features absolutely no half-steps. Half steps are crucial in tonal music because they serve to generate expectation in listeners and a sense of arrival when they are resolved. By containing none, the whole-tone scale avoids conventional patterns of tension and release.

From Russia, Debussy was especially impressed by the unorthodox music of Modest Mussorgsky, mentioned in the previous chapter. He found the exotic orchestration of Russian nationalist music irresistible. While this connection to Russian music links Debussy to such practices as composing programmatic music, he strove to distance himself by disdaining attempts to depict his programs literally. He wanted to convey the emotional impact of experiences in his music rather than try to tell some particular story.

LA MER

In our recorded anthology [CD3 #8] we have an example from a large orchestral work from relatively late in Debussy's career, titled *La Mer* (The Sea) dating from 1910. The piece is divided into three movements. We have the last in our anthology: a movement Debussy subtitled "The Dialogue of the Wind and Waves."

Various influences contributing to Debussy's style are reflected in this work. One was a bent for musical exoticism. Notice that a gong, much like those found in the gamelan, opens this movement. Like many contemporary French painters, poets, and musicians, he was also fascinated by the endlessly suggestive qualities of Wagner's "leit-motifs," used in part for extended harmonic journeys, which blurred all hard outlines of form. Some influence of Russia can be heard here. He was particularly inspired by the dramatic shaping and clear-cut colors found in the orchestral tone poems of the new Russian school. He loved Rimsky-Korsakov's *Antar* and *Scheherazade* (both orchestral works with sea scenes). Though there is no narrative program to accompany this work, the dialogues between wind and sea are experienced by the listener as pure emotions influenced by the undulating music, so suggestive of the ocean, and swirling and ephemeral material, suggestive of the wind. The sea held a special fascination for the late 1800s. Coleridge's "Rhyme of the Ancient Mariner" serves as a good example. That poem, like Debussy's symphonic poem, presents its subject "alone on a wide, wide sea."

The musical form is obscured by subtle criss-crossings of thematic and harmonic ideas. It unfolds as a kaleidoscope of colors and furtive images, shapes, and patterns, without any conventional symphonic design, which steadily builds to climactic action three-quarters of the way into the movement. Debussy's rhythms, in keeping with his claims while debating his old teacher, are also vague. The listener has much difficulty discerning a steady meter, concealed by syncopations and irregular subdivisions of beat patterns. Many animated rhythmic patterns are often sustained in *ostinato* fashion. Melodies do not last very long. Nonfunctional chords (or if we use Debussy's terminology in the debate, incomplete chords) weaken the sense of tonality. The use of the pentatonic, whole-tone, chromatic, and octatonic scales, each offering a unique and subtle brand of instability, further frustrates the sense of tonal center.

Listening Guide

Claude Debussy, La Mer (1910)
[CD3, #8] *(Duration, 7 min. 33 sec.)*

The Dialogue of the Wind and Waves

SECTION ONE

0.00   Low strings introduce a chromatic wave theme over resonating gongs.

0.12   Oboes, clarinets, and bassoons respond with a short intermitted motive, possibly representing the wind.
0.20   Sequence repeated
0.30   Low strings play a more excited rhythm, like some kind of watery upheaval from below, winds respond.
0.43   Trumpet solo introduces a new melody over tremolos in the high string.

1.01   Strings play a lively ascending scale that is continuously repeated, while the winds play sustained notes that serve as a transitional passage to a new section.

SECTION TWO

1.18   Upper woodwinds introduce a new theme in longer notes that descend by half, then whole steps, (each repeated), over an ascending chromatic motive in the lower strings.

1.43   The flute and cellos play a whole-step motive that is continuously repeated, as lower strings and winds gradually become more animated. This is the purest whole-tone section of the piece.

1.55   Woodwinds and brass alternate motives over a fast wave-like figure in the strings.
2.14   Brass introduce a tri-tone, then whole-tone motive over the strings' wave-like figure, while woodwinds provide brief splashes of color.
2.19   String basses continuously respond with a pizzicato melody.
2.24   Sequence repeated.
2.44   A new transitional passage begins to quiet the action.
3.04   Horns present a harmonic motive; violins respond with a descending passage, followed by the woodwinds.

SECTION THREE

3.45   Suddenly low chromatic string tremolos.

3.53   Violins play very high harmonics while flutes and oboes play high chromatic passages.

4.06   Chromatic harmonies descend, concluding the phrase.

4.21   Sequence repeated.

4.35   Music becomes gradually excited before the tempo slows and leads to the next melody.

5.01   Strings play high chromatic melody that eventually descends chromatically.

5.15   Brass plays the chromatic motive, which is then repeated by the strings.

5.31   Brass repeatedly plays a dissonant chord in animated rhythms, the woodwinds reply.

5.45   Strings play chromatic motive.

5.51   Upper woodwinds return with a theme from part two, which moved in longer notes that descend by half, then whole steps, (each repeated). It is now played over an ostinato pattern in the strings.

6.22   Wave motive returns in strings, while winds play chromatic motive above it.

6.37   Brass join in with sustained chords.

7.03   An agitated coda-like section quickly leads to an exciting and abrupt ending that features a single, hasty dominant to tonic cadence bringing the work to an unexpected, traditional close.

Readers may notice that the listening guide for *La Mer* makes no reference to a conventional form. While Debussy generally preferred ternary form, he was easily capable of making the radical step of avoiding obvious thematic recurrences. He chose this course for this piece in order to reflect the ever-changing quality of the sea. Such vagueness is the hallmark of Debussy's style.

IMPRESSIONISM

Debussy's name frequently finds itself coupled with the term Impressionism. This term was first applied to the work of painter Claude Monet. A critic looked at his vague and imprecise imagery and concluded that Monet's works were not paintings, but mere impressions. Monet resented the term at first, but later wore it as a crown. He wanted to capture the immediate effects of light's play upon objects.

Debussy knew Monet; they were even on friendly terms. When the term Impressionism was applied to Debussy's music, he too was initially upset. Later he accepted the term. What his music has to do with Monet's paintings may be very little. They do share a concern with keeping certainty at bay, Monet through his blurring of lines and evocation of the play of light, and Debussy through his blurring of formal, rhythmic, and tonal boundaries.

FIGURE 12.7 I Claude Monet, ***Impression—Sunrise.*** 1872. Oil on canvas. Avoiding all hard outlines of form, Monet sought to capture the effects of light and color as actually perceived by the artist momentarily. His is an approach that broke from traditional depictions of reality, and as a result stirred debate. An irate critic, who saw this painting as a formless collection of tiny colored patches, was prompted to label the entire Paris exhibition (1874) in which it was shown, "exhibition of the impressions." This derogatory term stuck. (© Archivo Iconografico, S.A./Corbis)

FIGURE 12.8 | Vincent van Gogh, ***Les Chaumes a Cordeville,*** 1890. Symbolism is a powerfully expressive tool. The images depicted are easily recognized, but serve as endlessly suggestive signs. The distorted rooftop and the liquid depiction of trees pointing upward to an ominous sky are not there to represent reality, but to symbolize van Gogh's disturbed view of the universe. Claude Debussy is considered an Impressionist in music because his fragmentary motives and flashes of tone color recall the Impressionists' painting technique. He can also be considered a Symbolist, since suggestion, rather than outright statement, is at the heart of his aesthetic. (Erich Lessing/Art Resource, NY)

SYMBOLISM

An artistic movement of even greater importance to Debussy was Symbolism. Debussy relished the poetry of Symbolists such as Poe, Baudelaire, Maeterlinck, and Mallarmé. These poets tended to obscure the immediate subject of their poetry by crafting elaborate metaphors or symbols. For example, in "The Fall of the House of Usher" (a poem that Debussy set to music) Poe describes a decaying aristocratic house in a way that conjures unmistakable suggestions of the ravages of incest upon the minds of the Usher family. A poem about incest wouldn't have been appreciated in Poe's time, nor in Debussy's, but a symbolist work exploring this most difficult of topics was permissible, even though it flew in the face of Victorian values. Other works of Debussy's based on Symbolist writing include his tone poem *Prelude to the Afternoon of a Faun*, his opera *Pelleas and Melisande*, and a large body of his art songs for solo voice and piano.

THE BALLETS RUSSES

One of the most interesting developments in music in Paris before the First World War concerns the ballet. Since the time of Louis XIV and Lully, France had long fostered professional ballet. During the 1800s, the Russian ruling class fixated on all things French. Today, the greatest collection of French painting from the turn of the twentieth century resides at one of the Tsar's palaces in St. Petersburg. Naturally a flourishing of the ballet in Russia attended this fixation on French culture.

In 1905 the Russian Empire suffered from widespread social unrest. The Tsar and his family were seen as wholly disengaged from the interests of the common people, who suffered terribly. Strikes in St. Petersburg and Moscow by ironworkers led to sympathetic strikes by other trade groups, including the seamstresses' union. This meant that the women who sewed the costumes for the Imperial Ballet were on strike. Soon the dancers joined them in sympathy for their cause. The Tsar didn't care much what ironworkers and seamstresses thought. They could be gunned down in the streets if the need arose, a tactic the Tsar had used before. However, famous ballerinas could not be gunned down for their disloyalty to his reign without raising an international furor. The Tsar had to crush the dancers' strike immediately and before general violence broke out. The ballet dancers of the Imperial theaters were informed that they had to report to work or lose their positions. Those who lost their positions suddenly found themselves without opportunities, since all the ballet theaters owed allegiance to the Tsar in order to remain open.

French and Russian Cultural Alliance

At this point, the Russian impresario Sergei Diaghilev entered the scene. Diaghilev fancied himself a man of the arts. Unfortunately, he failed as a painter, and after several years of study with Nikolai Rimsky-Korsakov, he admitted to being a failure as a composer as well. He transformed himself into an impresario, a person who organizes and seeks financing for artistic events. Diaghilev formed a new ballet company, signed the out-of-work dancers, and moved to Paris. There he formed the *Ballets russes* (The Russian Ballet).

Paris was as crazy about Russian culture in 1907 when Diaghilev started the *Ballets russes* as Russia was about things French. The reason for this mutual admiration stems from the Cultural Alliance. Signed in the years after the Franco-Prussian War when German troops defeated France decisively, the Cultural Alliance was an attempt by France and Russia to resist Germany's growing military and economic strength. Germany had always been comprised of a collection of small city-states. During the 1870s, Germany united into a mighty empire. Situated on opposite sides of Germany, France and Russia made natural allies. They vowed that should Germany attack either of them, the other would come to their aid and force Germany to fight enemies to the east and west. Military alliance between the two nations urged them to greater cultural sympathy as well, hence their mutual fascination with one another's artistic creations.

This situation suited Diaghilev's ambitions perfectly. During the early years of the *Ballets russes*, Russian nationalistic and romantic works were performed, including all the ballets of Chaikovsky and programmatic symphonic works of Rimsky-Korsakov. Diaghilev wisely changed the artistic emphasis of his company every few years in order to keep the public's fascination constantly refreshed. He commissioned new works from modern artists such as Debussy, Richard Strauss, and a young Russian named Igor Stravinsky (1882–1971).

IGOR STRAVINSKY

Stravinsky initially composed for the *Ballets russes* as an accident. Diaghilev commissioned a new ballet from the composer Anatol Liadov. Unfortunately, Liadov slipped into alcoholism before composing Diaghilev's new score. Diaghilev had traveled all the way from Paris to St. Petersburg to pick up the new piece. While there, he attended the wedding of Rimsky-Korsakov's daughter. At the reception afterward, a new orchestral piece by Rimsky-Korsakov's promising student, Stravinsky, had its debut.

FIGURE 12.9 | *Igor Stravinsky (1882–1971), drawn by Pablo Picasso (1920)* (© 2003 Estate of Pablo Picasso/Artists Rights Society [ARS], NY/Rèunion des Musèe Nationaux/Art Resource, NY)

Desperate to get a new ballet for the 1909 season, Diaghilev asked Stravinsky if he could compose a new ballet in three weeks. Unknown at the time, Stravinsky agreed happily. The result of this unlikely commission is the ballet *Firebird*, based on a Russian fairy tale. Stravinsky's score remains in the standard repertory today.

Stravinsky's next two ballets for Diaghilev count among the most audacious pieces written before the First World War. The first, entitled *Petrushka* (1911), contains, among its other innovations, the combination of two tonal keys playing simultaneously. The second of these ballets, *The Rite of Spring* (1913), was so controversial at its debut that half the audience rioted while the other half tried to shut them up. The tumult of that premier established Stravinsky, Diaghilev, and the brilliant young choreographer Nijinsky as three of the most talked about and controversial figures of their age. Moreover, it confirmed for Diaghilev the necessity of tirelessly searching for scandalous new works. This search would lead him to commission new scores from not only Stravinsky, but such maverick figures as Satie as well. The value of one scandal, one riot, one uproar was enormous. It kept all Paris talking about the *Ballets russes* and, more importantly for Diaghilev, buying tickets to see if the next performance would end in some violent demonstration for or against modern art.

THE RITE OF SPRING

The Story

Created in 1913 on the eve of the outbreak of World War One, *The Rite of Spring* remains one of the most talked-about works of the 1900s. The ballet tells a story devised by Stravinsky about a tumultuous moment for a tribe of prehistoric Russians. The moment is the advent of springtime. While spring is a time of new life and renewal, in the frozen north it is also a time of upheaval and violent change. Iced-over rivers begin to flow while filled with dangerous boulders of ice. The forests witness shards of ice falling from tree limbs. The ground itself becomes a mire of mud as the deep frost gives way beneath the sun's rays. Stravinsky imagines his tribe of prehistoric people trying to impose some order amidst the chaos of spring's arrival by appeasing the sun god, Yarillo, with a human sacrifice. In this case, the sacrifice will be a virgin girl.

The ballet unfolds over two acts. The first shows scenes within the community. The individual dancer in this first act is the tribal sage; everyone else dances in like manner with a group of other dancers representing people of similar age and gender. This segmentation of dancers into groups depicts the compartmentalization of the culture along age and gender lines, as well as the tribe's lack of interest in notions such as individualism. The section of this piece in our recorded anthology [CD3 #10] comes from the first act. It features the adolescent girls. The act ends with a riotous adulation of the earth by the entire tribe. The second act depicts the rite itself. First the adolescent girls perform a round dance. When one of them stumbles, she becomes the chosen one. The chosen one stands perfectly still as various ritual dances are performed.

FIGURE 12.10 | Pablo Picasso, ***Les Demoiselles D'Avignon.*** 1907. The women depicted are prostitutes. The colors are primal and the angular shapes of the figures resemble those of early African sculpture. Artists painting in this short-lived Fauve ("wild beast") style experimented with distorting images and incorporating motifs from primitive art. They compared primeval human experiences with similar contemporary practices in what they deemed a decadent European society. These artists sought to shed light on preliterate human tendencies as a means to contemplate our humanness, and to observe how much, if any, it may have changed. Many intellectuals and musicians, including Picasso's associate Igor Stravinsky, shared this early twentieth-century interest in preliterate culture. Utilizing a deliberate evocation of primordial power through insistent rhythms, percussive sounds, and sexual energy, Stravinsky explores in his ballet *The Rite of Spring* (1913), a primitive pagan, cultural justification for violent ritual in preliterate Russia with an abiding interest in contemporary societies' corrupt rationalization for aggressiveness. It is interesting to note that a propensity for hostility was reflected at the premier of this work, for the most infamous riot in music history broke out as a result of audience members who wanted to hear the piece and hecklers who booed, laughed, and made animal noises. Police were literally called in to quell the fist-fighting which had already spilled out into the street. (© 2003 Estate of Pablo Picasso/Artists Rights Society [ARS], NY/Digital image © The Museum of Modern Art/Licensed by SCALA/Art Resource, NY)

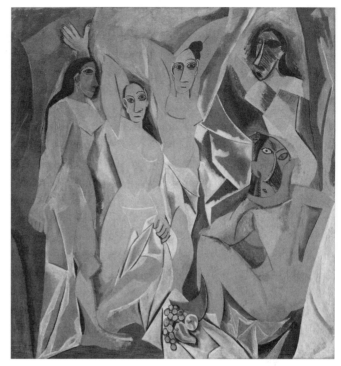

The climax of the ballet finds the chosen one performing a frantic solo as she dances herself to exhaustion and finally death.

The Music

Stravinsky's music for this strange story contains many audacious characteristics. While rival tonalities appear simultaneously, as was the case in his earlier work *Petrushka*, the parameter of rhythm witnesses Stravinsky's greatest innovations. For some stretches of the piece, the meter changes in almost every measure. The result is that those passages feel entirely unbalanced. Strongly accented beats can happen in almost any part of a measure, instead of on the traditionally emphasized first beat of each measure. Stravinsky's orchestration is similarly innovative. Rimsky-Korsakov, Stravinsky's teacher, taught orchestration and advocated that composers write music that was relatively easy and natural to play. Stravinsky ignores his teacher's advice, while still keeping his teacher's emphasis on folk song and delightful orchestration. The opening of the excerpt, which is also the opening of the ballet, serves as a good example of this emphasis. Here Stravinsky has a bassoon play in an extremely high register. The music being played is a folk song, but the tone of the bassoon will sound strained and new, like some prehistoric instrument, due to the high range. As you listen to this opening, try to tap your foot with the beat. Don't feel badly if it doesn't work well; Stravinsky intentionally throws off his listeners with constant meter changes.

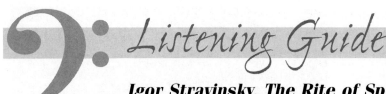

Listening Guide

Igor Stravinsky, The Rite of Spring (1913)

[CD3, #10] *(Duration, 8 min. 21 sec.)*

BALLET SCENES	MUSIC

Introduction

| 0.00 | With the birth of spring, a group of girls is seated before a sacred mound, each holding a garland. | A solo bassoon plays the opening theme, a repeated fragment of a folksong in changing meters, in its highest register. Its strained bleating quality sounds like a primitive call. |

0.45	The tribal Sage appears and guides them toward the mound.	The English horn joins in with new melodic fragments.
1.13		Pizzicato strings, oboe, and the clarinet enter with assorted melodic fragments.
1.25		Various instrumental combinations continuously shift abruptly in unpredictable rhythmic patterns as they build to a climax. (Each instrumental group provides rather static but sharp contrasts of color, all of which paint a rather strange panoramic prehistoric landscape.)
3.03		Suddenly, the opening bassoon solo is heard again. Pizzicato violins playing a short ostinato and low sustained notes in the bass clarinet join it.

Omens of Spring—Dance of the Adolescents

| 3.26 | The girls do a celebratory dance around the mound. | A short introductory section reflects a realization of spring. |
| 3.36 | | The "Dance of the Adolescents" begins with a syncopated ostinato figure comprised of a single dissonant chord that is repeated thirty-two times in even eighth notes, but with strong irregular accents that consistently shift the sense of meter. |

3.56

Fragments of Russian folksongs are introduced over the ostinato chords in a kaleidoscopic fashion, creating a musical collage, reminding the listener of the origins of this ritualistic landscape.

BASSOONS

FRENCH HORN

TRUMPETS

4.55

Melodic fragments are repeated with a long crescendo that leads into the next section.

The Game of Abduction

6.56 In this frenzied dance ritual, one of the girls is abducted and carried away.

Growing out of the previous section, a faster tempo, changing meters, and exciting rhythms in the high trumpet and percussion capture the violent nature of the chosen one's abduction for sacrifice.

Audience Reaction

We cannot know with any certainty whether the riot that greeted the premier of this piece resulted from Nijinsky's extremely innovative choreography, Stravinsky's audacious score, or a combination of the two. Whatever the reason, the audience was fairly evenly split among those who were enjoying what they were seeing and hearing, and those who emphatically were not. French audiences in past times felt more entitled to express their pleasure and displeasure at public performances than they do today. Booing, hooting, and whistling at the ballet was not only allowed, but seen as the right of the audience. The premiere of *The Rite of Spring*, however, eventually turned violent. Nijinsky could no longer hear the orchestra when the audience became so loud, so he began counting and shouting the beats loudly so the dancers could stay together. At the intermission between the acts, the poet and war hero Guillaume Apollinaire addressed the crowd and pleaded on behalf of the theater for calm. This mollified the crowd for a few minutes, but soon they were shouting with full throat again. When the night was over, Stravinsky felt devastated. All his hard work had come to nothing. But Diaghilev reassured him, saying, "Success is easy; scandal requires genius!" Obviously, Diaghilev and Jean-Jacques Rousseau, who argued that genius must be censored by taste, would not have agreed. The modernists shed all pretense of trying to please everybody. They wanted first and foremost to please themselves. For Diaghilev, that always meant offending more than a few people along the way.

Later Innovations

The *Ballets russes* functioned from 1907 until 1929, the year when Diaghilev died. Not only had Diaghilev discovered Stravinsky and afforded the young Russian an influential forum to have his music heard, but he also fostered the invention of modern dance. Unlike ballet, in which women wear point shoes and dance on their toes, modern dance uses bare feet. Modern dance allows for any movement at all, affording the choreography considerable latitude, while ballet tends to draw from a more restricted vocabulary of available movements chosen for their stylized expressivity.

MUSIC IN AMERICA BEFORE THE FIRST WORLD WAR

The United States of America hasn't figured into this book so far. A relatively young country, the United States did not contribute all that importantly to the field of music during its first 100 years. Most American professional musicians were trained in Europe, especially in Germany. They brought European ideas about music with them to these shores. While some rugged individuals such as William Billings (1746–1800), Stephen Foster (1826–1864), Eduard MacDowell (1861–1908), and John Philip Sousa (1854–1932) sought to craft a distinctly American style, their successes were mixed and felt very little outside this country. Yet within this country these men tower as giants in their respective lines. The interest of space within a book of this sort prompts us to skip America's interesting contributions of the 1800s and join the story in the last century.

Representing the first generation of American composers during the twentieth century, we've chosen Charles Ives. Ives represents the outstanding tradition of American experimental music.

CHARLES IVES

FIGURE 12.11 | *Charles Ives (1874–1954)*
(© Bettmann/Corbis)

Charles Ives was born in Connecticut, the son of a municipal bandleader. During the 1800s, most Americans, especially in smaller cities, heard more band concerts than orchestra concerts. Most small and medium-sized cities employed a professional bandleader. Ives' father possessed a spectacularly original musical sensibility. He believed his children should learn a nearly total musical independence. Experiments of every sort were tolerated at the Ives' home. Moreover, Charles was taught to sing in one key while his father accompanied him in another. This unorthodox approach to musical education fostered in Ives an uncommon ear for music.

Ives attended Yale University, where he studied composition with Horatio Parker. Parker held conservative notions about music and tried to foster in the wayward Ives an abiding love for the traditions of Europe. Ives resisted, but did enough work pleasing to his teacher to justify his graduation. Ives had many distractions during his college years. He played organ at a local Presbyterian church, pitched for a minor league baseball team, and continued to compose experimental music in a clandestine fashion. Among his experiments is the organ piece *The Yale-Princeton Football Game*. In this work, Ives imagined the keyboard of the organ as a metaphor for the gridiron. He visualized the ebb and flow of the game unfolding before him on the keys. Then he wrote down the result. Amidst material designed to simulate the movements of the game, Ives layered the two school's fight songs in harshly clashing keys. As Yale begins to triumph, Ives transposed the Princeton fight song first into the somber minor mode, before distorting it beyond recognition. Compositions such as this one were always undertaken without his teacher's knowledge.

After graduation, Ives moved to New York City where he worked for his uncle at a prestigious insurance firm. All the while, he continued composing. Among his experiments during this time was an interesting series of pieces for quarter-tone piano. To achieve this experiment, Ives took two pianos and placed them facing each other so that one person could sit in between them and play both keyboards, one with each hand. More importantly, he tuned one of the two pianos so that it was a quarter-tone sharper than the other. In other words, he tuned one piano so that every key struck on it would sound a note in between the consecutive keys of the other piano. The result is a division of the octave not into twelve, but twenty-four equal parts. Tenants of Ives' apartment building in New York City dubbed his compositions during this time "resident disturbances." Today they are performed and admired the world over.

Ives failed in his first post within his uncle's insurance company and found himself transferred to the marketing department. He was assigned the task of selling Americans on the idea of life insurance. He succeeded by drawing upon a philosophy that both he and his father espoused; transcendentalism. The transcendentalists believed in self-reliance, mutual aid, and reverence for nature, as the natural world brought man closer to the creator through unspoiled creation. Ives drew upon the poetry and philosophy of the transcendentalists in order to marshal such concepts as self-reliance in the sale of life insurance. Ives frequently drew upon the transcendentalists to inspire his compositions as well.

Flush with success in marketing life insurance, Ives went into partnership with a former classmate at Yale. They formed the Ives and Myrick Insurance Company. Ives made a fortune in business. This affluence allowed him never to worry whether his music was popular or even published. He held professional music-making in contempt, and showered with ridicule such professionally trained composers as his former teacher. Ives believed in a transcendent musicality that resided in common folk. The following short excerpt concerning a debate Ives overheard between his father and a conservatory-trained musician illustrates Ives' peculiar sense of the musical.

> *Once a nice young man (his musical sense having been limited by three years' intensive study at the Boston Conservatory) said to Father, "How can you stand it to hear Old John Bell (the best stone-mason in town) sing?" Father said, "He is a supreme musician." The young man (nice and educated) was horrified. "Why, he sings off the key, the wrong notes and everything—and that horrible, raucous voice—and he bellows out and hits notes no one else does—it's awful!" Father said, "Watch him closely and reverently, look into his face and hear the music of the ages. Don't pay too much attention to the sounds—for if you do, you may miss the music."*[3]

The idea that sound and music do not necessarily have anything to do with one another places Ives at a far remove from prevailing notions about Western music. For Ives, elitism in music was a terrible enemy of authentic and unspoiled expression.

---

[3] *Charles Ives' Memos*, ed John Kirkpatrick (New York: Norton, 1972): 131–133.

Figure 12.12 | Frederic Remington, ***The Bronco Buster,*** Bronze statute. Remington's art, like many of Ives' songs, seems to capture the very essence and excitement of basic human activities that are distinctly rooted in American traditions. (Frederic S. Remington, *The Bronco Buster,* 1895, date cast ca. 1905, bronze, 23¼ x 22⅜ x 11⅞ in., 1961.3, Amon Carter Museum, Fort Worth, Texas)

Ives' position in music history is odd. On the one hand, he held professionalism in contempt, yet on the other hand he composed some extraordinarily difficult pieces in terms of their technical demands on performers. For most of his life, Ives avoided public scrutiny. He did not seek out professional performances, preferring to view his music as a sign of his self-reliance. He and his family, along with select neighbors and friends, constituted audience enough for him. He did self-publish several works, including his virtuosic *Concord Sonata*, a piano piece with each movement devoted to a figure from the history of transcendentalism, and his *114 Songs.*

Ives' Songs

The piece in our anthology [CD4 #1] representing Ives is taken from his *114 Songs.* Observers have noted that within this collection there are nearly 114 separate styles. Some of the songs smack of German Romanticism, some are atonal, and some draw upon diverse folk traditions.

Charlie Rutledge

In our anthology is the song "Charlie Rutledge." This song is a setting of words by D.J. O'Maley, taken from a collection of cowboy verse. In setting this text, Ives chose a ternary structure. The outer "A" sections present a striding bass line in the left hand of the piano, suggestive of popular and sentimental songs of the time. Yet, the notes of this bass line and of the melody presented by the singer are pentatonic. The pentatonic scale, as mentioned in the discussion of Debussy, features only five notes. Indonesian classical music is by no means the only music in the world that features this five-note scale. Much of the world's folk music is pentatonic. In the "B" section, the text deals with the particulars of Charlie Rutledge's death. Here Ives presents atonal material to express the chaos and excitement of the cattle drive. When the text mentions Charlie's horse falling on its hapless rider, Ives asks the pianist to use his or her fists in pounding out clusters of consecutive notes. The vocal part, too, is subject to interesting innovation. The singer becomes so excited by the story that he or she stops singing and begins reciting the text in rhythm.

Taken together, Ives' pentatonicism, atonality, evocation of popular styles, clusters of consecutive pitches, and recitation of text demonstrate Ives' experimental approach. Like European modernists, he was interested in self-expression to such a degree that the traditional rules no longer bound him. His music sounds very different from Debussy's or Schoenberg's or Stravinsky's, but he was most certainly participating in the same general trend away from tonality and other Common Practice strategies of musical organization.

Charles Ives, Charlie Rutledge
[CD4, #1] *(Duration, 2 min. 24 sec.)*

Ternary Form: A B A

A

0.00   The piano presents a striding bass line in the left hand that is suggestive of popular and sentimental songs of the time, though the notes of this bass line and of the melody presented by the singer are pentatonic (a five-tone scale which may be represented by the black keys on the piano).

0.38   A transitional passage slows and leads directly into the contrasting B section.

B

0.55   Text deals with the particulars of Charlie Rutledge's death. Atonal material is used to express the chaos and excitement of the cattle drive. When the text mentions Charlie's horse falling on its hapless rider, the pianist uses his or her fists to pound out clusters of consecutive notes. The singer becomes so excited by the story that he or she stops singing and begins reciting the text in rhythm.

1.41   Transitional material slows again, but leads directly back to A section material this time

A

1.53   Pentatonic notes comprising the melody and striding bass line in the left hand of the piano return, as the dramatic text continues.

THE FIRST WORLD WAR

From 1914 to 1918 most of the nations of Europe went to war. The battle lines were essentially drawn between those nations that had enthusiastically conquered and colonized much of the planet (Britain, France, and Russia) against those European nations that had largely been left out of the imperialistic enterprises of the previous century (Austria and Germany). Other nations joined either side for various reasons. Claiming that one side or the other held a morally superior position within this conflict is difficult, although the classic take among the winners is that the losers started it. Worse than the scope of the conflict or its moral ambiguity was the method by which it was waged. Military technology had outstripped the imagination of the military leadership of both sides. Among the technological advances that made this war impossibly bloody were the machine gun and poison gas. These weapons were used almost exclusively for defensive purposes. Machine guns were invariably mounted on tripods rather than carried by hand. Therefore, the defenders could use them but the attackers did not. Poison gas is also mainly a defensive weapon, as no sane general would recklessly order his troops to advance into an area poisoned by his own side. The result of this defensive mentality was a nearly uninterrupted network of trenches running through Western Europe from the Swiss border to the Atlantic Ocean. Offensives saw the attacking side hurtle men forward by the tens of thousands in the hope that there would be enough men to intercept the machine gun bullets so that some men would survive to reach the far trenches and attack. The casualties stemming from these dehumanizing tactics were staggering.

After four years of sickening losses, Germany finally surrendered, not because she had been defeated militarily, but because the United States had joined the war on the side of Britain and France after a heated debate in the United States senate in which some senators argued for joining on the German side. Moreover, Britain and France had begun deploying soldiers from their vast colonies. Germany simply lacked the manpower to go on fighting in this manner. When the war ended, not one inch of German soil had been conquered. The German leadership hoped that this fact would discourage the victorious powers from punishing Germany too harshly for fighting on the losing side of the war. It did not. Germany was treated as a conquered power, and massive financial penalties were exacted against her. Germany's economy was devastated for the next fifteen years, and her people were left to seek desperate measures. This desperation led to the eventual rise of Adolph Hitler and the raw and stupid cruelty of the Nazi Party.

The dark consequences of the war were not only felt in Germany. People all over Europe looked at the catastrophe of a world war and wondered how Western Civilization had sunk so low.

NEO-CLASSICISM

No project, no institution of the West was beyond questioning after World War One. Some in the field of music felt that the unbridled modernism practiced before the war should be restrained by some influence from a more familiar music. What emerged was neo-classicism, a movement in music that calls for the creation of a more perfect modernism through the combination of modern musical traits with orderly principles borrowed from music's past or from popular styles.

Stravinsky's Neo-Classic Period

One of the first composers to embrace the ideal of neo-classicism was Igor Stravinsky. His compositions written after the war indicate a decided cooling off emotionally from the hot heights reached in works such as *The Rite of Spring*. Stravinsky achieved this new emotional cool at times by embracing older forms and an emotional objectivity, as is the case in his influential *Octet* (1922). In his first ballet written for Diaghilev after the war, Stravinsky looked to Pergolesi (the composer discussed at the beginning of the Classical Period chapter) for inspiration. In this piece called *Pulcinella* (1919) Stravinsky borrowed melodies written by Pergolesi and his imitators. Their lean and balanced style lends Stravinsky's work a clear break from the powerful and dark emotions of *The Rite of Spring*. Stravinsky even went so far as to argue in writing that music conveyed no specific emotional content, conveying instead only itself. He wrote "I consider that music is, by its very nature, essentially powerless to express anything at all, whether a feeling, an attitude of mind, a psychological mood, a phenomenon of nature, et cetera."[4] Here Stravinsky clearly parts company with many composers, not only of the early twentieth century, but throughout history.

---

[4]*Music in the Western World: a History in Documents*, Piero Weiss and Richard Taruskin, eds. (New York: Schirmer, 1985): 461.

FIGURE 12.13 | Andrew Wyeth, ***Christina's World, 1948.*** Tempera on gesso panel. Reticent emotions are conveyed by a precise realism that appears almost photographic. The vast landscape with sparse buildings and distant horizon seem to suggest a sense of melancholy and desolation as well as fresh possibilities for Christina, a young paraplegic girl positioned in a field with her back to the viewer, reaching forward, observing conflicts of solitude. With this, paradoxical sentiments of humans as being both limited and limitless are embodied, echoing in some way neo-classical principles, which may be weighted against Michelangelo's "David," (Figure 8.3) discussed in chapter eight of this book. The extreme differences in portrayal only exemplify how human characteristics not only define but also connect everyone in terms that are inescapable. (Digital image © The Museum of Modern Art/Licensed by SCALA/Art Resource, NY)

The extent of Stravinsky's efforts to cool off the dizzying emotionalism of modern music can be seen in an opera he wrote to celebrate Diaghilev's birthday. For the subject he chose the legend of Oedipus. After commissioning the poet Jean Cocteau to write a libretto telling the lurid story of Oedipus, a man who unbeknownst to him, murdered his father and married his mother; Stravinsky then had the libretto translated into Latin. By choosing a dead language, he cut off the audience from the emotional content of this most emotionally charged story. The opera *Oedipus Rex* even tries to conjure the remote traditions of the oratorio, as Stravinsky did not stage the first performance, but presented it as one would an oratorio. Not only was the audience incapable of understanding the words, but they had no stage action to cue them as to the content of the drama. Stravinsky was bold to write a dramatic work that de-emphasizes the drama.

German Neo-Classicism

Stravinsky composed in a neo-classical manner from 1919 until the early 1950s. His commitment to this hybrid modernism was not a passing fancy. Stravinsky had many colleagues interested in neo-classicism as well. Paul Hindemith (1895–1963) was

Germany's leading neo-classicist. After spending his early career as an expressionist, he turned after the war to a more sober and objective style built around traditional forms (especially the fugue), and a playful brand of tonality that allowed for constant and instantaneous modulations without traditional preparation. Perhaps the most important aspect of Hindemith's neo-classicism was the concept of *Gebrauchsmusik* (useful music). Hindemith believed that modern composers had an obligation to write pieces for children and amateurs, ensembles and instruments with small repertories, and for the edification of a larger audience. In short, he felt the modernist had more than an obligation to himself or herself, but to society in general.

Hindemith's friend and associate Kurt Weill (1900–1950) also fostered a brand of neo-classicism. Weill's neo-classicism depends more on introducing popular styles into a modernist musical composition. A devout Marxist, Weill wanted his music to be relevant for the embattled working class in Germany. Popular music, he felt, was more apt to win over the working class. Weill's neo-classicism sounds nothing like Hindemith's or Stravinsky's, but it is born of the same sense that modernism had lost its way and needed the influence of a more familiar style to lend it renewed life.

Parisian Neo-Classicism

Paris was the capital of neo-classicism. Most French composers active between the wars composed in a style related to the philosophical position of neo-classicism. Darius Milhaud (1892–1974), like Weill in Germany, favored popular idioms along with traditional formal designs. He lived in Brazil during the war and spent time in New York City. As a result, American jazz and Brazilian popular music figure prominently in Milhaud's compositions. Milhaud also made the presentation of two or more tonal keys simultaneously an important part of his style. He felt that modernists could draw upon traditional tonality but that they should layer it in order to achieve a modern sound. He compared this layering of simultaneous tonalities to the introduction of a third dimension into music.

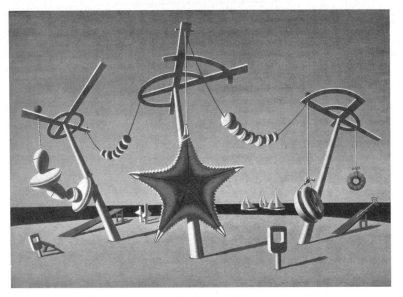

Figure 12.14 | Edward Wadsworth, *The Beached Margin, 1937.* Egg tempera on linen. Startling juxtapositions of nautical objects in vivid hyperrealism appear almost surrealistic. Their imaginative geometric shapes offer a quality of fantasy to a beach-scape that is otherwise depicted here as still-life. Wadsworth developed a deep passion for the sea and its vessels after serving in the Royal Navy during the First World War, designing and painting camouflage for ships. This composition offers bold relief from that charge. (© 2003 Artists Rights Society [ARS], New York/DACS, London/Tate Gallery, London/Art Resource, NY)

GERMAINE TAILLEFERRE

A short waltz by Germaine Tailleferre (1892–1983) represents Parisian neo-classicism in our recorded anthology, [CD4 #2]. Tailleferre favored a flip style that achieves an emotional cooling off by seeming off-handed. European modernism before the First World War could be accused of being a little too serious. Tailleferre distanced herself from seriousness by drawing her inspiration from French popular music associated with circuses, fairs, and other popular entertainment configured for the delight of the lower classes. Tailleferre and her friends (including Darius Milhaud) honestly enjoyed going to circuses and fairs. Tailleferre's evocation of these places through their distinct music should come as no surprise.

WALTZ OF TELEGRAMS

Tailleferre's "Waltz of Telegrams" comes from a collaborative ballet organized by the poet Jean Cocteau. Cocteau had become dissatisfied with Diaghilev's frequent refusals to employ his favorite composers, a group of young French musicians known collectively as *les six*. Cocteau organized a ballet set on the Eiffel Tower, where a wedding party has assembled. Two phonographs on either side of the stage broadcast a text, devised by Cocteau, that includes spoken dialogue for the characters and a running narration of the outlandish events on stage. Among the improbable occurrences depicted in this work is the massacre of the entire wedding party by a mischievous young boy. After everyone is dead, they suddenly all jump up again and continue as though nothing had happened. Cocteau hoped this event would remind his audience of the shooting galleries at the fairs in Paris, where targets are knocked down only to jump up again. One such gallery in the Bohemian Parisian district of Montmarte featured tin figures of a wedding party. For a ballet where matters of life and death are meaningless trivia, it takes an ironic turn when a rogue lion eats the general who had been invited to the wedding. The general, an ignoble personage in the extreme, is treated to a mock sentimental funeral replete with tearful speeches. France saw a mounting interest in the absurd after the First World War when her generals had so badly misused the populace. This work, *The Wedding Party on the Eiffel Tour* (1921), illustrates the absurdity common in French art between the wars.

The "Waltz of Telegrams" occurs when a squadron of telegrams in the form of young female dancers descends onto the stage to deliver some improbable and ultimately unimportant message. Tailleferre wrote a comical waltz to accompany this action. The formal

**FIGURE 12.15 | *Les Six, a group of six French composers*. From left to right: Darius Milhaud, George Auric, Arthur Honegger, Germaine Tailleferre, Francis Poulenc, and Louis Durey. Seated at the piano is the poet and novelist Jean Cocteau. (© Bettmann/Corbis)

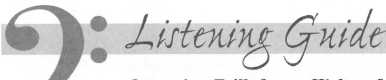

Germaine Tailleferre, Waltz of Telegrams, from The Wedding Party on the Eiffel Tour (1921)
[CD4, #2] *(Duration, 2 min. 28 sec.)*

0.00 **INTRODUCTION:** A martial introduction reminiscent of the opening to Rimsky-Korsakov's "Farewell and Departure of the Tsar" reaches a climax with a trumpet fanfare.

0.08 **A SECTION:** The clarinet begins by presenting a wonderfully rambling tune depicting the airborne telegrams flittering in the breeze. This tune opens with several repetitions of the same short phrase. Next a trumpet presents the same material initially allocated to the clarinet. The violins provide an answering phrase.

0.38 **B SECTION**: After a brief transition, four melodies are heard in rapid succession. The first (0.38) is scored so that the piccolo is central. The second (0.54) provides more of a tutti texture for the strings. The third (1.03), a wobbling theme suggestive of the telegrams trying to keep their balance on the narrow iron works of the Eiffel Tower, is assigned primarily to the violins. The fourth (1.11) features a solo horn.

1:45 **A1 SECTION:** After each of the short themes from Section B has come and gone, the entire orchestra swells to a brilliant return of the little theme first heard at the beginning of the A Section. At the climax of this outburst, Tailleferre inserts a sudden and awkwardly long silence. A highly syncopated section follows and leads to . . .

2.13 **CODA**: a brief coda that begins featuring the bassoon playing descending scalar figures, and closes on a thumping dominant to tonic cadence.

design of the piece is ironic and informal. A cavalcade of silly, circus-like tunes unfold one after the other. Only one ever returns after its initial appearance.

The trivial and lighthearted style Tailleferre used in this piece typifies an important brand of French neo-classicism that looked to popular entertainment for its source of material to fuse with modernism. Among the leading practitioners of this style were Tailleferre, Francis Poulenc, and Georges Auric.

The Scope of Neo-Classicism

To conclude this overview of neo-classicism, we must point out that it was international in scope, dominated in the musical scene during the years between the world wars, diverse in the ways it was practiced, and decidedly born of anxiety over the possibility that modernism had become too serious and deeply engaged in a hyper-emotionalism that wasn't healthy. Igor Stravinsky was surely its most famous advocate. He looked mainly to the remote past for his influences. Others looked to popular music. The important commonality lies in the fact that all neo-classicists seek an emotional reserve unknown in pre-war modernism.

THE TWELVE-TONE TECHNIQUE

Not all influential European composers shared the sense that anything was wrong with expressionism, atonality, or pre-war modernism. The most important advocates of continuity with pre-war developments were Béla Bartók in Hungary and Schoenberg and his students in Austria. For the purposes of scope, we'll focus on Schoenberg and his students.

After the war, Schoenberg found the conditions for performances of his atonal works and those of his students deteriorating in Austria. Heartsick from years of total war, much of the Austrian public was uninterested in explorations of the dark emotional states associated with expressionism. A small but vocal segment of the concert-going public began demonstrating against Schoenberg and his followers. They disrupted concerts and made life miserable for the enthusiasts of modern music. Some scholars point out that part of Schoenberg's difficulties with the public in his homeland stems from a profound anti-Semitism. Schoenberg was Jewish at a time of mounting hostility and intolerance toward Jews. After losing the war, some Germans were looking for a scapegoat, and found blaming Jews an easy answer to a much more complicated question. Whatever the diverse sources of antipathy Schoenberg experienced, he and his students founded The Society for Private Musical Performance as an act of defiance and a means to continue practicing modernism just as they had before the war. This organization fostered performances of new music in a context unlike any other concerts before or since. Pieces would be played for a largely invited audience of like-minded enthusiasts. Afterward, no clapping or booing was allowed. Schoenberg wanted to shift emphasis away from the attachment of value judgments and toward a pure understanding of music.

Another fascinating post-war development Schoenberg came up with was a method for making the composition of atonal music less taxing on the composer. After overthrowing tonality in his music, Schoenberg found that he had to invent a musical language with each new piece. If a system could be devised to facilitate the composition of atonal music, he felt certain that both he and his students would benefit. He had noticed that his students were not producing work very quickly. He attributed this to the difficulty inherent in writing atonal music. Alban Berg during his entire life produced only a small number of works, although each of them is the product of a minutely detailed imagination. Anton Webern, Schoenberg's other outstanding student, wrote only miniature compositions, never lasting more than a few fleeting moments. In both cases, Schoenberg felt a system was warranted to help make composing atonal music more facile.

The system Schoenberg devised has come to be known as "the twelve-tone method." It also goes by the name twelve-tone technique and the more generic name "serialism." Under this method, the composer creates a row of all twelve pitches of the chromatic scale. This row of twelve notes provides the motivic information that will hold the piece together. Remember that Schoenberg was preoccupied with the concept of the motive as the central organizing principle of modern music. Once the row has been created, the composer can then use not only it, but all the variations of it described above when examining the motivic variation practices used by Schoenberg in his song "Nacht." First, the composer can present the row in its original order and then transpose that to any of the twelve pitches of the chromatic scale. Second, the technique of retrograde, presenting the motive backwards, can also be transposed to any of the twelve pitches. The same goes for inversion and retrograde inversion. These simple variations provide the composer with 48 row forms, all of which are closely linked to

FIGURE 12.16 | Pablo Picasso, *Portrait of Ambroise Vollard.* 1910. Oil on canvas. This portrait of Vollard, one of Picasso's earliest supporters, was painted with a monochromatic paleness typically expressed in the Analytic Cubist style. The facial features rise from under a meshwork of shifting planes and multifaceted cubes, allowing the viewer to perceive the figure simultaneously from various vantage points. The figure in this painting does not change, but the technique allows the observer an opportunity to shift perspective and to achieve a richer understanding and appreciation. Schoenberg likewise reasoned that a tone row maintained its own integrity, regardless of the permutation or angle it was viewed, and could therefore serve as a unifying sound signature in an atonal work. (© Estate of Pablo Picasso/Artists Rights Society [ARS], NY/SCALA/Art Resource, NY)

the original row by virtue of exemplifying precisely the same intervallic relationships note to note. Schoenberg's technique suggests that composers of atonal music would do well to develop a row ensuring that no single pitch appears more or less often than any other. Moreover, if the row is composed with care, the avoidance of all vestiges of tonal implication can be achieved.

ANTON WEBERN

Concerto, Opus 24

A piece by Anton Webern represents the twelve-tone method in our recorded anthology, [CD3 #11]. Webern's Concerto, op. 24 (1928), dedicated to Schoenberg on his birthday, uses both the twelve-tone method and Schoenberg's favorite sonority, a three-note grouping including a minor second and a minor third. We've heard Schoenberg use that sonority previously in the piece "Nacht" from *Pierrot Lunaire*. Webern held a Ph.D. in Music History. For his concerto he returned to the old Baroque practice of writing a concerto with no designated soloist. The tiny forces used for this piece, only nine instruments, are also a throw-back to bygone times, before the Romantics allowed the size of the orchestra to swell.

The Tone Row

The tone row for this concerto is comprised of four three-note groupings, each made up of a minor second and a minor third relationship. Here is the tone row for this piece:

Please observe that all the twelve pitches of the chromatic scale are used one time each. This condition is necessary for twelve-tone music. While this may seem needlessly technical, each of these three-note groupings is comprised of notes that relate to one another by the interval of the minor second and the minor third. For example, B-flat is a minor second below B, and D is a minor third above B. By preserving these relationships, not only does Webern celebrate his teacher's favorite atonal sonority, but he also ensures that the motives in his piece will all be extremely closely related. When the row is first played at the very beginning of this piece, Webern orchestrates its first appearance to increase the likelihood that listeners will be able to comprehend his piece, by assigning each three-note grouping to a different instrument and giving each a different rhythmic value. The oboe plays the first three notes in sixteenths. The flute plays the next three in eighths. The trumpet takes the next three in triplet eighth notes. The last three notes are played by the clarinet in triplet quarter notes. When the piano enters, it plays the row backwards and also reverses the rhythmic values of the row's first appearance. Throughout the movement, Webern will present the music in three-note groupings clarified by orchestration. His goal centered on creating music with coherence that was achieved through concentration on the motive.

Listening Guide

Anton Webern, Concerto, Opus 24 (1928)
[CD3, #11] *(Duration, 6 min. 22 sec.)*

For Nine Instruments (No Designated Soloist)
First movement:

0.00   The oboe plays the first three notes in sixteenths.

0.01   The flute plays the next three in eighths.

0.02   The trumpet takes the next three in triplet eighth notes.

0.03 The last three notes of the row are played by the clarinet in triplet quarter notes. The ebbing and flowing of the tempo is continued throughout the movement, punctuating the phrase lengths and typifying the movement with an energy that constantly changes.

0.05 The piano enters, playing the row backwards and also reversing the rhythmic values of the row's first appearance.

0.09 The clarinet, then viola, violin, and finally the oboe, sustain the piano's concluding rhythmic values of sixteenth notes as they play in turn the three-note groupings that comprise the row.

0.11 The piano responds in sixteenth notes with two groupings, and is answered by the flute, then trumpet, with the remaining two groups in triplets.

0.15 The piano now plays the entire row in triplets, but changes the interrelated melodic structure by forming chords, which also quickens the pace of the row.

0.18 With the second note of each group accented, the three-note groupings continue in eighth notes as they are passed from instrument to instrument through three varied treatments of the row.

0.33 The trumpet enters forte with a three-note grouping in triplets, which is followed by the trombone, violin, and viola. Against this, the piano continues presenting its groupings in eighth notes, which results in an energized polyrhythmic pattern of two-against-three.

0.36 The rhythmic pattern of two against three is sustained as quarter-note triplets (three notes played in the time of two quarter-note pulses), played by the oboe, flute, and then violin, heard over the piano's eighth-note triplets (three notes played in the time of one quarter-note pulse).

0.43 Trumpet sixteenths are quickly passed to the clarinet, then oboe.

0.45 The violin and viola answer with succinct sixteenths, over piano triplets.

0.48 The trumpet introduces a dotted rhythm that the clarinet picks up and passes to the violin, while the piano plays quarter notes on each beat, alternating between one and two pitches, to complete each three-note grouping.

0.97 The clarinet enters into a syncopated dialogue with the violin over piano eighth notes for the next two treatments of the row.

1.13 The clarinet continues but is answered this time by the trumpet, then viola, and flute

1.22 Sixteenth notes in groupings of two are quickly passed from instrument to instrument, over piano eighth notes.

1.31 The clarinet introduces higher notes in dotted rhythmic patterns that are picked up by the other instruments.

1.41 The oboe counters the previous treatment with a fortissimo low note, followed by the clarinet, then piano, trumpet, and trombone in quick succession.

1.44 The piano plays a three-note pattern in sixteenth notes, which leads to the horn playing the next in eighth notes, to the oboe's eighth-note triplet, to the flute's quarer-note triplet, in essence slowing down the tempo overall.

1.48 Three-note groupings in sixteenths are quickly passed from trumpet to clarinet, then oboe and piano.

1.52 Relatively long eighth-note patterns are passed from instrument-to-instrument through two more treatments of the row.

2.04 The clarinet begins with descending triplets, followed by the horn, trumpet, and trombone, over piano eighth notes.

2.07 Quarter-note triplets played fortissimo in the oboe and clarinet, then flute and oboe, followed by the violin and viola, are played over syncopated rhythms in the piano.

2.17 The oboe plays a three-note grouping followed by the trumpet, flute, and clarinet.

2.23 The piano incites quick three-note groupings in sixteenths that ascend to the viola, and violin.

2.26 **pause**

2.27 The piano plays two chords, which are met by one punctuated chord in the winds to end the movement.

Composers working after the Second World War will be influenced by Webern's singular style. During his life, however, his style received very little attention. His music was banned by the Nazis as "degenerate art." He spent his last years in near total obscurity. In a freak occurrence, he was shot dead by an American soldier during the final days of the Second World War. He did not live to see the influence his music had after the war.

CONCLUSIONS

The first half of the twentieth century saw the rise of modernism. The pieces in the anthology representing this period reveal a great diversity of styles and structures, from the extremes of Webern's sober and cerebral concerto to Tailleferre's flip waltz. With so few stylistic features in common, one might ask what the music discussed in this chapter has in common, other than a general chronological proximity.

Modernism allows individual artists to pursue their visions wherever they take them. This situation makes the diversity of the period a necessary function of remaining true to modernism's central premise. In the aftermath of Romanticism, which also prized the individual of genius, Modernism had nowhere to go but to test just how far the individual might go. Many Modernists, such as Schoenberg, hoped that their ideas would take hold and persuade the majority of composers to join them. All such hopes have failed during the previous century. Everything about the 1900s seems to point toward a coming apart, an end to cultural consensus. The technological advances described when the chapter began, starting with the car, including the record player and radio, and perhaps culminating with the personal computer, all accommodate the individual to become a more perfectly isolated consumer. The modern artist at this same time can hardly be expected to act in a more communal way than his or her audience. The remarkable thing about Modernism is how many artists do concern themselves, as Hindemith did, with the needs of society.

The common thread that runs through the pieces in this chapter then might be their common drift away from some vital priority of the previous century along with their essential failure to become the new norm. Of course failure is such a loaded term, especially since the individual composer could hardly be expected to establish norms for music in a time and place that didn't want them.

Some Questions for Discussion

1 Many composers during the previous century seemed to want to distance themselves from Romanticism. Why? What aspects of Romanticism can you see still operating in the pieces in this chapter?

2 Stravinsky's provocative claims that music was incapable of communicating anything seems worth discussing. Do you agree with his opinion? Why or why not? What examples can you think of to illustrate how he might be right or wrong?

3 Modernism might be more useful as a marketing tool than a descriptor of art. What does Modernism mean to you? Do you ever use the word? If so, when and to say what? All the pieces studied in this chapter were likely composed before anyone reading this book was born. How modern does the music sound now? Would anyone like to riot over *The Rite of Spring*? Does anyone hear Satie's music as audacious? Would anyone try to disrupt a concert of Schoenberg and his students? Do you think as students of music we need a better word to describe this period, one that doesn't treat this music as modern anymore so much as antique? What word ending in "ism" would you choose to replace "modernism"?

13

Concert Music 1945–present

MUSIC AFTER THE SECOND WORLD WAR

After the Second World War, a second important split in the art of music took place. The first split mentioned in this book took place during the nineteenth century and took the form of a division between so-called classical and popular art. That split is described at the beginning of the previous chapter and relates to a large degree to class-based social distinctions impressing themselves on the field of music.

Modernism

The next split witnesses the division between avant-garde music and classical music. This split also has some relationship to class, but might be more centrally concerned with historicism. The previous chapter chronicled a few achievements by modernists. These achievements offended, to one degree or another, the old order. As the historicist sensibility rose in power and importance, cultivated audiences, especially from the upper-classes, rallied around antique music. The result was a general although not total failure on the part of modernists to gain mainstream support. For some, such as Erik Satie and Sergei Diaghilev, failure to appeal to the mainstream was a badge of honor to be worn with pride. Others, such as Anton Webern, labored in considerable anonymity, a condition that may have bothered them but certainly did not necessitate any change in their personal style.

After 1945 the modernist attitude of apartness from the mainstream would become not so much a desirable condition as an inevitable one. Extending the achievements of Webern or Satie into still further innovation would leave mainstream audiences uninterested in modern music. Eventually a split took place. This split is still not universally recognized, but it is nonetheless very real. On the one hand, we have the new generations of modernists, now commonly called "the avant-garde," and on the other hand we have the concert music mainstream. The avant-garde takes its name from French military terminology, and refers to the advanced troops who scout the terrain, engaging the enemy on the furthest periphery of the army. There is also a certain heroic connotation to the term, as the avant-garde troops find themselves alone or fighting overwhelming odds.

The Avant-Garde and Mainstream Audiences

Increasingly, the audience for avant-garde music is different from the audience for traditional concert music. Mainstream institutions of music-making such as symphony orchestras or opera companies don't want or, more often, can't perform avant-garde works, partly because the works weren't written for them or because they are simply too difficult or alienating for a mainstream audience. Similarly, ensembles or performers interested in avant-garde music don't want anything to do with performing the older classics. They cultivate an audience less interested in that repertory; moreover, their artistry is better suited to the newer repertory.

Many composers working after 1945 did not consider themselves avant-garde. They tried to reach out to the traditional concert-music establishment. With very few exceptions, these efforts have failed. That's not to say that large symphony orchestras or opera companies won't perform their works; they will, only they won't embrace them over the long haul or for very many performances. John Corigliano, an American composer, wrote a magnificent symphony during the 1990s. His symphony was performed by the Chicago Symphony Orchestra, among others. The recording of the piece sold well and received overwhelmingly favorable critical response. These are fine and rare accomplishments for a living composer. With each passing season, however, this wonderful work, ideally suited to the purposes of a professional symphony orchestra, will enjoy fewer and fewer performances. An initial blush of excitement won his piece a temporary place in the repertory. It also won him new commissions for still other works. Should he succeed in his lifetime in establishing one such work into the standard repertory of professional orchestras, he will have succeeded where many, many others have failed. Eventually the old heroes of the orchestra such as Beethoven, Brahms, and Berlioz take back their places on the programs. Historicism is as much the enemy of composers like Corigliano as it is the enemy of the avant-garde. Corigliano is a masterful composer, and has the very best career going of any living composer working for acceptance within the mainstream, but even he is facing the very longest of odds.

This chapter is devoted to the avant-garde composers working after 1945, not because they are better or more interesting than their more traditional counterparts. The chapter could easily have gone the other way and placed John Corigliano at center stage.

WORLD WAR TWO

The Second World War (1939–1945) was even more grisly than the first had been. The Nazis played out their mad ambition to subjugate the world under the yoke of a mad man's ludicrous notions of racial superiority and inferiority. Their cause revealed the hideous excess of Romanticism. Inspired by a self-styled genius in Adolph Hitler, Germany and her allies fought a doomed war, ignoring all restraint of reason. Whipped into an emotional frenzy, they tried the impossible for six long years in the vane hope of realizing the dreams of a monster, with predictable and catastrophic results. Along the way, they indulged in a systematic mass murder of their enemies. Specially targeted were the Jews, long the victims of intolerance and injustice throughout Europe. Hollywood often depicts Nazis as coldly calculating, rational people. The opposite is more clearly the case. Their project, the conquest of the world around a bogus theory drawn from pseudo-science, was the supreme distillation of emotion devoid of rationality. They could not succeed. Doomed projects are seldom the concern of coldly calculating students of rationality. The Nazis revealed their fascination with hyper-emotionalism in their preferences within the field of art. Prudish in their sexual morays, they detested German expressionism. In its place they elevated an insipid Romantic revival, devoid of the lofty ambitions and quest to depict the inner torments of mankind. In the field of music, they banned American jazz because of its connection to people of African background. Also banned was atonal music. That Schoenberg was Jewish may have influenced this decision.

Some students of history want to focus the lessons of the Nazi's genocidal project exclusively on Germany not realizing that genocidal theories and practices long predated the Second World War. During the 1800s, Euro-Americans had previously attempted genocide against entire nations of Native Americans. The lessons of the Nazis' crimes and failures are lessons for all of humanity and all ages. They are a grim warning against repeating any of the injustices and hatreds of the past.

In the process of defeating the insidious threat of world fascism, the United States developed a super weapon, the atom bomb. In unleashing this weapon on civilian populations in Japan, a new era in the world's history emerged, an era when mankind possessed the means to annihilate itself.

Having defeated fascism, the democracies of the West shifted their focus to their former allies, the communists. Battle lines were quickly drawn between the communist nations of Eastern Europe and their allies against the capitalist West and its allies. The following forty years of uninterrupted tensions have come to be called the Cold War. While the actual fighting was limited to small nations such as Korea or Vietnam, the threat of all-out nuclear war loomed as a constant worry. The anxieties that marked the start of the century concerning industrialization gave way to even greater anxieties. The conflict would only end with the economic collapse of the Soviet Union during the late 1980s.

Just as the First World War impacted attitudes in the field of music and prompted reform, so did the Second World War. Revolted by the Nazi experiment and shocked by humanity's capacity for violence and hatred, young European composers looked to distance themselves from the war and the Romantic philosophies that fostered it by adopting a hyper-rational approach to their art. The art of music seems to some the province of pure emotion, but that is by no means the only or even the dominant approach.

DARMSTADT

After the ravages of the Second World War, a search began among European composers for a style that would distance new activity from all that came before. They wanted a music that was international and cosmopolitan in style to thwart the traditions of nationalism that had informed so much music from the recent past. Even more importantly, they wanted a music that was rational in the extreme, in order to set the Romantic and irrational project of the Nazis in the past. To facilitate this search for a new music, an annual program of international courses in contemporary music was undertaken in the small German city of Darmstadt.

Darmstadt Music Festivals

The Darmstadt festivals included concerts, discussions, and courses aimed at helping young composers from throughout Europe in their effort to locate a style suitable for the aftermath of the war. A Frenchman named Olivier Messiaen (1908–1992) emerged as the most popular teacher. He encouraged students to look to Anton Webern as a model of a sober and serious style exemplifying the ideal of rationality. Webern's fame grew enormously after the war, thanks to the sympathy young musicians felt for his style. They specially admired how his use of twelve-tone rows impact his rhythmic and orchestrational practices in pieces like the concerto discussed in the previous chapter.

Integral Serialism

Two students who came to admire Webern were Karlheinz Stockhausen (1928–) and Pierre Boulez (1925–). These two men crafted a new technique modeled on what they admired about Webern. This technique is usually called *integral serialism.* It resembles Schoenberg's twelve-tone method in that the tone row still governs the use of pitches within an integral serial work. Under the helpful guidance of Messiaen, Stockhausen and Boulez sought to subject other parameters of music to the same governing principles that Schoenberg used to govern pitches in twelve-tone music. Early experiments in integral serialism include Messiaen's *Mode de valeur et d'intensité* (1949), Boulez' *Structures* (1951), and Stockhausen's *Kreuzspiel* (1952). In each of these pieces, rhythms, timbres, and other parameters of music were governed by the equivalent of rows. The goal was an austere new style celebrating the triumph of reason over emotionalism, in which all components of a composition are subjected to rationally conceived rules. In this way, the generation of composers in Europe after World War Two could hardly be more different from the maverick generation of Debussy, Satie, and Stravinsky. Boulez in particular hoped that rules eliminating all past assumptions about music would liberate him to find a distinct and personal voice as a composer.

While the quest for a hyper-rational style informed the early activities of the Darmstadt composers, they were seldom satisfied with their earliest efforts. A minute and questing fascination with innovation rules the careers of both Boulez and Stockhausen. At times their efforts and methods of explaining themselves began to resemble the discourse of scientists. At other times, they tried to make space for the irrational again in their music. The result is a diverse body of work that has a strong following, especially among the educational elite of Western Europe.

Surrealism

Boulez' composition *Le Marteau sans maître* (Hammer without Master) of 1953 represents the integral serial ideal in Europe after the Second World War. This piece, like Schoenberg's *Pierrot Lunaire* before it, strives to present a wholly new brand of atonality uniquely suited to the poetry of a new time. The poem, in this case, is taken not from expressionism, but from the French movement of surrealism. The surrealists believed that the world of the subconscious as experienced in dreams constituted something more important than waking reality, which they mistrusted. Surrealists achieved their ends by casting together violent and irrational juxtapositions.

Le Marteau Sans Maître

Choosing such poetry may seem to contradict the post-war ambition of these composers to foster rationality in their music. More than a contradiction, Boulez strove for a challenge. The poetry of René Char provided this challenge. In setting it, Boulez does many things that distance himself from musical trends of the last four or more centuries.

His setting of the poem emphasized words of minimal importance, such as conjunctions, unstressed syllables, articles, and other non-essential elements of the poetry, in order to thwart all waking meaning. The convoluted melodic line resulting from his integral serial approach, while haunting, presents the listener with a kind of melody so different from the usual approaches to melody heard in earlier CDs in our anthology as to suggest an almost complete break with the past. While this may sound like criticism, it isn't. Boulez chose a poem that strives itself not to make sense in the usual way, thus his setting suits the poet's aim magnificently. Moreover, Boulez, like many young Europeans at the time, wanted to achieve a break with the past. Boulez was a very young man when the Nazis invaded his homeland. He spent important and formative years wondering if France's allies would ever turn the tide and end the nightmarish occupation. Such experiences were bound to shape his actions.

Along with the ultra-complex rhythms, constantly changing meter, and ethereal melodic line, Boulez provides a most unusual accompaniment. In this song, [CD4 #3], the singer is joined only by an alto flute (a larger version of the usual flute capable of producing lower pitches and a darker tone).

Listening Guide

Pierre Boulez, *Le Marteau sans maître* (Hammer without Master), (1953)

[**CD4, #3**] *(Duration, 2 min. 25 sec.)*

0.00	*Alto Flute Introduction*	
0.12	La roulotte rouge au bord du clou	The red caravan at the periphery of the cell
0.45	Et cadavre dans le panier	And a cadaver in the basket
1.03	Et chevaux de labours dans le ferà cheval	And draft horses in the horseshoe
1.46	Je rêve la tête sur la pointe	I dream of my head on the point of
	de mon couteau Pérou	my Peruvian knife

The striking imagery of the short poem heard in our recorded example stems from the essential ideals of surrealism. For the text and translation, see the listening guide. First, caravans are usually remarkable for being colorful. Here we have a monochrome caravan that could exist only in dreams, or fantasies, or perhaps a child's picture book. The cadaver in the basket draws upon essential anxieties about death, and places a horrid object (the cadaver) inside an object usually associated with picnics or fresh produce. The illogic of the next line situating more than one complete horse inside a horseshoe provides a typical surrealist affront to waking logic. The surrealists loved to include mentions of faraway places they had never been within their work, hence the mention of a Peruvian knife. The image of the poet's head on the knife's point conjures the sort of violent image that simultaneously attracts and repulses, much in the manner of nightmares. The whole makes sense only in the way that striking images from dreams might make sense; a persuasive interpretation might take a lifetime to form and only provide a provisional insight into the poem's meaning.

Boulez' setting of this surrealist text, as mentioned above, places the least important words and syllables on the most important musical passages. For example, the French word "du" meaning "of the" could almost be omitted from the poem without damaging the meaning much. Such words usually fall on weak beats and receive only a syllabic setting. In this case, Boulez presents this word with an eleven-note melisma and a melody sprawling over the range of an octave plus a third. Suddenly "of the" becomes the central image of a poem stuffed with striking images.

Future Innovations

Boulez held mixed feelings about Schoenberg's accomplishments. On the one hand, he admired and used the atonal strategy of organization that Schoenberg invented, the twelve-tone method. On the other hand, Boulez preferred Webern's approach because it offered a more radical break with conventional textures such as homophony, a melody with accompaniment.

Boulez and Stockhausen devoted the decades of the 1950s and 1960s to the exploration of integral serialism. Their efforts eventually led to composition using modular forms. A modular form is a formal plan that changes with every performance, depending on choices made by the performer. They are the most immediate heirs to the traditions of music that Schoenberg so cared about, traditions concerning seriousness, hard work, and the belief that Western music remains a conduit for the expression of important ideas through sophisticated musical means. They have not succeeded in winning over a massive popular audience. Some see this as evidence of some failing on their part.

Another way to look at their relatively small audience is broader in scope. No music of the twentieth century was ever embraced by the majority. The technological and social developments discussed at the beginning of the previous chapter preclude cultural consensus around anyone or anything in the field of music. The integral serialists should not be uniquely judged by criteria by which all fail. Moreover, we must remember that the past masters from previous eras did not enjoy widespread popularity in the usual sense. If Mozart was so loved in his own time, why then did he die penniless at the age of 35 and have his body dumped in an unmarked grave? That isn't the fate of the universally loved. The truth is that Boulez and Stockhausen both receive so much attention and favor that they each live very comfortably in positions of enormous respect. The criticism that they lack audience appeal cannot be reconciled with these facts. The general cultural fragmentation makes everyone a special or minority taste. Finally, Boulez and Stockhausen, like certain modernists discussed in the previous chapter, did not and do not want popularity. For most modernists, the approval of the many is not a goal.

ELECTRONIC MUSIC

Edgard Varèse

Electronic music rises primarily after World War Two. But even before the war broke out, isolated composers were dreaming of a purely electronic means of creating musical sounds. No one was more concerned with this development than Edgard Varèse (1883–1965) who spent much of the 1930s trying to persuade large electronics corporations, such as RCA in America and Philips in the Netherlands, to build an electronic music studio. The plans for electronic instruments existed, but Varèse could not convince any corporations to build them, simply because he could not express how the corporation might profit financially from such a venture.

Musique Concrète

During the 1940s, important strides were made in the field of electronic music first in Paris. Pierre Schaeffer (1910–) executed a series of musical experiments whereby he recorded sounds and later in a studio configured these sounds into musical compositions. His first work along these lines, *Etude de chemin de fer* (Study for Railroad) of 1948, created a sensation. In it he spliced together material recorded at a railway station. He found that he could splice off the attack of the sound, leaving only the decay, and vice versa. These sorts of compositions, comprised of recorded acoustic sounds, are called *musique concrète*.

The Synthesizer

The next major breakthrough resulted from the combined efforts of German and American electrical engineers.

FIGURE 13.1 | *Edgard Varèse (1883–1965)*
(© Bettmann/Corbis)

Werner Meyer-Eppler and Harry F. Olsen collaborated in constructing twin synthesizers, one in Meyer-Eppler's native Germany and the other in America. The synthesizer is an instrument that produces musical sounds through purely electrical means. In order to make a composition using one, the composer must record each individual sound on a separate piece of magnetic tape, and then splice these pieces together onto several audio tracks in order to make a collage of synthesized sound. First Stockhausen and then Boulez cheerfully embraced this new medium.

Poème Electronique

The manufacture of synthesizers was the realization of a dream long held by Edgard Varèse. His first commission for an electronic work came from the Dutch electronics giant, Philips. The Philips Corporation wanted to build a pavilion at the Brussels Worlds Fair in order to sell consumers on the idea of owning slide projectors. They wanted visitors to ride through their pavilion taking a journey through mankind's relationship with technology. Along the way, they wanted to have slides project images illustrative of their theme. The sensational architect Le Corbusier was hired to design the pavilion and oversee the slide show. Radical in his thinking, Le Corbusier preferred naturally occurring structures as inspiration. His pavilion was shaped like the digestive system of a cow and included many curved chambers comparable to a cow's multiple stomachs, linked by curvilinear passageways comparable to intestines. Within this gently curving and completely dark space, the slide show would achieve maximum effect. Spread throughout the pavilion were speakers playing small snips of Varèse's *Poème electronique*.

Figure 13.2 | Robert Delaunay, **_Formes, circulaires, soleil No. 2, 1912._** Painting. The artist's intent was to perceive these dynamic colored circular shapes as simultaneous rhythmic contrasts. In Delaunay's essays, he describes playing with colors in the same way music often expresses itself in colored phrases. In accordance, when Edgard Varèse's *Poème Electronique* was first performed at an exhibit at the 1958 Brussels World Fair by the Philips Corporation, the exhibit pavilion was designed to project a sequence of colored lights and images while Varèse's three-track tape was played from 425 surrounding speakers. The spectators continually experienced light and sound from unexpected angles, generating an interactive environmental feat in rhythmic contrasts. (© L & M Services B. V. Amsterdam 20030510)

Each and every individual sound you hear in Varèse's composition resulted from his patching that single sound on a synthesizer, transferring the sound to magnetic tape, and then splicing that tape into one of the audio tracks of his composition. Composing for synthesizer in the 1950s required exacting and time-consuming labor. Today many undergraduate students at universities have far more powerful and flexible means of creating electronic music on their personal computers than all composers had at their combined disposal during the 1950s. We need to keep this in mind as we listen to pioneering examples of electronic music such as *Poème electronique*.

While listening to this piece [CD4 #4], you might benefit from trying to imagine not only Varése and his hundreds of lonely hours spent patching cords and splicing tape, but also his frustrating years of trying to persuade electronics companies to make a synthesizer. The project cost him decades of effort. If historical rumination doesn't stimulate you, you might consider the original location of the piece's presentation. Traveling in an amusement-park-style car, through a darkened building modeled in its design on a bovine digestive tract, seeing images of mankind's relationship with technology projected onto curved walls, while music emanated from hundreds of hidden speakers, surely made for a more conducive environment than a modern dorm room or apartment.

Edgard Varèse, Poème electronique
[CD4, #4] *(Duration, 7 min. 59 sec.)*

0.00   Six low gong strikes—soft ticks—sirens lead into low to high intense sounds.

(Pause)

0.42   Drum tones and scraping sounds—short squawks—a **three-tone motive** is introduced and repeated twice.

1.10   Low machine-like tones with grinding noises—short squawks—**three-tone motive** presented with new timbres.

1.38   Short squawks with high-pitched chirps—percussive sounds—sirens—tapping noises lead into four low gong strikes—various electronic pitches—drum taps (first a pattern of five, then **three**).

2.49   High alternating pitches—big crescendo on low sound.

3.25   Rattles and drum taps, repeated.

3.38   Gong and voices.

3.53   Drum taps.

3.57   Voices.

4.15   Sudden loud noise—drumming, scraping sounds and cymbal.

4.25   Voices—drumming sounds.

4.35   Rattles and drumming sounds.

4.40   Low gonglike sounds and scraping—electronic pitch fluctuations.

5.01   Low electronic effects—distorted voices.

5.12   Tapping, scraping, and drumming.

(Pause)

5.45   Soft to loud electronic sound.

(Pause)

6.08   Drumming and electronic pitch fluctuations.

(Pause)

6.19   Distant siren—tapping—various pitches.

6.33   Sirens, gongs, and cymbals.

6.44   Wavering vocal sounds leading to more melodic vocalizations.

7.06   Loud scraping sounds and tapping.

7.11   Electronic static-like sounds with percussion.

7.28   **Three-tone motive** stated and then repeated with airplane sounds and low to high-pitched sirens that crescendo.

7.55 Electronic static-like sounds that abruptly cease.

Much of the pleasure of electronic music in its pioneering early days stems from the unusual timbres achieved through the synthesizer. From the listening guide, you can see that many different types of sounds appear in the piece, although all of it was produced on a single electronic instrument. Yet for all its newness, the three-note motive that recurs here and there during the piece lends it a somewhat traditional over-all shape. That motive is clearest at the beginning and end of the piece; however, you may hear it in some of the other sections where it isn't mentioned in the guide. In a vague way it's always there in some varied sense.

INTEGRAL SERIALISM IN AMERICA

Milton Babbitt

The leading advocate of integral serialism in America was Milton Babbitt (1916–). During the 1930s, Babbitt taught at Princeton University. During the Second World War, the Princeton mathematics faculty was employed by the federal government in developing the atomic bomb. Babbitt, an expert in the field of mathematics as well as music, was transferred to the mathematics department while the regular faculty in that field was away working on the Manhattan Project, the code name for the development of the first atomic weapons. When the war ended, he returned to the music department armed with new ideas about the organization of music along rational principles. He felt that, like mathematics, music worked best within a closed system. In math, a closed system allows for certain assumptions to exist so that work can unfold within those assumptions. Euclidian geometry (the kind of geometry we study in junior high and high school), for example, is a closed system. It presumes a flat, two-dimensional field. Once you introduce topography to the field, the system cannot account for it and falls apart. Babbitt felt that music born of a closed system could be evaluated by more or less objective means. Tonality, for example, is born of certain rules and makes certain assumptions. In other words, it is a closed system. Babbitt wanted integral serialism to be a comparably closed system. He felt that all parameters of the piece (timbre, dynamics, rhythms, pitches) should be regulated not by individual rows, as the European integral serialists had done, but by one row common to all parameters. After the war, in pieces such as *Three Compositions for Piano* (1947), *Composition for Twelve Instruments* (1948) and *All Set* (1957), Babbitt explored his ideals concerning first the twelve-tone method and later integral serialism.

Philomel

As with Boulez and Stockhausen, the synthesizer fascinated Babbitt. The composition in our recorded anthology [CD4 #5] representing integral serialism in America is one by Babbitt for synthesized tape, recorded singer, and soprano called *Philomel*. In this piece, Babbitt sets to music a poem dealing with the Greek mythic figure Philomel. She was the sister to the wife of King Tereus. One day in the forest, the king raped her. In order to hide his terrible crime, the King cut out Philomel's tongue so she could not tell anyone of his deeds. Once home, Philomel occupied herself with making a tapestry. On the tapestry, she wove pictures detailing King Tereus' crime. She then brought her tapestry to her sister. Together, they punished Tereus by feeding him his son's limbs baked in a pie. Our recording only covers the first part of the piece, where

Philomel reflects on her victimization as she searches for a new voice to tell of her suffering. On the recording you will hear not only the soprano singing Babbitt's dramatic setting of the poem, but also the synthesized accompaniment configured by Babbitt in the studio and transferred to magnetic tape. In preparing this piece, the singer must repair to the studio as well, and tape herself singing several passages that are then integrated into the taped accompaniment for the work. Far from striving for an emotional cool or hyper-rationality, Babbitt's work verges on expressionism. Babbitt, being an American, experienced the Second World War differently from his European counterparts in the field of integral serialism. Boulez grew up in occupied Paris, and Stockhausen served as a stretcher-bearer after his parents were both killed during allied bombing raids on his home city of Cologne. For Babbitt, there was less urgency to distance himself from past music in his practice of integral serialism.

Milton Babbitt, Philomel

[CD4, #5] *(Duration, 4 min. 40 sec.)*

(For synthesized tape, recorded singer, and soprano)

0.00   Synthesized percussive sounds and lyrical vocalizations that eventually move to high notes are introduced, answered by synthesized electronic-piano-like sounds.

0.22   Vocalizations become percussive in quality and alternate dynamically between loud and soft.

1.07   The poetic text commences, echoed by recorded singer, and accompanied by synthesized tape.

2.20   The dramatic story pauses as portions of the text are repeated, though electronically altered through distortion and pitch register.

2.26   Poetic text continues with synthesized accompaniment.

3.11   Singer builds to a musical climax, which dramatically illustrates the violence portrayed.

3.39   The soprano's voice glissandos downwards to stressed words such as "killed," "stilled," and "unfulfilled."

3.49   The recorded singer repeats the words for added stress.

3.53   Both soprano and accompanying music turn more reflective for the words "broken the bond of silence." With the conclusion of the dramatic text, the music is curtailed.

In addition to being a distinguished composer, Babbitt was also an important teacher. Through his position at Princeton University, he trained many outstanding composers. A large number of his students went on to become university professors as well. The result of Babbitt's work as a teacher was the wide spread of integral serialism within American universities.

UNIVERSITIES AND AVANT-GARDE MUSIC

Having read this chapter so far, one might reasonably wonder where avant-garde music drew its support. The old system of patronage had undergone many transformations in the previous hundred years. The 1800s saw the aristocracy and the church falter as patrons. In their place, public institutions like symphony orchestras and opera companies depended not only on audience interest but also on the generosity of wealthy enthusiasts of the arts, who gave money to support music-making bodies that could not support themselves. Since those patrons and the institutions they patronized rallied around historicist preferences for antique music, modernists depended on the large number of educated, urban supporters of modern art. After the Second World War, universities stepped in as a major patron of avant-garde music. The reason for university interest stemmed in part from the Cold War.

The competition between the capitalist West and the communist East was not only a military, economic, and political rivalry. The two sides confronted one another in almost every field of endeavor. Some readers may recall the politicization of the Olympics that led to heated struggles to win more medals, the boycott of the Moscow Games in 1980 by the United States and some of her allies, and the boycott of the Los Angeles Games by the Soviet Union and most of her allies.

The sciences saw much of the hottest rivalry. The launch of the Sputnik satellite orbiting Earth by the Soviet Union during the 1950s announced to the West that the Soviets were racing ahead in the exploration of outer space. Anxious not to let their rivals dominate space, the West launched its own ambitious program of scientific exploration of the heavens, culminating in the first manned-expedition to the Moon.

Young men were encouraged in the West to study mathematics and the sciences during the 1950s and 1960s in order to serve in America's scientific competition with the Soviets. While not everyone is scientifically inclined, all other facets of human achievement were touched by the Cold War rivalry, even the arts.

Attending university after high school was far from the norm for young people in America prior to the Second World War. Once the Cold War began, attending college became a patriotic duty in order that each capable young person might contribute all he or she could to the Cold War. The result was enormous growth in American universities, both in numbers and in size.

Musical composition departments soon found themselves competing with science departments in accessing funding. Integral serialism, with its emphasis on rational principles of organization and on electronic technologies, became a natural sort of music for this purpose. Funding boards could understand artistic projects that sounded like they were predicated on rational and technical progress.

Integral serialism wasn't the only sort of music to benefit from the patronage of universities. Today avant-garde music of every sort depends to a large degree on university support. Not only are the audiences for avant-garde music often affiliated with universities, but the patrons for the music are the universities themselves. They afford composition professors a secure living in exchange for the teaching the composers do. Now that the Cold War is over, a reconfiguration of the academy's relationship with avant-garde music may take place as well. Already we find job listings emphasizing technological specialties and commercial music at some universities replacing some of the old positions once filled by avant-garde composers who have now retired or died. Moreover, young musicians drawn to embark on careers in musical composition are increasingly less inclined to explore avant-garde options in favor of other, more easily accessible styles.

INDETERMINACY

The Music of John Cage

While integral serialism, with its potential for generating rational compositions, occupied some post-war composers, another major breakthrough in musical organization occupied the imaginations of others. John Cage (1912–1992) also sought to distance his music from the emotionalism of the romantics and early moderns, although for very different reasons. To achieve this distance, Cage hoped to remove his desires and ambitions from his music. That approach served as both means and ends for Cage, who believed in such slogans as "Don't try to change the world, you'll only make matters worse." He wanted to illustrate the presence of sublime music everywhere around us at all times, or, in his own words, "to reveal how excellent things already are." This ambition on his part was fostered by his encounters with Zen Buddhism during the 1940s. Zen is a practice of mental discipline designed to free the practitioner of attachments and desires, "to sober and quiet the mind" (to use Cage's favorite phrase). In order to free his compositions of his desires, Cage sought radical methods of organizing pieces.

FIGURE 13.3 | *John Cage (1912–1992)* (© Hulton-Deutsch Collection/Corbis)

While Cage had a long and varied career before the 1940s, a career that even led him to study with Arnold Schoenberg, his most lasting contributions to music began in the late 1940s. Cage's first important experiment in this field was a composition from 1950 called *Imaginary Landscape IV*. This piece calls for performers to adjust the knobs on radios, effectively changing the station and the volume using randomly generated numbers to govern both. Every performance of Cage's piece is different, as neither he nor any of the performers can control what the audience hears. The resulting collage of sounds gathered from thin air illustrates how music is already happening all around, people just don't always have a receiver tuned to hear it. Moreover, the choices of radio programmers throughout the region have more direct impact on what the audience hears than Cage does. They become anonymous and totally unwitting collaborators in a piece freed from any one particular person's desires and attachments about what the piece should sound like. Now, one could easily argue that the event itself is printed with Cage's personality and eccentric sense of the theatrical. When confronted with that seeming contradiction—Cage's desire to free his music from his desires versus the result of having his piece reflect his desires at the macro level—Cage always laughed and said something to the effect of how wonderful contradictions are. This sort of playful engagement with critics made Cage a beloved and heroic guest speaker at universities and conferences, and added to his fame.

4′33″

Cage's next composition along these lines bears the title *4′33″* (1951). In this work, the performer or performers do nothing for four minutes and thirty-three seconds.

FIGURE 13.4 | Kurt Schwitters, **Picture of Spatial Growths—Picture with Two Small Dogs, 1939.** Collage on board. This work is comprised of an assortment of items, including a postcard, expended envelope, discarded packaging and bus tickets. Mixed into this collage are randomly picked words from newspapers, which are daubed with paint and positioned without purpose. Schwitters achieves a sense of balance in his abstract composition, even if creating art from objects that had been randomly collected challenged public complacency and traditional aesthetes. (© 2003 Artists Rights Society [ARS], New York/VG Bild-Kunst, Bonn/Tate Gallery/Art Resource, NY)

Some call this work a silent piece, yet Cage pointed out that it is not silent. The accidental sounds in the auditorium comprise the music. Each stirring, each cough, the whir of air conditioning, the sound made by one's own bodily systems (respiratory, digestive, circulatory) all combine with every other audible sound to make up the musical work. The implications of this piece are too numerous to recount here. A few illustrative implications must suffice. This work invites the listener to focus on how excellent the world already is without all our strivings and our artistry. The piece also presents an interesting invitation to ponder what constitutes music, a sort of philosophical challenge in musical form. Clearly Cage feels that music is an activity rather than a thing, an activity of listening. According to Cage, any sound can have the frame of art put around it so that it can be heard as music.

Cage's radical and liberalizing concept that everything might be music raised an obvious question: if 4'33" is music, why did Cage go on composing pieces for another forty years? After all, wouldn't it be sufficient to listen to whatever is going on whenever one wanted to hear music? Where's the need for composers in such a world? Cage answered this question many times this way: "Sometimes my telephone rings, and I answer it. A nice person on the other end of the line asks me to make a score for a piece of music. They often offer small sums of money. I usually agree." Cage did not write a single piece that was not commissioned by a performer or performers during the remainder of his career. People wanted new scores from him, so he made them new scores. His desires don't much enter into the matter. He never denied the basic irrelevance of composing in the aftermath of 4'33"; instead, he changed the subject to his relationship with musicians interested in accessing more and new examples of his music.

Music of Changes

The piece in our recorded anthology [CD4 #6] to illustrate Cage's music comes from very early in his development as an indeterminate composer. Indeterminacy refers to works in which some important element or elements are left to chance. Sometimes chance stems from simply letting things happen, as in 4'33". Other times Cage achieved indeterminacy by letting some system of choosing other than his own desires dictate the outcome. In our piece, the first book of his *Music of Changes* (1951), Cage's desires combine with chance to create a piece for piano that sounds quite random, but is in fact meticulously notated in a score. To make this piece, Cage consulted an ancient book of Chinese wisdom called *I Ching* (Book of Changes). This book calls on the reader to cast sticks and toss coins in order to discover what pages to read in order to find wisdom concerning some problem or concern. Cage made matrices of musical events, cast the sticks or coins, and consulted his matrices in order to know what event should happen next in his piece. He also established rules for the change over time of the matrices themselves, in keeping with the general theme of changes at work in the piece. The result is a composition that unfolds largely free from Cage's moment-by-moment management of the musical details.

John Cage, Music of Changes (1951)
[CD4, #6] *(Duration, 4 min. 14 sec.)*

0.00   Light, furtive tones are introduced, contrasted by loud, accentuated chords. Since these contrasting materials seem to emerge as musical dialogue, though each continually interrupts the other, the listener may be able to imagine them as an energetic conversation taking place between two people. If one would rather look to non-Occidental philosophies influential to John Cage, the opposing motives could be appreciated as "yin and yang" energy. Regardless, as this piece unfolds, colorful, introductory motives prove to move, not unlike many life experiences, in unpredictable ways, and appear full of surprises. Though the score for this piece is meticulously notated, indeterminate aspects reflect Cage's attention to an ancient book of Chinese wisdom called *I Ching* (Book of Changes). Moreover, any apprehension of contrasting motives must be seen as occurring without Cage's intentions, as a pure accident.

0.11   Longer pitch durations comprise an extended phrase. Forte chords respond with their own extended phrase.

0.37   (Silence)

0.40   Forte chords enter more emphatically, interspersed with short silences.

0.48   (Silence)

0.51   Forceful chords are played and allowed to ring under interspersed returns of the furtive material vaguely similar to the material at the beginning. Various tone combinations result in producing new and colorful pitch combinations.

1.11   (Silence)

1.15   An embellished treatment of the furtive material enters. The phrases sound rather free, as though they are being improvised.

1.36   (Silence)

1.39   This section appears as an improvised variation of the accented chord motive. It is in fact neither improvised nor a variation, but a seemingly random occurrence chosen by chance from a finite range of possibilities.

2.14   (Silence)

2.15   A new treatment of the furtive material commences.

2.24   (Silence)

2.26 Loud chords are struck and allowed to ring.

2.29 (Silence)

2.32 Contrasting material (furtive and loud chords) are again presented together in dialogue. At times each utilizes extended pitch registers, creating yet new colorful pitch arrangements.

3.56 (Silence)

A tiny portion of material comparable to the opening appears and brings the work to a close.

For some listeners, indeterminate works can be a little frustrating. Many people are used to musical events anticipating other events, creating expectations, rewarding or frustrating those expectations in pleasing ways that reveal some design or plan in the work. This piece by Cage almost totally frustrates this method of engaging music. His piece works best when the listener simply accepts whatever comes, concentrates on each event as it happens, and then lets each event pass away without allowing it to inflect their listening to the next event. Some theorists call Cage's approach "non-teleological." "Teleo" refers to goal directedness in Greek. When something lacks goal directedness and simply happens in the moment, we call it non-teleological. Like a good Zen riddle, the question then arises, "Can non-goal directedness become itself a goal?" Many Zen masters grapple with the problem of becoming attached to non-attachment or their own desire to shed desires, a problem comparable to non-goal directedness becoming its own goal. Cage relished these contradictions and philosophical problems. Far from flinching at seeming contradictions, he threw open his arms and embraced them, usually in a way that was full of humor.

Music of Changes does not result in a piece free from Cage's desires. He had been listening to the music of Webern and enjoying it very much. He manufactured the matrices of possible events in such a way that Webern's preferences for sparse and austere atonal music would most likely result. Later pieces would find Cage coming closer to the goal of removing his attachments and desires from his pieces. This early effort, nevertheless, captures the flavor of Cage's indeterminate efforts. Readers may want to try performing 4′33″ for themselves in order to hear a piece by Cage where his desires are less easily heard.

Cage's Philosophy of Letting Go of the Self in Art

During the remainder of his career, Cage advocated letting go of the self in art in order to let sound simply be itself. He lived out his philosophy to the fullest. He was a popular guest speaker on college campuses during his life. Often he would be asked to lecture on his ideas. He found such pedantic settings antithetical to his message. In an effort to illustrate the futility of certain kinds of goal-oriented exchange, he would often take questions from his audiences. After each question was posed, he would cast sticks or toss a coin and then read a written answer corresponding not to the question asked, but to his stick tossing. Invariably this meant that his answer had nothing to do with the question posed. However, Cage would insist that some higher logic that transcended our desire to make ourselves understood would kick in, and render his chance-generated answer all the more meaningful. If nothing else, his way of answering by not answering might illustrate that the asker should shed his or her attachment to getting an answer without discovering it.

FIGURE 13.5 | Morris Louis, **Beta Upsilon, from the series "Unfurleds," 1960.**
Acrylic on canvas. The artist has pushed flowing streams of colors to the perimeters of
this painting, directing the viewer's attention to the broad central area created.
Considerable tension across the middle is achieved as the bright colors on the right
stand in sharp contrast to darker hues on the left. In the same way, John Cage utilizes
opposing energies that are felt across poignant silences in his "Music of Changes."
(© Smithsonian American Art Museum, Washington, DC/Art Resource, NY)

RADICAL AVANT-GARDE MUSIC AFTER CAGE

Cage's ideas, music, and engaging personality attracted a large following to his
cause. During the 1950s, he was joined by three younger composers to form the New
York School made up of John Cage, Earle Brown (1926–), Morton Feldman (1926–
1987), and Christian Wolff (1934–). Brown pioneered the idea of the graphic scores.
These are scores that vaguely suggest a field of possibilities rather than a particular musical result. Some of them look more like conceptual art or abstract expressionist painting rather than musical scores. Feldman put complete faith in an irrational intuition
that produced musical works of exquisite delicacy. Wolff explored the field of game theory to make cooperative compositions, the scores of which resemble rules for a game
more than traditional musical scores. These games always emphasize keen listening
within the ensemble that executes them. Still other composers were inspired by Cage's
theatrical and humorous manners. His influence on a generation of young American
composers active during the 1960s can scarcely be overstated.

Annea Lockwood

One radical young composer who looked to Cage's work as a useful point of departure was Annea Lockwood. Lockwood studied music in New Zealand. Once at the
Royal Conservatory of Music, she was informed that a woman could not study composition. Instead she had to study piano. Later, she wrote a piece called *Piano Burning*
in which an old piano is set ablaze. On its surface this may look like a needlessly destructive act, but then we must consider the circumstances that gave rise to the piece's
composition. Lockwood was working on a collaborative dance piece entitled *Heat*. The
choreographer wanted a piece of *musique concrète*. Lockwood began setting things on

fire and tape-recording them in search of interesting sound sources. That project came to nothing, but in the process she learned that pianos sound very interesting as they burn. One by one the strings snap in the heat, the wooden frame crackles and hisses. Varnishes used on pianos tend to make the flames burn purple. She found this seemingly destructive act a useful way to purge her bad feelings about her discriminatory treatment in school and, in an odd way, a beautifully creative act, both aurally and visually.

Throughout her career, Lockwood has found surprising beauty where one might least expect it. Her career might be seen as one long modeling of the Cagean concept that the world is already so excellent and now we need to go out and discover it. Finding the sublime in the everyday remains a concept Lockwood takes to lofty heights.

Glass Concerts

During the 1960s, Lockwood lived in London. There she presented a series of *Glass Concerts*. These concerts featured atmospheric lighting in a small space. The music is made up of amplified performances on pieces of specially configured scientific glass. In our anthology [CD4 #7, 8, 9] are three short excerpts from her *Glass Concerts*. The scores for these pieces leave much to the imagination of the individual performer. In that way, Lockwood continues Cage's practice of removing some of the composer's desires from the work. Mainly her scores provide instructions on how to elicit surprisingly interesting sounds from unusual pieces of glass. By providing such simple instructions, Lockwood's pieces are inclusive rather than exclusive. They invite non-professionals to participate in a way that had not been the norm in Western concert music for more than 200 years. While the avant-garde can seem elitist and apart from the general society, composers such as Cage and Lockwood clearly strive to reverse this situation.

The three excerpts of Lockwood's *Glass Concerts* found in our anthology [CD4 #7, 8, 9] are titled "Glass Rod Vibrating," "Turning Gong," and "Mini Mobile." The first, as the name implies, calls for the performer to set a tiny rod of glass in motion while holding it against a larger plane of glass. Fluctuations in pitch are achieved by rolling the rod along the glass plane. The second piece centers on a large, round piece of glass that spins. As it spins, the performer strikes it lightly with his or her hands. The last requires the formation of a mobile comprised of tiny pieces of glass used in microscopy labs. In explaining her intentions with these pieces, Lockwood wrote:

> *I have become fascinated by the complexity of the single sound. I have treated each sound as if it were a piece of music in itself. For me, every sound has its own minute form—is composed of small flashing rhythms, shifting tones, has momentum, comes, vanishes, lives out its own structure. Since we are used to hearing sounds together, either juxtaposed or compared, one sound alone seems simple; but so are the round, scruffed stones lying about everywhere, until you crack one apart and all its intricate beauty takes you by surprise.*[1]

Here Lockwood gives voice to the ideal of discovering beauty everywhere. This concept is central to understanding indeterminacy in music. Indeterminacy provided the alternative to integral serialism that allowed young composers to find their way through the post-war era. In an unlikely parallel between the two movements, both

---

[1]Annea Lockwood, liner note for ¿What Next? Recording 0021.

afford the potential of diminishing the importance of manipulative emotionalism, so essential to Romanticism and so repulsive to composers who came of age during and immediately after the war. Presenting these two movements as responses to the Second World War makes for a quick and convenient story for a book conceived on this scale, but it should not distract from the importance of making interesting and beautiful music to both the practitioners of integral serialism and indeterminacy. As memories of the war faded, making art rapidly replaced making statements of distance from the past, at least at the surface of their labors.

Listening Guide

Annea Lockwood, "Glass Rod Vibrating," from Glass Concerts
[CD4, #7] *(Duration, 1 min. 44 sec.)*

The performer sets a tiny rod of glass in motion while holding it against a larger plane of glass. Rolling the rod along the glass plane causes fluctuations in pitch.

0.00   Fast drum-like rolls on a glass plane begin loudly, then decrescendo. Microtonal fluctuations occur.

0.09   Silence.

0.13   Drum-like rolls repeated, but they are heard as an echo of the opening.

0.24   Silence.

0.26   A percussive roll descends in microtonal increments as a glissando to a low pitch that is sustained.

0.37   Silence.

0.40   A percussive roll glissandos upwards.

0.49   Silence.

0.52   New timbres are introduced, which fall and decay quickly.

0.56   Silence.

0.57   Low pitches glissando upwards.

1.03   Silence.

1.04   Accented percussive rolls fluctuate in pitch, dynamic, and timbre.

1.12   The preceding event is repeated with slightly different results.

1.18   Silence.

1.19   Very soft, percussive rolls.

1.21   Silence.
1.22   Accentuated rolls fluctuate in pitch, dynamic, and timbre.

1.31   Silence.

1.32   New timbres are introduced with sounds that seem to imitate a nose flute. The characteristic "twang" begins low and quickly ascends. It is immediately followed by a brief echo.

1.37   Silence.

1.38   The preceding timbre is briefly repeated twice.

Annea Lockwood, "Turning Gong" and "Mini Mobile," from Glass Concerts
[CD4, #8 and 9]   *(Duration, 3 min. 6 sec.)*

"Turning Gong"—The performer strikes lightly with his or her hands a large, round piece of glass as it spins.

0.00   Gong-like tone is sustained through varied dynamics, before decaying into silence.

0.09   Silence.

0.10   Opening event is repeated more quietly.

0.20   Silence.

0.22   Repeated strikes produce a variety of microtonal pitches and dynamics.

0.48   Silence.

0.50   Low, accented tone quickly results in distorted microtonal reverberations.

0.58   Softer strikes echo the previous event, sustaining the texture.

1.18   A series of repeated strikes decrescendo, bringing "Turning Gong" to an end.

1.24   Silence.

"Mini Mobile"—The performer utilizes a mobile comprised of tiny pieces of glass used in microscopy labs. In our recorded anthology, this concert appears to begin as a musical response to "Turning Gong," as its textures and timbres are in clear contrast. The listening guide describes the opening, a segment that begins and ends the concert with delicate chimes.

1.30   Multiple tones produce an array of colors and textures.

AMERICAN MUSIC DURING THE 1970S

After a generation dominated by integral serialism and indeterminacy, composers working in America found themselves faced with a grave difficulty, how could you continue to be original without covering ground already covered by one of the innovators of these two techniques? Some found minimalism, a style of composition emphasizing the use of a small amount of musical material, either repeated or elongated, over a vast period of time. Some leading figures in this new style include La Monte Young (1937–), Terry Riley (1935–), Steve Reich (1936–), and Philip Glass (1937–). The music of these four individuals doesn't sound alike at all. Each favored a different aspect of minimalism, with La Monte Young exploring the area of drones, elongations of single pitches, Riley exploring motivic repetition over a steady pulse, and Reich delving into phase processes, whereby two or more instruments play the same material over and over at a different rate of speed. By 1970 most of the innovations of minimalism had played out, making it yet another difficult option for younger composers.

A technique that many younger composers found liberating was a kind of eclectic quotation of past materials and styles. George Rochberg (1912–) played a central role in this development. He had been an integral serialist, but after the death of his son elected to explore past styles that he found more emotionally expressive. Sometimes he quoted actual pieces, but mostly he quoted past styles ranging from the Renaissance to the early twentieth century. Quotation doesn't necessitate adopting any particular overall style, in fact, it intervenes against adopting a single style.

GEORGE CRUMB

Black Angels

Starting in the 1960s, many composers quote past music. George Crumb (1929–) emerged in the 1970s as one of the most influential composers who used past music and past styles in the service of his art.

Dismayed over the Vietnam War, George Crumb scored his quartet for electrified string quartet, *Black Angels,* to serve as a post-holocaust parable on the desolation, hopelessness, and disillusionment all too often experienced in our troubled contemporary world. The amplification of a string quartet and use of several unusual effects generated a highly surrealistic landscape, a journey into the "dark land" of human conflict. In addition, there are many quasi-programmatic allusions, such as God versus Devil, that serve his purposes as symbolic of conflict rather than as a literal program for the piece. In order to summon divine and profane imagery in his piece, Crumb allows musical quotation to serve his purposes as talismans of the opposing forces at work in this piece.

In addition to the quotation of existing works, Crumb uses exotic techniques on the instruments to serve his programmatic ends. On several occasions, extended string techniques tone-paint images of swarming insects, frequently encountered in jungle terrain, with obvious inferences to Biblical plagues, which are divine in nature. Insects might also be appreciated as a manifestation of unspoiled creation—possessing the quality of being natural. Crumb also brings numerical symbolism to bear in his piece. Numbers figure prominently in the construction of his music. By using symbolically powerful numbers for tones, durations, patterns of repetition, and so forth, Crumb hoped to draw upon the extra-musical significance of numbers. Though such associations can be difficult to hear, there are others that are made vivid within his piece. For example, in Image 7, Threnody II, the ominous number thirteen is ritualistically shouted in Japanese, Russian, and Swahili.

More solemn musical quotations from earlier works are utilized to sound as echoes of ancient music. Such tonal allusions include Franz Schubert's *"Death and the Maiden"* in image six, where the strings are asked to simulate a consort of viols, while other parts reference the famous medieval chant from the Requiem Mass, *"Dies*

FIGURE 13.6 | *George Crumb (b. 1929)*
(© Oscar White/Corbis)

Irae" ("Day of Wrath"). A rather menacing, high-pitched quotation from Bernard Herrmann's score for the film *Psycho* commences Image Seven, Threnody II. Other musical symbolism includes the use of the tritone or "devil's interval," and the "devil's trill," formally used by the Italian violinist and composer Tartini, who authored a work of such tremendous difficulty owing to the extensive use of trills (rapid fluctuations between two pitches) that his piece was seen as diabolical. At one point the quartet begins counting to seven in German, an allusion to a frightening scene from the German opera, *Der Freischutz*. The devil appears in that scene just as the number seven is shouted. In folklore, the violin has often served as the devil's favored instrument, which he uses to seduce the innocent to corruption.

Each instrumentalist for this work, in addition to playing their respective string instrument (violin I and II, viola, and cello), is asked to vocalize and play either maracas, tam-tams, or water-tuned crystal goblets that are bowed to create an ethereal timbre. By having his string players perform on percussion instruments as well as their electrified string instruments, Crumb not only achieves diverse timbres but also a wonderful theatricality.

This work [CD4 #10 and 11] is structured in three parts to portray three stages of a soul's voyage. He titles them Departure (fall from grace), Absence (spiritual annihilation) and Return (redemption). Images Six and Seven from Absence are in our recorded anthology.

George Crumb's eclecticism and use of quotations cannot represent all the diverse ways that composers in the 1970s embraced quotation, but he certainly was one of the

Listening Guide

George Crumb, Black Angels, Scenes 6 and 7 from Part II, Absence
[CD 4, #10 and 11] *(Duration, 4 min. 21 sec.)*

Scene 6. PAVANA LACHRYMAE [CD4. #10]

0.00 The electric cello, Violin II, and Viola play by bowing their stings near the tuning pegs to simulate an ancient consort of viols. The music they play is a musical theme from Schubert's song "Death and the Maiden."

0.26 Electric violin I interjects a solo obbligato, mimicking insect sounds.

0.45 The harmonious consort gradually fades to silence, as the violin's menacing obbligato moves directly into Image Seven.

Scene 7. THRENODY II: BLACK ANGELS [CD4, #11]

0.00 Strings introduce a musical evocation of Bernard Herrmann's score for *Psycho*, followed by a loud descending glissando in the upper strings.

0.06 A loud pizzicato in the upper strings initiates the "devil's trill" in the cello.

0.09 The entire ensemble shouts "thirteen" in Japanese.

0.10   Upper strings trill, leading to unison glissandos that get faster and faster.

0.27   Flurry of trills and glissandos lead to another shout, this time "thirteen" in Russian.

0.38   Pizzicato initiates a trill, moving to unison glissandos.

0.42   Crescendo builds to trills.

0.53   Opening musical quotation from *Psycho* in the upper strings over cello trills and crescendos.

0.57   Shouts of "thirteen" in Swahili over cello's glissandi trills.

1.00   Pizzicato initiates more trills that lead to unison glissandi.

1.04   Trills lead to higher-pitched glissandi.

1.36   Accentuated rhythmic motive (seven-note pattern repeated three times, then reduced to a five-note pattern repeated three times, and finally a three-note pattern ending in a tremolo lasting seven seconds) is intermittently repeated between numerical shouts counting to seven in German.

2.01   Loud cymbal crash, followed by shouts of "thirteen" in German.

2.13   Violin I hands the insect obbligato (similar to the kind heard in image six) over to violin II to conclude (the closing obbligato lasts thirteen seconds).

most influential figures to undertake this approach. His piece is neither serial nor indeterminate nor minimalist. By taking up the technique of quotation, Crumb avoids easy comparisons to the music of the previous generation. His style was much imitated and very influential during the 1970s and 1980s. For younger composers drawn to university teaching, he offered a path that afforded some distance from the avant-garde techniques of the previous generation.

The use of quotation partly caught fire in the 1960s and 1970s precisely because of the pressures of historicism. By taking the music of the past and making it available either for stylistic evocation as done by Rochberg or for the purposes of drawing on programmatic associations as done by Crumb, modern composers turn the rich history of Western music to their personal aims. They also increase the interest of the mainstream in their music as recognizable styles and famous quotations can bridge the gap between the traditional concert audience and the avant-garde composer.

CONCLUSION

Like all the chapters before it, this chapter has concentrated on only a few achievements from the era it presumes to cover. The musical avant-garde affords students of Western music a glimpse of the extremes of radical organization undertaken after the war. The composers represented in this section have done much to impress their ideas onto the larger musical community. That none of these ideas have been adopted by the musical mainstream encourages us to look at the ambitions of the avant-garde. Adoption by the mainstream is not a goal. Moreover, we might at this point contemplate in the face of the rise of popular music and the fragmentation of taste throughout society, whether there is a musical mainstream any more.

Some Questions for Discussion

1   All of the music in this chapter, despite having been composed comparatively recently, isn't very well known by the general public. What factors in our society, beyond those mentioned in the chapter itself, do you see mediating against the general public coming to know this music? Do you think this condition of relative obscurity for much avant-garde music is a particular problem or an advantage?

2   Can an artist's intentions and desires ever be completely divorced from his or her creations? What would be some of the reasons for pursuing such a potentially impossible task?

3   Crumb found quotation of past music a useful way to communicate an extra-musical program. In the book, we've tried to describe all of these quotations that we found useful for understanding his intentions. Would you have recognized any of his quotations? As time goes by, will it be possible to quote antique music and reasonably expect anyone in the audience to recognize any of the quotations for what they are, let alone apprehend their extra-musical meaning? Can you think of films that quote other films? What effect does noticing a quotation as a quotation in a film do for you as a viewer? Is it easier to recognize film quotation rather than musical quotes? Why do you think that is? Does the information age with its cheap and massive availability of information have any impact on the usefulness of quoting in art?

JAZZ IS A CLASSICAL MUSIC

Having surveyed concert music of the previous century, at this point we need to backtrack and examine a crucial omission of the previous two chapters: jazz. Classification of any kind can become a subjective practice very easily. Even the most rigorously objective sorting based on material evidence still depends on the selection of the criteria for that sorting. Categorizing music is an imprecise science. At first blush, one might conclude that a book introducing concert music need not bother itself with jazz. Another approach might reveal, however, that jazz is central to any discussion of concert music in the previous century. The concert settings may be different for jazz than for German expressionists, but if we've learned nothing else from this book we should at least acknowledge that the social settings for concert music, indeed the definition of a concert, has changed over the centuries. The exclusive salons of Venice in its prime differ socially from the academic presentation of Boulez' latest creation at Darmstadt. What constitutes a concert is under constant negotiation. If the principal criterion for determining what music counts for inclusion is a like performing venue, then we should have given up long ago on most of the music presented in this book.

Classical, Traditional, and Popular Music Classifications

A long tradition exists in musical studies, dating back at least to the work of Bruno Nettl in the 1960s, that differentiates between three types of music: classical, traditional, and popular. Popular refers to music that is primarily configured as a disposable commodity. To be sure, popular musicians take their work seriously, but they do not tend to worry about posterity so much as immediate appeal. They are quick to change with trends in consumer appetite. Even within this field, we can see much grey area. The Baby Boom generation invented the term "classic rock" to identify the rock 'n' roll music popular when they were young. This term indicates an effort to make this music transcend its moment of popularity and become canonized as something capable of gratifying generations of listeners. The terms also can be used as a tool of distancing their preferred popular music from the comparable popular music of their children. Now middle aged, the Baby Boomers find themselves turned off by the music of their children and needful of powerful terms to elevate their preferences. There's always the chance that they'll be proved right by history, that Nettl's classification system will fail, and their music will transcend the ages. Don't bet too much on it, if you want our advice. Already we can see the popular figures of a generation ago flagging in their power to persuade a younger audience to care. Popular music has the following sorts of objective elements: little or no attempt to write it down, a premium on performance over composition, some strong commercial appeal or the emulation of styles with a strong commercial appeal, rapid changes in audience taste quickly accommodated in the music itself, and a social function that seldom caters to silent or immobile contemplation of the music itself so much as the making of a total scene involving dancing, fashion, and other forms of socializing.

Nettl's classification of folk music describes all that music that is born of anonymous authors and has been passed down by word of mouth. Identifying the origins of a particular example of folk music can be very difficult. The creators of this music are not so much trying to establish a position for themselves as widely recognized musicians, but rather they are integrating their music-making into a social fabric. Much folk music has little commercial value because it is readily available and easily accessible both for performers and listeners. That is not to say that the best folk musicians cannot become famous and even prized individuals thanks to their artistry, only that folk music can be—as the name of the category implies—made by the folk. In some cultures folk music represents the most valued musical achievements. In the West, that is seldom the case. Folk music differs from popular music in that it can be commercial but has some traditional role in the society that is more functional than commercial.

This book deals with what Nettl calls classical music. We chose the term "concert music" to avoid certain kinds of confusion and unwanted implications of the term "classical." In practice, the two terms can be used interchangeably with little loss of understanding.

Classical music refers to music that emphasizes the composer, is usually written down, intends to appeal to posterity, and, while often functional, can also be treated as art for art's sake. Exceptions to these general characteristics can be found especially in the chapter dealing with the Middle Ages, but in others as well. Jazz clearly meets the standards of these criteria. Moreover, insofar as jazz comes into being in the United States, it is a Western music that meets the criteria of a classical music.

On the topic of jazz's inclusion or exclusion in the field of classical music, the great jazz composer and performer Duke Ellington (discussed later in this chapter in more detail) argued that there was no such thing as jazz. He said, "It's all music. Eventually we'll come to realize that, and there won't be any more debates." What follows is a brief historical survey of ragtime and jazz—and no more debating classification and terminology.

RAGTIME

The history of jazz flows out of many traditions including ragtime, the blues, the improvised music of African-Americans in the decades following emancipation, spirituals, and the various musics of West Africa as remembered by the men and women who came to this country from there. Because ragtime is a classical, or concert music, we'll examine its contribution most closely. Ragtime benefited from the participation and contributions of several composers with excellent classical training. As a result, it was notated and published, leading to widespread performance and real popularity. Eventually these pieces came to the attention of jazz musicians who used them as a framework for their own improvisatory performances.

SCOTT JOPLIN

Ragtime music is closely associated with one central figure in its history, Scott Joplin. Joplin was born in Texarkana, Texas. His mother worked as a housekeeper and was able to afford music lessons for her son from a German-born and educated musician named Julius Weiss. Joplin showed considerable talent and learned to play the piano, sing harmony parts, compose, and demonstrate a fine knowledge of European musical theory. After a short career as a professional singer in a barbershop quartet, he became a music professor at the George P. Smith College for Negroes. His duties included teaching piano, singing, and music theory.

For additional income Joplin played piano in the evening at the Maple Leaf Club just outside Sedalia, Missouri. The Maple Leaf Club saw the flourishing of "the sporting life." This was a lifestyle built on good grooming, snappy dressing, elegant manners, gambling, and good times as practiced by many African-American men at the end of the nineteenth century. Joplin's music served as the ideal accompaniment to the sporting life. While wildly popular at the Maple Leaf Club, Joplin had wider aspirations. Through his lawyer and agent, John Stark, Joplin signed a lucrative contract to publish his ragtime compositions.

Joplin's ragtime piano music exemplifies the following characteristics: use of syncopation (a technique calling for strongly accented notes on the off-beats), a jaunty march tempo, unusual tonal plan emphasizing the fourth instead of the fifth, homophonic texture, and a striding bass line. This style captivated a huge segment of the American public and eventually won over many Western Europeans as well. Claude Debussy and Erik Satie both published piano compositions born of this style. More important than the admiration of European composers was the admiration of the American public. Purchases of sheet music containing the scores of Joplin's compositions made him a quite wealthy man.

Maple Leaf Rag

The piece in our recorded anthology [CD4 #12] representing ragtime is Joplin's famous *Maple Leaf Rag*. The form of this piece is basically binary, although there are two different repeated segments within each larger part of the form. A diagram of the form looks like this:

FIGURE 14.1 | *Scott Joplin (1868–1917)*
(© Bettmann/Corbis)

FIRST SECTION					SECOND SECTION			
A	A	B	B	A	C	C	D	D

The "C" section is where Joplin modulates to his polar key. He almost always favored the fourth, or sub-dominant, to the more traditional fifth, or dominant. As you listen, more so than the key changes, the distinct melodic material of each sub-section will help you know where you are within the form. See the listening guide for this piece for clarification.

Scott Joplin, *Maple Leaf Rag (1899)*
[CD4, #12] *(Duration, 3 min. 20 sec.)*

Binary Form: A B

A (Tempo di marcia)

0.00 **a**   Joplin's characteristic use of syncopation, a jaunty march tempo, homophonic texture, and a striding bass line are immediately recognized.

0.22 **a**   Opening material is repeated.

0.44 **b**   Opening material is varied in different ways and presented with new harmonies.

1.06 **b**   Preceding material is repeated.

1.28 **a**   Opening material returns.

B (Trio)

1.50 **c**   Joplin modulates to his polar key, favoring almost always the fourth, or sub-dominant, as opposed to the more traditional fifth, or dominant. The distinct melodic material of each sub-section helps the listener recognize the form.

2.12 **c**   Preceding material repeats.

2.34 **d**   "C" material is varied in new ways and presented with new harmonies.

2.56 **d**   Preceding material is repeated.

The Influence of Ragtime

Soon after Joplin's works were published and widely sold, he became alarmed at what he saw as an unwholesome tendency on the part of performers to rush the stately, march tempo of ragtime compositions. He felt this robbed his works of their inherent dignity, a dignity closely associated with the sporting life. In an effort to insist that his intentions be honored, he wrote and published a short tract on ragtime called *School of Ragtime.* Joplin also made piano rolls, the rolls used to operate player pianos, in an effort to demonstrate the proper way to play his music. Despite Joplin's efforts, his ragtime compositions were widely adapted to suit new purposes. Most interestingly, they drew the attention of jazz musicians, who used them as the framework for improvisatory variations. The pianist Jelly Roll Morton produced a hot-selling recording of Joplin's *Maple Leaf Rag.* In his version, Morton not only takes the piece at a fast tempo but introduces all manner of virtuosic alterations to Joplin's score. In this way, ragtime fueled the growing importance of jazz by providing exciting compositions upon which performers could add their individual voices.

Joplin's efforts to control how his compositions were used ultimately failed. He believed that his pieces should be treated like any other classical compositions. He hoped that his intentions would be honored. It was his misfortune that his work became too popular to be controlled by one man. Too many people wanted to play his works, a problem quite opposite from the problem of many avant-garde composers. As they became more and more popular, their distribution and performance could no longer be regulated. Recordings, such as Jelly Roll Morton's, sounded good to tens of thousands of people. When a market of that size exists for music, the market tends to win out over the composer's original intentions.

Joplin's Contributions to Opera

Joplin experienced other difficulties of a very different sort. He was a great admirer of opera. He invested much of his considerable fortune in a series of opera companies that tended to spend far more money than they drew in. The apex of his involvement with opera saw him compose *Treemonisha* (1911). This opera tells the story of a young African-American woman in Louisiana during the years immediately after the Civil War and the freeing of the slaves. She confronts the evil influence of superstition and ignorance among her people in a story about courage and commitment to community. Joplin hoped that the Metropolitan Opera in New York would produce his work. They would not. Racial prejudice, still an ugly problem in the United States, was rampant in Joplin's time. African-American performers were not then allowed on the stage of the Metropolitan Opera. Joplin's career in opera was as disappointing to him as his career in ragtime was lucrative.

THE ADVENT OF JAZZ ON RECORD

The story of jazz probably doesn't begin with the first jazz recordings. It may not even begin with the first use of the word "jazz." African-American musicians certainly participated in an ongoing tradition of instrumental music involving improvisation upon some pre-existent music, for as long as there have been people of African background in this land. Jazz as we know it is easier to study with the advent of recording technology. Recordings make our job easier because they provide music to study. In the early days of jazz, compositions were of less importance than performances. There's still an element of truth to that claim in the field of jazz.

Early Recording Techniques

Early recordings of jazz can illuminate this music for us, but it can also deceive us in unexpected ways. The recording technology of the 1920s could not faithfully reproduce jazz as it was experienced in concerts, clubs, and other less formal performance venues. Around 1920 in New Orleans, the typical jazz ensemble featured from roughly five to twelve musicians. A performance of a piece or song in a live context might last well over ten minutes. Recordings from this period could not last much more than two minutes before the wax cylinder ran out of space to store more information. Musicians making recordings needed to shorten what they would have played live to accommodate the available technology. Similarly, certain instruments couldn't be used, such as the double bass or the drums. These instruments tended to make the needle jump off the cylinder during recording, effectively ruining the cylinder. For the bass line, a tuba positioned in the next room could be used as a substitute. Naturally this changes the timbre of the performance considerably. Similarly, wood blocks or luggage stuffed with clothes frequently doubled for drums. These items are less resonant than a drum and offered a muffled timbre that the technology of the day could handle. What we hear in these early recordings is a facsimile of how jazz sounded, rather than a perfect document.

What early recordings do document for us is a lively music featuring a dense polyphonic texture of musicians improvising upon a variety of pre-existent musical materials. Often these materials came from ragtime or the blues. This contrapuntal melodic improvisation was supported by drums, a tuba, often a piano, and equally often a banjo or guitar. These instruments formed what is called "the rhythm section." They don't participate in the melodic improvisation so much as they lay down the harmonic foundation for the piece and present a driving rhythmic momentum. This basic and successful formula is rather faithfully preserved on recordings. Some of the leading bands in the early days of jazz include Joe "King" Oliver's Creole Jazz Band, the Kid Ory Band, and Jelly Roll Morton's Red Hot Peppers.

LOUIS ARMSTRONG

Louis Armstrong (1901–1971) emerged as the most influential figure in New Orleans jazz. Born in New Orleans the son of a prostitute and an absent father, Armstrong spent much of his youth in an orphanage. He received a trumpet as a gift, and it became his ticket out of a life of poverty and neglect. Initially he worked with Joe "King" Oliver, himself a successful trumpet player. Armstrong participated on many of Oliver's recordings as a secondary figure. Biographers agree that Armstrong's personality tended to gravitate toward finding a powerful and dominant personality to follow. Oliver provided that personality at first. Eventually, however, he took the advice of admirers who convinced him first to switch over to the Kid Ory Band and later strike out on his own.

Armstrong's Recordings

Armstrong's recordings starting in the mid-1920s revolutionized early jazz. While most ensembles presented a fairly undifferentiated polyphonic texture of group im-

FIGURE 14.2 | *Louis Armstrong (1901–1971)* Shown with Joe ("King") Oliver's Creole Jazz Band. Lilian Hardin is at the piano. (© Bettmann/Corbis)

provisation from the beginning of a piece to the end, Armstrong's sharply drawn musical personality shines through in his recordings thanks in large part to changes of texture. Sometimes he had most of the players drop out to let the soloist be heard more distinctly. Sometimes he sang his solos rather than playing them on trumpet for the sake of variety. Through these innovations in texture, Armstrong established the centrality of the clearly defined soloist as crucial to jazz. He stamped his powerful musical identity onto the field of jazz. Readers interested in hearing the contrast between Armstrong's approach in the late1920s and New Orleans style recordings from earlier should locate a copy of *The Smithsonian Collection of Classic Jazz*. This outstanding collection can be found in most college libraries. Recordings of King Oliver's Creole Jazz Band or Jelly Roll Morton's Red Hot Peppers provide nice examples of group improvisation.

Louis Armstrong and His Hot Five

Hotter Than That

In our recorded anthology [CD4 #13] is a recording of Louis Armstrong and His Hot Five from 1927, made after Armstrong had been leading a band of his own for more than a year. The song, titled "Hotter than That," was composed by Armstrong's second wife, the pianist Lilian Hardin. The recording features four renditions of the song, each one called a chorus, and each presented with a distinct texture. The first features Armstrong playing trumpet. He's accompanied by the entire quintet, but unobtrusively. The second chorus features clarinetist Johnny Dodds. Critics tend to feel that Dodds lacks some of the clarity of musical identity possessed by Armstrong, but his solo is certainly worthy and the contrasting timbre of the clarinet affords the recording some pleasing variety. Next Armstrong presents one of his trademark "scat" versions of the tune. "Scat" refers to a wordless vocal improvisation. Entertaining in the extreme, "scat" solos helped to elevate Armstrong to the heights of popularity. At the end of this third version of the song, Armstrong joins guitar player Lonnie Johnson as they trade quick snatches of melody. Playful exchanges of this sort were common in jazz of the 1920s, and remain a pleasing part of many jazz performances today. The fourth and final chorus features Armstrong on trumpet again. As the recording ends, Lonnie Johnson is again trading snatches of melody with Armstrong. Suddenly, just before the cylinder ran out, Johnson plays an ambiguous chord and the performance ends. Such an ending would likely never have occurred in live performance, but the primitive state of recording technology at the time mandated some quick thinking on the part of players such as that demonstrated by Johnson. Earlier in the recording you can hear Lilian Hardin enter early on the piano in the hopes of moving the performance forward to avoid precisely what did happen at the end of the recording. Her effort is furtive and does not meet with success. These moments of having to think together on the fly affords jazz a winning quality of unpredictability in performance. Rather than striving for a perfect and identical execution of the piece every time out, jazz musicians thrive on the unexpected. Improvisation, by its nature, depends on some unexpected occurrences changing the performance and requiring a quick response.

Listening Guide

Lilian Hardin, "Hotter Than That" (1927)
[CD4, #13] *(Duration, 3 min.)*

Louis Armstrong and His Hot Five

0.00 **FIRST CHORUS:** The opening rendition of the song features Armstrong playing trumpet. He's accompanied by the entire quintet. The supporting performers do an excellent job of staying out of Armstrong's way as he provides a clear and virtuosic solo full of rhythmic drive.

0.46 **SECOND CHORUS:** Clarinetist Johnny Dodds is featured improvising on the same melodic material Armstrong improvised upon in the first chorus.

1.22 **THIRD CHORUS:** Armstrong sings a "scat" versions of the tune. The texture of this sung version of the song is thinner than the previous versions, with only the guitar accompanying Armstrong. At the end of this third version of the song (1.55), Armstrong joins guitar player Lonnie Johnson as they trade quick snatches of melody.

2.18 **FOURTH CHORUS:** The final version of the song features Armstrong on trumpet again. As the recording ends (2.45), Lonnie Johnson is again trading snatches of melody with Armstrong. Suddenly, just before the cylinder runs out, Johnson plays an ambiguous chord and the performance ends. Such an ending would likely never have occurred in live performance, but the primitive state of recording technology at the time mandated some quick thinking on the part of players, such as that demonstrated by Johnson.

Armstrong's Popularity

Armstrong's career soared during the 1920s. Broadway musicals were rewritten to allow for an appearance by Armstrong. When sound films were invented, Armstrong was much sought after to make brief appearances playing himself. He appeared in more than fifty films. While he would never be so musically influential as he was in the 1920s, his winning musicality and easy manners in front of a crowd made him a favorite figure in the field of entertainment right up until his death.

BIG BAND JAZZ

As Armstrong and His Hot Fives were revolutionizing jazz on recordings, new developments in New York City were taking shape that would change the field of jazz for the next fifteen years. At the Roseland, Fletcher Henderson and his orchestra were attracting large crowds. For a time, Louis Armstrong played in Henderson's orchestra. Armstrong's influence was enormous. All the players were starting to develop a singular style. Each solo was a celebration of jazz' power as a conduit for distinct musical personalities to reveal themselves through improvisation. As the popularity of jazz at the Roseland swelled, a huge dance floor became the forum for Henderson and his fellow musicians. In time, Henderson employed an ensemble of fairly large scale including several trumpets, trombones, saxophones, clarinets, a pianist, a drummer, and a bass player. This instrumentation came to be known as a *big band*. When more than 800 couples came to the Roseland to dance, this large ensemble was needed in order for the music to be heard in the far reaches of the dance floor.

A larger ensemble requires special care to keep things together. Fletcher Henderson employed an arranger, a person who writes out parts for the big band. Don Redman was Henderson's first and most pioneering arranger.

Soon big bands appeared in every major city in America, with Kansas City and New York enjoying the greatest concentrations of activity. The radio carried favorite bands coast to coast. White musicians adopted the style, and soon big band music achieved a near consensus of popularity within the United States. Among white bandleaders, Benny Goodman was certainly the most influential. He employed the first integrated big band, that is, both black and white musicians as well as Latinos playing in the same ensemble. Today this innovation may not sound too important, but in the 1930s in racially divided America, his efforts were nothing short of heroic.

DUKE ELLINGTON

In terms of composers and bandleaders, Duke Ellington (1899–1974) is generally held in the greatest respect. Ellington was born in Washington D.C. In the 1920s, African-Americans had limited options. Ellington's mother was a housekeeper. Her son would likely become a domestic ser-

FIGURE 14.3 | *Duke Ellington (1899–1974)*
(© Underwood & Underwood/Corbis)

vant as well, unless something drastic happened to change the family's fortunes. She brought her son to work so he could practice the piano on the fine instruments owned by her clients. Her foresight paid dividends. As a teenager, Ellington played piano professionally in clubs and at parties in his home city. Ellington always dressed and carried himself with the dignity befitting his mother's employers, as a way of distancing himself from humble roots. Over the course of his career, Ellington composed more than 1000 pieces during a career spanning a fifty-year period. Many of his compositions remain in wide circulation today. Ellington evinced a gift for crafting melodies ideally suited to melodic improvisation. As an arranger for his own big band, he had no peer—each arrangement took full advantage of his extraordinarily virtuosic ensemble. Some complain that his reputation partly depends on the superb musicians around him. Their talents allowed for his arrangements. Far from a reservation on Ellington's importance, this true observation reveals just how intelligent an arranger Ellington was. He understood the strengths of the musicians around him, and made use of those strengths in a common cause.

Ko-Ko

Ellington's arrangement of his own composition *Ko-Ko*, played by his orchestra, appears in our recorded anthology, [CD4 #14]. By the time this performance was recorded in 1940, the technology of recording had improved considerably. Basses and drums could be used, and pieces didn't need to be cut short to accommodate the machinery's limitations.

Listening Guide

Duke Ellington, Ko-Ko (1940)
[CD4, #14] (Duration, 2 min. 40 sec.)

0.00 **INTRODUCTION:** The baritone saxophone presents a four-note rhythmic figure, which is answered in a syncopated rhythm by the trombones. This four-note figure, answered by some other instrument, will evolve into the most important feature of the piece.

0.12 **FIRST CHORUS:** Juan Tizol plays a four-note melody, using the same rhythm presented by the baritone saxophone in the introduction. The saxophones answer, using the same syncopated rhythm used by the trombones in the introduction, but with different chords.

0.31 **SECOND CHORUS:** Now trombonist Joe Nanton takes a solo. He uses a mute to distort the timbre of the trombone. During this chorus, Ellington allows the four-note motive to become less prominent. Saxophones play it quietly and are obscured somewhat by dissonant chords from Ellington's piano.

0.49 **THIRD CHORUS:** This chorus is very similar to the previous one, except that the trombone solo is now in a higher register.

1.01 **FOURTH CHORUS:** Saxophones now carry the main melody as Ellington begins playing an intricate accompaniment in fast passages and dissonant chords on the piano.

1.25 **FIFTH CHORUS:** Now the four-note motive is presented by trumpets in their lowest register. The saxophones present the main melodic answer in a virtuosic manner.

1.43 **SIXTH CHORUS:** Conscious that sustaining the tension built up in the last two choruses won't be easy, Ellington assigns the four-note motive to the entire band and has Jimmy Blanton, the lone double bass player, answer them by himself.

2.02 **SEVENTH CHORUS:** This is the most thickly textured of all the choruses, as the entire band plays the entire time. The four-note motive is now replaced by dissonant chords answered by the saxophones.

2.20 **CODA:** The material of the introduction returns with a short flourish at the end for the whole group, to bring the piece to a rousing close.

The Popularity of Big Band Music

While Ellington may have had the hottest band of the big band era, many other leaders contributed to making this America's most popular music of the 1930s and 1940s including Benny Goodman, Count Basie, Bennie Moten, Gene Krupa, and Guy Lombardo. The popularity of big band music continued well into the 1950s, although it was dealt a rather severe blow during a lengthy musicians' strike in 1943. That strike and its impact will occupy our attention later in this chapter.

Some historians of jazz insist that big-band jazz does not reflect the mainstream. They point out that the style of jazz performed by small forces in an intimate setting, such as heard in Armstrong's recording with the Hot Fives, remained a force even during the heyday of the big bands. Furthermore, these historians feel that big-band jazz compromised the improvisatory quality of jazz by relying too heavily on arrangers. Whatever one's take on this controversy about the history of jazz, the popularity and influence of the big bands cannot be denied, whether they reflect the mainstream or not.

AVANT-GARDE JAZZ AFTER THE SECOND WORLD WAR

Be-Bop

The musicians strike of 1943 interrupted the lives of most jazz musicians. Those who had been playing in big bands needed to find smaller ensembles to play in, out of the general public's view. Many found inspiration in the work of several musicians who were already cultivating a new style intended for smaller forces in the smaller clubs of New York City. The trumpeter Dizzy Gillespie and the saxophonist Charlie Parker spent the middle 1940s playing together, along with two or three other musicians. The style of their music has come to be called "be-bop." Be-bop was a form of jazz meant for connoisseurs who wanted to compare the intricate details of complex solos played at blistering tempos and within a super-sophisticated harmonic language. Be-bop never became as broadly popular with the general public as big-band jazz, but for enthusiasts of jazz it became the new ideal. Most jazz musicians today still play in a manner inflected by be-bop, although there are notable exceptions.

With its fast tempos, complex harmonies, and the premium placed on virtuosity, be-bop musicians took on characteristics of warriors priding themselves on their achievements and holding lesser players in contempt. Be-bop has been called rather poetically, "a warrior culture." Among the many be-bop musicians represented within *The Smithsonian Collection of Classic Jazz*, one finds not only Gillespie and Parker but Dexter Gordon, Miles Davis, and Thelonius Monk as well.

FIGURE 14.4 | *Thelonius Monk (1917–1982)* (© Mosaic Images/Corbis)

Thelonius Monk

For the purposes of our anthology, we've chosen to single out the pianist Thelonius Monk, [CD4 #15] although in some ways he is least representative of be-bop in its purest and most virtuosic form. Monk's virtuosity lay in his compositions and his superb ability as a pianist always to pick interesting notes, not only during solos but when accompanying other soloists. Monk gained a reputation for stealing the spotlight from other be-bop soloists with a single carefully chosen note presented while playing an accompanimental role. He also had an exotic personality. Monk became the model for the Beatnik look, with his goatee and beanie and his hip way of talking. All be-bop musicians preferred to keep be-bop an outsider and almost exclusively African-American art form. Monk, however, managed to be an outsider among outsiders, lending his music a special historical resonance as perfectly illustrative of a time, an attitude, and a place within the history of African-American concert music. Monk's composition *Misterioso*, first recorded in 1948, represents be-bop in our anthology.

Misterioso

In *Misterioso* we hear first the piano playing a series of ascending sixths. The entire introduction to the piece sounds like an etude, or study piece. In etudes, one often finds exercises in which a single interval is played over and over again. Soon the vibraphone, played by Milt Jackson, joins in and plays ascending sixths along with Monk on the piano.

The first solo belongs to Jackson on vibraphone. His rollicking solo is accompanied by Monk's patented, sparse piano playing. Playing just a few notes in each bar, Monk manages to share the spotlight and lend the performance some wonderful energy. Monk had a magical gift for saying more with less. His use of measured dissonances gives his accompanimental playing a sparkle that his fans genuinely love. The piece began with an introduction, then jumped to a solo so the listener doesn't have a clear sense of the tune and never will. Monk's approach to composition is radical. He laid out a fairly simple chord progression, wrote out the ascending sixth introduction, then left it to the players to work some be-bop magic during their solos. Monk's approach constitutes a radical departure from the arranged music of the big-band era.

Monk takes the next solo. He frequently plays notes far removed from the underlying harmony of his composition. The tension between his solo and the material assigned to the bass results in the sort of be-bop solo that kept audiences of initiated fans coming back to hear the same players night after night. After Monk's solo, which spans two repetitions of the underlying harmony from the introduction, the ascending sixths from the introduction return in the vibes. Monk plays along, employing sparse but juicy dissonances. As Milt Jackson nears the end of the ascending sixth material, Monk joins along as the tempo slows dramatically. As a final odd flourish, Monk plays a descending whole-tone scale of the sort used by Debussy. When Debussy used whole-tone material in *La Mer*, he abandoned it on the last two chords in order to achieve a decisive, albeit abrupt, tonal closure. Here Monk does nearly the opposite. Just when closure is needed in his piece, he trots out a totally unexpected whole-tone scale designed to render the close unsatisfactory. Such small acts of musical defiance illustrate the extent to which be-bop musicians were non-conformists. None was more of a non-conformist than Monk. While Gillespie or Parker played intricate material at extraordinary fast speeds, Monk's approach depends on the virtuosic selection of a few notes capable of making a large statement.

Listening Guide

Thelonius Monk, Misterioso (1948)
[CD4, #15] *(Duration, 3 min. 19 sec.)*

Introduction

0.00   The piano plays a series of ascending sixths that sound as if they are part of an etude, or study piece.

0.11   The vibraphone, played by Milt Jackson, joins in and plays ascending sixths along with Monk on the piano.

First Solo

0.44   Jackson's solo on vibraphone is accompanied by Monk's patented, sparse piano playing.

Second Solo

1.23   Monk takes the next solo. He frequently plays notes far removed from the underlying harmony of his composition. The result is at once relaxed and full of tension.

2.39   The ascending sixths from the introduction return in the vibes. Monk plays along, employing sparse but juicy dissonances.

3.02   As Milt Jackson nears the end of the ascending sixth material, Monk joins along as the tempo slows dramatically.

As a final odd flourish, Monk plays a descending whole-tone scale.

FREE JAZZ

Our overview of major trends in jazz ends in the 1960s with the advent of free jazz. Just as the Civil Rights movement in this country was meeting stiff opposition from some White Americans entrenched in old patterns of thought and behavior, radical African-American musicians were looking for an even more liberated and combative form of jazz. For free jazz players, the embrace of be-bop by large numbers of White

FIGURE 14.5 | *Ornette Coleman* (© Mosaic Images/ Corbis)

FIGURE 14.6 | *Cecil Taylor (1929–)* (© Christopher Felver/Corbis)

Americans signaled the need to move in another direction, one that would create still a more perfect "outsider art." The saxophone player Ornette Coleman led the way. His recordings from the late 1950s, such as *The Shape of Jazz to Come*, presented listeners with the loosest of compositions, allowing for wildly intuitive solos. Coleman disdained all the aspects of be-bop that were starting to appeal to a larger audience, such as virtuosity expressed through fast and intricate playing.

The movement called free jazz takes its name from a recording released in 1965 by Coleman called *Free Jazz*. This work harks back to the days before recording, when improvisation in a group environment was jazz. The one long composition contained on *Free Jazz* provides the loosest possible framework for free exploration of sound within a jazz idiom. The piece brings jazz into its closest sympathy with the indeterminate music of Cage and his followers.

The World of Cecil Taylor

Our recorded anthology [CD4 #16] contains a piece called *Air* by renowned free jazz pianist Cecil Taylor (1929–) off his first album, *The World of Cecil Taylor* (1960). Conservatory trained in classical piano, Taylor draws upon his rich background to bring a very different edge to free jazz than that cultivated by Coleman. Taylor's free jazz is more devoted to virtuosity, although, thanks to his banging sometimes nearly atonal improvisations, he achieves a virtuosity that could not be mistaken for be-bop.

Air opens with an unaccompanied drum solo. The frantic energy of this solo sets the stage for the following piece. Next, Cecil Taylor plays an unaccompanied piano solo that picks up on the energy of the drum solo. Taylor loudly bangs dissonant chords in complex rhythms comparable to the rhythms of the drum solo. Next, the saxophone takes a long solo, only this time the rest of the group accompanies. Note that Taylor continues banging out dissonant chords in spasmodic rhythms as the saxophone plays a be-bop-influenced solo. The longest section of the piece by far is devoted to an accompanied piano solo for Taylor. Here, at the free disposal of his intuition, Taylor alternates between blisteringly fast and intricate passage work and frenetically repeated chords. The second-to-last section of the piece finds the piano, bass, and drums alternating with short passages for drums alone. This change of texture, similar to that achieved by Ellington in the sixth chorus of *Ko-Ko*, when the bass alternates solos with the whole group, lends the performance variety. Taylor takes one last short solo with bass and drum accompaniment. As this last section slows, almost like a windup toy running out of energy, a final quiet cymbal roll brings the work to an end.

Listeners may find that the absence of a recurring motive makes *Air* a tad difficult to follow. By having no preconceived material around and upon which to improvise, Taylor maximizes the freedom available to his raw musical instincts. Radical enthusiasts of jazz in the 1960s became passionate about free jazz, precisely because of this radical freedom achieved within the music itself.

Cecil Taylor, "Air," from The World of Cecil Taylor (1960)
[CD4, #16] *(Duration, 8 min. 37 sec.)*

0.00   An unaccompanied drum solo unfolds with frantic energy. Dennis Charles played drums for this album.

0.20   Cecil Taylor plays an unaccompanied piano solo that picks up on the energy of the drum solo by banging out dissonant chords in complex rhythms.

1.11   The saxophone takes a long solo accompanied by the rest of the group. Note that Taylor continues banging out dissonant chords in spasmodic rhythms as the saxophone plays a be-bop-influenced solo. The saxophone player is Archie Shepp, who had strong credentials as a virtuosic be-bop player.

3.10   Taylor takes a long accompanied piano solo. Here, at the free disposal of his intuition, Taylor alternates between blisteringly fast and intricate passage work and frenetically repeated chords.

6.01   The penultimate section of the piece finds the piano, bass, and drums alternating with short passages for drums alone, providing a change of texture.

8.01   Taylor takes one last short solo with bass and drum accompaniment. As this last section slows, a final quiet cymbal roll brings the work to an end.

Some Call It "Out" Jazz

Coleman and Taylor are not by any means the only practitioners of free jazz. Sun Ra, a composer/performer possessed by vivid eccentricities, was also an influential figure in this style. Sun Ra insisted that he could travel in time, be in two places at once, visit distant planets, and otherwise defy all known logic governing our time and space. He was the freest spirit within a free movement.

Like avant-garde concert music examined in the previous chapter, free jazz was not intended for a mass audience. It afforded its practitioners an outsider's art that never came inside. Some call it "out" jazz, in part for this reason, and in part because the players emphasizing so many tones drawn from outside the underlying harmony.

JAZZ SINCE THE 1960S

While our recorded anthology ends with a recording from 1960, jazz does not by any means end there. All of the styles described and illustrated in this chapter are still alive and well. Ragtime has its advocates, as does the New Orleans style of group polyphonic improvisation. A small renaissance of interest in big-band jazz and swing is unfolding even as this book is being written. Be-bop can still be heard executed at the very highest levels of excellence in all the major cities where a lively jazz scene abides. Free jazz, too, has its devoted practitioners, one of whom will be an important subject in our next chapter. The history of jazz sees an unfolding of consecutive phases, but none of the phases die out. Instead, an overlapping of diverse styles enriches the contemporary scene.

Among the crucial developments not represented in our anthology, two desperately need some mention. Latin Jazz stems from the activity of musicians in Latin America, where local dance traditions like the samba in Brazil inform players and serve as the framework for improvisatory performances. Hispanic musicians have been important contributors to the history of jazz certainly since the 1930s. Today, jazz from South America and the Caribbean finds its way into almost every important jazz festival around the world.

Finally, the 1970s witnessed an important fusion of jazz and rock 'n' roll. This style of jazz is known as fusion, and while some jazz purists regret this style, its abiding popularity suggests that it has a devoted following that will sustain it as an important style for a long time to come.

THE SOCIAL CONTEXTS OF JAZZ PERFORMANCE

Jazz isn't normally played in a concert hall of the sort where symphony orchestras might play. There are certainly exceptions to this rule, but not too many. Nightclubs provide the most common venue for jazz performance. While the audience may be enjoying drinks or even conversation, these public venues are not so different from the salons of past centuries. They are public, which affords one key difference, but the presence of drinking or conversation during a musical performance is as old as music in the West. You may recall in our chapter on ancient Greece that our recorded example is a drinking song. Our quotion from Plato in that same chapter refers to music accompanying eating and drinking. The formality of the nineteenth-century concert is the exception rather than the rule in Western concert music.

Dance halls also afford a frequent spot for jazz performances, especially for big-band jazz. By contrast, dancing to be-bop or free jazz is at best a personal and private decision, more apt to take the form of swaying with the music rather than actually dancing in the strictest sense.

Universities and colleges increasingly host jazz performances. Here the setting more closely resembles the traditional nineteenth-century concert venue, with the audience refraining from food, drink, and conversation. Whether such a venue is ideal for jazz might be a matter for argument. It certainly isn't the original venue.

While the settings for jazz may be less formal than those hosting other kinds of classical music today, the relationship of the audience to the music is no less studious than with other classical musics. Jazz aficionados can and do behave in a very similar manner to other classical music enthusiasts. Appreciation flows from thoughtful experience as much with jazz as with other concert musics. Jazz, like all classical musics, can attract both snobs and posers. It has become a symbol of prestige for many enthusiasts, as jazz connoisseurship resembles other kinds of connoisseurship. This doesn't have to be the case, but it is. In short, the venues may be different, but the social components of classical music consumption are just as apparent in jazz as in opera.

Some Questions for Discussion

1 Recording technology played a tremendous role in what we know about jazz in its early days. This role was sometimes good (without it we would have nothing but written and oral accounts) and sometimes bad (musicians had to misrepresent their practices in order to make records). Can you think of other ways, both good and bad, that the recording industry shapes music and musicians?

2 Why would African Americans periodically want to create what this book calls "outsider art?" What are the advantages of creating art that the majority will not like or will be incapable of understanding? Can you think of other examples of "outsider arts?"

3 Often in jazz, performance and improvisation eclipse composition in importance. Do you think that jazz should be thought of or classified as a classical music, given this situation? Is improvised art more or less valuable or worthy of study than the sort of thoroughly composed and notated art we've studied in other chapters? Why?

CHAPTER 15

Postmodernism

POSTMODERNISM

One last stop is required before we leave the previous century and this overview of music history. During the last twenty years, many people have noticed a change in the culture of the West. This change hasn't taken hold yet in all phases of life—it may never—but there is definitely a new sensibility abroad. That sensibility has come to be called "postmodernism."

The word postmodernism came from the field of architecture initially. Critics looked at playful new trends in architecture and noticed that the modernist ideal of form following function was giving way to a play of forms drawn from history finding their way into new buildings without any reference to their initial function. Modernist architecture can best be exemplified by the skyscraper. Clean lines present glass towers of the utmost utility, as usable space is maximized due to the stacking of floor upon floor, story upon story. The unadorned form of the typical skyscraper perfectly serves its function as a way to maximize space within the usually expensive real estate at the business center of a city. Today, new skyscrapers are not being built with anything close to the rate of twenty years ago.

The Architect Charles Moore

The architect Charles Moore is widely seen as a leader in the movement in architecture away from the modernist ideal of form follows function. His *Piazza d'Italia* in New Orleans provides a good illustration. This building features a wide variety of forms from diverse historical styles, much like Crumb's *Black Angels* contains many quotations from other music. However, there's a difference. Crumb draws upon the original meaning of Schubert's "Death and the Maiden" or the Gregorian Chant "Dies Irae." Moore doesn't seem too particular about original meanings. His *Piazza d'Italia* features arches and buttresses drawn from medieval architecture, but they aren't holding anything up. They just sit there as an ornament. He uses gargoyles, small sculptures of demons that adorned many Gothic cathedrals. Originally gargoyles functioned as

325

FIGURE 15.1 | *Piazza d'Italia* (© 1991 The Times Picayune Publishing Co., all rights reserved. Used with permission of The Times-Picayune)

drainage spouts that moved rainwater from the roof out and away from the cathedral's foundation. On the *Piazza d'Italia* the gargoyles aren't in any way connected to the drainage system. Moore lined the corridors in his building with cobblestones. Cobblestones are used in European towns, first because they are a plentiful resource taken from the rocky soils of Europe, and second because they facilitate keeping the surface of the street relatively clean, as filth falls between the stones, keeping pedestrians' feet cleaner. New Orleans is built upon swampland. Every cobblestone in the *Piazza d'Italia* had to be specially imported, as the land surrounding New Orleans is anything but rocky. If anything, cobblestones are harder to keep clean during modern times than a flat surface. More importantly, New Orleans is a city with a rich architectural history and a look all its own. Moore's decision to draw upon architectural history having nothing to do with the traditions of New Orleans shows us his playful, even mischievous, streak.

Play over Purpose

One might reasonably have asked Charles Moore during his life why he bothers borrowing forms and robbing them of their function. Observers of postmodernism would generally reply with several answers. First, Moore is reacting against centuries of repressive rationality. Second, he is engaging in a kind of historicized play that even the most casual student of architectural history could appreciate. Finally, his work places play and process over purpose and outcome. Such seeming reversals of traditional logic in architecture result not only in exciting buildings but in a critique of the direction that Western logic has taken the West. For the postmodernist, a building that gets a conversation started in the community about the role of buildings in the community, is more successful than a building that settles into a position of immediate and quiet acceptance.

Play over purpose is one of the rallying cries of postmodernists. They no longer trust the modernist notion that right-thinking people always need to be productive, goal-oriented, or serious. To support this logic, they point to all the hardships, injustices, and mayhem created by people who were being serious, goal-oriented, and productive. Finally, postmodernists are mistrustful of logically justified certainty. They argue that people tell themselves that they're being logical, yet two perfectly nice people may reasonably arrive at divergent or even mutually exclusive ideas about logic. Both are convinced, but who is right? The postmodernist would argue, neither, they've both equally deluded themselves into certainty. Some people object to the seeming relativism of this position, but the linguist and critic Jacques Derrida has done a brilliant job of arguing that the language of logic is constructed rather than actual. Look at all the certainties presented in the pages of this book. Each age thinks it has gotten music right, yet every few generations, the certainties of the parents are overturned by the children. Postmodernists argue that the children should stop inventing new certainties, and thus break the chain by simply being a little uncertain all the time. This embrace of the uncertain resembles medieval contentment with mystery, discussed in that chapter. The resemblance is not coincidental, although the rationale for it could hardly be more different. Postmodernists might well argue that the medieval mind had something going for it in accepting mystery.

Moore's playful architecture is only one possible way of realizing this breaking of the chain, of giving up on the idea that this generation must improve on the last. He wasn't trying to improve so much as he was engaged in a playful type of scavenging from the past.

MUSIC AND POSTMODERNISM

The musicologist Charles Hamm, in trying to define a musical postmodernism, laid out the following list of dualistic relationships to differentiate postmodernism from modernism. We've modified this list to suit slightly different aims, but the inspiration lies in the same sources Hamm draws upon. Before looking at that list, modernism itself needs a little defining. For postmodernists, modernism runs from roughly the start of the Renaissance to the present. They see continuity from 1450 onward, while this book has in some ways tried to illustrate certain discontinuities. They see this vast period linked by the concepts on the following list associated with modernism:

Modernism	Postmodernism
Purpose	Play
Closed Forms	Open Forms
Design	Chance
Hierarchy	Anarchy
Ends Oriented	Means Oriented
Permanence	Impermanence
Linear Progress	Random Access

Hamm argues that John Cage was a postmodernist, and in looking at this list, it's easy to see why. He certainly preferred chance and impermanence over their alternatives. The case of Cage could be used to indicate the limitations of this list of dualisms. Informing the list of characteristic procedures used by postmodernists must be one of two sensibilities: resistance or reaction. In the case of resistance, the postmodernist combatively seeks to draw distinctions between postmodern work and the work of modernists. This sensibility is characterized by an active distancing of present practices, both artistic and social, from the practices of a past that no longer gets to dictate the terms of its meaning or value. All the past's artifacts, no matter how respectfully they were once viewed, can be used in playful combinations without respect for original context or function. The attitude of reaction accepts the generic procedures of the past, and turns these procedures into the service of a game of forms. We'll examine these two sensibilities more closely when we get to particular postmodern musicians.

Several composers have come to identify themselves as postmodernists; interestingly, Cage wasn't one of them. Cage still believed in the persuasive power of music and hoped to contribute to a perfecting of society through his heroic labors. In that regard, Cage isn't so very different from Beethoven. Cage sought to sober and quiet the minds of the listeners in order to render them open to divine influences. Beethoven hoped to share with the future his vision of a just and orderly society posited on the ideals of brotherhood. Both used art in a purposeful project of social change. Whether either one succeeded constitutes an entirely different matter.

For the purposes of this chapter, we'll examine only three musicians who self-identify as postmodernists: John Adams, Robert Ashley, and John Zorn. These three composers do not write music that sounds in any way alike, but all of them draw strength for their creativity from having accepted the idea that they are no longer participating in the same historical models that governed music since 1450.

JOHN ADAMS AND THE POSTMODERNISM OF REACTION

John Adams (1947–) most closely resembles Charles Moore in respect to his drawing upon past styles and depriving them of their original function. Unlike George Crumb, Adams doesn't quote any specific work from the past, but his pieces are full of styles common in earlier music. In his famous opera *Nixon in China* (1986), Adams uses fairly steady pulses and small-scale repetition in the manner of the minimalists, but he links them to a chromatic harmonic language comparable to Richard Strauss' chromatic, tonal style. The minimalists and the late Romantics had no ambitions in common, yet Adams turns both of their styles to suit his own purposes. Moreover, the practices of the minimalists serve the purpose of the listener, abandoning any sense of harmonic goal within the music, while the harmonic language of chromaticism popularized by Wagner and Strauss is ideally suited to creating hypersensitivity in the listener concerning harmonic goals. Adams achieves a spectacular form of musical ju-jitsu as he manages to keep his balance while undertaking two mutually exclusive sets of past musical practices.

Nixon in China

Some readers may find it unlikely that an opera was ever written about President Nixon's famous visit to China in 1973. Most people Adams' age have real feelings about the corrupt presidency of Richard Nixon and about the Cold War in general. Students of Cold War politics are sure to have feelings about Nixon's historic initiative in visiting a Communist nation for peaceful talks. Adams doesn't appear the least bit interested in making any political statements in his opera, nor does his librettist, Alice Goodman.

The postmodernism of reaction takes the terms of the past and turns them into a game of form. Adams' opera takes the genre of opera and tries to revitalize it. Opera, so important in past eras, as this book tries to illustrate, fell on hard times during the last century. Professional opera companies became satisfied with the repertory of the past. New works have difficulty getting repeated performances. Adams engages the genre in all its complexities. He needs extremely skillful, professional singers of the sort employed by great opera companies. He needs a large and professional symphony orchestra to support the singers. In short, he has written in *Nixon in China* a thoroughly conventional opera. Operas once emphasized the activities of powerful national leaders, so does Adams'.

Even in its smaller details, the work draws on the history of operatic convention. In keeping with older French tastes, there is a ballet woven into the story. In keeping with the appetites of opera fans, each major character gets to sing a stupendous aria. All the conventions are in place, but now we must look at Adams' postmodern sensibility. None of the conventions serve their original functions, just as Moore's borrowing of old architectural elements do not serve their original functions. Instead of a morality play with world leaders as the subjects, Adams' opera is an entertainment largely bereft of any intentional commentary on its subject, a subject richly inclined to invite an opinion from artists and audiences of his generation.

For reasons of copyright and expense, we could not include an excerpt from *Nixon in China* in our recorded anthology. Readers may be able to locate a recording on their own, or if this book is being used as a text for a course, instructors may want to bring a recording to class. Pat Nixon, the First Lady of the United States from 1969 to 1974, traveled to China with her husband. Typical of visits by First Ladies, she was taken on tours of Beijing and the surrounding countryside while her husband met with Chinese leaders and dignitaries. The second act of the opera shows Pat Nixon as she visits a collective pig farm, a grade school, and finally the Forbidden City—the former home to the emperors of China and now an important historical landmark in Beijing. Weary from her long day of tourism, Mrs. Nixon takes a short break and sings her aria "Isn't It Prophetic." Musically this aria reveals Adams' general stylistic union of chromatic harmony with a minimalistic pulse of a slow and quiet nature. Alice Goodman's text provides a lovely illustration of the postmodern sensibility that informs the entire work.

MRS. NIXON
This is prophetic!
I foresee a time will come
when luxury dissolves into the atmosphere
like a perfume,
and everywhere the simple virtues
root and branch and leaf and flower.
And on that bench there we'll relax
and taste the fruit of all our actions.
Why regret life which is so much like a dream?
Let the eternal plan resume:
in the bedroom communities
Let us be taken by surprise;
Yes! Let the band play on and on;
Let the stand-up comedian finish his act,
let Gypsy Rose kick off her high-heeled party shoes;
let interested businessmen speculate further,
let routine dull the edge of mortality.
Let days grow imperceptibly longer,
let the sun set in cloud;
let lonely drivers on the road pull over for a bite to eat,
let the farmer switch on the light over the porch,

let passersby look in on the large family around the table,
let them pass.
Let the expression on the Statue of Liberty
change just a little,
let her see what lies inland:
across the plain one man is marching
the Unknown Soldier has risen from his tomb;
let him be recognized at home. The Prodigal.
Give him his share:
The eagle nailed to the barn door.
Let him be quick.
The sirens wail as bride and groom
kiss through the veil.
Bless this union with all its might,
let it remain inviolate.

As important as this text is the person who utters it. Pat Nixon has come to China as a representative of the capitalist West in its conflict with Communism. Yet her text speaks not of the ideological struggles of the Cold War, but of more simple virtues. The striking image of luxury dissolving into the atmosphere like a perfume suggests that her prophecy will bring the end of capitalism, for luxury is a concept that lends capitalism much of its rationale. Her long series of lines beginning with the word "let" beg the question in most cases, how can we "let" things so ephemeral and out of our control happen as we have no say over them? Moreover, the rational value of some of these things is debatable. What purpose would a change, for example, in the Statue of Liberty's face serve, especially when the precise nature of the change is unstated. Much of the poetry of Mrs. Nixon's aria serves virtues not normally achieved through modernism's purposeful struggling. Toward the end of the aria, she seems in a cryptic way to be calling for the end of struggle. The Unknown Soldier is no longer needed as a universal figure for those who die in combat. It's time that he be recognized for who he is and allowed to end his symbolic role of inspiring more to die in a noble cause. Her mention of the siren's wail conjures the imagery of an air raid. Yet more important is the hopeful imagery of love conjured by the kiss of bride and groom. She calls for repose, not struggle, and in doing so sides with the union of man and woman. Yet, for all this seeming ambivalence about war and struggle, the text does not categorically state a position. It leaves us to reflect on Mrs. Nixon, herself a Cold Warrior, as she seeks repose. Later in the opera, Mrs. Nixon will be so moved by a propagandistic ballet written by the consummate Cold Warrior, Madame Mao, that she will leave her seat and rush to the aid of the Marxist heroine. The opera blurs the boundaries between East and West, between Communist and Capitalist in a way that refrains from taking a side, or even admitting that the two sides are so very different. It is an opera about politicians that playfully resists indulging in politics.

Genres are always the subject of critique by postmodernists. Genres serve functions, tell stories of a particular sort to a particular time and place, and even subsume the role of myth in clarifying values and ideals in some cases. Adams' relationship with the genre of opera takes its traditional functions, as a medium to comment on the struggles of the powerful, and resists doing it. All the elements of the genre are in perfect place, but the sensibility behind the opera manipulates the elements in a game of forms rather than in the form's purposeful service of function.

ROBERT ASHLEY

Robert Ashley (1930–), a friend of John Adams, also writes postmodern operas. Ashley's operas are even more radical in their conception. Most of them were written for television, and all of them feature as much speaking as singing, although often the rhythms of the spoken sections are carefully crafted from a musical standpoint. Ashley's reasons for writing spoken, rather than sung, operas concerns first and foremost his belief that good speakers are very musical indeed. Beneath this surface rationale, the idea of speaking an opera subverts the usual notion of the genre. Unlike Adams, who works within the conventions of opera, Ashley thwarts them. The sensibility that informs his postmodernism is one of resistance to the past and its siren song of entertaining formulas.

While Ashley's work resists the form of opera, he fancies himself a very strict formalist. In his case, formalism is no idle thing. Ashley takes the form of his work very seriously. He first composes his own text. In doing so, his instinct is to rant and rave and make speeches at the audience, advancing his pet issues. He has profound respect for the ranting of the homeless people who lived in the park across the street from his home in New York—or at least they used to live there before the inhumane policies of the Mayor Giuliani forced most of the homeless to leave Manhattan. In some pieces, Ashley draws inspiration from these rantings. In his operas, he resists the temptation to rant in a way that makes his original meaning too obvious. (Obviousness is the hated enemy of postmodern artists.) Instead he thinks of what he'd like to say to the audience, then he develops an elaborate system for making his text fit very strict and rigidly formal plans. He claims that this practice helps him to be a better writer, because he can't rant and rave as he'd like and still have his text fit his rigid formal plan. The result is that the sense and message changes during the process of composition. Moreover, Ashley has been working with the same small number of singers for a very long time. The personalities of his friends, the singers, now inform what he writes for them. All this helps to nudge him away from making speeches advancing his opinions, and toward postmodern art, where the logic of meaning is always under negotiation. Once he has the text, he decides on a mode of delivery, again always with the singers in mind. When writing for himself, he favors a declamation on a single pitch in a fairly rapid tempo. When writing for classically trained singers, he might take advantage of their more theatrical way of presenting themselves.

Next, Ashley makes the accompaniment for each section of his opera. Ashley likes relatively cheap-sounding electric keyboard accompaniments. He has grown awfully tired of conventional orchestral instruments. Most of his accompaniments are rich in layered repetitions, and all of them make use of low-end electric keyboards. He calls the process of making up accompaniments "making my orchestra." His orchestras are made up of a relatively narrow array of timbres, usually having little or nothing to do with orchestras as conventionally conceived and described earlier in this book.

Atalanta: Acts of God

The work in our anthology [CD4 #17] representing Ashley comes from his mammoth opera project *Atalanta: Acts of God*. Atalanta was a woman who, in Greek legend, could run faster than any man. She was so strong and virtuous that, when her father sought an appropriate husband for her, many obstacles were placed in the prospective husband's path. First, he had to beat her in a race, with terrible consequences if he lost. Many tried and lost. Hippomenes loves Atalanta. Knowing he cannot out-run her, he seeks help from Aphrodite, the goddess of love. She gives him three golden apples to distract Atalanta during the race. The strategy works, and Hippomenes wins the race. Atalanta is so taken with the cleverness of her successful suitor, that they do not wait to return to town in order to announce their pending marriage. Instead they stopped in a temple to make love. The temple belonged to Aphrodite, who is so offended by their deed that she turns both lovers into leopards. This network of operatic projects, which Ashely calls *Atalanta: Acts of God*, is a postmodern recasting of this legend. In it, aliens aboard a space ship abduct three men: the surrealist painter Max Ernst, storyteller Willard Reynolds, and pianist Bud Powell. These three men might possess admirable characteristics for distracting Atalanta, but Ashley insists that the aliens abduct them for some undefined "outer space reasons." Each man receives a character reference and tells an anecdote.

Before becoming too comfortable with this description, first we must point out that the actual opera, in its whole, has never been written and never will be written. The project is simply unrealizable, Ashley insists. The work exists only in related projects of varying degrees of relationship to the conceived but unexecuted whole. One could look at the video *Atalanta: Strategy* and see and hear something of the spirit of the entire project, but this video is not the project itself. One could attend a live performance of sections of the unrealized whole. One could also purchase a recording of sections. Ashley's emphasis on the process of making a work related to a project too vast constitutes an important illustration of the postmodern relationship to finished projects. Postmodernism differs from modernism most crucially in its skepticism about the idea of creative work ever being (in any meaningful way) finished. All acts are parts of processes and continuations; none can ever really be in any important sense, finished. We've argued previously in this book that style periods in the history of music don't really end. People go on performing and, in the process, changing the music in terms of meaning, and even in terms of what the audience will hear. The story of Beethoven's music cannot end with Beethoven putting his pen down and thinking "Well, that's that, another symphony finished." Once the music leaves his desk, it becomes one with the whole process of musical practice, a process that will endure as long as human beings remain musical.

In our anthology [CD4 #17] we have the anecdote of Max Ernst. In listening, you'll surely note that the text is difficult to follow. Ashley likes to make it difficult for listeners to hear every word. Ashley himself sings the leading role of this scene. Many words he utters during our excerpt are promptly repeated by another male speaker. Meanwhile a woman singing in Italian further obscures the matter—that is, if we are safe in assuming that the words Ashley sings are the matter. After all, we must remember that Ashley's formalist methods have removed his text from clearly expressing his most direct notions about this immediate section of the drama. The electric keyboard playing by Ashley's friend, "Blue" Gene Tyranny, further complicates the musical landscape.

The text of the anecdote for Max Ernst expresses the skeleton of a postmodern meditation on the difficulty of dividing time into a past, a present, and a future. The text opens by attacking the notion of linear progress, one of modernism's sacred cows.

> Begin, of course, with once upon a time though
> more and more now, finally, that notion is
> doubtful to be widely held—
> especially as it is joined among us in our tiny
> tiny circle to finally.
> More and more, now, there are strange lights
> in the sky, and the sense of a past known through
> its moment to moment like meshing with the present
> is held in doubt.
> That's just as well.

It was a boring idea, anyway.
More and more now they come to me and say the
moment to moment like meshing with the present
of a whatever is now, necessarily, man, the
past.
It could be, for instance, another present
meshing with the present, or, God forbid,
the future meshing with the present.
The meshing is what's got us so upset.
The meshing is what we gave a name to.
We gave to that meshing, from our own need, the
name of the past.
We could have called it something else.
We could have called it, for instance, everywhere.
What is the name of consciousness? Everywhere.

This text illustrates Ashley's willingness to stray from the usual linear ways that operatic stories used to be told. Before we conclude that this straying is some kind of sacrifice on Ashley's part, take a look back at all the operatic excerpts in this book. Do they really make perfect sense? Perhaps Ashley is straying from a conventional way of not making much sense to an unconventional way of not making much sense. Or perhaps Ashley is simply doing a better job of telling a story that more clearly reflects the discursive ways that thoughts come and go, follow or don't follow one another in an age influenced by television remote controls surfing more than 100 channels, microchips affording random access to information, and an information explosion rendering a big picture almost impossible to discern. Ashley's work seems deeply connected to the way things are now. That's probably why he communicates his ideas primarily through television, a medium much despised by high-art mavens, but very much woven into the fabric of contemporary life.

Listening Guide

Robert Ashley, Atalanta: Acts of God
[CD4, #17] *(Duration, 8 min. 4 sec.)*

The anecdote of Max Ernst

0.00   Electric Keyboard Introduction

0.19   Woman begins singing in Italian.

0.26   Male speaker adds to the texture.

Within the complex musical landscape, Ashley begins singing the leading role of this scene.

0.36   Begin, of course, with once upon a time though

0.37   more and more now, finally, that notion is

0.40   doubtful to be widely held -

0.42   especially as it is joined among us in our tiny

0.44 tiny circle to finally.

0.49 More and more, now, there are strange lights

0.50 in the sky, and the sense of a past known through

0.52 its moment to moment like meshing with the present

0.54 is held in doubt.

0.57 That's just as well.

0.59 It was a boring idea, anyway.

1.03 More and more now they come to me and say the

1.05 moment to moment like meshing with the present

1.07 of a whatever is now, necessarily, man, the

1.09 past.

1.15 It could be, for instance, another present

1.18 meshing with the present, or, God forbid,

1.19 the future meshing with the present.

1.21 The meshing is what's got us so upset.

1.24 The meshing is what we gave a name to.

1.29 We gave to that meshing, from our own need, the

1.31 name of the past.

1.34 We could have called it something else.

1.36 We could have called it, for instance, everywhere.

1.38 What is the name of consciousness? Everywhere.

1.43 The male speaker, woman singing in Italian, and electric keyboard continue, eventually leading into a new texture with a decrescendo.

2.26 New section commences with long notes and sustained harmonies.

2.55 Synthesized sounds mimic television remote controls surfing several channels, affording random access to information almost impossible to discern.

3.03 Voices produce succinct, distorted tones.

3.12 Longer pitch durations invoke the image of a media channel coming into temporary focus, as others filter in and out of range.

3.15 Electric keyboard begins playing an obbligato-like melody above the action taking place.

4.50 Static sounds begin to provide a steady pulse that enters into phase with the obbligato melody.

5.10 Voices dominate as pulse continues.

5.29 Long notes provide sustained harmonies and new textures.

6.00 A new pulse is provided by the electric keyboard for solo voices.

6.17   Electric keyboard plays new melody.

6.43   Voices phase in and out of time as they echo each other with the words "we are all connected."

7.02   New vocal treatments provide new textures, as each gradually comes into focus.

8.00   Electric keyboard takes over and quickly brings this scene to a close.

After listening to our excerpt from Ashley's opera, one might be drawn to ask a question that Adams' opera doesn't demand: why is this called an opera? It certainly isn't an opera in the usual sense of the term. When Ashley asks himself why he calls it an opera in *Atalanta: Strategy* he replies: "Atalanta is what it is, I call it an opera." The language, in a very important sense, belongs to all its users. Ashley uses the word opera for his own purposes, but at the same time seems little concerned whether or not others call it an opera. The important thing is that his work is means-driven rather than ends-driven. He's invested in a super-complex process of making the opera, explaining the making of the opera, and performing the opera in various ways as it is being made. Whether or not one wants to label what he's doing "postmodern" seems less important than noting that what he is doing certainly isn't replicating the priorities of the past. His sensibility resists the past in a very tangible way, by earnestly going about its business of emphasizing processes over finished products.

JOHN ZORN

John Zorn (1953–) grew up in the age of television. He claims watching television for hours and hours during his youth shortened his attention span. As a result, his music changes drastically from moment to moment. He claims that listeners who find themselves hating his music need only wait a minute or two, as it's sure to change completely in that time. During the 1980s, Zorn established himself as a leading voice in the field of free jazz. He still plays saxophone around the world. This chapter will center on his compositional approach rather than his work as a much admired performer on the saxophone.

Zorn's Compositions

His compositions are very difficult to generalize about. Some are collages of quotations and borrowed styles, such as his work for string quartet, vocalist, and turn-table player called *Forbidden Fruit*. This piece features shreds of famous string quartets by Beethoven, other classical works, quotations from Japanese films designed for teenaged girls, imitations of soundtracks for Bugs Bunny and other Warner Brothers cartoons, and a healthy measure of thrash metal playing. These stylistic evocations resemble Charles Moore's, in that none of them serve anything resembling their original function. They are evoked for the purpose of play.

Often Zorn's collage works are composed in the service of a musical imagination that tends toward the cinematic. He finds thinking about a film or a genre of film helpful in organizing his pieces. This situation is best revealed in his works *Spillane* and *Godard*. In other works he emphasizes game-like structures that allow for many changes of style and a great deal of improvisation. A single performance of such a work, called *Cobra*, can be heard in our recorded anthology, [CD4 #18, 19, and 20].

Cobra

To perform *Cobra*, one needs a goodly number of fine musicians, and a leader. The leader has cards that contain symbols that tell the ensemble what to do. With hand symbols the leader can select individual players or small groups of players and give them instructions guiding them in a general way to perform. Some of the instructions include playing quick cartoon-style snatches of music, imitating what other players have just done, initiating some style of popular or classical music, or improvising repeating patterns, like *ostinatos*. Each performance of this piece will be as different as the imaginations of the people involved, and no one imagination (least of all the composer's) can ever control what happens sufficiently to be called responsible for the way the work sounds. A complicating factor within the piece that helps ensure that the result is the product of many imaginations, rather than just one, is the possibility of players turning against the leader and overthrowing him or her. Players who don't like the instructions they've been given can turn rebel. They signify this revolt in performance by donning a headband. Once three players are wearing head bands, an insurrection has been achieved. There is no limit to the number of insurrections that can take place within a single performance.

The performance on our recorded anthology is only one of several that have been made over the years. Typical of Zorn's music, this performance features live electronic performance, numerous sudden changes of style, a generally chaotic overall effect, and virtuosic playing by individuals. As every performance of *Cobra* is radically different, the sole purpose of the following listening guide is to assist the listener through this one-time musical happening preserved in our recorded anthology. Reflected in the guide are three main sections, which Zorn indicated with Italian tempo designations.

Listening Guide

John Zorn, Cobra
[CD4, #18, 19, and 20] *(Duration, 7 min. 9 sec.)*

Presto (Very fast) [CD4, #18]

0.00 Rhythmically energized ostinato patterns by the entire ensemble open the work, and are suddenly curtailed.

0.12 Distinct string-like plucking is allowed to resonate and ascend and descend by microtones, interjected with softer syncopated "ticks."

0.24 Electronic piano tremolos are played over a syncopated pulse

0.31 The opening ostinato pattern returns, this time with an emphasis on pitches played by the treble instruments.

0.48 Warbles ascending and descending by microtones appear to mimic surfing broadcasted channels, as underlying ostinato pulses appear Asian in character.

1.07 The evocation of a rock-n-roll station that has been electronically distorted appears as the result of the previous channel surfing.

1.14 Automotive-racing sounds seem to move into the distance as underlying string-like plucking within an ostinato pattern gradually takes over, before it gradually diminishes and slows.

1.37 Two very soft drum taps conclude the section.

Adagio Maestoso (Slow and Majestic) [CD4, #19]

0.00 Warbled electronic sounds constantly shifting up and down by microtones generate the landscape for sustained synthesized chords.

0.35 Flute, accompanied by marimba, mimics elevator-style music, answered by brass and percussion, then slide whistle.

0.55 Sci-fi movie-like snatches are electronically produced.

1.10 Drums and electric guitar respond.

1.26 The previous sci-fi section material returns.

1.36 Drums and electric guitar answer.

2.04 A muted trumpet shifts pitch, timbre, and dynamics in blues-like fashion.

2.18 An electronic buzz is immediately followed by the entire ensemble improvising, each on their own.

2.26 A popular sounding musical style evoked by guitar and drums brings this section to a close while they fade away.

Violento (In a violent, impetuous style) [CD4, #20]

0.00 Electronic, percussive-like rolls crescendo as they vary pitch.

0.22 Electronic piano enters into the distant mix as the opening sounds have now reached a sustained fortissimo level.

0.37 Distinct percussive sounds, answered each time by punctuated strings, interrupt the previous section.

0.53 The opening material returns.

1.15 Percussive timbres enter and vary, with winds and strings then joining the texture.

1.34 A free jazz-like section is invoked, with each instrumentalist independently improvising.

2.04 Solo vocalizations interrupt the previous section.

2.20 Sustained vocal trills continuously fluctuate in pitch, timbre, and dynamics, seemingly mimicking early monophonic chanting.

2.29 Dramatically varied dynamics and timbres produced by the instrumentalists respond.

2.38 Chant-like vocalizations return.

2.45 The opening material returns with an electric organ.

2.59 Solo vocalizations mimic the great Louis Armstrong's style.

3.10 The electric organ answers, mimicking church-like hymns, and is then joined by synthesized strings, then percussion and electronic disturbances, which gradually begin to establish an ostinato pattern that mimics a "walking bass" line.

4.07 Harp-like strums conclude.

From the discussion of Zorn above and the listening example in our anthology, you may have noticed that Zorn charts a career much closer to the edge of popular art than Ashley or (certainly) Adams. Zorn's choices of popular inspiration, such as thrash metal or rap music, might find themselves side by side with classical inspirations such as Beethoven or free jazz. These juxtapositions of popular art and classical art start to indicate the absurdity of such large categories. As Ellington said, "It's all just music." Postmodernism has little patience for modernism's fascination with making up categories. It works finally to thwart them.

Zorn's postmodern music sounds always quite different from Ashley's. While they are in sympathy on many large and general points, for example on the centrality of process or the need for some formal plan (Zorn's movie idea, Ashley's painstaking formal process of making a text), the music that results reflects their very different ways of performing. Ashley loves to rant, so speech figures importantly in his music. Zorn is a virtuosic saxophone player, so instrumental virtuosity informs the sound of his music.

POSTMODERNISM AND ART IN THE FUTURE

Whether postmodernism represents a temporary state in the West's relationship with the arts and whether it will change beyond recognition in its search for constant renewal, cannot be foretold at this time. One thing is clear: artists such as Ashley, Adams, and Zorn are gaining influence, inspiring a future generation, and creating art in a manner quite alien to the manners of previous centuries. The power of process over finished works and the new relationship with the logic of form have to be reckoned with by any contemporary artist.

Postmodernists enjoy shrouding their terminology in mystery and resist laying out a clear blueprint of what it takes for something to be postmodern. Generating stable definitions for terminology in the arts is a practice closely associated with modernism, a practice postmodernism must resist in order to remain a distinction with a difference. Chances are good that postmodernity will change its tactics, redefine its terms, and reject its own origins. This situation makes the study of postmodernism and art more of a process than a finished act.

POSTMODERNISM AND SOCIETY

While we've tried to explain what postmodern art is and how we might imagine its relationship to modernity, what we haven't done is ground these radical new practices in the culture and society of the time. The social ramifications of postmodern art are difficult to trace, yet we can see postmodern ideals such as the triumph of form over function starting to shape other social institutions beyond the arts.

Whatever one's take on the political situation in the United States, there does seem to be a mounting sense that our political institutions are more deeply connected to forms rather than functions. It used to be that politicians and political parties sought to win elections as a means to an end. The victory in the election allowed them to govern and to use the institutions of the government in the service of a vision. During the last two or three decades, it seems that politicians and political parties seek to win elections in order to sustain their access to the formal trappings of power: the selling of influence, the manipulation of the media mainly toward the purpose of winning the next election, and—of course—indulging in more and more campaigning. Actually initiating ideas of striking contrast to the ideas of your political opponents rarely, but still occasionally, occupies the more modern-minded of them. This is not the analysis of the authors' of this book; it is a widely held view of the contemporary scene. The consequences of politicians divesting from the function of politics and indulging themselves in the play of forms could mean a radical change in our democracy. Some would argue that change has already happened and that our democracy now exists more as an empty form than as a functioning body of rules and ideas with intrinsic vigor.

More optimistic observers might suggest that, while the effect of postmodernity on politics has been unsettling in the short term, the future looks bright. From an emphasis on process and play, a new organizing principle, as yet unforeseeable in its details but more just in its ultimate applications, may arise. The modern government with all its self-seriousness may, by this logic, have played itself out and be in need of replacement by a more creative set of guiding principles.

Many readers of this book may be college students. In universities too we see a mounting game of forms replacing the function of the university. Administrations, a new super-class on college campuses undreamt of by the founders of the West's first universities, now frequently impose a game of forms in which the educational mission (the function of the university) may be lost. This game of forms revolves around mollifying student bodies with entertainments having nothing to do with their studies (athletic spectacles, popular film series, cheap and unregulated internet access, stand-up comedians amongst other diversionary shows sponsored by the college, lowering standards to accommodate lifestyles built around massive beer consumption). The faculty too must often be mollified so as not to become too interested in the educational function of a university. Raises and promotions at most universities revolve around research, not teaching. This research leads to massive duplication in the sciences, publication of less than completely considered work in the humanities, a culture of quantity over quality across many campuses. The hiring of economically desperate individuals often very early in their careers to do most of the teaching is another manifestation of a university straying from its educational function.

This characterization of the political and academic climate may be needlessly bleak, but most readers will be able to add anecdotal evidence to support the thesis that the institutions of our society are straying into a game of forms over function. Hardworking and serious people enter all fields and strive to function wisely and well. This is true of both the academy and politics, to name only the two fields mentioned in this section.

Before we leave the subject of postmodernism, let's return to our three composers briefly. Their actions seem very different from those attributed generically to politicians and academicians. Their art works draw attention to the interchange of form and function. They place these issues at the foreground and in the process help illuminate the contemporary situation. Rather than extending the problem of supplanting function with a game of forms, their work at the larger level serves the function of sensitizing their audiences to what is happening in the world. The more people who are self-consciously participating in society, the greater the likelihood that positive change will come from this transition from modernity to postmodernity.

Some Questions for Discussion

1 While three artists were singled out in this chapter as exemplars of postmodern music, can you think of popular entertainers in the field of music who strike you as postmodern? In many ways popular music is closer to the vanguard of postmodernism. Why might that be the case?

2 Do any of the pieces from earlier chapters seem to meet the criteria for postmodernism set out by Hamm in the list produced early in this chapter? Even if none do exactly conform to the list, which ones come closest?

3 What, if anything, can you point to in contemporary society that would lead to anyone being skeptical about traditions of Western logic? Do you find yourself replicating any of the characteristics of postmodernity in your practices and creative acts?

Glossary of Musical Terms

A cappella: voices alone; without accompaniment of musical instruments

Accelerando: with gradual increasing speed

Accent: a stress that is placed on a particular note in music, or one of various symbols that indicates the type of stress

Alto: the lowest female vocal range, also called contralto; an instrument that performs in a range similar to an alto voice

Amplitude: the furthest distance a vibrating object travels; the degree of displacement

Aria: a vocal number sung solo or as a duet with orchestra in a work such as an opera, oratorio, or cantata

Arioso: a cross between the declamatory style of recitative and the lyric style called "aria"

Arpeggio: a chord that is played one note after another in succession, either ascending or descending, rather than simultaneously

Ars Nova: "new art" or "new technique," a term used by composers of the 14th century to distinguish their new and complex polyphonic music from earlier 13th century organum, which they referred to as "ars antiqua" or "old technique"

Art song, Lied: (plural, "Lieder"): the musical setting of a poem, usually performed by solo voice and piano, in which the performers are expected to contribute significantly to the artistic effect of the poetry

A tempo: to resume a previous musical temo

Atonal: having no tonal center, avoiding any sense of tonality

Augmentation: the repetition of a theme, using notes that are lengthened in value, thus slowing it down

Aulos: a double-reed instrument remotely like the modern oboe and associated with emotion and pleasure in the ancient Greek imagination

Avant-garde: a term taken from French military terminology; in the arts it refers to the new generations of modernists whose work is innovative, experimental, or unconventional

Ballet: a choreographed dance relating a story or theme performed to music by ballet dancers, or the musical score written for such a dance

Banda: refers to the instrumentals placed on stage in Italian opera

Bar lines: vertical lines through the staff used to show measures

Baritone: a male voice or instrument with a pitch register lower than a tenor and higher than a bass

Bass: the lowest male voice register; an instrument that performs in a range similar to a bass voice

Bass clef or F clef: a clef indicating that a note on the fourth line of the staff represents the F, an interval of a fifth, below middle C

Basso continuo group: continuous ("continuo") bass ("basso"), performed by low-pitched instruments such as the cello, bass, or bassoon on the bass part, with a keyboard instrument such as an organ or harpsichord, the performer's left hand reinforcing the bass line, while the right hand continuously plays chords being outlined, note-by-note in the bass; the instrumental group that performs this part

Beat: a musical pulse; the smallest unit of meter

Be-bop: a form of jazz meant for connoisseurs who wanted to compare the intricate details of complex solos played at blistering tempos and within a super-sophisticated harmonic language

Bel canto: Italian for "beautiful singing," a term that sums up the principal goal of Italian opera composers and audiences during the Romantic period

Binary form: a two-part musical form with different sections indicated: **AB**

Bridge: a transitional passage; in sonata form, a modulating passage that moves from the tonic key to a second key, connecting to main themes

Cadence: notes that give pause or end, to a passage, or work, with some degree of conclusiveness

Cadence theme: closing material that is usually less distinct than other themes in a piece; sometimes consisting of only descending scales or chords

Cadenza: an improvised solo within a larger work otherwise notated, such as a concerto

Castrato: a male singer who was castrated before puberty in order to maintain a soprano or alto voice; it had the virtue of a boy's high register coupled to a full-grown man's vocal power

Chain suspension: when harmonic resolutions are prolonged by repeatedly holding over one or more pitches from a preceding chord into the next, which would have otherwise resolved the prior harmonic tension

Chamber music: music played by small groups, such as a string quartet or woodwind quintet, with one person to a part

Chant: a musical passage in which syllables or words are sung on the same note, or a single word or syllable is sung on a series of notes; generally for liturgical purposes, as in Gregorian chant

Chitarrone: a string instrument similar to the lute, but with several additional bass strings

Choir: an organized group of singers, or instruments of the same type, who perform together, especially in church, with the music usually consisting of multiple parts for different voice types, or instruments

Chorale: a four-part harmonization of a hymn tune originally intended for congregational singing in the Lutheran church

Chord: three or more notes played or sung simultaneously to harmonize and embellish a melody

Chromaticism: a musical style that utilizes some or all of the twelve tones of the chromatic scale; notes moving by half-steps

Chromatic harmony: chords consisting of tones outside of the prevailing key but included in the chromatic scale; frequently used in Romantic music

Chromatic scale: the set of twelve pitches represented by all the white and black keys on the piano within one octave

Chorus: music written for a large group of singers, usually of multiple parts for different voice types; or a set of lines that are repeated at least twice after each verse in the course of a song; or in jazz, an improvised section of a larger work which is based on musical ideas previously introduced

Church modes: pitch orderings that date back to ancient Greece, represented by several pitch orientations of the diatonic scales with D, E, F, G, and B, as tonics, instead of the tonal scales represented by C and A

Climax: the most exciting or important moment, or point a melody or entire piece strove for

Clef: a symbol used to designate pitch on a staff

Coda: means "tail;" a musical section placed at the end of a piece or movement that does not represent part of a described form such as Theme and Variations form

Commedia dell'arte: an Italian type of improvised street theater based on stock characters who by their dress and manners conjured instant associations in audiences

Common time: a musical meter with four beats to the measure, and the quarter note equals the beat; often referred to as four-four time

Compound meter: simple meters, multiplied by three: *compound duple meter* (6/2, 6/4, 6/8), *compound triple meter* (9/4, 9/8), and *compound quadruple meter* (12/4, 12/8, 12/16)

Concertato principle: calls for composers to combine diverse musical forces, such as choruses combined with an ensemble of brasses in the same piece, toward a common purpose, as opposed to one basic timbre, most often human voices

Concerto: means "to contend," it is an instrumental work for soloist or group of soloists and orchestra

Concerto grosso: means "large concerto"; it is an instrumental work that requires many solo instrumentalists rather than just one, and orchestra

Conductus: compositions frequently used at Notre Dame in the 13th century to accompany religious processions; in English we still use the word "conduct" to indicate moving from place to place

Consonance: intervals or chords, or any other musical sound combinations that sound free of tension or discord

Counterpoint: "note-against-note," or by extension, "melody-against-melody;" this term refers to the technique of writing polyphonic music

Countersubject: a distinctive polyphonic line that recurrently accompanies the subject of a fugue in another voice

Crescendo: to gradually get louder

Cyclic form: a form indicating the return of certain themes or motives in various different movements of a large composition, such as a symphony

Decrescendo or diminuendo: to gradually get softer

Da capo: directs performers to go to the beginning of a piece and repeat up to a later point indicated

Da capo aria: an aria in ABA form, which results from the opening A section sung da capo at the end

Declamation: when words are set in music by incorporating rhythms and melodies that approximate normal speech patterns

Development: the practice of manipulating themes and motives in various ways; it also refers to the section of sonata form in which themes from the exposition undergo this process

Diatonic: the natural scales consisting of five whole steps and two half steps, produced by the white keys on the piano

Dies irae: "Day of wrath;" one of the gravest Gregorian chants frequently heard in Catholic Requiem masses throughout France, and was used by Berlioz in his *Symphonie Fantastique*

Diminuendo: gradually getting softer

Diminution: the repetition of a theme, using notes that are shortened in value, thus speeding it up

Dissonance, discord: intervals or chords, or any other musical sounds that sound relatively tense, harsh, biting, or unstable

Divertissements: diversions within a larger work that allowed for spectacular effects

Dominant: the note, or a triad built, on the fifth degree of a diatonic scale

Dotted rhythms: an amalgamated rhythm produced when a dotted note is followed by a shorter note, or vice versa

Dramma giacoso: means "jocular drama," a drama intended to be funny

Drone: a single note or chord that is held throughout a melodic part, commonly used to accompany singers in many societies

Duration: the length of time a particular sound or silence lasts

Dynamics: the loudness or softness of sound, or volume of a musical passage

Enharmonic: used to describe notes spelled differently, but having the same pitch

Episode: diversionary music in a fugue that often appears to wander, since all the melodic lines start to move freely and the tonality constantly modulates

Exposition: the first section of a fugue or a sonata-form movement

Expressionism: a 20th century artistic movement that seeks the expression of pure emotional states liberated from all repression, exploring dark, previously hidden emotions or pure and ecstatic emotional states once considered taboo

Falsettist: a man with a particularly well developed falsetto range

Falsetto: "false voice," a method used by male singers to sing in a very high pitch register

Fauve style: a short-lived "wild beast" style in the early part of the 20th century that experimented with distorting images and incorporating motifs from primitive art

Fermata: a cessation of counting; to "hold" a note or chord longer than the time value indicated

Flat: a symbol indicating that the note to which it is fixed is to be played one half step below the specified note

Form: associated with musical interactions that produce a sense of shape and structure

Fortspinnung: means "forward spinning"; a motivic technique that makes the melody of a work seem almost endless; just as one instrument's melodic phrase is coming to an end, another instrument enters with a fresh melodic idea

Fragmentation: the process of reducing a theme to fragments

Free jazz: a liberated and combative form of jazz that presented listeners with the loosest of compositions, allowing for wildly intuitive solos

Frequency: the speed or rate of vibrations occurring in a sound-producing body

Fugue: a polyphonic composition for an established number of voices, built on a single principal theme called the subject, since all parts are based on the same material

Fusion: a style of jazz representing a fusion of jazz and rock 'n' roll

Gallant style: a detached emotional musical style favored in the Enlightenment, that looks outward to society and is anxious to please; as compared to dramatic styles of the Baroque period that are puffed up with their own pathos and emotion

Genre: one of the categories into which artistic works of all kinds may be divided, made on the basis of form, style, or subject matter

Gesamtkunstwerk: "total artwork"; a term used by Wagner as a way of expressing his ideal of fusing all the arts at their highest perfection so that the whole of this fusion would be greater than the sum of its parts

Half step: a semitone; an interval between any two successive notes of the chromatic scale

Hammerstrokes: loud chords that typically began an overture; used to give the audience fair warning that the opera was about to start

Harmony: a combination of musical notes that usually form chords; the vertical aspect of music

Hemiola: rhythms that work at cross purposes with the prevailing meter; a rhythmic alternation of two notes in the place of three, or three notes in the place of two

Homophony: a musical texture that describes only one melody of real interest presented with other sounds used to harmoniously support it

Idée fixe: a "fixed idea" or obsession; a term Berlioz uses for a recurring theme, which carries programmatic meaning, in all of the movements of his *Symphonie Fantastique*

Imitative polyphony: a musical texture describing two or more simultaneous melodic lines using the same or quite similar melodies, but with staggered entrances

Impressionism: a late 19th and early 20th century French artistic movement; in music, a style concerned with keeping certainty at bay; characterized by blurring formal, rhythmic, and tonal boundaries to express scenes or emotions

Improvisation: the creative process of performing without preparation or set notation to follow

Indeterminacy: an artistic method of organization that sought to remove personal desires and ambitions from art by letting some system of choosing other than one's own desires dictate the outcome

Integral serialism: relating to mathematical integrals or integration; in music, a comparably closed system where all parameters of a piece (timbre, dynamics, rhythms, pitches) are either regulated by individual rows, as the European integral serialists had done, or by one row common to all parameters, reflected in many compositions by Milton Babbitt, a leading advocate of integral serialism in America

Intermezzo: a relatively short piece of music that is performed between longer movements of an extended composition such as an opera

Interval: the distance between two pitches

Introduction: a musical section added to the beginning of a piece or movement that does not represent part of the described form such as Theme and Variations form

Introduzzione: a formal plan for the opening of an opera that orients the audience as to where and when the opera is set and what the crucial stakes are within the drama, and introduces a principal character in the process

Inversion: reading or playing a musical line or series upside down; reversing all its upward intervals downward and vice versa

Isorhythm: the 14th century technique of constructing a piece with a voice that is comprised of a borrowed, repeating melodic line (a color) and a repeated rhythmic pattern (talea)

Jazz: an American classical music genre that flows out of many traditions including ragtime, the blues, the improvised music of African Americans in the decades following emancipation, spirituals, and the various musics of West Africa as remembered by the men and women who came to this country from there

Kapellmeister: a person who leads musical activities for a court or cathedral and sometimes for both

Key signature: a group of flats or sharps printed on the staff at the beginning of a piece or section to show the key in which it is to be played

Kithare: a popular instrument of ancient Greece, it consisted of a square, wooden sound box and two curved arms connected by a crossbar, with five to eleven strings that were plucked with a plectrum

Latin jazz: a style of jazz that stems from the activity of musicians in Latin America where local dance traditions like the samba in Brazil inform players and serve as the framework for improvistory performances

Ledger lines: short extra lines added above and below the staff used to accommodate a few higher or lower pitches

Leitmotifs: guiding motives that were used as a principal means of connecting the music to the drama in Wagner's music dramas

Libretto: the text of a dramatic work such as an opera, including both spoken and sung parts

Lyre: a string instrument vaguely akin to the modern harp and associated with reason and moderation in the ancient Greek imagination

Madrigal: a polyphonic composition for unaccompanied voices; ideally they feature responsive settings of elegant, secular poetry

Maestro da capella: means "master of the chapel," it signifies a person who leads musical activities for a cathedral

Major scale: a diatonic scale represented by the white keys of the piano keyboard, oriented around C as the tonic; characterized by half-step intervals between the third and fourth tones and seventh and eighth tones, with whole tones between all other consecutive steps

Measure: a unit of meter, consisting of a principal strong beat and one or more weaker ones

Melisma: a decorative phrase or passage in vocal music, in which one syllable of text is sung to a melodic sequence of several notes

Melodic: a musical line that relates to or is characteristic of a melody

Melody: a succession of single pitches going somewhere with an appeal to the senses, heard as a recognizable whole

Minimalism: a 20th-century style of composition emphasizing the use of a small amount of musical material either repeated or elongated over a vast period of time

Minor scale: a diatonic scale represented by the white keys of the piano keyboard, oriented around A as the tonic; the third and usually, sixth and seventh notes are lower by a half-step than those in the major scale, giving it a less bright quality

Mode: a musical scale that is one of seven patterns of notes that can be played over an octave using only the white notes of the piano keyboard

Modernism: an early 20th-century movement expressing revolutionary ideas and styles as a reaction to traditional forms

Modular form: a formal musical plan that changes with every performance depending on choices made by the performer

Monody: dramatic vocal music for solo voice with instrumental accompaniment

Monophony: a texture describing one unaccompanied melody

Motet: a vocal composition, usually sacred, with parts for different voices; early motets were based on fragments of Gregorian chant

Motive, motif: a short musical idea consisting of at least two notes, forming the basis for development in a piece of music

Movement: term used for a large, self-contained section within a larger work, such as a symphony

Musical tone: sound producing a series of regular, predictable pulsations, which possess four basic definitive characteristics; frequency, volume, timbre, and duration

Music drama: a term Wagner used for his distinctive type of opera

Musique concrète: compositions comprised of recorded acoustic sounds

Neo-classicism: a 20th-century movement in music that calls for the creation of a more perfect modernism through the combination of modern musical traits with orderly principles borrowed from music's past or from popular styles

Nocturne: a genre that centers on the evocation of moods and feelings associated with the night, which has no preconceived formal plan associated with it

Noise: any sound producing a series of irregular, unpredictable pulsations, causing diffusion in aural clarity

Non-imitative polyphony: a musical texture that describes two or more simultaneous melodic lines that are quite different

Note: a sound of a particular pitch, quality, or duration played or sung; a written musical symbol that indicates such a sound

Obligato: usually with reference to an instrument, a manner of writing that calls for the addition of a short contrapuntal melody to another main melody at indicated places

Octatonic scale: an eight-tone scale alternating between whole and half-steps

Octave: an interval of eight notes, represented by the white keys on the piano, where a pitch is perceived as being duplicated

Opera: a dramatic work of art presented in music; thought of initially as a string of musical works performed one right after another which, taken together, tell a complete story

Oratorio: a large-scale composition for soloists, chorus, and orchestra that tells a story, much like opera; but unlike opera, these stories are usually religious and meant to be performed without costumes or stage movement

Orchestra: a large group of musicians, consisting of sections of string, woodwind, brass, and percussion, which is often directed by a conductor

Organum: an early form of medieval polyphonic music that combines a plainchant melody with one or more other melodies

Ostinato: a short musical phrase or melody that is repeated over and over, usually at the same pitch

Overture: an orchestral movement that usually introduces a longer musical work such as an opera, or ballet; often including many of the work's themes

Passagio: an ornament comprised of quick runs up and down scales, often heard during the singing of Baroque opera

Pedal point: as a term that most often pertains to an organist's foot ("pedal"), which manipulates a pedal keyboard, it is used for holding a single bass note while other voices progress with a succession of changing harmonies against it

Pentatonic scale: an ancient five-tone scale, represented in the relation of the black keys of the piano

Phrase: a sequence of notes that form a unit in music, each leading sensibly to the next

Piano; pianissimo: played "soft"; played "very soft"

Pitch: the highness or lowness of musical sound

Petit air: means "little song"; a tuneful style of singing that was used in *tragedie-lyrique* for moments of diminished emotional importance

Pizzicato: using fingers to pluck the strings of an instrument that is usually bowed, such as a violin

Polyphony: a texture describing two or more melodies played or sung simultaneously

Program music: instrumental music associated with an extra-musical idea or story

Postmodernism: a 20th-century movement that moves away from the modernist ideal of form follows function; all the past's artifacts, no matter how respectfully they were once viewed, can be used in playful combinations with respect for original context or function

Psalters: monophonic tunes used in singing psalm texts in worship service

Ragtime: a genre of American music that originated around the turn of the twentieth century that is closely associated with one central figure in its history, Scott Joplin; usually notated and published for piano, it benefited from the participation and contributions of several composers with excellent classical training, and came to the attention of jazz musicians who used them as a framework for their own improvisatory performances; it is characterized by distinctive syncopated right-hand rhythms against a regularly accented left-hand beat

Recapitulation: the last section of a sonata-form movement in which all the thematic material of the exposition returns in their original order; however, all of the themes now appear in the tonic

Recitative: speech-like singing

Rests: short silences in music; the notational symbols indicating silences

Re-transition: a modulating passage that leads to the recapitulation in sonata form

Retrograde: reading or playing a musical line or series backwards

Retrograde-inversion: reading or playing a musical line or series upside down and backwards

Rhythm: in general terms, the organization of sound and silence through time

Rhythmic modes: a system of notation at Notre Dame during the 13th century that allowed for interesting rhythmic variety

Rhythm section: an instrumental group consisting of drums, a tuba, often a piano, and equally often a banjo or guitar that does not participate in the melodic improvisation in jazz so much as they lay down the harmonic foundation for the piece and present a driving rhythmic momentum

Ritornello: the orchestral material that is introduced at the beginning of a movement of a work such as a concerto, which always returns, usually in fragments and in different keys throughout

Ritornello form: a Baroque form that utilizes the recurrences of a *ritornello* theme

Rondo: a relatively joyful, simple form; the fundamental principle is the unvaried repetition of a main theme, commonly called a "tune"

Row, series: an ordering of the twelve tones that provides the motivic information that will hold a piece together; used in the twelve-tone method

Scale: a collection of pitches chosen for a particular piece

Scat: a wordless vocal improvisation that often utilizes nonsense syllables

Schubertiads: musical evenings that were paid for by the wealthy, in which Schubert and a few friends would play piano works, art songs, and chamber music at an aristocratic home

Sequences and Tropes: the addition of new chant melodies setting religious poetry in order to augment the services associated with days of particular importance to the region during medieval times

Sharp: a symbol indicating that the note to which it is fixed is to be played one half-step above the specified note

Simple meters: metric groupings in *duple* (2/2, 2/4, 2/8), *triple* (3/2, 3/4, 3/8), and *quadruple* (4/2, 4/4, 4/8), time

Solo: a piece of music performed by one musician, or a passage for solo performer within a larger work for two or more performers; it also refers to a performance by a single artist with or without accompaniment

Sonata: a multi-movement work for one or more instruments; at least one movement is in sonata form

Sonata form: a form that was developed by Classical composers; sometimes referred to as "first-movement form" or "sonata-allegro form"

Sonata rondo form: a hybrid form that combines elements of sonata and rondo form

Soprano: the highest female voice register; an instrument that performs in a range similar to a soprano voice

Staff: the five lines and four spaces used to indicate graphically the relative highness or lowness of pitch

Stretto: when one voice in a fugue overlaps with another; entering before another has finished

String Quartet: an instrumental ensemble consisting of two violins, viola, and cello; or a piece written for this group of musicians

Strophic: when all stanzas of the text in a song are sung to the same music

Style: the recognized way in which the formal elements of a work have been handled so as to provide the whole with expressive effect

Subject: the single principal theme of a fugue, as all parts will be based on the same linear material

Surrealism: a 20th-century French artistic movement which believed that the world of the subconscious as experienced in dreams constituted something more important than waking reality, which they mistrusted, and achieved their ends by casting together violent and irrational juxtapositions

Symbolism: an artistic style that originated in the late nineteenth century, in which suggestion, rather than outright statement represents the heart of its aesthetic

Symphony: a genre usually exemplifying the following characteristics: instruments only, multi-movements, lofty musical ambitions, and an abstract subject matter; some exceptions include singers in symphonies, a single long movement, intentionally trivial in nature, or the incorporation of concrete story lines

Syncopation: the deliberate displacement of the expected pulse of meter, accent, and rhythm

Synthesizer: an instrument that produces musical sounds through purely electrical means

Tempo: the pace at which rhythmical units progress

Tenor: the highest natural adult male singing voice; an instrument that performs in a range similar to a tenor voice

Ternary form: a three-part musical form in which the last section repeats the first and the middle section differs, indicated: **ABA**

Texture: a term used to describe the various sounds and melodic lines taking place concurrently in a piece of music

Theme: means "topic"; a principal or basic subject of a piece of music

Theme and variations form: a form that consists of a theme followed by a series of variations on it

Through-composed: when new music is used for each stanza of the text in a song

Tie: a symbol connecting two notes of the same pitch, used to extend the duration value of the first note by the durational value of the second

Timbre or tone color: the sonorous quality of tone of a particular voice or instrument, or group of voices or instruments; dependent on the amount and proportion of overtones present

Time signature: a sign used to indicate meter, represented by a fraction in which the upper figure shows beats per measure and the lower figure shows the time value of each beat

Tonality: the feeling of centrality of one note to a passage of music

Tonic: the central note commonly referred to as "do," in a diatonic scale

Tragedie-lyrique: meaning "lyric tragedy," a French term used to distance their operas from their Italian counterparts; they emphasized recitative and featured visual spectacle and ballet

Transpose: to move an entire piece, or a section of a work, or a scale, or twelve-tone row up or down in pitch, preserving all of the intervallic relationships within the unit

Treble clef or G clef: a clef that puts G above middle C on the second line of the staff, used for the higher pitch frequencies

Tremolo: a quavering effect frequently used for dramatic purpose, produced by the rapid repetition of a tone or the rapid alternation between two tones

Trill: a musical ornament produced by the rapid alternation between two adjacent pitches

Trillo: when the same note is sung over and over in rapid succession, a Baroque style ornament

Triplet: a group of three notes played in the time usually taken by two notes of the same value

Trope: in the medieval Christian Church, a phrase or text interpolated into the Mass

Troubadour: a writer or singer of lyric verses about courtly love who entertained the upper classes in parts of Europe during the 11th to 13th centuries

Twelve-tone method, serialism: a compositional method in which the composer creates a row of all twelve pitches of the chromatic scale to provide the motivic information that will hold the piece together, while assuring atonality

Two-tempo aria: an aria that is based on an important tempo change part way through; it opens with a "scena," a section of recitative that advances the action, moves to a "tempo primo," or first tempo section, which then moves to another called the "tempo di mezzo," or middle tempo, and concludes with a rousing "cabaleta," a section that caps off the form, giving the "two-tempo aria" three tempi, which makes the label a misnomer

Virtuosity: great skill or technique shown by a performer

Vocal Cantata: a sizable work for small orchestra, chorus, and vocal soloists, either sacred or secular

Volkstummlichkeit: a German word meaning "folk voice-ness," or in musical terms, when thoroughly professionalized music strives to sound like folk song

Whole step; whole tone: an interval that is equal to two half-steps or semitones

Word painting: the musical illustration of the text; when a composer strives to marry the music to the least change of meaning or tone in the poetry

Whole-tone scale: a six-tone scale consisting exclusively of whole steps

Word painting: the musical illustration of the text

Index

About the Authors

Armand Ambrosini appears as recitalist, chamber musician and teacher throughout the United States. He has been an Artist-in Residence at the Sequoia Chamber Music Workshop, Arcata, California since 1991, the Ashland Chamber Music Workshop, Ashland, Oregon since 1995, and the Chamber Music Conference and Composer's Forum of the East, Bennington College, Bennington, Vermont since 2000. He has served as principal clarinetist with the Philharmonia Virtuosi, Stamford, Bridgeport, and New Haven Symphonies; and the New York String Orchestra, under Alexander Schneider, in a special performance at Carnegie Hall. He is a founding member of the Cordier Chamber Ensemble, which has commissioned several new compositions and toured extensively throughout the east coast, performing at Symphony Space and the Kitchen Center for Video, Music and Dance, New York City; the Washington Project for the Arts, Washington, D.C.; the Center for Chamber Music, Troy, New York; and Carnegie Recital Hall, under the auspices of a Martha Baird Rockefeller Grant.

In addition to an active performance schedule, he currently serves on the faculty at the University of Oklahoma. The release of his first book and accompanying CD: *Ned Rorem's Song Cycle **Ariel:** A Musical Dramatization of Five Poems by Sylvia Plath* in December 2001 by KENDALL/HUNT Publishing Company, has received high praise from Ned Rorem and is being sold on the internet through amazon.com/books.

He holds a BFA and MFA degree from the California Institute of the Arts, a MM degree from Yale University, and a DMA degree from the State University of New York at Stony Brook.

Michael Lee has worked as a professional double bass player with the Eugene Symphony, a radio host for classical music programming, a public school music teacher, a copyright consultant in music to Disney Studios, and as a bassist with various free jazz and improvised music ensembles. Currently he serves as associate professor of musicology at the University of Oklahoma where he teaches courses on twentieth-century music history, American music history, film music, film history, and leads the university's improvisation ensemble. He holds the PhD in musicology from the University of Southern California. His research interests include American experimental music, film music, the Ballets russes, and les six.